The Gospel of Leadership

An Unconventional Dialogue in the Pursuit of Truth
A Tale of Wisdom Inspired by a True Story

Dedicated to Aspiring Leaders

Ryan Krupa

Editor: Howard Gambrill Clark, PhD

First published by Dog Ear Publishing
4011 Vincennes Road
Indianapolis, IN 46268
www.dogearpublishing.net

ISBN: 978-145756-526-7

This book is printed on acid-free paper.
Printed in the United States of America

TABLE OF CONTENTS

EPIGRAPH

What do you say concerning yourself?
He said, I am the voice of one crying in the wilderness.[1]

- The Gospel According to Saint John

I am grateful and I am your friend, but I will obey the god rather than you, and as long as I draw breath and am able, I shall not cease to practice philosophy, to exhort you and in my usual way to point out to any one of you whom I happen to meet: 'Good Sir, you are an Athenian, a citizen of the greatest city with the greatest reputation for both wisdom and power; are you not ashamed of your eagerness to possess as much wealth, reputation, and honors as possible, while you do not care for nor give thought to wisdom and truth, or the best possible state of your soul?' Then, if one of you disputes this and says he does care, I shall not let him go at once or leave him, but I shall question him, examine him, and test him, and if I do not think he has attained the goodness that he says he has, I shall reproach him because he attaches little importance to the most important things and greater importance to inferior things. I shall treat in this way anyone I happen to meet, young and old, citizen and stranger, and more so the citizens because you are more kindred to me. Be sure that this is what the god orders me to do, and I think there is no greater blessing for the city than my services to the god. For I go around doing nothing but persuading both young and old among you not to care for your body or your wealth in preference to or as strongly as for the best possible state of your soul, as I say to you: Wealth does not bring about excellence, but excellence makes wealth and everything else good for men, both individually and collectively.[2]

- Socrates, Plato's *Apology*

To read well, that is, to read true books in a true spirit, is a noble exercise, and one that will task the reader more than any exercise which the customs of his day esteem. It requires training such as the athletes underwent, the steady intention almost of the whole life to this object. Books must be read as deliberately and reservedly as they were written.

- Henry David Thoreau, *Walden*

---

[1] The Holy Bible, Lamsa Translation.
[2] Plato, *Apology*, G.M.A. Grube translation.

PREFACE

This book is an odyssey into the truth of leadership's nature and essence. Written for aspiring leaders, teachers of leaders, and followers, the aim is to practice awakening a leader's potential. The book mirrors and reflects the inner nature of the leadership journey. It is written in a contemplative style and uses dialogue to exercise a leader's will, intelligence, and spirit. The techniques taught in these chapters are dialogue, meditation, and contemplation. The author seeks to teach leaders how to exercise the power of will and the power of intelligence to make the kinetic chain of knowing, willing, and acting morally and intellectually strong. Reading this book serves as a leadership development exercise.

This book is a teaching tool designed to demystify what takes place in the interior nature of a leader. It examines a leader's soul, as it is exercised and strengthened in preparation for the cardinal act of leading, and it analyzes the act of making practical judgments, an act that demands the cultivation of a discerning mind to see and know the truth to be acted upon.

Based on a true story, these chapters are a reflection on the formation of a leader and a realization of twenty years of research. The author studies the question: What does it take to develop a leader? Deliberations on eight years of guiding leaders on moral and intellectual quests in search of true freedom are revealed.

If you commit to reading *The Gospel of Leadership: An Unconventional Dialogue in the Pursuit of Truth*, read it at a leisurely pace, until you finish. Only reading the entire contents—from beginning to end—will allow you to see the truth you seek. Through strategic appreciation and patience, this work uses an indirect approach to achieve its objective: the understanding of the nature and essence of leadership development. There are no short cuts. If there were, this book would have only two statements:

1. Leadership is virtue, excellence and wisdom in the performance of actions.
2. Leadership lives in the pathless path of the unmoved movers in the knowable unknown.

Lastly, the author wrote this book, as an artifact—for posterity—to provide an account of one leader's struggle to understand the essence and nature of leadership and how to teach that essence and nature to his generation and future generations.

ABOUT THE AUTHOR

RYAN KRUPA is a Co-Founder of the MOSAIC INSTITUTE FOR HUMAN DEVELOPMENT. He is devoted to the pursuit of truth as a noble endeavor. His calling is to awaken leadership potential in aspiring leaders. He specializes in creating and teaching leadership development courses for US Special Operations units. He has studied and researched the domain of leadership development for twenty years. He has led development courses for eight years. Prior to MOSAIC, he served as an Officer in the US Marine Corps, a strategic account manager at the Center for Creative Leadership, and a consultant at Deloitte Consulting. He earned a Master of Science in Leadership from the University of San Diego, CA.

THE CONCEPTS TO BE AWAKENED AND REALIZED[1]

GUARDIAN: A keeper, a defender, a protector.

WARRIOR: A person experienced or distinguished in fighting. A hardy, courageous, or aggressive person.

INNER SIGHT: "The quick recognition of a truth that the mind would ordinarily miss or would perceive only after long study and reflection. An intellect that, even in the darkest hour, retains some glimmerings of the inner light, which leads to truth."

INNER DETERMINATION: "The courage to accept responsibility, the courage in the face of a moral danger. Determination proceeds from a special type of mind, from a strong rather than a brilliant one."

LIGHT: The quality of illumination. Vivacity, enthusiasm, or inspiration in a person's face and eyes. State of being visible or exposed. The power of vision. A source of illumination. A beacon. Spiritual illumination. Mental illumination. Elucidation, enlightenment, knowledge.

TRUTH: Disposition to speak and act truly and sincerely. Facts. The matter or circumstance as it really is. True Statement. Conformity to reality. Faithfulness to reality. Genuineness. Authenticity.

SOUL: The principle of life in humans. The principle of thought and action in a person, regarded as an entity distinct from the body; a person's spiritual as opposed to corporeal nature. The spiritual part of a human being considered in its moral aspect or in relation to God and his precepts. Intellectual or spiritual power; high development of the mental faculties. Also, deep feeling, sensitivity, especially as an aesthetic quality; zest, spirit. A person regarded as the inspirer or leader *of* some activity, cause, etc.; the chief agent, the prime mover, the animating spirit.

SPIRIT: The animating or life-giving principle in humans. The non-physical part of a corporeal being, especially considered as a moral agent; the soul. The divine nature or essential power *of* God, regarded as a creative, animating, or inspiring influence. The essential character *of* a thing, esp. a place, regarded as exerting an influence. The abstract intelligent or sentient part of a person as the seat of action and feeling.

FACULTIES: An ability, aptitude, or competence for a particular kind of action (sometimes natural as opposed to acquired). A power or capacity of a thing; an active property. An inherent power or

---

[1] All definitions from Shorter Oxford English Dictionary. Quotes are from Clausewitz, *On War*.

property of the mind, as reason, memory, etc.; a mental capability. The power, freedom, or right of doing something, given by law or by a superior.

WILL: The faculty by which a person exercises his or her capacity for initiating conscious and intentional action; power of choice in regard to action. Intention or determination that what one wishes or ordains be done by another or others; force or energy of intention. Control over one's own will; self-control; degree of deliberate imposition of this over instinct or impulse. Willpower.

INTELLIGENCE: The faculty of understanding; intellect. Sagacity. The action or fact of understanding something; knowledge, comprehension. An intelligent or rational being.

SPIRITED: Full of spirit. Lively. Vigorous. Energetic.

CONTEMPLATION: The action of thinking about or of pondering over a thing continuously; musing, meditation. A state or period of meditation or study. The action of gazing on or looking at attentively or thoughtfully.

MEDITATION: The action or practice of profound spiritual or religious reflection or mental contemplation. Continuous thought on one subject; (a period of) serious and sustained reflection or mental contemplation.

DIALOGUE: A literary work in conversational form; this kind of composition; the conversational part of a novel, etc. A conversation between two or more people; verbal interchange of thought, discussion.

VIRTUE: Conformity of life and conduct with moral principles. Moral excellence; uprightness. A particular form of moral excellence; a special manifestation of the influence of moral principles in life or conduct. Physical strength, force, or energy. Flourishing state or condition. The possession or display of manly qualities; manly excellence, courage, valor. Superiority or excellence; outstanding ability, merit, or distinction.

EXELLENCE: The state or fact of excelling; the possession of good qualities or abilities to an eminent or unusual degree; surpassing merit, skill, or worth. Outstanding. Supreme. Excelling in rank or dignity; exalted, highly honorable.

WISDOM: The quality of being wise, especially in relation to conduct and the choice of means and ends; the combination of experience and knowledge with the ability to apply them judiciously; sound judgment, prudence, practical sense. Knowledge, enlightenment, learning, erudition. Sound reasoning.

WISE: Of a person: having or exercising (the power of) sound judgment or discernment, especially in relation to conduct and the choice of means and ends; having and judiciously applying experience and knowledge; characterized by good sense and prudence. Of behavior, an action, a quality: proceeding from, indicating, or suggesting wisdom or discernment; sagacious, prudent, sensible, discreet.

CHAPTER ONE
THE CALL

A primordial fury forced me to call the mentor. I teach leaders how to practice justice and wisdom. The aim is to make them trustworthy in the cardinal acts of leading.

Why the fury?

I'm staring at a glacier of truth, and I can't see the route to the summit. I'm at an impasse.

Two decades of study and teaching, and it seems I've hit a mountain of opaque ice, an obstacle that cannot be surpassed. It speaks, "Turn back. To go further is not possible."

I don't turn back. I stay put and observe. I've been in similar situations in the past. Each day, I commit. I'd rather die here than turn back. I'm willing to die here, at this impasse. What am I not seeing? What needs to be developed? What skill is missing?

What is this glacier, this treacherous fortress barring further movement?

I steady myself as the interior thoughts begin their assault. All I've done is in vain. It's not possible to teach leadership. It's not possible to lead. Leadership is not possible. It's a made-up word and concept that does not exist in reality. Reality is strength. Reality is winning. Reality is suffering. Reality is harsh. Reality is nature. Reality is control. Reality is dominance. Might wins. Wealth wins. Goodness loses. Truth lost the war. Virtue lost the war. I am a casualty of the war of truth vs. falsehood.

I have failed. I chased a ghost. I chased an image. I chased an idea that is not found in reality. We've neutered the concept of leadership. We've turned it into a meaningless word. What is meaningless sells. What is truth does not sell.

> Truth is like poetry. And most people hate poetry.[1]

We want to consume leadership. We don't want to become the essence of it.

What led me to this despondency? I've not trained one leader that I would happily and willingly follow. It is not a question of talent. It's a question of sacrifice. They won't sacrifice their egos. They won't sacrifice their desires. They won't surrender the need to win. They won't surrender the need to achieve. They won't focus on truth. They are moral cowards.

---

[1] Adam McKay, *The Big Short,* screenplay, quote modified to remove profanity.

That is, except for the warriors. The warriors were not my concern. Everyone else was my concern. Especially the corporate and political and entertainment leaders.

The warriors I've worked with, yes, I'd follow.

Truth be told, I did not teach warriors leadership. I taught warriors how to unlock their tacit and intuitive knowledge to become better teachers and guides. You don't lead warriors. You follow them. Few are warriors. I'm lucky to have worked with these few. They exist, I've met them. Their existence saved me from insanity and madness. Why? They had to undergo rigorous training to wage war. They could comprehend that to lead, they also had to undergo rigorous training. To lead not only by their actions, but also by their wisdom (truth) and justice (goodness). They were willing to wrestle with the techniques that unlock potential.

The analogy of the sword of steel, the sword of truth, and the sword of wisdom illuminates their training. They knew steel; they were driving toward truth and wisdom. They were driven toward illumination. The first warrior who sought this work, when I asked what he thirsted for, said, "wisdom!"

What about the rest? The non-warriors, the majority of leaders?

The majority? They don't believe in something greater than themselves. I catch their arrogance and ignorance with one question: "What leads the leader?"

Blank stares. Then one responds: "I lead."

"You are in error," I answer.

I respond, "Truth leads the leader, full stop."

If you don't know how to seek the truth nor have had training to seek the truth, the seduction of power, wealth, and position cloaks you in darkness where everything is turned upside down but you think it is right side up—distortion, illusion, deception swirl around your mind and emotions. You don't even know it. You don't even know you live in the dark. You don't know you deceive yourself.

You deceive yourself because you don't wield your reason and intuition. You deceive yourself because you fear, rather than love, truth's sting of humility. You are a slave to feelings. You are a slave to emotions. You are a slave to desires. You are in bondage, and you think you are in freedom.

In bondage, you bend the light to your will instead of bending your will to the light.

I hunt for leadership in the souls and spirits of leaders. I hunt for the genius within. A wiser Daemon within. The God within.

Once I point this out to the majority of leaders, once I point out that they are in fact in prison and not free, what do you think they do? When the violence of truth strikes their souls, what do you think they do? They fail to embrace the pain, embrace the difficulty, and to use their will and mind to break their bonds. Instead, they cower, hide, and turn away from the sting of truth.

They turn back into the distortion. They turn back into oblivion. They hate the light of truth. They find comfort in the darkness. They can't take the inner rupture and the inner turbulence.

They won't transcend the ego. No, they run back into its grip.

Those non-leaders, the majority, refused to train in the true art of leadership. They refused to study—to become one with knowledge. They refused to read—to engage in intellectual weightlifting. They refused to meditate—to purify their souls. They refused to reflect—to become self-correcting. And why did they refuse? They could not endure the feedback that stings. They could not endure the nonstop inner demands of the virtuous life.

They crave and desire what I can and will not teach—expertise in the art of manipulation. Parlor tricks of the high-functioning trifecta of narcissism, sociopathy, and Machiavellianism, which predominate in multinational corporations as they kill the earth and kill the soul for one more dollar.

What do they desire? They want control. They want to live as tyrants. This is the secret in their hearts. And as long as they make money, we don't call them tyrants. As long as they achieve, we don't call them despots. Instead, we let them exercise control in their enterprises as tyrants. Why do we allow this? Because we are slaves to greater products and greater profits, not greater truths. When they don't produce what we want, we discard them as worthless.

The antiserum? It is incumbent on the leaders to exercise moral courage with authority and power. It is the burden of leadership to transmit moral strength, power, confidence, courage, and spirit to us, to uplift us and inspire us, until we can do the same. When the truth confronts these leaders, when I reflect it to them, they hate me for it. Truth is a bitter medicine. It is the medicine of and for the soul.

In willful ignorance, they refused to become pure. They refused to awaken what lives deep. They refused to develop discernment. They refused to exercise their intelligence. They refused the burden of a penetrating intellect—of seeing what they hide from, of seeing what they fear, of seeing what is true, and of seeing the true challenges and obstacles.

They hate what I do. They hate the pain of inner development. They hate the stinging truth. They hate that they are not pure enough and skilled enough to disclose the truth. And because they are not pure enough to disclose truth, they are not fit to lead. Truth will not be mocked.

On the scales of justice, I'm pure enough and skilled enough, just barely, to disclose the truth. And why is that? I'm devoted to seeking truth as a noble endeavor. I am a servant of truth. I am in pursuit of wisdom. I'm still light years away from the saints and their holiness or from the sages and their eternal wisdom. But I love truth's direction, wherever it may lead. And truth led me here, to this impasse.

True leadership training is not supernatural, yet the effect is supernatural—a more-than-human knowledge that can see the truth, the intelligible truth, the truth that cannot be seen with the eyes, only with the discerning mind.

Musashi, the great Samurai, laid down this principle with authority–

> Develop a discerning eye in all matters. And understand what cannot be seen by the eye.[2]

The majority of leaders, if not wise, what are they? Fools, successful fools, all of them.

I want to quit. That's the ego leading. It's brought on its full assault. I wrestle it into submission. How? I adhere to the principle, independent of feelings, never to quit the calling and vocation. I live the calling and vocation. Why? Because I can't quit what I am and I can't quit the purpose of my existence.

These fools, these achievers, have been rewarded for their strengths, their skill, and for winning. But, they were never rewarded for the truth. They were never rewarded for their character.

True leadership training takes aim at a person's character, the moral and intellectual fiber of the soul. It's startling how, in their first training experience, egotists who think they are strong implode. They stare at a stinging truth—leadership training never plays to strengths. The training discloses weaknesses, deficiencies, flaws, biases, and blind spots—the imperfections.

This is why reflection and inquiry are two weapons, two techniques, to learn and to experience the truth-disclosing art. This art leads to practical judgment. At the core, that is what they seek. This is the true skill they seek—more than manipulation, more than calculation, more than cunning—they seek to become skilled in the art of practical judgment. Why? As leaders, they are required to make judgment calls. That's the beautiful burden of leading.

What we wait for is the first visceral experience of truth revealing itself, when it stings the ego and awakens the soul. No one can prepare for it. Truth unveiled must upset the emotions. Truth unveiled must rupture the ego. Why? To produce humility and objectivity.

This is a necessity for the teaching of leadership—the sting awakens. When this happens, most quit. They shut down; they don't go deeper.

---

[2] Musashi, Miyamoto, *The Book of Five Rings*, W. S. Wilson translation.

The beauty of this work is that it is volitional. It cannot be forced. Truth does not force.

Those who persevere get the fruits of freedom and humility. This humility opens the gates of inquiry and allows us to peek through at truth. The master swordsman calls this an act of lightning spontaneity. It's a response that cannot be premeditated, only intuited.

This is why the training is designed to awaken the light and to produce humility. Most don't come in with humility; they come in with arrogance and ignorance. This revelation stings— they think they possess humility. The sting reveals their hubris. Until humility becomes a virtue, truth will sting instead of shining light.

> The aim is to live in the light.
> The aim is to lead in the light.

Those who train with rigor transform into a state of freedom. This state is produced by humility. It's a startling revelation, this true humility, to know how insignificant one is, to know how little one matters, to know the only thing that matters is the mission, the purpose, the calling, and leaving tracks.

Simply stated, leadership development crushes the ego, and most achievers are rewarded for inflating and projecting the ego.

I think Aristotle[3] would caution me that–

> No. Not fools. They sought goods that have some good, just not the highest good, truth, which is your aim. They sought pleasure. They sought wealth. They sought honor and fame. They sought achievement. They sought victory. They sought goods. You seek the highest good, truth. You seek the highest activity, contemplative wisdom.

Then I inquire–

> Is leadership required to seek this highest good, called truth?

Then I inquire, again–

> How should we define what is called leadership?

Then I inquire, once more–

> What kind of leader am I seeking to be, and what kind of leadership am I seeking to transmit to others?

Two decades in this pursuit and I'm still asking these foundational questions. Why is this? Why can't I see the truth about leadership development?

---

[3] Aristotle, *Nicomachean Ethics*, Sachs Translation.

I think Aristotle would offer an insight and then ask a question–

> You are seeking the highest truth as living and revealed wisdom. Is this necessary for basic leadership development?

I respond–

> So long as leaders exert authority and power over others, yes.

Now, I think Aristotle would caution me–

> Only the sages, philosophers, warriors, mystics, and saints who devoted their lives to such training can achieve this aim. These devoted ones are able to become the light of truth because they have undergone the most rigorous of all training: the perfection of spirit in mind, body, soul, and art.

Now, I hear *The Bhagavad Gita*[4] echoing from the depths–

> Unless the focus is on the warrior or guardian class of beings, what I've discovered is not meant for the majority of leaders.

> For the warrior, yes: "Courage, vigor, steadfastness, resourcefulness, and also an unwillingness-to-flee in battle, generosity, and a regal disposition."

> For the guardian, yes: "Calm, restraint, austerity, purity, patience, uprightness, real knowledge and worldly knowledge, piety (holiness)."

Now I am at a loss, I've already worked with the warriors, where do I go from here?

I think Saint John of the Cross would comment–

> Best to head towards the summit-abiding place in solitude and compassion.[5]

Now, I have to smile. I live in solitude. I practice but have not perfected the virtue of compassion, in its two-fold meaning–

1. To suffer with.
2. To see the light within.

I see a leader's light. I willingly suffer with leaders. I work to eradicate the suffering (as arrogance and ignorance) and awaken the light and the truth.

The Bhagavad Gita echoes again from the depths, the aim of illumination–

---

[4] *The Bhagavad Gita*, Feuerstein translation.
[5] Saint John of the Cross, *The Ascent of Mount Carmel*.

The disunion of the union with suffering.[6]

Why the effort? Because leaders exert incredible physical and psychological power and authority over human beings. In this light, they are sources and causes of needless suffering.

Why the effort? As a seeker of wisdom, I too, am still eradicating my own ignorance and arrogance and suffering. Ignorance as not knowing and seeing the source of the light and truth. Arrogance as self-will. Suffering as turmoil and torment. The saints said it best, the only criteria are to become pure in heart, poor in spirit, and unconditionally loving—the virtues of detachment, humility and charity. That's it. That's the conditioning we seek to actualize. Simple to write about, difficult to live and to become.

The Angelic Doctor mentors–

> There is no greater act of charity one can do to his neighbor than to lead him
> to the truth.[7]

You might be asking—why am I so driven to do this work? Why focus the effort on the corporate and political leaders? The answer—it's a calling.

The purpose—to ensure the economic, intellectual, spiritual, and moral security for our citizens.

No, the true purpose—the welfare of all human beings.

So, the question becomes, who is best to do this—to lead us to security, prosperity, and harmony? The warriors? The guardians? The sages? The saints?

I answer, only these devoted ones.

Now I ask, where do we find these devoted ones?

How do we find them?

Why find them?

Why? Because we need human beings who are worthy of admiration. We need human beings who are worthy to lead us. Few are called to lead. Few are called to pursue truth. Those who are called we need to find. We need them to accept the burden of leadership.

I know they are out there. I've met them—those worthy of our trust, worthy of leadership. Those who we can trust with power and authority over our institutions and enterprises.

---

[6] *The Bhagavad Gita*, Feuerstein translation.
[7] Peter Kreeft, *Socratic Logic*, Saint Thomas quoted.

Even with this knowledge, I'm in despondency. How did I even arrive here? What have I spent twenty years doing? Has it been in vain? Did my thirst lead me to mirages? Where is the well of truth? Where are the waters of truth? I'm dying of thirst.

In contemplation, I again look at this glacier of truth. No gear. No way forward. I don't see the route. The truth I seek is still veiled.

My mind is searching. What do I hate? Ah. There it is. I hate seeing egotists in command and authority manipulating others.

My mind is searching. What do I love? Ah. There it is. My freedom. Freedom of movement and freedom of being. I live in freedom. I am free.

My mind is searching. My freedom is not good enough. I care about you, my fellow human beings. I hate seeing you enslaved in the tyranny of the bureaucracy and in the tyranny of egotists and narcissists. I hate the toxicity of these tyrants poisoning the spirits and souls of all the world. It does not have to be this way. Any organization can be made noble by and through good leaders.

Dejected and in need of guidance, I called the mentor. The mentor I called is known as warrior, teacher, leader, guide, and guardian. He is a true sage.

I called. He listened. I shared with him what I shared with you. After a prolonged silence, he spoke. He began to share a dialogue that he had listened to, as a student, years before. From his perspective, what he heard could have been told three millennia before.

It began with a truth. Since the dawn of human history, roughly 70,000 BC, no evidence suggests human brains have evolved biologically. The implications—the human being and our human nature have not changed. The meaning—we are always experiencing the eternal return, each generation, each individual human being, from age to age, tasked with transcending the temporal and biological and entering the eternal and spiritual.

As he spoke, I listened. As I listened, I wrote down this story. The story is a dialogue between a warrior and a guardian. The story is a journey into the essence of light and the nature of truth. The story leads to the summit-abiding place, where the essence and nature of leadership reveals itself.

It is here, in this summit-abiding place, where my fury transformed into supreme joy.

Live in the light,

The Writer

CHAPTER TWO
THE BEGINNING

Guardian: We are called to discover–

How to teach leadership.
How to educate leaders.
How to develop leaders.

We discover "the how" by uncovering leadership's foundational structure. And its foundational structure is found in the essence and nature of the human being.

To uncover leadership's foundation, we must hunt in our own souls. We must hunt with prejudice. We must hunt like we're the last souls on the planet dying of hunger tearing across the plains, jungles, and mountains.

The terrain, though, is more treacherous than the longest desert and deepest ravine. The terrain is the soul.

What is a soul? What is it to be conscious? The physical and theoretical sciences, fine arts, humanities, and social sciences fall short; it cannot be described aptly.

Neurobiology and the study of artificial intelligence continue to raise more questions than answers. And rightly so. Artificial intelligence does not require consciousness, self-awareness, or a soul. And yet, it is produced by consciousness, self-awareness, and soul. This artificial intelligence is produced by a living intelligence. An intelligence whose nature it is to ask questions.

Warrior: What do you see?

Guardian: I can point to the signs that lead us to journey into the soul. The sign pointing to the path that must be followed says: the soul is the essence of our deepest interior nature; it is what lives deepest within us. The truth is, we live a composite conditioned life—yes, living and breathing and moving—but what moves us is something deeper, more mysterious and more powerful than any of our physical senses.

This is why we must hunt into the depths and heights of the interior ascent. But we must not fall into the temptation to observe other hunters.

Warrior: Why?

Guardian: Spectators starve to death in the passive state of observing. No, we must engage in the dynamic cycle of being and becoming. We must produce the awakening.

As Plato observed, behavior can hide our true nature. Behavior can hide and conceal the soul. A bad person acts saintly. We call him good. A good person acts criminally. We call him bad.[1]

To hunt deeper and deeper into the soul requires us to simultaneously transcend the perishable self, that which is mortal, that which dies with the body, the matter, that the soul gives form to. As we descend into the gorges of the soul, we must ascend beyond transcendence.

Warrior: Why?

Guardian: To reach beyond the edge of our composite-conditioned-existence.

To discover truth—and by truth we mean to reach the inner central 'nerve' laid bare—to discover essence and nature. And with this discovery, when we find it, we will understand how to 'lead' out of the depths of the soul; we'll receive leadership's nature and essence and power.

So first, we must know our innermost nature and essence. We must know ourselves. We must know the formal cause, the material cause, the efficient cause and the final cause.[2] We must find and feel the inner nerve. We must lay it bare, the soul, lay it out, in all its ugliness and beauty and hurt and pain. And only then can we begin to know what goodness is, what truth is, what beauty is. This goodness, this truth, once discovered and awakened, may then allow us to lead truthfully and objectively. And only then will we have earned the trust to guide others to discover the truth, the truth that guides us in the cardinal acts of leading. This truth is the light of wisdom.

This truth, this inner central nerve—detached from ego and desire—allows us to lead. Yes, we have ego. Yes, we have desire. But we need not let this weakness sour the soil of the soul.

The core technique of detachment will serve as our best weapon on this hunting expedition. In this way, when we look within, we can turn from the ego and not get ensnared by this 'king of mirages.' This 'king of deception' always waits in the shadows to disorient us and sting us; its goal is to collapse and paralyze us.

On this journey, there is an enemy—an enemy more dangerous than a thermonuclear intercontinental missile. This enemy is the ego. The ego is the source of desire. It lives within us and is wrapped around truth—our inner nerve—like a cancer that may ebb and flow but will never leave on its own. We render it powerless with detachment, discernment, and dialogue.

We need to be on guard to save ourselves from deception. We need to be on guard to keep ourselves from chasing mirages instead of truth.

---

[1] Plato, *Republic*, Joe Sachs translation.
[2] Aristotle, *Metaphysics*. Joe Sachs translation.

We need to temper the primordial desire in order to quench our thirst for knowledge. Let us be thirsty and see what happens when that thirst is denied.

This is why you, my blessed friend, have been called as a fellow explorer. You will see me erring, not quick enough to catch my own mistakes. You'll help me correct those errors, those miscalculations giving birth within the soul. You will save me from falling into crevasses, or when I do, you'll provide the gear to bring me back onto stable ground.

On this hunt, when we make a discovery we need the courage (the fire of our irrational nature) and the wisdom (the light of our rational nature) to let it change, to let it transform our instinctual behavior. We need the mettle and the might to let the principles and structures brand themselves into our being—the structure and principles that let us see and contend with truth.

We need to document these discoveries to create a domain of knowledge that can be taught and transmitted to others. We are not looking for the 'who' or the 'why. Instead, we are looking for the 'what' and the 'how.' What is it 'To Lead?'

What we are looking for is beyond opinion and fashion. It existed well before the light came in and will exist long after the light dies out. We are not looking for buzzwords. We are not looking to sell. We are not looking to gain stuff or new angles. We are seeking to know and understand. We are on the hunt. As the hunter requires weapons, our journey requires structures and lenses that make it possible 'To Lead' and then 'To Develop Leaders.'

In our quest, we seek to disclose the timeless and eternal structures that not even natural laws and gravity can affect. We are not looking to make something. There is no product or app. We are looking for what awakens the potential of the human being to lead. This exploring of ours is not a creative act; it is an act of discovery by a hunter on the hunt for his life. We are on guard against all miracle elixirs and YouTube charlatans. What we seek will be discovered when something within our nature awakens and is unleashed—something that will explode once we see and understand the core nerve of truth and goodness—a source of potent energy made to be released and realized. The potency of our nature.

In preparation, we need also to recognize where and when we have erred in the past.

In our arrogance, we thought we could, poof, create it, imagine it, and in doing so, we missed the mark. All the digital revolutions, technology, and ephemeral disruptive business modes will never produce or inspire good and just and wise leaders.

We have been greatly misled. We have allowed incompetent men and women to exercise unbelievable control in wealth, business, finance and government over our lives. We build nuclear-propelled, unmanned spaceships to probe the deepest reaches of the universe, and yet we cannot govern ourselves on our planet with the human qualities of beauty, freedom, and justice.

Why is this? The human being must grow. The human being must fulfill its purpose. Right now, we neither value nor nurture each human being's purpose. In our weakness, as Pieper[3] warned, we have led ourselves into the slave society of work. Work may be for the common need but beauty and truth and freedom are for the common good.

I call on you to focus on the good of man, not just the needs of man.

Emerson[4] reminds us that the secret of genius is to suffer no fiction.

You understand why I've called upon you. You are the only living being I've met who has the intellectual courage and depth of experience to help me discover the truth about leadership and how to develop leaders. And to do this, we must transcend fiction.

We have already demonstrated dedication in our lives to this pursuit. We have already sacrificed all else to this aim.

And yet this truth stings us–we have not discovered how to transmit this knowledge. Instead, we use sheer force of will and force of action to get others to follow us.

We know this is unsustainable. We know the knowledge and understanding dies with us. You can lead. I can lead. But, can we teach leadership? Can we develop leaders? Do we even have the right structures and signs and symbols to do so?

Warrior: As I listen, I wonder why we have neither taught leadership nor teach leadership in the same way as masters of other arts do—such as war, music, literature, architecture, and neurobiology.

Guardian: Because we are not masters and we have not met masters.

Warrior: Then, are we still students?

Guardian: Yes, we are students. But, we are also practitioners. Your concern, as is mine, is that this concept of leadership is still new, as an art, it's still in its infancy. Days past, the terms used were king, commander and governor. Why, now, is leadership revealing itself? I surmise, because democracy has taken root on the planet, a new way of being and relating is revealing itself. This has been a recent blink of an eye since the first Homo sapiens left East Africa to explore the world. This new way of being has been coined 'leadership,' but it draws heavily from war, business, and governance. The challenge now is that a person must not only master an activity, but also master the connecting and inspiring of free human beings, who at any moment can turn to a different organization with their time and energy.

---

[3] Josef Pieper, *Leisure: The Basis of Culture.*
[4] Ralph Waldo Emerson, "Representative Men."

Warrior: Okay. If leadership has been deemed a critical ability, why do we keep trying to teach leadership as a secondary activity instead of the primary activity?

Guardian: Good question. I cannot give the answer. Instead, let us hunt. Let the way of the warrior come into view. Let us look at the development process. First, there is basic training. Second, there is a pre-deployment training cycle of 18 months. Third, the warrior deploys to combat zones for 6 months. Fourth, upon return, the cycle begins again. Essentially their lives center around a two-year cycle: warriors train for 18 months, deploy for 6 months, and then repeat. This method of preparation leads to intuitive and embedded knowledge and the hard-earned instinct needed for warfighting. They train specifically for war.

Let the way of the musician come into view. The musician trains with a music master and can receive instruction for decades. The hope is that, after a decade of deliberate practice, the musician masters the techniques and mechanics to become a virtuoso performer. Skill and ability is monitored, measured, and assessed. Heart and inspiration are judged. Few reach the pinnacle of the solo seat in an orchestra.

Let the way of the artist come into view. The artist trains with a painting master, and then trains for a decade to develop mastery. Few reach the pinnacle of being master painters.

Warrior: How about the Martial Arts?

Guardian: The same goes with the martial arts. A revealing method is how the Shaolin monks dedicate their entire lives to the mastery of Kung Fu and Buddhism. They structure every hour of every day to this end.

And yet, with the way of the leader, this process of mastery is not applied!

If we are honest, leading is dreadfully more difficult than mastering one skill. Instead of making leadership development central, we treat it as a bolt-on activity. We treat it as a skill that can be learned on the job. Most jobs don't require leadership until there are strategic consequences. Most jobs require command and management. Why? There is not enough freedom to lead at the lower levels; this lack of freedom kills insights, initiative and adaptability.[5] You are told what to do, you are told the targets. You are not free to determine your own methods, targets, and skills. And how do you get ahead? By being a master of one thing and the tasks associated with that one thing. Then you're promoted. And once promoted, you learn, you are incompetent at leading, unless perhaps you micromanage those people that do that one thing that you once did. And you get promoted for this incompetence.

What I'm seeing is that we have made good human beings into conformists, and conformists cannot lead! Conformists do as they are told, and they serve what is the known, the status quo.

---

[5] Frans Osinga, *Science, Strategy, and War: The Strategic Theory of John Boyd.*

The known, the status quo, leads to destruction and death. The unknown, the potential to be realized, leads to freedom and vitality.

Instead of developing leaders, we buckle leadership training haphazardly to tactical and technical expertise, operational and managerial expertise, and command and strategic expertise.

How do we know we do this haphazardly? When we see this (the disease of today's leadership), when great experts fail to lead other experts.

> We see this too often—great tacticians failing in operational leadership.

> We see this too often—great operators failing in strategic leadership.

> And the worst failure of all—great strategic minds who failed in command.

Warrior: You see correctly. What do you suggest as a remedy? What is the antivenom?

Guardian: Before we offer a remedy. We need to ask what are we seeing and what aren't we seeing? You taught me this—to always ask: "what aren't we looking at?"

I can only offer what I'm seeing right now.

Warrior: Go on, tell me what you're seeing.

Guardian: It seems the building blocks of current leadership development do not lead to leadership at all, but are really organizational building blocks, focused on the structure and systems of the organization, not the nature and faculties of the human being.

What we have is horizontal development but no vertical development—the character and intellectual nature of the leader.

What I mean is, unlike in the martial and musical arts, most leadership thought is taken in the context of the enterprise: How to lead an organization or an enterprise.

What these thinkers[6] have failed to understand, and I'm reminded of Musashi[6], the great Samurai swordsman, is that whether engaged in a dual or in a war, whether with one person or with thousands of combatants, the principles remain the same. And it's here that I think we've failed in our thinking—we've created blind leaders, leaders who can only see what is tangible but cannot see what they cannot imagine (the intangible). And that intangibility leads to insights. And because these leaders do not know how to generate insights, they are blind to the truths revealing themselves.

---

[6] Miyamoto Musashi, *The Book of Five Rings.*

We keep looking at structure, systems, processes and skills that make the enterprises flourish. But, we have failed to develop the human principles that each human being in the enterprise must know and practice.

Pieper[7] would say, by allegiance to the conformity of values demanded by organizations, we have created skilled automatons instead of mature, virtuous, and freethinking human beings.

The irony, these skilled automatons think they are mature, free and virtuous!

I'm cautious to speak this way, but, because we are friends and *this is a sacred dialogue*, I must speak freely.

Warrior: Speak freely and truthfully.

Guardian: Does it not concern you and do you not wonder how it's possible that we create powerful systems and machines and yet it seems the human being is getting weaker in body, thought, and feeling?

I say weaker because of the obesity epidemic that has exploded. I say weaker because the number of prescriptions written for bodily and psychological weaknesses has exploded. It seems the human being, the good of the human being, the flourishing state of the human being, has been compromised. Is this not so?

Warrior: I won't say so publicly, but, because we are friends, yes, it seems the human being is getting weaker in mind and body. And that weakness is dangerous and yet at the same time easy to control. So, if you are asking me why things are as they are, I'd say that the controllers want weak people because weak wills lack the strength to resist and without resistance they obey. And if it's only about profiting off calculated combinations of white sugar, corn syrup, salt, and processed carbohydrates, then perhaps that is even worse.

Guardian: This is why I am hunting for this myself. And once I discover truth, then I'll find only the types of inner-natures that are capable of developing this way. I know this is not for everyone, but the war is against those few who exercise so much authority in the main—those few, that are, in my estimation, intellectually arrogant and morally corrupt.

To compete, to battle these few, we need to understand the structure of an organization's operational environment.

There seem to be two categories, organization and activity, with a total of six abilities that leaders must gain command of to compete.

---

[7] Josef Pieper, *Leisure: The Basis of Culture.*

Category I: Organization level

1. Tactical/Technical
2. Operational
3. Strategic

Category II: Activity level

1. Command
2. Management
3. Leadership

If we are honest, does this not look like too much for one leader to master? Why not just cut our losses, quit this endeavor, and be owners and investors? Why not just play the game?

Warrior: I played that game. I went to Harvard Business School and Goldman Sachs after going to war. I lasted only a few years. Silky, vile and villainous snakes, everywhere, who I physically and intellectually wanted to crush. But, man, did they know how to play the game—control by wealth drove them. They think wealth is hard power. But in reality, it is not power. It holds on by a string.

Guardian: Yes. It can be taken away. Anything that can be taken away, is not true power. Economic strength, not wealth, is power, the power to produce goods and services.

Warrior: Then, what are the sources of power?

Guardian: I see seven sources of power in society–

1. Military
2. Political
3. Economic
4. Technological
5. Social
6. Religious
7. Intellectual

From these sources, I see three primary levers of power–

1. Control by organized power.
2. Control by military power.
3. Control by economic power.

These are the three levers leaders use to win "obedience and consent." Most notably, one lever of power is missing.

Warrior: What do you see?

Guardian: There is one more lever of power, and this comes from the intellectual source of power–

> 1. To lead, not control, by influence, appreciation, and persuasion, led by truth's guidance.

Warrior: And that is why I am here. I want to learn how to teach leaders to fight with their minds so as not to control but to awaken and be guided by light and truth.

Guardian: That is why I fight this war too. In this age, we are in a cosmic conflict with our fellow Homo sapiens. The hope is to discover how to prepare leaders—to stand their ground in truth and lead. The hope is to teach leaders how to fight with the counterweights to manipulation, wooing, seduction, and coercion.

The counterweights are influence, inspiration, harmony and initiative.

To begin, do we agree that our search is narrowed to the intellectual source of power and the lever of influence? To prepare for this non-martial combat?

Warrior: Yes.

Guardian: Do you have the patience?

Warrior: Yes.

Guardian: Then, let the aim, the final cause, lead us, the efficient cause, to the source, the formal cause.

To orient us, for mastery, it takes up to ten years or 10,000 hours of deliberate practice to learn how to play one instrument.

Warrior: Yes. Ericsson's research suggests this is true.[8]

Guardian: Now, look again at the abilities a leader must gain command of to compete. Is it less or more demanding than learning one instrument or one skill?

Warrior: They are not less. They are more demanding.

Guardian: Then at maximum, we would need 60,000 hours of training, practice and experience required to master leadership in the activities of tactics, operations, strategy, management, command, and leadership.

Is this realistic?

---

[8] K. Anders Ericsson and Jaqui Smith, *Toward A General Theory of Expertise.*

Warrior: Not in the way we currently structure professional development in our institutions.

Guardian: Indeed. And we have not even mentioned where these leadership abilities are needed– Politics, War, Business, Finance, Commerce, Economics, Education and Technology. Let's add another 10,000 hours to master one of these domains.

Warrior: By this estimate, it looks like 70,000 hours of deliberate practice and experience is needed to lead at the highest levels.

Guardian: What does this reveal?

Warrior: Complete ignorance of the controlling class—the Generals, the CEOs, the Politicians, the Administrators, the Chancellors, and the Provosts. They act like they know how to lead when they have no idea. They were trained in domain skill, not leadership skill. They were trained to manage the knowledge, the organization, the status quo. They are highly prized automatons.

Guardian: Forgive them. Pity them. They do not know their own ignorance. They rule by wealth, they rule by power, they rule by force. But they do not lead.

Warrior: And you and I, do we know our ignorance?

Guardian: Yes. Which is how we even know that we must hunt for truth.

Warrior: Why?

Guardian: To eradicate our ignorance. To ascend into truth's knowing.

Saint Thomas mentors us here–

> Knowledge is the offspring of truth.[9]

Warrior: Then, can we claim that anyone who is currently speaking about leadership development is in error, and does not understand what they are saying and seeing?

Guardian: Yes.

Warrior: Then, all those New York Times best sellers are wrong?

Guardian: Yes.

Warrior: All of them?

Guardian: Yes.

---

[9] Josef Pieper, *Living the Truth.* Saint Thomas Quoted.

Warrior: But surely some of those books at the airport and required readings at Stanford, Sloan, Harvard, and Wharton have something of value to add.

Guardian: No.

Warrior: All those TED talks?

Guardian: No.

Warrior: All those conferences, libraries, and treatises by fortune 500 leaders?

Guardian: No.

Warrior: What is the better way?

Guardian: What are you seeing?

Warrior: Don't answer my question with a question.

Guardian: I cannot and will not tell you. You and I are on the hunt of our lives. You and I, both of us, must find our core nerve, our essence, our truth.

Warrior: Then, maybe there's a better way to think about 'leadership' instead of 'enterprise leadership.' Maybe we need to step outside of current systems and domains?

Guardian: Yes, you are closing in on the nerve center.

Warrior: What principles lead us inward, to the core?

Guardian: Let us propose these tenets or guiding principles–

1. Leaders need to be independent of any hierarchy.
2. Leaders need to live outside any system.
3. Leadership needs to be independent of the enterprise.

Warrior: In one stroke, you slice the 'Gordian knot' keeping the truths of leadership development in the dark.

Guardian: I do hope so. Managers, not leaders, need to live inside the enterprise. That is why we call them Executives. Generals, not leaders, need to live in their Commands. That is why we call them Commanders. But leaders, the kind that I have in mind, they need to live outside of any organizational structure. They cannot be beholden to the temporal and functional and transactional demands that keep a system or enterprise efficient and effective.

Warrior: Do you mean they are a law unto themselves?

Guardian: No, I mean they are detached from the tyranny of the technocrats and the tyranny of bureaucracy. They need to be free to speak their mind with impunity. They need to be free from subjecting themselves to another human being who has control or influence over them. They need to be free from organizational or institutional achievement so that they can see and understand how to respond to reality's unfolding. Our leaders fear no achievement and they fear no loss. They only seek to disclose the truth and know how to respond.

Warrior: Are you even sure we should call what you're describing leadership?

Guardian: Do you have a better term for the concept I'm seeing?

Warrior: Not yet.

Guardian: What if what I call leaders are not leaders at all, but functional and skilled experts and workers?

What if the beginnings of leadership development must be independent of:

1. The enterprise (organization)
2. The function (command and management)
3. The level (tactical, operational, strategic)
4. The domain (finance, war, business, education)

What if the eternal truths of leadership have remained hidden because we've been looking at what is concrete, what is brick and mortar, and only what we can see and touch and feel and smell and hear?

Warrior: I am not seeing the path of the hunt. You're losing me.

Guardian: What if what we are looking for is independent of enterprise structures, processes, systems and skills?

What do you think has happened because we make human beings subordinate to organizational objectives and requirements at the expense of their human development?

Warrior: We create company men. We create conformists. We kill creativity. We kill freedom. We kill insights. We kill the iconoclasts.

Guardian: This terrifies me.

Warrior: Then, have we made professionals in organizations servants to the organization instead of servants to the truth?

Guardian: Yes. If we remove the word servant and replaced it with slave, have we made human beings slaves to the organization? Bondage to truth frees and empowers.

Warrior: That is a bit of a stretch. They choose where to give their energy and minds as labor and skill.

Guardian: I've asked this question of professionals–

> If you were independently wealthy, would you still willingly give your energy and mind to achieve the organizational targets demanded of you?

Warrior: What do they say?

Guardian: 99 out of 100 say they would quit. What does that tell you?

Warrior: The coercive power of economic need reigns like a king. I'm reminded of the proverb, "he lived to be 100, he died when he was 30."

Guardian: That is why I love working with warriors, scholars, scientists, creators, and artists. They have to do their work. Their work is an extension of their being.

While I look for those who are called, my concern is with all beings.

Warrior: That is my concern too—all beings.

Guardian: Then what is the outcome of this current organizational way of being?

Warrior: We have made professionals and workers into submissive and obedient servants instead of freethinking leaders who pursue truth and then act accordingly.

Guardian: What do you think has happened to the character of these professionals after a decade or more of sacrificing their reason and what they know is right because of organizational or political pressures?

Warrior: The spirit and might of their souls has been crushed. Their character has been weakened and corrupted.

Instead of practicing courage by taking a stand, they buckled and imploded when faced with the artificial and fabricated pressures of organizational demands. They end up highly skilled cowards.

Guardian: Are we seeing this correctly? Are they, these conformists, worthy of becoming leaders?

Warrior: It is terrifying. I've been fighting and killing evil men for a long time—a sheep dog against the wolf to protect the innocent—but I never thought how dangerous executives could be until this moment. They don't kill people like the 'wolves' of this world; they are soul killers. That is a cosmic crime.

Guardian: Corporate wolves. Slave labor masters. Cowardly souls escaping the burdens of freedom, refusing the burden of wielding courageous axes–the axes of freedom.

A leader is no slave master nor is a leader a slave. A leader is self-governing and self-sufficient. A leader is no servant. Servants work for other men, not for themselves. Does this sting? Am I hitting a raw nerve? Are you drunk with the grey sobriety of the cold empty essence? Do we have the courage to look at this?

It's terrifying that the theory of servant leadership gets praised. It's an ill-conceived concept. Instead look to the powers of Christ's words and deeds.

Warrior: The analogy does not hold. This is beginning to sound sacrosanct, offensive, and odd given so many do not believe in Christ.

Guardian: For a Christian: Christ is Lord, Christ Sacrifices, Christ Frees, Christ Forgives, but Christ is no servant; he is the Eternal King.

Instead of servant leadership, it should be called Christ-like leadership—godlike leadership.

Warrior: Fine. But no Christian should be arrogant enough to think he can be godlike.

Guardian: The saints prove otherwise by the darkness of faith. They take part in the divine nature, with light and truth, a godlike quality of seeing, knowing, and loving.

Warrior: You are losing me.

Guardian: What are you seeing?

Warrior: I see cowardly conformists managing the enterprises by power and authority, by command and control, not by leadership and influence and appreciation.[10] The dignity of each soul has not been recognized and valued.

In this light, Josef Pieper mentors–

> His dignity is ignored; I concentrate on his weakness and on those areas that may appeal to him–all in order to manipulate him, to use him for *my* purposes.[11]

Guardian: And these blessed conformists, because of their political finesse, because of their cunning, because of their savviness, because of their bag of tricks, because of their reading of behavior, because of the ability to coerce and manipulate, they reach the top of their enterprises. And then, when they do, what do we call them?

Warrior: We call them leaders.

Guardian: Are they? Are they leaders? Are they free? Are they worthy of admiration?

---

[10] Frans Osinga, *Science, Strategy, and War–The Strategic Theory of John Boyd.*
[11] Josef Pieper, *Abuse of Language, Abuse of Power.*

Warrior: It all depends on how you define the concepts of leader and leadership.

By the common definition, "to be in charge," then, yes, they are leaders. I think where you are going is that you look at the soul of the human being and then make the judgment call, independent of achievements and honors.

Guardian: Ah ha! Rousseau may be of help here. He wrote his educational treatise with democratic societies in mind.

That fearless and lucid writer on education, and at the same time a deeply flawed father, wrote, in his treatise *Emile, or On Education* the most powerful point in but a fistful of words.

Rousseau said the purpose of education is to awaken a freethinking human being to be independent of the wills, emotions, and judgments of others. He wrote–

> I make his well-being independent of either the will or the judgments of others.[12]

I cannot call conformists leaders. They are not independent but dependent. This dependence strips them of true power. Corporate leaders give people what they want. They cater to the wills and judgments of others and then become wealthy and successful. I cannot call this kind of character a leader. They are demagogues. They create and sell "consumerism and eroticism, greed and lust."[13] And we reward them for it by buying their goods and buying the stocks.

Warrior: It seems we are surrounded by the opposite of what Rousseau aimed at in educating freethinking human beings. What we have are conformists. What we have are human beings who conform their own will and judgments to the will and judgments of others.

But why? To be liked and to be accepted and to fit in?

Guardian: This tendency, in previous times, may have been called for when *exile* was a common practice.

Warrior: But now what do we do? We make our well-being dependent upon the wills and judgments of others.

Guardian: Is that not bondage instead of freedom? Can we call this the trifecta of emotional-intellectual-spiritual slavery?

Warrior: Why do you keep using the word slavery? It stings. It's a crime against humanity. It implies bondage. It reminds me of the horrors of history that haunt our society. And rightfully

---

[12] Jean Jacques Rousseau, *Emile, or On Education*, Bloom translation.
[13] Peter Kreeft, *Handbook of Christian Apologetics*.

so. Can we not drop the term slavery? Let's use another word. This is offensive, out of place, and hyperbolic.

Guardian: Stop. We can be free externally under laws and government and still be slaves—living in cognitive bondage—internally in our relationships to other beings and to reality.

Warrior: Then we hunt for the truth of what lives hidden in ourselves. And we will expose a similar truth in the citizenry. And I'm telling you right now, this hurts. This is a pain, an ache that I can't drown with booze and pills.

Guardian: For consolation, I can't help but think of Aquinas' perspective–

> There is no greater act of charity one can do to his neighbor than to lead him to the truth.[14]

Warrior: And that is the aim, once we discover the truth, to lead others to it.

Guardian: That is the keystone principle–

> To lead others to see and know the truth.

I add another principle–

> To live and lead in the light.

For twenty years this has been my leadership 'battle cry.'

This is our endeavor–

> To endure as we guide leaders to seek the truth, to disclose the truth, and to wield courage to act upon the truth they know.

To steady ourselves, can we lay down these principles, and leap from them, as we hunt for leadership's truths?

Warrior: To what end?

Guardian: To lead leaders to know light and truth.

Warrior: I'd caution on the use of the word truth.

Guardian: I exercise no such caution on our hunt. We are hunting now, not just to live, but to awaken the light and truth in our souls. What is life if we have no soul? What is leading, if we don't lead souls?

Basil King's "Conquest of Fear" is echoing from the depths–

---

[14] Peter Kreeft, *Socratic Logic.* Saint Thomas quoted.

Go at it boldly, and you'll find unexpected forces closing round you and coming to your aid.[15]

Warrior: Then, let's roll, in boldness and strength and courage.

Guardian: If our aim is to lead others to light and truth, then the groundwork must first be to condition their character to be independent of the wills and judgments of others. This conditioning is critical–They must be able to take a stand against the tyranny of opinions, the tyranny of fears and the tyranny of judgments.

Warrior: This means, we need to teach leaders the freedom and burden of speaking one's mind. What you are driving at is the union of intellectual and moral virtues that direct the cardinal acts of leading. What do you call this union and act?

Guardian: Fortitude. To speak one's mind with discerning fearlessness.

To achieve this, we must teach leaders to be detached from the organization and from careerism.

Warrior: This is our first obstacle.

Guardian: What do you see?

Warrior: Instead of detachment and discernment, I see careerists. These careerists are organizational survivalists. And these survivalists are in nature and essence conformists. Let us call them "survivalist-conformist-careerists." These SCCs, known as CEOs and SESs[16], are rewarded for behaving this way—the conformist artist, aka, the confidence artist. In essence they are con artists. They rely on deception instead of truth. They manipulate instead of lead. They create false wants disguised as needs. They are obsessed with promotion. They are obsessed with income. They are obsessed with wealth. They worry about losing. They worry about failure. They worry about losing wealth. Their worries are primal. This makes them dangerous. They don't seek truth. They don't seek to know truth and act accordingly.

Guardian: Our way of being—to lead others to light and truth—triggers an emotional storm that wreaks havoc, confusion and devastation on the con artists' fragile and imagined reality. Their hallucinations and their shared narratives are shattered and disintegrated by our methods. It seems that a psychological death occurs. And yet this death, this loss of identity, awakens them to their true essence and nature—to a true source of power and freedom that they must now learn to strengthen and take command of.

---

[15] Basil King, *Conquest of Fear*.

[16] The Senior Executive Service (SES) is a position classification in the civil service of the United States federal government, somewhat analogous to general officer or flag officer ranks in the U.S. Armed Forces.

Warrior: I see why you don't hunt within enterprises.

Guardian: Once the fiction is cleared out, once they are able to see their essence, we need to anchor them on the path of virtue, excellence, and wisdom. We need to demonstrate a way that leads to high ideals and high mindedness—yet exposing their nerve laid bare to the brutal essence of reality.

Warrior: This means we need to make ourselves and others strong enough to bear the wills and judgments of others, every day. You mean, we need to live these principles, not just know them. It's a way of being we aim for. And we hit our aim by converting principles into practice.

Guardian: Yes.

Warrior: Do we not see the opposite tendencies today? Organizations and managers using their wills and judgments to control others, to make them obedient, and to make them submit to forces outside of their own nature?

Guardian: Yes. That is why I do not want to train leaders at their organizations. I need nature's sacred ground.

Warrior: We need nature's freedom and beauty to inspire their souls. Nature as a helper?

Guardian: Yes. I must ask it again. Before we go any further. Do you agree that the first principle of leadership development is to make yet-to-be leaders independent of the will and judgments of others? With the aim to make their well-being, their sense of self, their self-esteem, strong and powerful by building moral and psychological strength?

Warrior: Yes. First, we build strong foundations. We do not bypass self-esteem and moral courage. No, we make them a priority. We lead development with this priority. Learning skill is easy. Developing character is difficult.

Guardian: I agree. Our leaders must achieve independence from the assaults of the wills and judgments of others. And yet, simultaneously, we must be on guard against the vice of this independence—arrogance and ignorance.

To be on guard, we cross-examine leaders to reveal interior inconsistencies and incongruities. By this feedback method, we teach leaders to strengthen their character.

Warrior: Instead of this method, what are you seeing, in the realm of leadership training and development?

Guardian: At the core, we do not teach leaders to connect soul to soul nor mind to mind. We teach them to manipulate emotions instead of transcending them. We teach tricks to become likeable. We teach tricks to exhibit behaviors that are rewarded. This always seemed false, artificial and fake to me. I don't want to conform myself to some unnatural pattern. I want to exercise my interior nature, the soul, and condition it into an excellent state of being. I want to become virtuous, in my innermost nature, where I violently and forcibly take command of my desires and feelings, and transform them by the powers of spirit. Only growing the spirit achieves the core of our art. Behaviors make us closer to brutes than angels. By developing the faculties of spirit, the powers of the will and intelligence, we don't conform to an external pattern. No, we awaken our innermost potencies to become the essence of beauty and truth and goodness. Do you see the difference?

Warrior: Ah. We create hollow beings instead of hallowed beings.

Guardian: Good God, yes. Empty shells with soiled and atrophied interior natures. Instead of becoming virtuous, we obey external values. This kind of obeying strips the soul of her powers.

Warrior: Then, what have we discovered? Have we, as a society, forgotten dignity, virtue, excellence and wisdom? Do we, as a society, only value achievement, wealth, honor and glory?

Guardian: It seems to be so. Let us look, again, at the enterprise functions. I'm uneasy with this framework. I'm tempted to leave it behind. It's a closed system. Being in this system keeps us in bondage. We need to be outside of any man-made systems. We need to enter nature's freedom.

Warrior: What are you seeing that others don't see?

Guardian: We need to discover a true leadership development framework.

Warrior: Why?

Guardian: This is what I see—

We take a human being and drop him into these organizational requirements, and in doing so, we lead him into a cell of imprisonment. The cell, the box, the cube, the office, the building, the walls by nature restrict and conform us. We go from an open system, the individual responding to the demands of reality, to a closed system, a cog in a machine, reduced to the way of the automaton.[17] We lose the freedom to think, will, and act to the best of our ability. When we drop ourselves into the bureaucratic functions of the enterprise, we lose our freedom.

By doing this, we are not detached but attached; we are not free, but in bondage; we narrow our vision instead of widening it; instead of being nature, we put our souls into man-made prefabricated constricted containers. These containers dim and weaken—instead of awakening and strengthening and testing—our powers.

---

[17] O.E.D. definition for 'automaton': A living being whose actions are purely involuntary or mechanical; a person behaving without active intelligence or mechanically in a set pattern or routine.

Warrior: Are you saying the modern way is, essentially, the man in a cage?

Guardian: Yes. At least, that is how I felt in an office. I felt caged.

Warrior: Then, is it true to say, you 'felt' this, because you experienced the office as a caged cell?

Guardian: Yes. I had to break free.

Warrior: And now, being free, your vision has awakened?

Guardian: Yes. And this sight is painful. Yet, I do not know a better way.

Warrior: That is why we are hunting?

Guardian: Yes. Most of us are not called to lead. Most of us do not have the inner nature to undergo the rigors of true development.

Warrior: Just as most are not called to be warriors. People 'think' they want to be warriors until the training begins. Once the training begins, most willingly quit.

Guardian: Yes. That is how I am seeing our art. I want it to be hard. I want it to be challenging. I want it to weed out the posers and wannabes. That is why I can't stand current training models. It's fast food for the mind. And it's profitable! It's a billion-dollar racket of charlatans.

That said, maybe I am in error. Maybe enterprise functions are necessary for non-leaders. Maybe this is a good thing.

Warrior: As an analogy, in athletics not everyone has what it takes to become a professional athlete or an Olympian. Yet, we have organizations filled with helpers to support their training and performance.

Guardian: Yes. And yet, even in professional athletic organizations, don't we see non-professional authorities controlling professionals?

Warrior: You mean the ownership class?

Guardian: Yes. A just society would be led by owner-operators, not owner-controllers. I aim to strike at the weakness of the bureaucrats, the lobbyists and the technocrats, who wield power in our pluralistic and lobbyist economy, yet possess no true excellence.[18] We have fools controlling the wise instead of the wise guiding the fools.

Warrior: I don't follow.

---

[18] Carroll Quigley, *Tragedy and Hope*.

Guardian: We have 'managers', who want to 'appear' and 'look' and 'seem' to be leaders, without 'being' leaders. These managers ride on the backs of the experts, innovators and creators.

Warrior: I sense resentment from personal experience. I never experienced that kind of injustice. I felt free as a warrior even though I had to interact with the bureaucracy that supported the mission.

Guardian: It is true, I hated corporate and bureaucratic life. I felt this way of living as complete spiritual oppression. Yes, my basic necessities were cared for; no, my spiritual necessities not only were not cared for, but were trampled on. I felt weak, confused, in a state of darkness. Had I known what I am, I would have resigned within a week, instead of spending a decade in a voluntary spiritual and metaphysical purgatory.

The kind of leader I admire, I could not find in professional organizations. I found great managers and good souls who were pivotal mentors, but, I never wanted to be like them. I never wanted to lead 'inside' an organization. I needed to find a natural and creative wilderness. I needed freedom to develop, untethered from administrative activities. I resonated with creators, with warriors, with artists, with musicians, with statesmen, with sages, and with saints. They had to become something. They had to awaken the daemon. The daemon speaks to all of us. It leads to the awakening. The daemon led me to the perspective that leadership development needed to be seen in the same light as the development of warriors and sages. This search led me to techniques that combined the physical, intellectual, and spiritual. It is here that I discovered a different pathway to training. It is here that I discovered the 'battle skills' of leading.

Warrior: I'm not clear. Why did you experience freedom in sports and oppression in organizations?

Guardian: The organization is too controlling, too mechanical, too administrative, too focused on the organization at the expense of individual. I felt the organization should be there to free the human being to pursue more freedom in virtue and excellence, not less.

In athletics, you trained and competed. Your performance and your growth mattered. The means and ends of athletics are the same.

Warrior: Ah. Okay. What you are saying, in athletics, you had to train and master skills and then compete and demonstrate and display those skills. Most importantly, you loved the activities of competitive sports and of leading warriors. Compared to these experiences, you hated the activities that led to bureaucratic and management achievements.

Guardian: Close. Let me be clear then. I don't mind management functions if I love the mission. In the Marines, one had to exercise leadership by integrating the functions of tactics, operations, strategy, and management.

Warrior: Then, why did the way of management not resonate with you?

Guardian: Why not? The entrepreneurs are free. The builders are free. The creators are free. I love the creators. I love small businesses. I love small government agencies. I hate massive organizational structures. To me, they seem to be leviathans, crushing the freedom of citizens into a life of total work instead of freedom. These organizations are totalitarian structures cloaked as free and necessary enterprises.

Warrior: Then, what is your aim? What kind of leader are you aiming to produce?

Guardian: Striking at the Gordian knot, if these enterprises, these leviathans and totalitarian structures, were led by worthy men and women, we would be spared from the rigors of this expedition.

What I am striking at is not the structure. No. What I am striking at is the viciousness that takes place in the modern organization. They are places where souls are fearful to speak their mind, places where souls encounter incompetent, insecure, and unstable mangers. Now we must ask, why would souls put up with these injustices? Why?

Warrior: Economic pressure and fears.

Guardian: Rightfully so. My aim is not to change the systems or structures, but to change the spirit and souls of those leading these enterprises. My aim is to see more noble and wise leaders leading all citizens, in any and all work, be it bureaucratic or not. In truth, my aim is all souls.

Warrior: Your hope is to see managers who possess the qualities, presence, and command of a statesman?

Guardian: Yes, that is the hope. What if nothing needs to change, except the moral and intellectual virtues of our leaders? What if it is as simple as teaching managers how to pursue truth? And, what if the real test for the manager is the fortitude to act on the truth thus discovered? What then? Would this not change the entire fiber and fabric of the living bond between human beings in each and every profession?

Warrior: Good God, you are idealistic. You're striking at the failures of our educators, not our managers. Our educators have failed to educate and produce strong and powerful citizens.

You aim to strike the power of spirit, to equip leaders to lead by following the truth. You seek to develop leaders to be educators who know how to awaken light and truth in people.

Guardian: Yes.

Warrior: This is not realistic. You are asking too much of an average person.

Guardian: Why? Let me frame it this way. You are a warrior and you trained for combat. What if the needs of the military made you a submariner, and you hated being on a submarine?

Warrior: I'd hate it. I'd have to leave. I'd have to find a different environment. A different way of being. A different way of working.

Guardian: Exactly. And yet, some leaders loved being submariners.

Warrior: True.

Guardian: Then, a true and realistic aim is to teach professionals, who will one day be leaders, to go in the direction that they deem most important.

Warrior: Yes, that is realistic. That is justice. You seek true justice. You seek to remind people that the virtue of justice includes doing one thing well and doing what one is naturally fit to do well.

Guardian: Yes. For me, basic business life is no way of life at all. But, for many it's a beautiful life and way of being that provides economic security for their families. My aim is different from the aim of economic security.

In nature and essence, the way of the leader is similar to the way of the warrior. You fight martial wars. I fight intellectual, emotional and spiritual wars. The way of a leader, as I see it, is not needed to manage organizations. Administrators are needed to manage organizations.

Warrior: Wait. I'm confused. What are you seeking?

Guardian: I am seeking potential leaders, who can lead independent of any skill-based function. I'll take a lawyer who wants to train. I'll take an administrative assistant who wants to train. I'll take a construction worker who wants to train. What I am seeking is to distinguish the power of the soul from the power of organizational authority.

Warrior: You seek human beings, independent of any professional skill and ability?

Guardian: Yes. I'd rather be incompetent professionally and awakened spiritually.

Warrior: And yet, you've never let yourself be professionally incompetent.

Guardian: I aim at excellence in anything I'm entrusted to do, even if I hate the work.

To be clear. I am in search of those called to awaken their potential. I am in search of those called to fight not economic wars, not political wars, not martial wars, but, spiritual, intellectual and emotional wars. I seek a return to the democratic virtue of liberty. I fear this liberty is being destroyed by the modern way of working.

Warrior: You seek leaders, at all levels, at any place in society, not just at the senior and strategic level?

Guardian: Yes. That is what I'm seeking.

Warrior: You are seeking to know the types that can awaken leaders as warriors who fight non-martial wars?

Guardian: We are getting closer.

Warrior: I'm concerned. What is it about business life that you hated?

Guardian: I hated routine superficial and administrative work. I hated a professional routine where it was demanded by my managers that I show up, 5 days a week, 8–12 hours a day. And during that time, I was told what was important and what to do, all the while being caged in an office. To top it off, as a dog bone, I'd get 4 weeks of vacation. And I don't see how a leader would lead that way of life or accept that way of life. All this human potential wasted.

I'm not interested in working 'in' an artificial man-made system, as a cog in a machine, as a means to the end. Where my spirit, as the means, is a servant to the end, to produce 'things and products.' I hate that way of life. And if we are honest, most do. Most submit out of economic necessity. And I understand this, for parents. The vocation of parenting demands economic security.

Warrior: You remind me of a noble savage.

Guardian: So I've been told.

What we call business leadership is the way of the administrator. That is not dynamic. That is not magnetic. That is not geared to training and developing for some great test or challenge.

That is why I want to explore the true art, so we can be honest about our aims. To be clear, I have no contempt for people who live this way and use it as a means, an economic means, to provide for their living. This is fine. However, I cannot call people who live this way leaders. They are functional managers providing for the common needs and wants.

Warrior: What about entrepreneurs?

Guardian: They are like creators until the organization enters a level of maturity and becomes a bureaucracy. For a leader, the action is 'the way' and 'the means' and 'the end.' That should be our elementary test.

Warrior: What are you aiming at?

Guardian: I'm terrified to admit this. **I seek mastery of a sacred art, the art of leading souls.**

Warrior: Ah ha. You said it. You see leadership development as a sacred art, the art of leading souls. **You see this art as the mystical calling to lead souls.**

Why do you call it leadership development instead of spiritual development?

Guardian: Because of the term "lead," which means to guide and direct and to cross thresholds. What are we leading when we say we are leading the human being? We are leading what lives in their inner nature. I do view this as a sacred art. I do think that true leadership is the leading of souls by souls, independent of theology and religion. And instead of this, we have leaders, leading, no, manipulating the irrational desires of human beings instead of their souls. This must change for truth to be awakened.

What I see now is not leadership. I see managers using human beings and their energy as human capital in the form of a skill. They manage skills; they do not lead souls. Nor could they, because they do not even know their own soul. They are in total lack of true knowledge, self-knowledge, which is the keystone to awakening light and truth.

I'm a bit nervous to speak my mind freely. But, because it's just you and I trust you, I'll do my best to speak with courage and freedom in a spontaneous and emergent way.

Leadership is about leading souls. Any other attribute is not leadership. That is why it remains so hidden from view. When I say soul, I do not mean it solely in a theological sense. But I do mean metaphysics—the study of being.[19]

Our current leaders, who are non-leaders, do not know being. If you do not know being, you cannot lead a being. If you do not know yourself, you cannot lead another self. Aristotle[20] equated existence, that which is alive, with being. If there is no being there is no existence. If there is no existence, there is no being. Do you see?

Warrior: In those terms, yes, I do see what you mean as the aim of leading—to lead beings.

Guardian: When I use the term soul or the term spirit, I mean the inner nature of the human being.

Warrior: What is the inner nature of the human being?

Guardian: The inner nature comprises 1) will, 2) intelligence, and 3) spiritedness—expressed as feelings, thoughts, perceptions, wants, needs, desires, pains, pleasures, joys, sorrows—all aimed at meaning, purpose and calling, more than just survival and care of the body. I mean the urge to transcend the physical and the temporal. Most human beings sacrifice their soul to provide for the body instead of sacrificing the body for the soul. That is why we see grotesque cowardice in our citizens. The survivalist-conformist-careerists feed off of this cowardice.

Warrior: Harsh judgments.

---

[19] Aristotle, *On the Soul*, Sachs Translation.
[20] Aristotle, *Metaphysics*, Sachs Translation.

Guardian: Which is why I exercise silence and solitude now. Long ago, I initially hoped once everyone heard this is possible—to lead the spirits of men and women—every manager would seek this training. This hope led to my greatest miscalculation–

I soon realized my aim terrified leaders instead of liberating them.

I loved the demands placed on the soul by taking a hard look within. I learned to love to take a hard look within. I wanted to be with leaders as they learned this ability. I did not realize that the practice of self-knowledge would terrify them. Why? I did not realize how weak their interior natures were. They had lived by exercising external sources of power instead of inner sources of power. They valued power sources like wealth, authority, and achievement. They lacked the power sources of justice, sacrifice, compassion, and wisdom. They hated knowing how weak they actually were, and how insignificant they actually were, and how only two things matter: doing important work and making oneself trustworthy.

Once, in a heated conversation, a company leader asked, "what are we actually doing, I don't get it."

I said, "We are crushing egos and awakening souls." He got up and left.

Warrior: Wow. The weakness of those with authority is terrifying.

Guardian: My mentor warned, as a way to always be on guard, "the strength of weakness is dangerous within the individual."

Warrior: In this light then, do you have an example that is not as threatening as "crushing the ego and awakening the soul?" I say this because in war, a key principle is using the indirect approach as a strategy and tactic. It seems your lessons of experience, in the form of failures to resonate with leaders, were from using the direct approach instead of the indirect approach.

Guardian: My good man. This is where I've failed the most. I did not realize that in seeking truth, first as self-knowledge, it's best not to take a head shot at the ego, but to take an indirect line to the soul. This is another principle–

We aim to educate leaders in methods to guide them to see the truth for themselves.

I am reminded of the difference between the torch bearer and the candle holder. I've learned to be a candle holder in the darkness. I've learned to exercise patience and resist the temptation to tell leaders what they don't see but need to see. This is easy to state and difficult to practice. There is no accelerating human development. It is a constant grind.

When it comes to seeing truth and light, chess is the best metaphor for what we are aiming at in the development methods. To begin, I think we have it all wrong, this study of leadership

34

and the preparing of leaders. I'll use chess to highlight this statement. I don't know if it will resonate, but this is what I'm seeing.

Warrior: Go on, I'm following.

Guardian: Let's look at the game of chess. Imagine you are a leader being prepared in the game of chess, and this is your progression.

For four years, you train as a Pawn and you are directed to move as a Pawn. This is your skill.

Then you are promoted to a Knight. You train for four years as a Knight and you are directed to move as a knight. This is your skill. Then you are promoted to a Rook. You train for four years as a Rook and are directed to move as a Rook. This is your skill. This process continues, until you are promoted to King. Even then, in the game of chess, the King is directed to move as a King.

Then, after 24 years of skill-based knowledge, you are taken off the board, to lead as a chess player. Now you enter into the strategic and tactical and abstract waters. Now you face other chess masters. Up until now, after 24 years, all you know is being on the board, seeing the environment from a skill-based perspective. You've only learned skills and individual moves but not strategy. You never organized and moved the players in concerted attacks and defenses.

Now, you need to learn to play the game. Playing the game lives in a different dimension. It is a different reality. No longer are you on the board, sticking to your position, sticking to your swim lane, as the saying goes.

Now, you are removed from the board. Your view is now total, whole and complete. Now, you live in an abstract dimension of patterns, potentials, strategies and counter strategies, where every move changes the dynamics at play.

Now, you have to lead. Now you have to think deeply. Now you are the decision maker. Now you must create the strategies, orchestrate the movements, and set the pieces in motion as a coherent whole with the aim of winning.

Now, after 24 years of thinking you see truth, you know you are in the dark. You literally can't see what is going on, even though you see what's on the board. How do you make sense of it? How do you learn strategies? Who teaches you? Where do you get feedback? How do you learn this strategic art? You don't have 10 years to train; it's real time and you are battling.

Then true fear grips you. You become paralyzed. Then you get angry. You reflect—I could have been playing the game of chess for the last 24 years!

Now, it's like starting a new profession. Your previous experiences do not matter.

Now, the memories of your superiors assault your mind–

You need to pay your dues.

You need frontline experience.

You need to be a good teammate.

You need to meet the demands of the board.

You can't be a strategist without experience in the trenches.

Now, the truth reveals itself–

You've been told a lie. You were controlled by inferior beings.

Eisenhower, one of the greatest souls of these United States, never led men in combat, yet he became one of our greatest commanders, presidents, and statesmen of history. Same with George Marshall.

Warrior: What can we learn from history?

Guardian: You realize that leading is not sports; it is not music; it is not martial arts; it is not success; it is not achievement; it is not expertise in one activity. It's something more demanding that takes total devotion and effort and had you to do it over, you'd have designed the training from your formative years onward. You realize most will never have the ability to play leadership, the way a chess player plays chess, without a revolution in the development of leaders.

You now laugh when leaders quote Bill Belichick: "Do your job". It's the wrong analogy.

A better analogy is a quarterback—a quarterback for 20 years. The quarterback as leader gets closer to the truth. The head coach can, in theory, get even closer. And the strategist, in theory, if awakened, can get closest. When we take a hard look at leadership it's a wholly different activity.

Why don't we train with the end in mind?

To lead, from the perspective I'm taking, you don't need to be on the board. It's more like math; you need to study the elements, the patterns, the structures, and then you need practice.

Now, I did not have this perspective until I stepped off the board, when I left organizational life and created a think-tank to study this problem–

What does it take to develop leaders?

Stepping off the board opened up my thinking. I don't have the answer now, but I do know, and this infuriates me, I wanted a different kind of training in my formative years and in my professional years. Now, I had to start all over again. The anger ignited the awakening.

Warrior: Buddha smiles now—through suffering we awaken.

Guardian: Now, awakened, I hope, with your help, to discover the best methods of leadership development. Only in suffering and reflection did I realize what I wanted most in my formative years–

> I wanted to be taught to play the true game and the true art. The art of leading souls.

I did not want to be on the board. I did not want to be shackled to a skill that I did not need.

Only in suffering and reflection did I learn why I experienced life as a disoriented, fragmented, and veiled reality instead of an ordered and united and illuminated reality–

> My inner being, the soul, had not been educated, developed, ordered and made free!

Only by the blessing of athletics did I have an experience of this illumination and freedom. I experienced in athletics a sense of flow and timelessness and union.

Warrior: Please explain.

Guardian: When I played sports, I knew the game and the training and what needed to be done.

There is a beautiful cycle of development. This cycle consisted of training, competing, measuring, and recovering. It seemed beautiful to me as a kid. The beauty and the competitiveness inspired me. As a kid, I experienced beauty in the athletic arts. I loved living that way: deliberate practice, skill, measurement, competition, growth, repeat. Then, when I entered the workforce and started to work *in* an organization, I thought–

> This is not pursuing excellence.
> This is not a beautiful existence.
> This is not a beautiful use of my energy and spirit.
> This is not meaningful work.

Viscerally–

> I felt in bondage—I had become the means instead of the end.
> I felt lost.
> I felt, this is not *living*.
> I felt called to lead.
> I felt called to find some noble purpose.

I felt called to find some lifelong quest.
I felt called to what?

Then, the calling echoed from the depths—

Prepare to develop leaders.

And it's been calling ever since. The calling transformed into a lifelong purpose—

Develop leaders to lead souls.

After 20 years of studying the depths of this calling, now it's time to lead out of the depths of my understanding. I think leadership needs to be figured out and modeled like the game of chess by a chess player, so we can train from our youth onward.

Warrior: That's quite a challenge. It's not realistic.

Guardian: Plato did not think this quest unrealistic. There's an insightful passage that captures the same end we are after—an end that I've not reached, but that I think possible and worthy of our best efforts.

Warrior: This eternal return is the divine comedy after all.

Guardian: I'm fine serving in disguise like Don Quixote as long as we reach the aim.

Look at what Plato states is the aim of his Guardians—

> And when they are fifty years old, those who have preserved throughout and are in every way best at everything, both in deed and in knowledge, must at last be led to the end. And, lifting up the brilliant beams of their souls, they must be compelled to look toward that which provides light for everything. Once they see the good itself, they must be compelled, each in his turn, to use it as a pattern for ordering city, private men, and themselves for the rest of their lives. For the most part, each one spends his time in philosophy, but when his turn comes, he drudges in politics and rules for the city's sake, not as though he were doing a thing that is fine, but, one that is necessary. And thus always educating other like men and leaving them behind in their place as guardians of the city, they go off to the Isles of the Blessed and dwell...And ruling women too... Don't suppose that what I have said applies any more to men than to women, all those who are born among them with adequate natures.[21]

He uses the term "soul" and the term "guardian". What happened? Why are leaders not trained this way? Have you been trained this way?

---

[21] Plato, *Republic*, Allan Bloom Translation.

Warrior: No.

Guardian: Neither have I. This passage hit me deep in the soul. The crucial point is that the critical training that Plato speaks of, is from ages 35–50. My God, I thought, we are not training at all during those ages. Most are on cruise control thinking they've already arrived. I no longer wonder why our leaders are the babblers of nonsense. They are in the cave of ignorance and arrogance.

Warrior: By this measure, you and I would have been ejected because of our crudeness, vices and corruption.

Guardian: That's what I thought too, until I meditated on the passage. Now, I don't think so. I've read deeper into the text. Leadership is not after perfect beings, but beings who have been purified and illuminated to see the source of the good and the true. Awakened. Transcended.

In fact, it seems imperfect beings with wreckages and recoveries are the types of character who would endure this training. In fact, all human beings are imperfect beings, engaged in a living cycle of being and becoming, of awakening and actualizing potentials. This is the joy of being—awakening the deepest potencies.[22]

Warrior: I'm always on guard when I meet a leader without wreckage, one who has never fallen from grace. I look for those that have fallen and recovered. I've been in the darkness and I have wreckage. And I have recovered.

Guardian: Me too. We need the wreckage to awaken in the soul detachment and humility. Now, with this aim in mind, let's create a new framework for leadership. As with chess, let's keep 'leadership' outside of the grid and off the board. Let's use the analogy of a football coach in the skybox calling plays. From the elevation he's able to take a fuller perspective. This might be controversial because you've never heard of a coach who never played football. So, the analogy may fail, but with the game of chess it does not fail. The leader trusts the experts of levels and functions but provides strategic guidance.

Is this controversial? Will it work?

To further the controversy, the leader needs to be detached no less than in "the way of death" of the Hagakure. What did Yamamoto have in mind when he taught that only by being deathless, free of the body, could the warrior move with lightning speed…an ability that revealed itself after decades of training? Does not this principle hold for leaders?[23]

---

[22] O.E.D. definition of potency–A person or thing wielding or possessing power or influence. Potentiality, inherent capability or possibility.
[23] Yamamoto Tsunetomo, *Hagakure: The Book of the Samurai*. W.S. Wilson translation.

What I'm getting at, my blessed friend, is that we need to learn how to wield metaphysical swords of truth and light and wisdom.

We need to free Excalibur's sword of light and truth and use it to cut free leadership from its Gordian knot. Just as a chess master hovers over the board like some invisible spiritual being, so we must learn to hover over the domain for full perspective. Knowing full well that, just like the chess player, we will be tested and suffer the most. We will seek to establish a fellowship of leaders, a community of truth-seekers modeled after the knights of Excalibur. All equal. Let me be clear, I don't mean leadership by boards or commissions. I mean by merit.

As Taleb stated, all leaders must have soul in the game.[24] They must take risks and there must be something to lose. There is no security. There is no net. We are free climbers making the ascent. Taleb adds, never in the history of humanity have so few exercised so much power with so little accountability. We need to counter this bitter truth. It seems we've gone from empires by blood to empires by wealth, to empires by religion, to empires by corporations. If you can't quit your means of employment, you are not free. And we seek freedom.

This is how I envision the look of leadership. It's outside of the organization. Being outside, we must not be tempted to look at Management, Command, Organization, Strategy, Operations, and Tactics. They are secondary. We are after primacy. The primacy that lives within. The primacy of the soul. The inner nature of the leader.

Warrior: Wait, is your aim to create guardians, or I dare say, philosophers, lovers of wisdom, cloaked as leaders?

Guardian: No. My aim is truth. Not terms. Not Identities. Not one way. My aim is to free leadership to its highest aim and ideal. It's not something new. We are rediscovering, not inventing, because the need has returned.

My challenge is to share how I think and how I make sense of this domain. It's going to be jarring, fragmented, unclear, and hidden until we reach the summit and look back in understanding. But the work, the journey to the summit, is what will be most rewarding for leaders to study. They'll see how we wrestled with knowledge to make it known and to make it an extension of our being, so that we could see light and truth.

The reason I contacted you and why it's necessary for the two of us to make this ascent is that after leading hundreds of leadership development programs, I cannot point to one student who has become an awakened leader. I cannot point to one student who trained to become noble, wise, strong, and just. And it's not because they don't want it; it's because they don't know how to train. They say they need more guidance and yet I do not have the structure to train them. My hope is that what we document will serve as a baseline to further their development.

---

[24] Nassim Nicholas Taleb, *Antifragility: Things That Gain From Disorder.*

Let me ask: can you point to anyone who leads this way?

Warrior: None. Not even ourselves.

Guardian: I know. We failed. This is why the weight of the cosmos is upon us to hunt it for ourselves, and maybe by becoming it we'll be able to teach it effectively.

Warrior: What made you so driven to seek out this truth?

Guardian: So that our sons and daughters will know who to follow, and so that if they themselves are called to lead, they'll know where to go for direction to find their inner selves. To awaken the nerve center. To transcend. To be prepared to lead.

Warrior: I have three boys. I'm driven to explore for that aim too.

Guardian: Then, onward we move.

CHAPTER THREE
THE ART OF DIALOGUE

Guardian: A truth: I am a failure. I have failed in arguably the most important mission of mankind—to help people transcend themselves and reach toward the light of wisdom. That is to say, in the main, I've been an utter failure in developing leaders. I haven't even neared the summit of truth; I haven't even neared the depth of our essence. I have failed to go high enough; I have failed to go deep enough. I'm talking about what it is to be a human unshackled by unseen chains, silent bullets, and invisible corporate swords that kill our souls and damage us far more than any improvised explosive device.

Warrior: Yes. We failed. Full stop. We all failed by your definition of success—training other leaders to become teachers of leaders who are self-realized and wise. By this specific definition of yours, then yes, we failed.

Guardian: Am I wrong to think this way? Am I in error to aim for this? Am I missing the mark to demand this of our leaders and ourselves? Am I getting too existential and philosophical and leaving the orbit of the practical, leaving the orbit of what is possible? What can be accomplished by our sentient muscles and brains? What can be accomplished with our little slice of time on this terra firma?

Warrior: I was taught that we have only two options. Victory or death. So, no, this journey is not for naught. It is indeed a noble aim. Check that. It is a necessary aim. No challenge is unconquerable. This is one that I'm willing to explore. It should be explained beforehand that this path is treacherous, and the aim almost never attained, but that nonetheless the effort is justified.

Robert Browning mentors–

> A man's reach should exceed his grasp, Or what's a heaven for?[1]

What are we here for if not to transcend ourselves?

Guardian: I've set this aim before the leaders of the great religions too. I've asked them–

> How many saints and sages have you produced in each generation?

It's a shocking conversation to have with these leaders as they are not Saints nor are they Holy ones.

---

[1] Robert Browning, "Andrea del Sarto".

Warrior: We'd be in good company then. I'm no saint. I'm not holy even as I've seen bullets and flak and body parts and white-hot metal burst all around me. Sure, I felt invincible, and guilty, for a moment. But then the mortal bell rings. I look at myself and see a hill of flaws. A mountain of weaknesses even as I trust my mind and body to reach the unreachable.

Guardian: Are we, as practitioners, the ignorant leading the ignorant?

Warrior: At least we know we are without this knowledge. At least we are hunting for it. That we know we are without the knowledge may well be a galaxy-wide step. The world is overflowing with ignorant people who are completely convinced they are brilliant, without flaw, and know everything worth knowing. If we're hunting for the depth of essence and the height of transcendence, then we are on the right path and fighting the good fight. I can't help but remember my childhood lust for the rebels of our fathers, the iconoclasts, the destroyers of the status quo.

Charles Bukowski prods us–

> If you're going to try, go all the way. Otherwise, don't even start. This could mean losing girlfriends, wives, relatives and maybe even your mind. It could mean not eating for three or four days. It could mean freezing on a park bench. It could mean jail. It could mean derision. It could mean mockery— isolation. Isolation is the gift. All the others are a test of your endurance, of how much you really want to do it. And, you'll do it, despite rejection and the worst odds. And it will be better than anything else you can imagine. If you're going to try, go all the way. There is no other feeling like that. You will be alone with the gods, and the nights will flame with fire. You will ride life straight to perfect laughter. It's the only good fight there is.[2]

I don't want to be in ignorance and not know I'm in ignorance. I want the hunt.

Guardian: Christ highlighted to his disciples that ignorance is the last sin to overcome.

Warrior: And Socrates demonstrated how to overcome it.

Guardian: Let the greatest teachers of truth guide us. These titans, Christ and Socrates, taught us how to seek. These wise ones taught us how to hunt. To not stop until we know and viscerally experience the light and the truth. To summit to the realm beyond belief, to know by becoming the known. It's a seeking that culminates in the beatific vision–

> Knowing and loving as we are known and loved.[3]

---

[2] Charles Bukowski, *Factotum*.

[3] Ralph Martin, *The Fulfillment of All Desire: A Guidebook for the Journey to God Based on the Wisdom of the Saints*.

If you will allow it, I'm pulling from these titans of truth to discover a pedagogic and andragogic structure to develop leaders.

Warrior: I accept. I will allow it for your aim of discovery.

Guardian: Very well. Then I'm making a judgment call, right out of the gates, that the only ones in our era who have not failed us are the great scientists, innovators, and business leaders. The truly great, not just the empty legends and those with the most twitter followers.

But, I cannot pull from these domains, because they create 'things' and uncover and create 'knowledge.' They do not discover the truth of what we are, how we were created, and what we are here to fulfill as transitory beings on earth, as flashes of stardust in a stubbornly three-dimensional world.

Warrior: What about neurobiologists? Are they not scientists of all we can't see of ourselves? What about psychiatry? Are they not doctors of the soul? What about psychologists? Are they not scientists of the soul?

Guardian: Ah. Yes. The beauty of colliding perspectives. The only psychologist I will pull from is Maslow.

Warrior: Why?

Guardian: His thinking on Eupsychian management and self-realization can be traced back to metaphysical roots. If, that is, you know where to look.

Warrior: Eupsychian?

Guardian: Maslow coined the concept from the Greek, *eu*, which means "good" and *psyche* which means "soul and spirit."

As a psychologist, in the study of the human spirit and soul and animating part of the human being, he said, managers must make themselves responsible for Eupsychian Management, or "good psychological management."[4] And I resonate with this aim as it leads to well-being for all.

This concept can be traced back to the ancient Greek philosophers. The concept of happiness meant living in a flourishing state. And I resonate with this concept. You don't earn a certain amount of money and become a state of happiness. Rather, it is living and breathing in a flourishing nature, truly flourishing for the mind, spirit, soul, and body.

The ancient philosophers said the virtues of soul, when highly developed, lead to a flourishing state. Virtues lead to happiness. Happiness is the second order effect of being virtuous. They coined the term *Eudaimonia*, what we now call happiness. Breaking down the etymology, *eu*

---

[4] Abraham Maslow, *Eupsychian Management.*

is "good" and *daemon* is "spirit." By this definition of happiness, it means we are called to grow and live in a flourishing state rooted in an attitude of good-spiritedness—that the only thing we truly control is our attitude of either being in good or in bad spirit.

And when we speak of hunting in and across a leader's soul for leadership development, to find its source, we are hunting for the daemon, or the god-within, or the genius that speaks when awakened.

Warrior: That is a noble aim. That is an aim worth fighting for and hunting after.

Guardian: This is why I cannot pull from "moderns" for our journey. They are beautiful makers and creators of temporal and transient goods, but they are not the educators of beautiful souls. They make 'stuff' out of stardust that will be stardust again.

Warrior: And we want to know how to develop beautiful souls.

Guardian: This is why I don't hunt in the business schools, nor in the psychology departments, nor in the neuroscience departments. And I caution others not to look in business schools and corporate leadership ranks for guidance and answers.

Warrior: Who makes you the judge of where to look? What makes you the judge of where to hunt?

Guardian: Do you respect and admire these teachers for their ability to grow your soul?

Warrior: No. But, I admire their intelligence and industriousness. I admire their seriousness and their ability to get things done, their ability to deliver.

Guardian: I do too. But I don't look to them nor to their souls for answers.

Warrior: But you look to philosophy and metaphysics. You use concepts like soul, light, and truth. You even look to theology.

Guardian: Mystical theology of the saints. Yes. But not apologetics. I hope for the day of leaders who are saints, sages and statesmen instead of priests, scientists, and politicians. The latter may be critical for material success and bodily needs on earth. But I'm after eternal knowledge and understanding—the timeless wisdom and truths that each soul must journey to awaken, transcend, and then share in.

Warrior: You mean first and foremost, self-knowledge.

Guardian: Yes. Our creators and makers are at best servants who provide goods. But they lack the wisdom to lead souls.

They are makers of goods, not liberators of souls.

We need to be builders of free souls and not janitors of the unliberated.

And these leaders, who we train, these freedom-seeking souls, have the burden of responsibility–

> They must do the inner work. And the work is painful by design. It cuts right to the nerve center of the body and the soul. It hurts like a pain that no drug can assuage. There is no opium for this hurt.

For a framework, the saints and sages mapped it out best. Here are the three pillars of the transformational process–

> Purification, illumination, and union.

Warrior: Hold on. I agree to training in the liminal space.[5] But, we are not making saints and sages. We are instead making leaders. Your view of leadership development is too idealistic, too spiritualistic, and too unrealistic even by my standards. And I'm the one whose reach exceeds his grasp.

Guardian: Hold on to that judgment. Can we at least explore and see what we can learn that would benefit a leader's development? I'm not asking for leaders to become sages and saints, but, I am demanding that our training awakens the light and the truth in our leaders, to be able to lead in the light.

I'm not concerned right now with everyone else. I'm not concerned if it's realistic or practical. I am concerned with exploring and seeing what is revealed. That is, what we can do to discover the truths of leadership development. In this light, I'm studying other domains that demand an interior transformation, be it the saint or the sage—the saint in love, the sage in intelligence. Both combined. Leaders must become more sagacious. But, let's venture to see if we will be awakened and transformed in the process. Then we can speak from 'knowing' instead of 'knowing about.'

For a rhythm, let's move like Lewis and Clark in unmapped territory and charter the route for our next adventures. What we need to do is to take, or enter, into an intellectual and spiritual adventure, not a physical adventure.

Warrior: A metaphysical adventure?

Guardian: Yes. Greater in danger and greater in joy than traveling abroad or mountaineering. I need to make that clear. It is arduous and challenging work. It is hard. There is no panacea.

---

[5] O.E.D. definition of liminal–Of, pertaining to, or situated at a limen; occupying a position on, or on both sides of, a boundary or threshold.

Warrior: I only enjoy challenging work, putting my body, mind, and soul to the test. This is who I am, what I do.

Guardian: This is why I work with warriors like you. You are prepared to go on this type of adventure. I've been doing it alone for two decades, but I still can't explain and teach what I've learned. I have failed thus far.

Warrior: I still don't think the work we've done in the past has been in vain. You are seeking an apex, a summit so high the sun will blind you. I love climbing, and not everyone needs to be like Reinhold Messner, solo climbing up Mt. Everest without oxygen, but mountaineers must climb, and leaders must journey.

Guardian: Yes. As teachers, our aim is to plant seeds—seeds for the leadership arts.

Warrior: Our hope, then, should be to connect with the soul of a leader, not create enlightened ones. Which, by the way, we can't because we are not enlightened ourselves.

Guardian: Then we are playing the long game. Those who we train, by pursuing development in a self-taught (autodidactic) process, may years from now grow into flourishing leaders.

Warrior: Maybe then, by your definition of leadership, we'll have succeeded. But, it's on the leader to take the journey.

Guardian: Indeed, that is why I want to document our journey. Leadership development (and this is painful) is largely an autodidactic process, a self-taught, self-directed process.

Warrior: Hold on. How many leaders do you know who are autodidactic? Where is the autodidactic training manual?

Guardian: There is none. We need to create one. My point is it's not our responsibility to force our will on leaders to produce their development.

Warrior: And some warrior cultures are notorious for forcing their will onto others, even their own teammates.

Guardian: We need to be on guard about this. We aim to strengthen the faculty of "will." We need to forge the "will" of the leader to do the work, most of which will be done in "silence" and "solitude" in early mornings, late nights, and weekends.

The saints are a good reminder of why this is critical, Sertillanges writes–

> Solitude enables you to make contact with yourself, a necessity if you want to realize yourself—not to repeat like a parrot a few acquired formulas, but, to be a prophet of the God within you who speaks a unique language to each man…a mental training which is education, that is the drawing and unfolding of a soul…I should like to add the bath of silence, in order to tone up the

organism of the spirit, to accentuate the personality, and to produce the active consciousness of it…[6]

Warrior: This silence and solitude is where the leader learns to listen to the light and truth within, to let it reveal itself, to build authenticity. We need to hammer this out. Too many leaders think they are wasting time in silence and solitude (meditation and contemplation) and in reality, they are hiding from themselves.

Guardian: I want to stress that "will" is of greatest importance and it grows strong in silence and solitude, not weaker. A leader must learn to balance independence and interdependence simultaneously and seamlessly.

Warrior: I think this is where the struggle lives, as you pointed out. We use our being— our energy, our passion—when we make contact with leaders. And your concern is with the leaders, those unborn, who we will never work with in person. This is why you want to explore and document. You want to leave an artifact.

Guardian: Yes. If we are to explore, do we need to set a measure, a focus, and an aim? What is our aim?

Warrior: Our aim might be to provide the knowledge that is embedded in you and me to others.

Guardian: Our first aim then is to take not only our experiences, but the knowledge we learned from experiences, and lead it out through a metaphysical journey.

Warrior: As you say, the hope is to lead out the tacit and intuitive knowledge and make it concrete with terms, concepts, frameworks and theories in an artifact called a book.

Guardian: We can leverage the great works that others have done before us and highlight how to activate these truths in one's being. We need to integrate knowledge and techniques that can be studied and practiced like an art, independent of any system. I'm interested in creating an art form, similar to the musician, athlete, and martial artist. Yes, that is our aim and that is our challenge.

Warrior: I think that is why you're contacting me. You're stuck. I'm stuck. Not in our journey but in our journey to train others.

Guardian: Let's here and now identify our first technique as "The Art of Dialogue."

This technique teaches truth-seekers how to enter the depths of intelligence in order to lead out truths, principles and structures, what we call knowledge. In our case, leadership knowledge. We will document what "dialogue" actually means. The Latin roots are *Dia* which means "to

---

[6] A.G. Sertillanges, *The Intellectual Life: Its Spirit, Conditions, Methods.*

flow" and *Logos* which means "meaning." And our aim is "to flow in meaning" and transmit that meaning to others.

Warrior: Yes.

Guardian: What is the vice of dialogue?

Warrior: Sophistical and rhetorical and demagogical manipulation. The abuse of language.[7]

Guardian: We are getting closer. The vice of dialogue is to flow in untruth. What are the rules to guard against becoming combative and antagonistic about controversial issues? My meaning: dialogue is one technique in the art of truth-seeking. This means: I don't want to be right; I don't care if I'm wrong. I want to know what is right and to act accordingly. If our leadership art lives in truth's competitiveness, we want to engage in a competitive spirit, one that is *agonistic*, not antagonistic, to collide ideas, opinions, and perspectives with the goal of catching truth as it reveals itself. Worlds collide and reveal new light.

I want us to demonstrate what it means not to dominate or be better than others but to use our intelligence freely to see what it reveals. My point is that dialogue is a great leadership technique to unveil the truth. And this leads to developing practical judgment, which is our aim in leading— the transcendent anchored by the harsh reality of gravity.

Warrior: What do you have in mind to demonstrate and document how to do this?

Guardian: I'll lead with a beautiful insight from Sertillanges–

> If besides lectures in the afternoon and study following on the lectures, they could talk in the evening, at supper, of all of these noble things, so as to learn more by drinking them in in conversation, than by the very lectures.[8]

Our attitude shall be–

> Without pride or the spirit of rivalry, seeking only the truth.

That is my aim. To seek truth and learn the truth by drinking it in in dialogue.

Warrior: Now, we have the aim, we know the "what." But "how" do we actually practice this? I think this is a challenge we all face. We know we need to be better, we know we need to shed the ego, we know we need to be better listeners, we know we need to be virtuous, but, how do we practice? How do we learn to teach the practical skills?

Guardian: For the "how" of dialogue, I think we've discovered four principles.

---

[7] Josef Pieper, *Abuse of Language–Abuse of Power*.
[8] A.G. Sertillanges, *The Intellectual Life: Its Spirit, Conditions, Methods*.

Warrior: We? I don't see it yet.

Guardian: You may not see, but you are practicing them.

Warrior: What do you see?

Guardian: First, I see that we are using only high-minded thoughts and high emotional energy. I sense nothing antagonistic coming from you, nor coming from me. This sets us at ease. You are no threat to me and I am no threat to you. We should be on guard against negative "rants". We should always focus on what's highest. Negative thoughts and emotions crush any hope of seeing truth. Did you happen to notice the jab I took against servant leadership? I wanted to see if you'd check me.

Warrior: I hardly noticed.

Guardian: I demonstrated ignorance. You did not catch it. You should have asked "did you read and study Greenleaf's work?"

And I would have said, "No." We should not comment or have opinions about that which we never studied or that which we have not experienced. We should have the courage only to talk about what we know or what we've studied or what we've experienced. Why?

This keeps us from the proverbial leadership sin–

Acting like we know when we have no idea.

Warrior: One thing on which I'd caution you is that I've not studied this question of "what it takes to develop leaders" for 20 years. But, I have 20 years of experience leading warriors in combat. The way we can team up is that when you share a concept and it lands in me intuitively, I can acknowledge the revealed spoken truth from concrete experience. You are the lead guide on this ascent and I am here for support. All the pressure is on you to discover and bring leadership truths to light. I know from working with you, your nature is to be a solo alpinist, but because you are past your edge, you need me to catch you when you fall, especially when it's into a crevasse. I'm still learning how to team with you because I'm normally the leader. Now, I must be the anchor here lest you float away, fall, or stray off your own course. I appreciate your point about dialogue as I'm drinking in the dialogue and growing in understanding. And I'll do my best to check you if you're making faulty and ignorant statements.

Guardia: Please keep me accountable.

Warrior: You're the lead on this journey. You're leading every pitch. As we climb, when I follow the route you've created, I'll learn the moves and the holds too. This is good. In a way, we are practicing how to discover and transmit knowledge together. I'm happy to support as I do need the break from leading.

Guardian: Do you see how we increase clarity by drinking in thoughtful and noble dialogue?

Warrior: I never saw how important it was till now. Because of time constraints, I spent more time commanding and giving orders instead of building intellectual depth and understanding.

Guardian: This is emergent, is it not? I have a general aim, but, as we explore we grow in our being and in our understanding. We can drink in Musashi's wise counsel on this ascent–

> You should investigate this thoroughly.[9]

We should demand this of ourselves as we investigate how to develop leaders—we must have the intellectual strength to investigate thoroughly and not dumb it down. It is terrifying when leaders say that I am too intellectual, that what I say and how I teach is too academic and theoretical. What they are really saying is that their intelligence has not been developed enough. What they are saying is that they have only learned to see what is tangible, physical, and concrete. At the core, they fear the truth—the truth that they have not been trained properly to see what is intelligible, intangible, and abstract. And yet, using concepts and language itself is abstract. It's the union of intuition and reason, abstracting the intelligent patterns of beings.

Warrior: Warriors seek mastery. You don't need to dumb it down with me. Speak from soul to soul and awaken the truth in us.

Guardian: Then it's set. The perennial technique on this journey is dialogue.

Warrior: Set.

Guardian: And the first principle to master this technique of dialogue is to command our being to use language that is winged with goodwill in thoughts, emotions, and words.

Warrior: Set—speak with truth, goodness, and justice.

Guardian: The second principle of dialogue is to command our being to discuss ideas, terms, concepts, theories, models, frameworks, issues, concerns, challenges, and problems, *but not people*.

Warrior: And this means to develop intellectual depth and strength, because if you are not a student of the game, you will complain about a person's behavior because you can't see "intelligibly and intangibly" what is going on. Your mind is not seasoned. You are blinded and you don't even know it. You don't understand character, experience, strategy, and objectives and how they must be orchestrated together.

---

[9] Miyamoto Musashi, *The Book of Five Rings*.

Guardian: There is a nasty tendency, a form of injustice, to gossip and complain about people instead of looking at the qualities in human nature that lead us into error and that must be corrected.

> Men and women range themselves into three classes or orders of intelligence; you can tell the lowest class by their habit of always talking about persons; the next by the fact that their habit is always to converse about things; the highest by their preference for the discussion of ideas.[10]

Eleanor Roosevelt made this quote famous–

> Weak minds discuss people, average minds discuss events, and great minds discuss ideas.

We are here to explore truths and ideas, not the weaknesses of people. We are all ascending the path from imperfection to perfection by being and becoming. The conformists and careerists experience frustration because they are not prepared to have noble dialogues; they've never studied the art, and they are never still enough to listen. What I aim to do is highlight their arrogance and ignorance and their lack of humility and discernment.

Warrior: I see why you focus on warriors. Warriors have the discipline and courage to wrestle with the challenge of seeking truth. It takes a fearless individual to do what you are doing. I see why it's challenging working with those who've never been to war.

Guardian: Human beings who have been to war, or who have hit rock bottom, or who have suffered a great loss, tend to resonate with what I'm doing because the grip of their ego has been detached. People who suffer from the delusion and deception of their ego can't even see what I'm doing. They don't see it. They get frustrated. They give up. They go make money or they go get fame.

Warrior: It's because they refuse to take a hard look within. They resist being self-reflective because they fear truth. They fear the truth that they are unimportant; they fear their true insignificance. As Genghis Khan is thought to have warned–

> If you can't swallow your pride, you can't lead.[11]

To counter my ego, and God knows, it's still there, lurking, I've always led by stating this basic proposition to my team–

> If you kept a camera on me 24/7, you'd find enough faults and failures to fire me and banish me from leading.

---

[10] Quote attributed to Henry Thomas Buckle by Charles Steward.
[11] Jack Weatherford, *Genghis Khan and the Making of the Modern World.*

Guardian: That is humility. You are demonstrating the virtue of humility. That's why I look for people who have wreckage. That sting of failure releases the grip of the ego.

But, my hope is that—for the younger generation—they don't need wreckage. But, of course, they do need rigorous training. We need to train leaders how to push past their edge, fail, and recover quickly from failure. To be more than resilient. To be anti-fragile and seek anti-fragility fearlessly even in moments when it seems like all is lost. Even in the deepest depths of the darkest hours. That is the real lesson of practical judgment. The courage to act. You never have enough information. You will fail, and in failure, you still need to act. That is why we need to teach leaders to wear life lightly. Nothing is grave, not even death.

Warrior: The Spartans taught contempt for death–

> His heart truly has achieved contempt for death, and with that he transcends himself and his actions touch the sublime.[12]

And Mongols did not even have a saying because to even whisper the word "death" would be to give it too much credence.

What you are saying is that we must be tasked with growing souls straight instead of crookedly. We want them when they are young, when they have a chip on their shoulder, when they are not fully formed, in order to educate them to experience mistakes, to have regrets, to experience unbecoming conduct. Then they will receive the truths we speak, not before, but after they have failed.

Guardian: And we are there not to keep them from failure, but to trigger it. And then, in failure, we are there to help them recover. Let me ask you, when were most of your failures?

Warrior: Good God, in my 20s. Cocksure in ignorance.

> Education is man's going forward from cocksure ignorance to thoughtful uncertainty.[13]

Guardian: And when did you have the least amount of guidance and mentoring?

Warrior: In my 20s.

Guardian: It's absurd, when we see the truth that in our 20s, when we are the least mature and most vulnerable and unstable, we are left alone the most. This is when we need the most mentoring and guidance, not the least. It's not supernatural, the success of McArthur. His mother moved to West Point to ensure he received the guidance and support he needed to thrive during those critical and vulnerable years. His father, a General, brought him to Japan

---

[12] Steven Pressfield, *Gates of Fire*.
[13] Kenneth G. Johnson, *Michigan Education Journal*, Volumes 36-37, Page 285, 1958.

to be his aide-de-camp. He had been prepared almost every step of the way.[14] Then, in the World Wars, iconoclastic in temperament, he demonstrated intelligence and valor. Despite his victories and achievements, he is still a flawed and imperfect human being. As it should be.

Warrior: Education, not school, is time intensive.

Guardian: Yes. We still do not take education seriously enough. What is called education is mass socialization.

Warrior: Are you saying that every yet-to-be leader, should have a mentor in the form of a "handler?"

Guardian: What I am saying is, why do we drop our children off at college and leave them to their own devices? They are in sheer ignorance. We create an injustice by saying–

> What do you want to be in life?
> What do you want to study?
> What do you want to do?

In those formative years, from ages 18–26, they need to be directed in the fundamentals of becoming a mature being, independent of skill and vocation. The basic building blocks of education are being neglected, which a century ago we called "the liberation arts" of thinking, speaking, reckoning, and acting. The modern university is the worst place to liberate souls. Students need teachers as mentors and guides and most professors can't even guide themselves. This is why I am focused on a narrow set of beings, the future and current leaders. We will place them in the rigors of training and the burden of leading.

Warrior: Now I see why we are setting these ground rules. These rules honor the dignity of the human being. These principles serve as broad strokes to leave room for failure, forgiveness, and recovery.

Guardian: Then it is set. We don't judge people. We identify the qualities that lead to error or lead to correct action.

Warrior: Set. Our aim is to create self-correcting souls.

Guardian: The third principle of dialogue commands that we exercise intelligence and logic as we wrestle with what we are seeing, in terms of concepts, models, frameworks, and theories. To get out of subjectivity and into objectivity. Yes, as psychological beings, we need to know the kinetic chain between motive and action. But, as reasoning beings, to transmit this art, we need to know the kinetic chain between knowledge and knowing.

Warrior: I like how we are practicing the art of command in these principles. If I understand correctly, what you are demanding is that we use understanding, judgments, and reasoning

---

[14] Arthur Herman, *Douglas McArthur: American Warrior*.

when we have dialogue about anything we set our mind to. This gives the conversation depth and rigor and richness so that we counter the tendency to engage in superficial thinking. What you are saying is that through dialogue, we need to go beyond superficial thinking and get to the depths to see what needs to be revealed. Or in your language, to disclose the truth that is hidden from superficial thinking. Leading is a thinking game. I'm glad you used the chess analogy. We are not after tactical skills; we are after operational and strategic skills.

Guardian: The way we can practice this, even with beginners, is to ask them to speak their mind, to be courageous and tell us what they are thinking. And the way to do this is to teach them not to be attached to their thinking. Instead, we teach them to view a thought or an idea as the raw material to wrestle with. And the way we wrestle with this raw material is to throw the idea up in the air, and then let our intelligence look at it and wrestle with it. This is why I love clashing ideas. I want to see what happens when they wrestle with each other. Thinking is alive to me. It is a living being; it has substance, I dare say, spiritual substance.

Warrior: We can practice this by observing our reactions to new ideas and controversial issues.

Guardian: The aim of doing this is to discover, not the reactions, but the frameworks that help us to make sense of what we are seeing in reality. And then, to help us respond effectively to that reality. Joseph Campbell's "Hero's Journey" is one such framework.

Warrior: I've studied it, but how is it important to leadership development?

Guardian: For our purposes, it serves as a framework to guide use from the known to the unknown, from the surface to the depths, as a living framework that is active in the soul. Our challenge is to awaken these frameworks in our being, in our intelligence, to give them life so that we can use them to see the beauty and truth of our intelligence coming into correspondence with reality. We have the ability to make our inner reality harmonized with outer reality—the marriage of the subjective and the objective, of the knower and the known.

Warrior: Wait. Is that what must take place for truth to arise and for practical judgment to be developed?

Guardian: Yes. When mangers study with veracity, the deeper meaning of the numbers, reveal the true story. And the story, once seen, has a pattern. Once the pattern is seen, managers, the true ones, make the hard calls by decisive acts.

I learned the following from the "Michelangelo of Management," Harold Geneen[15]–

> The truth is that the drudgery of the numbers will make you free.

> What you are seeking is comprehension of the numbers: what they mean.

---

[15] Harold Geneen and Alvin Moscow, *Managing*.

That (comprehension) will only come with constant exposure, constant repetition, retention of what you read in the past, and a familiarity with the actual activities the numbers represent.

You cannot speed up the process. Comprehension seeps into your brain by a process of osmosis and gradually you will find yourself at ease with numbers and the facts, no matter how remote they may seem at first, bring comprehension; somehow the pieces begin to fit together.

Warrior: This might be a bit too abstract for students to follow.

Guardian: That is why they need teachers to guide and light the way. Unlike a business which is more quantitative, with numbers that are critical to effectiveness, when it comes to development, we live in a qualitative environment. Instead of numbers we are dealing with ideas and concepts. What transforms in education is the strength of our will, our intelligence and our spiritedness. Do you see? Our spirit is not a number, it can't be calculated, it must be developed.

Warrior: I can see why people love business and wealth; it's a quantitative numbers game.

Guardian: And for us, it's not the drudgery of the numbers, it's the drudgery of purifying the soul to see light and truth.

Warrior: This is getting abstract for me too.

Guardian: Me too. How do we bring this truth to light? How to we take concepts and ideas and awaken them in our being? That is the beauty of our intelligence—we have the ability to take knowledge in and make it an extension of our being. This is a divine blessing. We can qualitatively increase our light and truth by the way we train. And we do this by changing the way we react, by changing the way we respond, by changing the way we act, by changing the way we think, by changing the way we work, and by changing the way we live.

Warrior: And by studying different models and frameworks and embedding them in our being, in our intelligence, they then become an extension of our being that we can employ like a weapon, as we face different obstacles and challenges in the adventure of living. This is how we open our minds, how we awaken our intelligence to see what is hidden from the eyes but what is visible to the mind. This is how to practice what Musashi[16] said–

> Develop a discerning eye in all matters.
> Understand what cannot be seen by the eye.
> Consider yourself lightly; consider the world deeply.

Guardian: Are we beginning to see more deeply?

---

[16] Miyamoto Musashi, *The Book of Five Rings*.

Warrior: Yes.

Guardian: That is why you and I are wrestling. This art of intellectual gymnastics is how we train and condition our spirit to become these leadership principles—not learn but become.

Warrior: We become the principles?

Guardian: That is what I'm seeing. Somehow, and I'm not sure how this is possible, by using our intelligence to explore truth's principles, we become the truth by becoming the principles.

I've not stated this before, but the reason why we study wisdom literature is not to read about wisdom, rather it's to make ourselves the living embodiment of the wisdom that we read. We can make the wisdom come alive in our being, and the wisdom literature is humanity's continual reminder.

Warrior: Good God, this is intense. We become the wisdom of the wisdom literature? What you are saying is that power and authority is dangerous if it's controlled by human beings who have not become wise by the light of wisdom?

Guardian: Yes. This is exactly what I am saying. Twenty years ago, I 'tried' to read and study Plato, but I was not ready. What I read did not let me in. It's wild to discuss with you because now when I read Plato and the writings of the wise, it not only lets me in, it lights my soul. When I am confused and discouraged, I know that all I need to do, to remedy my spirit, is to enter into silence and solitude and read a Platonic dialogue or a Gospel of light. I can speak of this all day, but, until a soul has this experience, it will not resonate. That is why I make leaders transcribe, word for word, passages from ancient wisdom. It's one of the only ways to get them to pay attention and to get them to deepen their being.

Warrior: How did you learn this or get this idea to study or transcribe ancient wisdom to awaken it or embed it in our soul?

Guardian: I first got the idea from sports training. When I trained and competed, it seemed the skills became an extension of my being. It seemed I could play and move in an intuitive manner. I loved that experience. Then, when I trained in yoga, it seemed I could move in the same intuitive manner. The movements seemed to become an extension of my being. It seemed body, mind, and spirit united in a timeless and eternal and immortal expression. I must confess, this experience in yoga did not happen in the beginning. In the beginning each movement seemed uncomfortable and painful. Then, after years of training, the movements seemed to awaken the light of my soul, and my body itself seemed to be an extension of the soul.

This led to the insight that developing virtue and wisdom demands the same kind of training as an art. Only this sacred art does not involve the body. I searched for methods, with the aim to make virtue an extension of being. This led to the highest aim–

To make virtue, excellence, and wisdom an extension of being.

I searched for methods to make virtue an intuitive movement—a movement that led to lightening spontaneity in the known, and intuitive discernment in the unknown.

Warrior: I'm lost.

Guardian: How many wisdom and sacred canons have you transcribed?

Warrior: None.

Guardian: What I mean is, this movement and flow of becoming wise or virtuous seemed to be an active condition of a spirit responding naturally and spontaneously to reality as it unfolded. I started to train with the wisdom literature as I did with sports and yoga, in the early mornings and the late nights. I practiced meditation and contemplation as techniques to awaken light and truth. I sought exercises to make the spirit and intelligence, "sharp, discerning, and developed." I hoped these practices would awaken something deeper in my being. This is when I started to transcribe, word for word, the wisdom and sacred canons. Specifically, Saint John's Gospel, Plato's *Republic*, and *The Bhagavad Gita*.

Warrior: And what did you discover?

Guardian: Because I approached it from a leadership perspective and not a speculative perspective, I found that I could see or speak or act from soul to soul, and that I could see what others could not see. I remember my peers commenting, "How did you know how to act?" And I responded, "I could just see." And they said, "How could you see?" And I said, "I don't know, I think it's from the way I study at home with the wisdom literature."

Warrior: Wait. You are describing the process of awakening the moral and intellectual faculties, the aim of education, instead of just talking about the faculties and the virtues. What you are saying is that you learned how to exercise the faculties that produce virtue?

Guardian: Yes. Not perfectly, but pursuing perfection. I think if you seek wisdom, wisdom gives you a deeper sense of sight. I'm just able to see and I thought everyone could see. I'm no better. I only train differently.

Warrior: It's similar to what people say about clairvoyance, that they can just see what is hidden from others.

Guardian: Yes, though I am not clairvoyant. I was speaking from a leadership development perspective where I have studied the craft of management and leadership. And then, when I went to work, when I set my intelligence on work and on the people doing the work, I could just see.

Warrior: This is similar to the way we train in tactical teams. We train so much that we can just see and move and respond, intuitively.

Guardian: That's the thing, leadership development demands that kind of intense training.

Warrior: And because you did not have the training you wanted, you sought it in the wisdom literature. Meaning, you knew the experience from sports, the military, and yoga and you wondered why you still felt unprepared as a leader.

Guardian: Yes. I had to study human nature. I had to study how to pursue truth. I am fortunate—my first commander told me that to be an effective leader I must not only study war, but I must also study human nature and history. He said that the military will supply the study of war but that I had to study human nature and history. He said I had to do this early in the morning and late at night. This implied that when not at work, I should be studying.

Warrior: Which is why, now, when you read the ancient wisdom, your intelligence is prepared to receive it and practice it.

Guardian: Yes.

Warrior: This is good and I am following. I always wondered about the absence of formal leadership training and the difficulty of teaching leadership.

Guardian: Now do you see how difficult this knowledge is to obtain?

Warrior: It's very mystical and metaphysical to me, and we are rewarded for what is physical and mathematical.

Guardian: I wonder if the leaders who read our dialogue will experience an awakening?

Warrior: That is a noble aim. By our example and our dialogue, I hope they do.

Guardian: We are entering deep waters of truth. We are entering the deep waters of consciousness. We need to become, spiritually and metaphorically, Orcas, killer whales, and demonstrate what it is like to swim in the depths, diving deeper and deeper, increasingly free in our truest nature and essence. I imagine that most human beings are in life boats, scared to death to dive into the deep ocean and become one with the living waters. We need to inspire them to leap in because if they stay in the boats, they are like self-sentenced prisoners who will never become what they truly are.

Warrior: I can see why you terrify others. If you are in essence an orca and they are in essence a timid soul, you can be terrifying.

Guardian: That is why I want to document what we do so we don't shock our fellow human beings, who are still in rafts. They don't see what we see. I never understood that until my peers kept saying, how did I know how to respond? And I kept saying that I just saw it.

Warrior: We need to get them out of the boats and into the waters, so they get experience. I am beginning to understand. It's not enough with just us; we need to teach others to swim in the depths.

Guardian: They don't realize the power of their intelligence. They don't realize the potency that lives in each one of them.

Warrior: And they need to know that to realize potency, they must go through the pain of transformation. That it's no different from the pain that a warrior goes through, so that the gate keepers of the brotherhood let them in.

Guardian: Only, our gatekeepers are not other human beings; our gatekeepers are the potencies that awaken when truth and light reveal themselves. Our intelligence, our being, our nature, seems to have an unending ability to realize potency in light and truth, in virtue and knowledge, but we've not been trained in how to realize our truest potencies. That is what drives me. Thank God, the sages and the saints and the mystics left us not only writings, but techniques which anyone can practice once they know they exist.

Warrior: Just like music. Someone needed to teach the musician that not only does music exist, but, there is a way to read and write music with sheet notes and there is a way to play music with instruments.

Guardian: And we are playing a form of music, in that we are interested in the harmony and resonance of intelligence awakening and responding to the challenges of living.

Warrior: Then we must identify the knowledge and the techniques and teach them to others.

Guardian: Once we teach, then it is up to them to engage in deliberate practice to master this art. We need to make this clear. Our aim is not about acquiring knowledge. Our aim is to prepare and strengthen each individual intelligence to have the courage and wisdom to make judgment calls. Aristotle called this ability practical judgment, and he defined it as–

> A truth-disclosing active condition involving reason.[17]

This is my greatest hope, that leaders develop this ability and that others who do not have the ability trust leaders when they make this call. This means, the intelligence needs to learn to see and needs to learn to respond to reality as it reveals itself. We must purify ourselves of ready-made prescriptions and pre-fabricated solutions. The beauty of this ability is that living itself is the adventure and this living is always mysterious and marvelous and emergent.

Warrior: This focus on living intelligence, on using the thinking ability to exercise practical judgment, hits home because when I've failed most is when I've been pressured by other leaders to use pre-fabricated solutions instead of trusting my insights. And it's always ended

---

[17] Aristotle, *Nicomachean Ethics*, Sachs translation.

badly, and I regretted not taking a stand more firmly in those situations, because I knew and I could see and I didn't realize that those around me were blinded and could not see. No one explained to them or to me that truth can be hidden, that truth needs to be discovered and that this truth-disclosing activity is the cornerstone of great leadership.

Guardian: I remember when I first met you. When I asked you if you could be anything what would you be, and you replied "a blinder remover." I had wondered how you came to that insight, and now I know.

Then we are set, the third principle of dialogue–

> We will lead with reason and intuition to wrestle with what we are seeing. We will do our best to stay clear of opinion. We will use concepts, frameworks, and theories and guides to understand our experiences and aim to disclose the truth.

Warrior: Set—when engaged in dialogue, we will command our intelligence to wrestle with concepts and theories in exercises, experiences, and decision making.

Guardian: For the last principle of dialogue, and the one I think is most important–

> To seek what might be right, and not to lay claim to rightness in premeditated and prefabricated opinions, but to seek for rightness and truth that reveals itself, not before, not after, but *in* the inquiry itself.

Warrior: Few of power and authority do this. They command. I doubt they have dialogue, truth-seeking, inquiries to observe a problem. No. They act on past experiences with limited and superficial understanding and they bark orders.

Guardian: That is why I did not last in the military.

Warrior: The only reason why I lasted is that on operations we were left alone and entrusted to execute the mission.

Guardian: That is why I suffer when I hear that the leader must be the expert, must know the answer, and must be right, before actually studying the problem. We are running counter to conventional wisdom. We are hunting to discover truths that we do not yet see and know.

Warrior: We hunt for Wisdom. What is powerful about this principle is that it reduces the psychological pressure on the leader to always know or always have the answer.

Guardian: Our leaders will have the courage to ask questions and work with others to seek out answers. Why is this so important?

Warrior: To be on guard against the perennial leadership sin–

Acting like we know when we have no idea.

Guardian: More specifically–

Thinking that we know when, in fact, we have no idea.

This is total ignorance. And the most dangerous kind of total ignorance. Ignorance masked in certainty, resolve, passion, and seemingly unassailable scientific fact. All further caked in the makeup of confidence. That is why I lead by problem-solving sessions. That is why for these sessions, teammates are required to study problem sets, discover facts, and create possible solution sets. This means I free them up from transactional actions. My perspective is that operational and strategic leaders need to delegate all known actions that make the organization run, and then use the freed-up time to study obstacles and challenges, and create solutions that destroy obstacles and challenges as they arise. This takes tremendous operational and individual discipline.

Warrior: I've rarely seen non-combat military units operate that way.

Guardian: When professionals don't deeply study specific problems, they have only their instincts and opinions, which are useless to the truth-seeking nature of leading. We need to get used to doing deep study and research to focus on the transformational work. Transactional work should be for administrators, not leaders.

Warrior: I see why you never got an MBA—you're no administrator. I see why you also never aimed at generational wealth—you're no wealth-seeker. You are a truth-seeker. All this aims at developing the leader as truth-seeker.

Guardian: If a person does not know how to seek the truth, I do not trust them in the art of leading.

Warrior: But, you trust doctors in the art of health and lawyers in the art of law and businessmen in the art of business.

Guardian: I trust them if they have good character.

Warrior: Good God, you really don't trust most people.

Guardian: Have they made themselves trustworthy in truth?

Warrior: Possibly. Some of them.

Guardian: I trust my ability to respond in good faith with all beings.

Warrior: Until they betray you.

Guardian: Even then, I forgive but move one. I say this because I live a spiritual life and do not claim much in the form of material goods. It's enough to live. I'm not an ideologue about living life spartanly. I do it because I want to and also must.

Warrior: This is why you have so much time and freedom to study this art. You don't play the game.

Guardian: I don't play the temporal game; I play the eternal game.

Warrior: And this is how you are able to lead others fearlessly into the unknown.

Guardian: Yes, because I do my best to live there. I do my best to live in the depths. We always live in the known and the unknown—that is what makes living so dynamic. That is why I love the leadership arts; it's to discover something in the unknown. It's exhilarating to live and lead this way. What we do as leaders, if leading is essentially paving the way, is that we create a pathway that becomes a simultaneous giving and receiving experience with reality and human beings.

That is a divine experience to me.

Warrior: This is similar to martial arts. Between two martial artists and the reality they share, there is a real giving and receiving, there is a harmony and flow that takes place between the two combative artists. The martial artist that can take hold of reality and flow with more lucidness and speed ends up victorious. Brute force and perfect form will not substitute flow and art.

Guardian: This is essentially the same as martial arts, except leaders get everyone in harmony and flow to aim at a shared goal. In our exploring, we aim to literally come into correspondence with reality, and dance with reality, and play in harmony with reality. I am not exaggerating.

This means there is an active and dynamic quality at play with our living and responding in our leadership activities. This is why we live in both the known and unknown at all times. And the quicker we accept this and the quicker we learn to live this way, the more harmony and understanding we will be able to create.

Warrior: What do you mean by known and unknown?

Guardian: That life must be lived. That life is moving us forward and growing us. That we've already experienced deaths in the form of growth–

> From infant to toddler
> From toddler to adolescent
> From adolescence to adult
> From student to worker
> From trainee to expert
> From manager to leader

In our seeking, we must discover techniques to simultaneously live the active life and the contemplative life. Aristotle frames both those ways of living as the active conditioning of our soul, of our intelligence, of our being.[18]

Warrior: Are you looking for the way of the leader as distinct from the way of the warrior or the way of the sage?

Guardian: I am seeking to understand how to awaken and activate our faculties—our sources of power—will, intelligence and spiritedness, so that leaders can move with fluidness and lucidness in the adventure of living, as they charge towards important goals, critical problems, and noble challenges. I don't see the leader as distinct from the warrior and the sage. I see the essence of all three natures as the same; but the work they do I see as different.

Warrior: Again, I must remember, you are aiming at developing souls.

Guardian: Yes. I always aim at that. When I hope, and I am hopeful, both in the negative sense of *The Bhagavad Gita*, and the positive sense of the Gospels, my hope is for all human beings to learn leadership principles and awaken them in their being so they can dance and flow with that reality, whether they experience joy or sorrow. I have faith that these dialogue principles will benefit all, with leaders setting the example.

> Renouncing all actions in Me, with mind turned toward the basis-of-self, and having become without hope, without sense of "mine," with your fever of anxiety departed—fight.[19]

> Hope always pertains to the unpossessed object. If something were possessed there could no longer be hope for it.[20]

Warrior: It seems that on our quest to move in the unknown, to move in the darkness, you are called to wield the theological virtues.

Guardian: Yes. The great sages are the guides. I am inspired by the teachings of Saint John of the Cross.

> Faith is a dark night, it illumines the soul that is in darkness.[21]

That is why dialogue is a means. This is the target we hit with dialogue–

> Not just to seek what is right. Not just to know what is right. But, it's the action. It's the courage to act on the revealed truth and the rightness of that

---

[18] Aristotle, *Nicomachean Ethics*, Sachs translation.
[19] *The Bhagavad Gita*, Georg Feuerstein translation.
[20] Saint John of the Cross, *The Ascent of Mount Carmel*.
[21] Saint John of the Cross, *The Ascent of Mount Carmel*.

truth. That is fortitude. That is moral courage. That is what we desperately hope to make manifest in the souls of our leaders.

Warrior: Powerful. What you are really saying, in a gentle way, is the technique of dialogue is designed to shed the ego, to enter a place of egoless intelligence. This would revolutionize professional relationships. You are not aiming at winning or acquiring; you are aiming at what is right and to act in rightness—truth and goodness.

Guardian: That is the aim of leadership development. I'm glad you are seeing it and calling it as you see it. That is why we need these techniques, to keep the ego in check and to keep us from getting stung by it.

Warrior: What makes us dangerous is what we can't see in our own being.

Guardian: Which is why leadership is a team sport.

Warrior: And that is why feedback, dialogue as cross-examination, is critical.

Guardian: Dialogue is a dynamic feedback practice. A practice that moves in fluidity and lucidity.

Warrior: Good God, I never saw dialogue as a living and fluid and lucid feedback practice. We are shining light and sharing that light with one another.

Guardian: Yes. You see correctly.

Warrior: Then to summarize what we covered, these are the dialogue guidelines that we will use for "protection", as we climb this glacier of leadership truth–

1. Only use positive and constructive language (aiming for goodwill in thoughts, words, emotions, and actions).
2. Discuss ideas, issues, concerns, and problems (not people) and do our homework so we can act based on fact, evidence, and concepts.
3. Use will and intelligence and logic to wrestle with concepts, models, techniques, exercises, and examples and see if we can disclose hidden truths.
4. Seek what might be right instead of having to be right, and then respond accordingly (to be responsive instead of reactive, to get into dynamic and living thinking, to aim for the joy of using heightened awareness).

Guardian: Elegant summary—concise and clear. We must have the courage to let these guidelines protect and guard us as we advance towards truth. We are a long way from discovering truth-seeking principles but these guidelines are strong foundations, to move and leap from, as we climb.

Warrior: These guidelines can act as firm footholds as we climb. They can also serve to protect and anchor us in case we fall. Especially in those moments when we leap into the unknown toward a hidden and elusive leadership truth.

Guardian: Because our journey is a continual leap into the unknown, we still need additional gear and knowledge and techniques. Now is the right time to bring in Joseph Campbell's "Hero's Journey" and use it as a framework, no, more of a map, to guide us in the darkness of the unknown.

Warrior: Impressive. You are teaching us how to study the terrain of truth-seeking much as we study the terrain for combat. As the scout sniper studies the valleys, fingers, and hills to decide the optimal location to execute his mission, we must look at the terrain of truth-seeking with equal prejudice. After all, it's not our life that's on the line. It's our very soul.

CHAPTER FOUR
THE JOURNEY

Guardian: We are not ready to journey and enter the darkness of the unknown. We need more skill, more understanding, and more techniques.

Warrior: Are we ever ready to enter the unknown? Won't it always seem too soon?

Guardian: Would you go on a solo mountaineering expedition without first training with guides and gaining experience in mountaineering? If I had all the gear but no training, would you trust me to go on a combat mission with you?

Warrior: No. You'd be a danger and a liability.

Guardian: Exactly. I've made the mistake of leading students to the unknown before they were ready. Instead of helping, I created confusion and anxiety. I learned the primacy of preparation. I learned the importance of preparing a leader's mind and spirit. This leads to a level of readiness to begin the journey within. This goes for you and for me.

The first step to readiness is training in principles, techniques, and knowledge. This serves as both a teaching strategy and a risk mitigation strategy. Risk cannot be erased. But it can be managed.

Being ready, we will not be deceived by illusions, distortions, and deceptions as we climb. They are sirens' calls to treacherous rocks in a treacherous sea. We must first close our ears and tie ourselves to the mast to avoid such traps.

Before we climb–

> We need to cover the principles and techniques. We need to wrestle with them and take command of them. Then, we can head out and climb with confidence. Then, we will be ready for truth when it reveals itself

Warrior: Got it. I never understood how much preparation this work took. I am a man of action. But I know the importance of preparing, practicing, training, and drills. And this mission is more complicated than simply taking a hill.

Guardian: And we are learning to temper our spirit of action with the spirit of contemplation.

Our first technique is dialogue—we've made good use of it and will continue to do so. Our first model is the Hero's Journey. Have you heard of this model?

Warrior: Yes. But, I want to hear what it means to you, and its implications for our expedition.

Guardian: Then, if you'll be the virtue of patience, I'll share what I'm seeing. I share this and other models for teachable points to awaken the intelligence of students, whether they are inexperienced or seasoned. To master skills, we need to spend time studying and mastering the domain of knowledge. I never understood this until I studied Csikszentmihalyi's research on creativity.[1]

He said that one key aspect of mastery is mastering a domain of knowledge. Back then I was not a student of leadership, though I was leading. I didn't study books and thought it was a waste of time—time wasted when I could have been taking action! I didn't want to study; I wanted to be doing.

The joke was on me once I started studying. I learned there is very little that we need to do, in terms of actions. I learned that the art of leading demands the study of emergent situations. I learned that the art of leading demands the creation of strategies to solve emergent problems. I learned that the art of leading is to empower resources and people to solve the unexpected and the unforeseen as it emerges. This was eye-opening. When I studied my activities, all I saw was wasted energy, as my actions were not critical.

Warrior: You are speaking from a strategic perspective.

Guardian: Yes. One of the challenges for me was that I loved physically moving my body, and I spent my formative years engaged in physical activities. But, when I started to study leadership and management I learned, it really is a thinking game. And this thinking game moved through various skills, many skills that I would never master. And when I started teaching leadership, I saw students struggling with what I too had struggled with—their 'leadership intelligence' was highly underdeveloped. They were good at doing tasks, at doing activities. But they were weak at 'thinking' in the realms of tactics, operations, strategy, and management. I notice that students resisted the difficulty of sharpening their minds intellectually. Meaning, they were good in math, they were good with numbers, they were good with calculations. But they struggled with concepts, frameworks, principles and ideas and using those to season their minds in the leadership acts of thinking tactically, operationally, and strategically. They were not used to feeling 'weak' at something. They had been rewarded most of their lives, be it at school or at work, for being good at something, for being superior to others at something, but they knew and I knew: they were not superior in the intelligence to lead others by the power of their insights, to see what was hidden and to make action plans to overcome unforeseen obstacles.

Warrior: Ah. That's why you like working with warriors. All we do is overcome problems

---

[1] Csikszentmihalyi, *Creativity.*

that occur in combat. We relish challenges and find honor in overcoming them. Shame and alienation sneak into our psyche otherwise.

Guardian: Those experiences awakened your intelligence. They made your mind lucid.

In our quest, we need to study the domain of knowledge. We do this by studying the theories, models, frameworks, and the experiences of our predecessors as the foundational work in order to leap into the unknown. This first model, the Hero's Journey, serves as a guide to prepare ourselves for this expedition.

Warrior: How?

Guardian: At its core, it serves to guide us into the unknown, instead of avoiding it. We can leverage this model as an instrument when we are in the unknown. It can serve as a map of what we will encounter and help us to see in the darkness. For this and all the models we cover, I have one aim: to make them live in our being. To awaken them as neural avenues ready to be driven down. These models are living and dynamic to me. I cannot stress this enough. I hope to discover how this is possible. The models are a way to bring sight to the life and the reality we are seeing and encountering—which is not just physical but intelligible in an intangible way. Any time that I'm confused, it's usually not physical. Instead something intelligible and intangible is taking place, and I can neither see it nor understand it. Because I study the domain of leadership, I can draw upon different instruments and see if they help disclose what is hidden.

Warrior: Wait. Do these, the models, act as your weapons to hit your targets?

Guardian: Yes.

Warrior: Intellectual weapons?

Guardian: Yes. Let me share why I think the hero's journey is critical. For context, this model was discovered during the great depression. While the model is new, the pattern discovered is ancient—which is why it resonates with me.

Warrior: How was this model discovered?

Guardian: During the great depression, a professor named Joseph Campbell found himself at St Lawrence College, with no work, no students, and no money. He had a small room on the campus. For five years, with very little to do, he pursued an interest that drove him—the study of myths. I dare say it was his Daemon, his god-within, that called to him to study myths. And did he ever heed this call! He studied every myth, from every culture, that he could get his eyes on. His Daemon, his calling, had to lead him. He could have studied any other topic, but he followed a living drive in his being to study one domain—myth. Hidden in myths, it turns out, are the living and truthful patterns about the purpose and meaning of human life.

Warrior: What is a myth?

Guardian: A myth is a story, a story clothed in fiction used to explain truths that are unexplainable. Where did we come from? Why do we exist? What is the purpose of our existence? They were used to help teach and inspire human communities to endure the challenges of living. But the genius of Campbell's discovery is that he abstracted a pattern and a structure that are universal to most myths. Now how is this possible? Most of these myths were created thousands of years ago in civilizations that had little contact between one another and were separated by oceans and mountains. And yet, as he discovered, the same basic pattern emerges again and again. He discovered a universal common pattern. He coined this universal structure the "Hero's Journey".[2]

Now what is of critical importance is the insight and revelation I saw in this structure–

This structure does not live outside of us, but lives inside of us.

Aristotle[3] said that "plot, then, is the first principle..." In other words, structure gives the story meaning. Many storytellers disagree from metaphysical perspectives. A Sunni may believe that history is over and there should be no hero journeys left. Hindus see cycles. Western pagans saw parables and sometimes stories with no structure. But the first civilizations of Mesopotamia and Egypt wrote Christ-stories long before the story of Christ. And enduring myths stubbornly have structure, giving them meaning and purpose. We find the hero's journey in the stories of the Pashtuns, Arabs, First Nation Peoples of the Americas, and every religion and civilization. This implies that every human being is living this journey, no matter how significant or insignificant his life is to him. Meaning that all human beings, both you and I, are living a conditioned and mortal existence. This existence has a beginning and has an end. We are all on a journey. As the wise say, God makes use of the fertile soil of daily life to teach us and to grow us. The myths and the heroes are used as simple reminders. Before I understood this or took hold of this, I thought something was wrong with me or that I was weak, if I encountered challenges where I failed and did not succeed or if I had a fall from grace because of a weakness in character. Now, I understand that this is how life is growing and challenging me and that I am part of an interactive living experience all the time.

Do you understand?

Warrior: I understand that I'll be more forgiving of my weakness and wreckage and laugh a little more about it...when it happens again.

Guardian: Humor is a living goodness needed for the hardships we'll undergo. The Quran tells us that God loves the humorous. This is critical to understand—we need to have a vigorous

[2] Joseph Campbell, *The Hero with a Thousand Faces.*
[3] Aristotle, *Poetics.*

attitude to lead while we're in the ups and downs and cycles of living. The hero's journey is a pattern for these cycles. This is not some dead model to me. It's living in me, in you, in all of us. I hammer this point home with leaders. I use the model as a balm after I've taken a sledgehammer to the psychological armor around their psyche. Both leaders and warriors experience this journey with more frequency and intensity. Let's cover the framework of the Hero's Journey.

Warrior: Let's wear the framework like armor for battle.

Guardian: My good man, yes.

The journey. The framework is a circle, a cycle, an eternal return. Let's start at the top of the cycle, and flow in a clockwise direction. There are seven gates and gatekeepers on this journey. We either pass or fail. Not everyone succeeds. Failing for us means our purpose has halted. Passing means that our purpose continues.

Warrior: The only attitude is *don't quit* and *don't turn back.*

Guardian: The bitter truth is most fail in purpose but do not fail in life—the perennial cycle of birth and death. By the cosmic measure, we all pass into death. But, not so, for the purpose-driven life—the life of living a calling.

Warrior: What do you mean by calling?

Guardian: I mean the calling to be–

> Warrior, Artist, Musician, Healer, Teacher, Writer, Spouse, Parent, Farmer, Builder, Creator, Innovator, Scientist, Politician, Manager, Leader, etc.

We need to know what we are called to do and then devote our being to it.

Warrior: What if you don't know the call?

Guardian: We are called. We need to listen. Then we need the courage to act on the calling. We cannot underestimate the primacy of courage. It takes courage to live the call, if we are honest. The first gate initiates the journey. This first gate is called "THE CALL."

For any noble endeavor, especially 'the call to lead,' we need to understand this concept of 'calling.' This is what leads us in the direction of our purpose. This is what leads in the direction of a way of living and a way of acting that is suited for our nature and essence. The perennial calls are marriage, parenting, farming, healing, teaching, making, and protecting. These are the highest-level calls that can be overlaid on almost every action known to man.

You've heard the biblical verse, "many are called, but few are chosen?"[4]

---

[4] The Holy Bible, *Book of Matthew*. Lamsa translation.

Warrior: Yes.

Guardian: The deeper meaning is that all are called, but few listen to the call. Our aim is to discover the call, not only for ourselves but also for everyone else. Not all are called to lead. Not all are called to fight. But all are called to a way of living and a way of being. You ask, how to know the light? The call is the first light. We all need to reflect and examine our life to discover this first light that lights the way. Now, even if one knows the call, this first gate is a formidable gatekeeper. Not everyone passes through this gate. And why? Because of fear. Fear paralyzes the soul. Passing this first gate requires willpower displayed as courage. It's the first test. We need to know this. Courage, not ability, sets the journey in motion. We need to know the calling is a choice. A choice, in that it asks for the will to say yes or no.

The fact that we are souls or conscious beings is marvelous. This is the beauty of the journey—We either affirm or deny the movement. It is crushing every time I hear one of our elders say in hindsight that they wish they had made the journey differently. They did not know what was going on; they did not know they were being tested. They did not have good teachers. What drove me is precisely this experience—I experienced subtle fear and did not even know it until I had an awakening. And even then, I'd get lulled back to sleep, only to be awakened again. No one even asked if I was experiencing fear. Odds are, we don't act because of fear. Fortitude, to overcome fear, awakens the soul from her sleep into the light of her powers. This is why it's critical in education to explain and map out the terrain—to prepare and steady students for when "the call" makes contact. Once there is contact, students know their most powerful weapons—willpower, courage, choice and endurance—need to be unleashed. That is how they shoulder the burdens placed on them. That is why the wise ones say, "listen, act, and don't quit." Quitting on one's purpose is a defamation of truth. Truth makes no guarantees. Failure is lurking all around and the only central task is to wield courage when listening to the call. This first gate is bearing down on us as we speak. The calling is "to discover the essence of leadership development."

Warrior: I thought you were explaining the model?

Guardian: I am. In the context of preparing us. Not as some abstract theory but as something that is actively engaging us right now. We've agreed to accept the call. Now we pass through the first gate. Do you experience this?

Warrior: Yes.

Guardian: We are now being guided on a journey, but we don't know where it will lead and when it will end. In our set of tools, along with dialogue and courage, we will need the virtues of faith and endurance to hammer into the granite of the climb.

Warrior: Climb? Journey? Which is it?

Guardian: Can't you see? The climb is the journey. We are beginning to leave the known and create distance from what is comfortable. We need to be led into the unknown, which is foreign and uncomfortable.

Warrior: The liminal space.

Guardian: Yes. The known is what is normal, easy, comfortable, without challenge and without test. The known is a common and an unhealthy kind of boredom and uneventfulness. But, where do we go? Do we have a map? Who guides us?

Warrior: Wait, I thought you were leading this. I thought you were the guide. Do we need a guide?

Guardian: Yes indeed. The second gate of the hero's journey is called "THE MENTOR." We need a mentor. Guess where we get the term "mentor" from.

Warrior: From guide?

Guardian: Homer, in his *Odyssey*, named Telemachus' tutor "Mentor."

This term, *mentor*, is old and significant. We human beings are the least equipped to survive without guidance, education and protection. In our leadership journey, did we have the best training and education?

Warrior: No.

Guardian: And if we are pioneers, if we are trailblazers, we still need some help? Is that fair?

Warrior: Yes.

Guardian: Then what do we need? If we had good mentors, what would they do?

Warrior: They would set the example. We would follow them. They would teach us and guide the way. They would demystify the art. They would provide training. They would get us skilled.

Guardian: And they are gatekeepers. Not everyone passes; not everyone is skilled enough.

Warrior: We would have to trust them. They would have to be trustworthy.

Guardian: No man is an island.

Warrior: Donne echoes from the depths—

> No man is an island entire of itself; every man
> is a piece of the continent, a part of the main;
> if a clod be washed away by the sea, Europe
> is the less, as well as if a promontory were, as

73

well as any manner of thy friends or of thine
own were; any man's death diminishes me,
because I am involved in mankind.
And therefore never send to know for whom
the bell tolls; it tolls for thee.[5]

Guardian: We need teachers. We need one another. This is why it's important to be a good student, a good follower. But more importantly, we must seek good teachers.

Warrior: Then who are our mentors going to be?

Guardian: The mentors? Don't you see? Our mentors will be the wisdom literature and the sacred literature. These canons will be our guide. It may seem difficult to imagine, but the ancient texts are living thinkers. We can have a lively dialogue with them. They are not meant to be read passively. No. We can experience their depths and their souls because the wisdom is eternal and it's waiting for us.

Warrior: That might be too abstract. Can you make it more concrete?

Guardian: Yes. We must study the domain. We must study the great thinkers who wrote about awakening the depths of our being. We must wrestle with these thinkers until they let us in. By wrestling with those who have gone before us, by making sense of what they struggled to know, maybe the depths of our intelligence will open and this opening may reveal hidden truths that we need to know in order to teach our art.

As an example, were you ever frustrated without knowing why?

Warrior: All the time in bureaucracies. All the time with the non-stop friction and resistance that acts like the force of entropy killing creativity, initiative and freedom of action.

Guardian: Pay attention. How does the frustration go away? Tell me what you do, supposing that you don't quite fix the situation.

Warrior: I practice self-reflection and study every angle of the situation to get to the core of what is frustrating me.

Guardian: Good.

Warrior: When I take time to study the phenomenon, what I observe begins to reveal itself, begins to explain itself, from moment to moment. Then, it is revealed: the errors in actions, the misfires in systems, and the ineffectiveness in strategies.

Guardian: Good.

---

[5] John Donne, *No Man is an Island* poem.

Warrior: I notice that I have to distance myself and detach myself from the situation to open up my field of observation.

Guardian: Good. Musashi's principle–

> Keep what is close, far; keep what is far, close.[6]

Warrior: When I do this, when I practice detachment and I create distance from the situation, I notice I become still, and when I become still, a heightened yet calm intelligence begins to create insights through my perceptions. Then with increased contemplation, I begin to see what needs to be corrected.

Guardian: This my good man is an example of truth-seeking. This is an example of disclosing the truth. You explained what happens when the intelligence comes to us at rest—it awakens. What you demonstrated is how our intelligence can come into harmony, can come into correspondence, with the reality. This is a critical skill, the art of truth-disclosing. Do you see why I asked you on the journey?

Warrior: I don't follow.

Guardian: Yes, the wisdom literature mentors. But I needed a peer-mentor.

Warrior: Good God, the blind leading the blind.

Guardian: You are serving as a martial arts sparring partner. To engage in the dynamics of feeder and receiver, giver and taker, mover and counter-mover. Only that we are in the dynamics of spirit and intelligence instead of spirit and body. We are learning to deepen understanding through dialogue, and you just demonstrated what it means to be lucid—to shine the light of intelligence on a situation.

Warrior: I'm reminded of Clausewitz's "On War," when he described as a necessity the commander's ability to grasp the essence of the situation, and to take decisive action by that grasping, by that understanding of the essence of reality as the battle is unfolding.

He called this ability *coup d'oeil* and he defined the concept as–

> The quick recognition of a truth that the mind would ordinarily miss or would perceive only after long study and reflection.[7]

Guardian: Good God. That is our aim. To learn how to do this with living itself, not just warfighting. He uses the word "truth." That *is* practical judgment—the art of 'truth disclosing.' It takes courage to remember that truth is reality and that reality can be hidden. I'm reminded of Emerson's perspective on truth—that it will not reveal itself to cowards.

---

[6] Miyamoto Musashi, *The Book of Five Rings*.
[7] Clausewitz, *On War*.

Warrior: I see how you leaped from Emerson–

> God will not have his work made manifest by cowards.[8]

Guardian: Deepening the significance, Clausewitz writes that to lead in battle, three qualities of character are of paramount importance: light, truth, and courage. He writes that the commander must make his intelligence strong, so that he has command of–

> An intellect that, even in the darkest hour, retains some glimmerings of the inner light, which leads to truth.[9]

Warrior: Your instinct and intuition to search for light and truth, spirit and intelligence, as the central task in forming leaders is hitting the mark. I did not think it possible to teach this. I never thought about how to teach this.

Guardian: Do you see how Clausewitz is mentoring us on our search to discover the essence of awakening light and truth?

Warrior: Yes.

Guardian: Peter Kreeft[10] stated that in the history of education, there has been no better instrument than a book. I pray leaders will read and study the books of wisdom to educate and awaken their soul.

Warrior: You believe books can awaken the soul?

Guardian: Beyond belief, I've had direct experiences of wisdom and sacred literature illuminating the soul.

Warrior: And we are hunting for this inner light in the soul of the leader.

Guardian: Yes. Do you wonder why we weren't taught this?

Warrior: Yes. I suspect it's because we live in the age of materialism—matter before consciousness.

Guardian: And I am a soul of idealism—spirit, then consciousness, then matter.

Warrior: Then you might not love this, but I need the courage to say this–

Clausewitz said, most soldiers (and we can add, most citizens) lack the genius within to achieve this skill. He said most need to be led, to be commanded, to be told what to do, because they do not have the willpower, and courage, and intelligence to endure the struggle to bring forth the fire of inner light to seek the truth.

---

[8] Ralph Waldo Emerson, "Self Reliance".
[9] Clausewitz, *On War*.
[10] Peter Kreeft, *Socratic Logic*.

Maybe he meant that it's not the lack of genius, but the lack of willpower to study and train to bring about this ability. He said most have false opinions. He said most get tripped up because they don't have the conceptual ability to harmonize concepts with reality. He said most use concepts incorrectly and mistakenly as they overlay them on reality, and then instead of creating insights they create distortions, and end up in the delusion of self-deception.

Guardian: Without rigorous education, that is expected. We will counter this perspective with rigorous education and development. That is why I focus on leaders. I have faith that if an individual is called to be a leader, she has the nature to awaken her potential to lead. Our task is to find those with the fire to train this way—to unlock this capacity. This is the purpose of our journey, to become trustworthy teachers.

Warrior: Leadership development as one of the highest teaching arts?

Guardian: Is it not looking that way? This is why first we are training and exploring, so that we can transform 'knowledge about' to 'knowing.' Then we need to find others and take them through the same training. We need the training to be rigorous, to discover those who have the drive and ability to become truth-seekers, and to cast out the image-seekers.

Guardian: What is the second quality Clausewitz wrote about?

Warrior: Emerson would appreciate this. Clausewitz wrote that once a commander experiences *coup d'oeil,* he must have "the courage to follow this faint light wherever it may lead."[11]

He called this ability *courage d'esprit* and defined the concept as–

> The courage to accept responsibility, the courage in the face of a moral danger.[12]

Further, he calls this courage "determination" and writes that–

> determination proceeds from a special type of mind, from a strong rather than a brilliant one.[13]

If we take these concepts to heart, the implications become serious when selecting leaders. What do we do now?

Guardian: We select the most brilliant ones, not the strongest ones.

Warrior: And what happens in a crisis?

---

[11] Clausewitz, *On War*.
[12] Clausewitz, *On War*.
[13] Clausewitz, *On War*.

Guardian: They fail.

Warrior: Why do they fail?

Guardian: Because they lack light, truth, and courage?

Warrior: And why do they lack these qualities?

Guardian: Because they were measured on the calculative ability, on their cunning and not on the character of their soul.

Warrior: Yes. That is what drives you to understand. That is what drives me too.

Guardian: That is why the journey begins with the light of the call and the courage to act on the call. Do you see why we study the great and powerful thinkers, so that they can mentor us, since we don't have mentors, since most in command do not have *coup d'oeil* and *coup d'esprit*.

Warrior: Yes, my good man, I see.

Guardian: To pass through the second gate, "THE MENTOR," means we need to rely on the mentoring of the wisdom and sacred canons. These are our expedition guides.

Warrior: Yes. I see.

Guardian: And we will also be peer-to-peer mentors.

Warrior: Yes. I think peer mentors, when virtuous and wise, are some of the best mentors we will have, because of shared hardships.

Guardian: Then, as we follow this path of the hero's journey as a living pattern, the next gate, gate 3, is called "CROSSING THE THRESHOLD." First the call, then the mentor. Now it's time to cross the threshold.

Warrior: Ah ha. To go from the known to the unknown. This is by design?

Guardian: Yes. We need to expect this. The unknown is where we are challenged and tested, not in the known. That is why the experience of the spectator is different from that of the participant in the arena.

Warrior: I have to share Theodore Roosevelt's perspective here. Even though I've read it again and again, it's important, because if you are not in the arena, if you are not in the unknown, you are not being tested. Not being tested, you are not growing, you are not being transformed, and you are not trustworthy. You are just a pundit. If I pray (though I don't) I pray for the pundits to be silenced. Daily, they commit the injustice of acting like they know, but they have no idea.

Guardian: You don't mean investigative journalists?

Warrior: Good God no, we need them. They are our truth-reporters. I mean the talking-heads, the babbling class, on the screen. They seem helpful. But they darken and distort and poison the mind with their seductive, hypnotizing and venomous language.

Unlike the babbling class, who lack the depth of soul to inspire, here are inspiring words to guide us.

> It is not the critic who counts; not the man who points out how the strong man stumbles, or where the doer of deeds could have done them better. The credit belongs to the man who is actually in the arena, whose face is marred by dust and sweat and blood; who strives valiantly; who errs, who comes short again and again, because there is no effort without error and shortcoming; but who does actually strive to do the deeds; who knows great enthusiasms, the great devotions; who spends himself in a worthy cause; who at the best knows in the end the triumph of high achievement, and who at the worst, if he fails, at least fails while daring greatly, so that his place shall never be with those cold and timid souls who neither know victory nor defeat.[14]

Guardian: I'd follow human beings like this. What most people do not do is read his 14-page speech, called "Citizenship in a Republic."

Warrior: We don't read or study. We quote and don't understand. But, man, are we skilled.

Guardian: I sense the irony aimed at us. All humor aside. What we are getting at is that we must develop and change our inner nature and make our character strong in courage and intelligence. We don't need to be brilliant but we need to be skilled in our art, the art of leading and developing souls to endure hardships and challenges in arenas worthy of their effort.

What I find interesting is the definition of the term "*lead*."[15] For our journey, two statements express the meaning of the term "*lead*"–

"to guide the way" and "to lead on a course."

Our guides are leading us: the writings of the warriors, sages, saints, and philosophers.

Warrior: We are following their lead. They've left a pathless path.

Guardian: By doing our homework, we demystify as much as possible and strike into the unknown with courage, wisdom, and strength. Are we seeing with more depth?

---

[14] Theodore Roosevelt, "Citizenship In A Republic", speech delivered in Paris, France, 1910.
[15] O.E.D. definition of 'lead.'

Warrior: It seems simple.

Guardian: Do you experience more insights by activating this model in our being?

Warrior: Yes.

Guardian: Then, when we journey and we hit an impasse, we won't quit, we won't turn back, we will seek out guidance by studying these texts that aid us in overcoming the impasses.

Warrior: Intellectual and spiritual mountaineering. Who knew they joy of this work?

Guardian: Soon we will cross the threshold. When we move into the unknown, we will not be following the wisdom and sacred canons. No. We are charting a new course. The canons are guides, walking side by side with us, but we are not aiming at mastering their body of work; we are aiming at awakening new truths and charting new courses and making fresh discoveries.

We are the leaders on this course. We are the guides on this course. It seems to be a paradox, but it's not. We are the explorers. We are not following another being unless that being is light and truth itself. This is the burden of ownership. This is the burden of responsibility. We are aiming at forging a way forward to create enlightened leaders. Our predecessors faced different challenges than what we face. We aim to carve out leadership knowledge in the granite of truth. And for this, we need to develop our inner light and determination. I hope you see why we spent time planning and mapping out the knowns. We do this to counter the intellectual weakness of blind faith and of leaping out into the unknown blindly without preparation, knowledge and skill. Our faith is anchored in truth. That is why we have courage on this adventure.

We need to deepen our understanding and experience of gate 3, "CROSSING THE THRESHOLD." This is where most yet-to-be adventures get stuck. This is where most who are called get paralyzed in fear. Most seekers quit before the journey begins. Why? They fear the unknown. They fear letting go of the known. And this fear crushes their destiny's calling. This is where we journey from the ordinary, the common, the known, into the extraordinary, the uncommon, and the unknown. This is where we begin to live with fear, a good fear, a fear that needs courage, because failure is a possibility.

Warrior: I love living in the unknown. That is why I loved training for combat and engaging in combat.

Guardian: Now, I love living in the unknown. I love entering the unfathomable abyss of being. But, when I was younger, I did not know what was going on. In ignorance, without the armor of courage, fear assaulted my interior nature. My intelligence became blinded by the storm of hidden and subtle fears. I did not know I had inner fear. I did not know the role of fear as the telltale sign of being on the journey. I needed a guide to explain this to me. The internal stress, caused by fear, did not match the external stress of the journey. It seems so simple in hindsight.

Warrior: Ouch. I never experienced internal stress like that.

Guardian: That is why your mantra of "be cool and live deep" is powerful. It's an attitude that we can bring to bear on all things, which is tough to do. For context, and to cross the threshold, let me explain what I'm seeing. As you trained for combat and went to war, I see what we are doing as intellectual and spiritual warfare. It is as serious and strenuous on mind, spirit and emotions. I don't know if I can express what I'm seeing, but I need to makes sense of this to further the journey. The soul, to me, is intangible. The intelligence to me is intangible. It seems to me that the real war is the war to know the truth and fight against deception and falsehood. The real war, the real combat, is to find and develop good human beings and get them into positions of authority and power so they can lead mankind, in truth and wisdom.

Warrior: Flower Newhouse wrote–

It will take men who live in the light to bring peace and harmony to mankind.[16]

Guardian: And our aim is to lead in the light. There is a war, a spiritual war, raging in the soul of every human being and they don't even know it. Between shame (which leads to alienation, psychological crisis, and an early death) and honor (which leads to high esteem, admiration, nobleness, and magnanimity). Now, if there is a spiritual war raging in every soul, do we see the primacy of developing leaders? Leaders who develop their souls to lead in the light?

Plato echoes from the depths–

Why, right here, stranger, is the first and best of all victories, the victory of oneself over oneself; and being defeated by oneself is the most shameful and at the same time the worst of all defeats. These things indicate that there is a war going on in us, ourselves against ourselves.[17]

Warrior: Yes. We won't say this publicly, but we aim at crushing the ego and awakening the soul.

Guardian: So, we aim to crush our ego and awaken the powers of soul?

Warrior: Yes.

Guardian: Instead of crushing souls, we crush egos.

Warrior: Yes.

---

[16] Flower Newhouse, *Songs of Deliverance*.
[17] Plato, *The Laws of Plato*, Pangle translation.

Guardian: When it comes to crushing the ego, we are not taking a head shot. We are not taking a direct aim. We are taking the indirect approach.

Warrior: Wise move.

Guardian: Unlike in combat, were you use weapons and tactics to crush an enemy morally and physically, we are aiming at creating weapons and tactics to free the soul.

Warrior: Which is why dialogue is a key weapon. The ego seeks control and dialogue seeks truth. And the soul, not the ego, powers dialogue.

I can't help but think of Musashi's writing on "Crushing."

> Smashing your opponent completely, even if he seems weak and you are strong, is called Crushing. This mentality is important. In martial arts situations…when you perceive that your opponents are few in number…or once you have confused them and found their weaknesses, you crush them. In other words, from the very beginning, you are intent on intimidating them and crushing them completely.[18]

> If your crushing is weak, they will be able to rally. The heart of this is to grasp what you have in hand and crush them. You should investigate this thoroughly.[19]

Guardian: I think you've lucidly highlighted the challenge. With both our ego and our enemies, we must crush them. However, I have found that warriors, because they spend their lives training to crush the enemy, tend to bring that energy to their own teammates and to themselves. This causes too much internal friction and thwarts efforts at leadership development. I have also found this with businesspeople and athletes. They spend so much time competing that they forget how to coach and teach and create harmony with the team.

Warrior: Their egos get in the way.

Guardian: And they think it's a good thing, to have big egos.

Warrior: And in truth, this is what makes them dangerous and is what usually leads to their downfall.

Guardian: They don't even understand the difference between will, spirit, intelligence, and ego. The ego does not like discomfort.

Warrior: It's terrifying how frenetic and spliced our being is from lack of education.

---

[18] Musashi, *Book of Five Rings.*
[19] Musashi, *Book of Five Rings.*

Guardian: That is why I'm wrestling with the idea of leadership development as a form of mixed martial arts.

Warrior: How? Soul vs. Ego?

Guardian: No. We can't take a head shot at the ego because it's a fraud, it's a delusion, it's mirage. Just by focusing on it, it wins.

Warrior: Why do we think it's real?

Guardian: Because we are both beast and angel in this temporal composition called the body. What if we could create mixed martial arts for the intelligence and spirit?

Warrior: What are you seeing?

Guardian: What are we actually doing in seeking to develop the soul of the leader?

Warrior: Self-knowledge vs. self-deception?

Guardian: Yes. We will cover that in detail, downstream. But, what are we doing? What is the action we are undertaking? It seems to me that we are agonistic competitors, who need to wrestle with ideas, who need to learn how to disclose the truth, who need to learn how to make just decisions. This is nothing new. Socrates invented this method. Only it seemed, Plato never had an opponent equal to him, to Socrates. It seemed his opponents were always weaker and ignorant. Our aim is to create trainings to build strong intelligences to wrestle with one another and disclose the truth. We need one another in this art. Only, the aim is not to make one another submit. The aim is for each to develop and trust his or her inner light and then ignite that inner light to discover a new truth. The aim is then to teach others to develop that inner light and do the same. That is how we learn to live in the light. That is why there is no 'winning against' in this art, only seeing 'what is.'

Instead of this, what do we have? We have everyone trying to control and dominate everyone else. That is human madness instead of divine madness. Money is not real. Movies are not real. Professional Sports are not a necessity. CEOs, Movie Stars, Statesmen, and Generals are not powerful. They are simply men and women. Mortal. Vulnerable. Imperfect. And yet they seem to exert power over mankind. How is this possible?

Warrior: You're striking the core problem with current leaders. They continually commit the greatest leadership sin–

    Acting like they know when they have no idea.

Guardian: And we empower them in their ignorance. That is why I resist the practice of 'one leader at the top.' Let's adhere to the practice of tertiary leadership, three leaders of mettle, who make decisions by clashing ideas and opinions against one another until the truth reveals itself.

Warrior: That is a counter measure to smoke out the egotists and narcissists. My experience in small combat units attests to this. These small units are self-governing and self-correcting and learn to maneuver as one.

Guardian: You taught me this, with your study of immunization, that the goal is to make beings free and strong to counter any disease in the form of deception or delusion.

Warrior: I see why you are bringing me along and not soloing.

Guardian: We find freedom in the unknown. We will dive deeper and deeper into the depth of the unknown as we make the ascent. The way I'm seeing this, as we climb higher in knowledge, we are going deeper into our being, and the deeper we go into the unknown, the better our chances of disclosing the truth. To do this, we need to learn to see in the dark.

Warrior: I'm seeing what you are seeing now. You are now going to point out that to see in the dark means to see with intelligence, to see with discernment, to see what cannot be seen with the physical eyes.

Guardian: Exactly my blessed friend. Aristotle taught me the value of friendship. He reminds us that there are three kinds of friends. The first kind of friend is the one we seek for pleasure or what they give to us by means of affection. The second kind of friend we seek for advantage or what we can gain by the friendship. The third kind of friend is one who we admire for their character. It is only this last kind of friendship that I seek. These are the kinds of friends that leaders need. This kind of friendship wants what is best for the character of his friend and seeks nothing in return. This kind of friends seeks no reciprocity. This is why Aristotle said, these kinds of friends share the same soul. He meant, they share in the same essence and power of soul—goodness, truth, beauty—independent of the composite self.[20]

Warrior: The world would be healthier if we demanded to let go of the two former kinds, and aimed only for the latter.

Guardian: Without friendships based on character, leadership development in the form of developing the soul is not possible.

Warrior: There would be too much unwarranted competition, egotism, antagonism, and jockeying, instead of demanding what is best for each friend.

Guardian: That is why I pray the Novena of Humility.

> That others our chosen and I set aside.[21]

The purpose of becoming virtuous and noble is to make oneself worthy of friendships.

---

[20] Aristotle, *Nicomachean Ethics,* Sachs Translation.
[21] Novena of Humility.

Warrior: And because of this friendship, we can freely speak our minds and pursue this endeavor.

Guardian: Now we arrive at gate 4, which is called "THE TESTS".

This is where the trials, tribulations, challenges and temptations reveal themselves. We must steady ourselves. We need to know that we must not retreat. We must not turn away. We must not avoid these tests, but rather engage them and combat them. These are the enemies. We welcome these enemies—this is where we are formed. These obstacles are how we know we've entered the deep waters of the unknown. Through them we will see and learn truth. Our mindset must be that we either overcome, or we expend all energy and spirit until there is nothing left, until the spirit leaves. That is why we are instructed to have contempt for death. There is no quitting. There is no turning back.

Warrior: The tests then, if we understand them correctly, are the truth, are the baptism, are the initiation. God, it seems so matter-of-fact when we map it out.

Guardian: Then, let us welcome the tests instead of fearing them. We need to make this known, it is the fighting spirit that destroys self-doubt and creates self-esteem. Fear loses its grip when there is understanding. Our aim is to nurture self-esteem, not in the absence of tests and trials, but *in* them. In the struggle of the tests and trials is where self-esteem and self-knowledge and self-discipline are born. We need to welcome the initiation phase in calmness and coolness. A coolness that grins with contempt for the necessary pain and suffering of transformation. Are we seeing clearly? I wanted this understanding. I wanted this training.

Warrior: Yes. We see clearly. Instead of keeping students in the dark, we will light the way. All they need to do is use their will, intelligence, and energy to gain knowledge and skill.

Guardian: We need mentors to demystify the work. Instead of mentors, we have bureaucrats throwing convention, coercion and control at neophytes. I hated the initial experience of military training. It was not challenging. I did reveal my incompetence. And I feared my incompetence. No one told me to be patient with learning the craft. I did not understand development. A mentor should have said, "in ten years, maybe you'll experience mastery; now, you just need basic skills. Just don't quit." I did not quit. But, without guidance, assaulted by fear and lack of mastery, I lived in a torrent of confusion. And I still scored high marks. I did not care about the marks; I cared about mastery and I knew I lacked mastery.

Warrior: That is wasted energy. You probably made it look easy.

Guardian: No. I rolled my eyes at instructors and they swarmed me the rest of indoctrination. Even back then, I did not care if they were in charge; I did not respect them. It all seemed like an act.

Warrior: It is an act.

Guardian: Why is it an act? That seems like an injustice to me. It's not real, it's training, and they are acting like it's real.

Warrior: The military plays to a baseline. You must remember most people only do one tour and one tour is nothing in terms of mastery. They need people to do what they are told to make the machine run.

Guardian: Why are living beings made the servants of a machine?

Warrior: Now you're getting too philosophical. Let's get back to the tests.

Guardian: I thought we were discussing tests. I want to make sure what we do never gets twisted and fabricated. We are the guides that point out we are living beings—that our inner nature and its development are more important than some machine. Our test is to take a stand and not get ensnared in the mechanization of living, but to use machines to aid in our living.

Warrior: What you are saying is, we are not going to change external systems effectively unless we change the beings, the souls, operating those systems.

Guardian: Yes. It's our principle that true growing pains take place in the soul. We aim at a human nature and a human experience that are superior to mere survival. We aim at a human nature that is designed to grow into perfection by the education and development of the inner faculties, and inner nature of each human being. I keep stressing this and I will continue to stress this on our journey. What is being grown is the soul.

Warrior: Can you describe this in more detail so I have a better understanding of your perspective on developing the soul of the leader?

Guardian: In this part of the test? I need the mentor, Meister Eckhart, to help me explain why I focus on the inner nature, the soul of the leader.

Warrior: Who is Meister Eckhart?

Guardian: He is a German Mystic from the 15th century.

Warrior: You do know, after two decades of combat, I'm agnostic.

Guardian: You seek the truth.

> You are a deeply religious man who doesn't believe in God. God will seek you out. You'll come back. Whether here or elsewhere only God can tell.[22]

Let's not get tangled up in concepts of belief—atheist, agnostic, theist. Let's just look at what has been written by discerning thinkers who explore the essence of our nature.

---

[22] Somerset Maugham, *The Razor's Edge.*

Warrior: Go on.

Guardian: To anchor us, I'd like to study a passage from this mystic–

> Concerning this, you should know what the masters say, that in every man
> there are two kinds of man. The one is called the outer man, that is the life
> of the senses: this man is served by the five senses, though, the outer man
> functions by the power of the soul. The other is called the inner man, that
> is man's inward nature. You should understand that a spiritual man, who
> loves God, makes use of the powers of the soul in the outer man only to the
> extent that the five outer senses need it: the inward nature is not concerned
> with the five senses except insofar as it is a guide or ruler of those senses,
> guarding them so that they do not yield to sense objects...[23]

Warrior: I'd caution you in our journey to forgo the use of terms like "Love of God."

Guardian: Can we just use "love of truth" every time we read "love of God?"

Warrior: For you, I will grant this request, because I know you love God and see God as the source of light and truth.

Guardian: Thank you. I've been seeking the truth of God for over two decades and you know this seeking has led to what I see and what I write. I've never 'seen' God, but, when I pray and contemplate the great mystical works, they affect me deeply enough to share what I now see, in terms of developing the soul of a leader. This body, that I am in, is a conditioned existence. This body, that I am in, is perishable. If I'm seeking eternal truths, I'm seeking what is not perishable. I'm not a preacher.

Warrior: You seem like one to me.

Guardian: Seeming and being are two different concepts. If I seem like a preacher, what am I, if we remove the seeming?

Warrior: I grant you, you are a truth-seeker and that is why I trust you.

Guardian: I'm doing my best to speak freely. I don't force people to seek truth or God. I look to concepts, and if they resonate, I investigate. After twenty years of seeking God's truths, I've never seen God, buy I pray and study scripture daily. And what you might find important, from a mystical perspective, is that every time I hit a wall or a ceiling in my journey, I pray until I see the light of an insight that can guide me.

Warrior: You pray. I meditate. The effect is the same. Just as I described earlier how I overcome frustrations.

[23] Meister Eckhart, *The Complete Works of Meister Eckhart*. On Detachment.

Guardian: That is what I am seeking—the transferable practices and techniques, independent of beliefs. I am looking for how a soul uses its intelligence to break free from frustrations and obstacles.

Warrior: Then we are making strides.

Guardian: I take this to mean that we should encourage people to trust themselves and not follow blindly after the beliefs and ideas of others. I mean, we must encourage people to "investigate things thoroughly for themselves." I don't want to be right; I want to discover what is right and then act accordingly.

The Bhagavad Gita, that sacred song to God, warned us–

> Better is one's own-law imperfectly carried out than another's law well performed. It is better to find death in the performance of one's own-law, for another's law is fear instilling.[24]

Warrior: Seeking truth is dangerous business. It's the opposite of coercive power. It's the harder road, but the road worth taking.

Guardian: This ancient text cautions us not to follow a theory of truth but to investigate and learn for ourselves so we become the wisdom it speaks. This ancient text is critical for annihilating all coercive authorities that use fear instead of truth, to control the ignorant, the weak, and the fearful. We seek freedom of being.

Warrior: That is why I'm cautious and hesitant when I hear you say you seek God. I've seen the horrors of men living in faith's blindness killing in the name of God, religion, and truth. That is why if I could have any vocation, it would be a "blinder remover." That is why I am truth- seeking with you, to remove the blinding darkness.

Guardian: I love that metaphor. I find that freedom in seeking God and truth because I want to know if I can make contact with the source that created nature and living beings. I value freedom above all else. Even when some say I am obedient to God it's because I experience freedom in what God reveals.

Warrior: …What truth and intelligence reveal.

Guardian: Yes. I am a lover of truth. I've lost all other great loves along the way. I've lost the soulmate along the way. Had I wisdom and not ignorance, I would have married her. Let our aim be to remove our own ignorance, blindness, darkness, and bondage. As we hunt, let us learn to see with vision, light, truth, and freedom. In our search we hunt for direct experience, not something that lives outside of ourselves, not something we can point to, but an experience

---

[24] *The Bhagavad Gita*, Feuerstein Translation.

of what we have become. For I, too, am cautious of the domain of theology as a means to control instead of liberate. I learned that the core of theology is truth and divinity and beauty, but the humans that lead theology and religions are corrupt, weak, ungodly, unsaintly, and all too human. My point is, the wisdom is correct; the souls leading it are incorrect and unwise.

Socrates–wise. Christ–wise. Buddha–wise.

Buddhi is a Sanskrit term and it means "wisdom-faculty."[25] The goal of practicing the techniques is to awaken the wisdom-faculty. And leaders, to develop the truth-disclosing ability of practical judgment, must awaken this wisdom-faculty to become trustworthy. Truth won't be mocked.

Warrior: Insightful. The essence and nature of what takes place in the soul's transformation is what you are aiming at. That resonates with me. On the adventure of wisdom-seeking we go. What awakened you?

Guardian: Being raised Catholic and still a practicing Catholic (the practices of the mystical saints), I grew up with a tremendous fear of hell. My parents had no idea, as early as grade school, that I felt gripped in a fear of hell. The saints say this fear is a gift of the Holy Spirit. The torments of this gift make sleeping unbearable, which is why I always sought the comfort of a woman. Until the virtue of chastity came calling.

In my early twenties, as a military leader, I contemplated, how could an all-powerful being endow weak and fragile human beings with the intelligence to create atomic weapons that assured the 'mutual suicide' of mankind if opposing armies engaged in full scale war, one that ends in intercontinental thermonuclear annihilation. I contemplated, how could Christian nations lead the way in these developments? Where were the Christians of Christian nations? I contemplated, how could I marry and bring forth children into an existence I did not understand nor an eternal principle that I could not believe? How could I live a family life when mankind still cannot live in peace and harmony twenty centuries after the Lord of Light? It led to such despondency that I refused to marry, let alone have children, and I went in search of truth.

Warrior: Were you always this existential?

Guardian: Yes. During this first period of despondency, I sought the guidance of a Catholic Priest. At the time, I was stationed in Japan and worked for a military leader who was Buddhist and who married a former Buddhist monk. He met her when he served as part of a Japanese Officer Exchange program and visited a Buddhist monastery. During the visit, they locked eyes, she left with him, and a beautiful love story and family was born.

Warrior: Beautiful.

---

[25] *The Bhagavad Gita*, Feuerstein Translation.

Guardian: It was strange to see this depth of love amidst the soul's anguish on a dark night. I scheduled a session with the Priest. I knocked on his office door.

Priest: Enter

I opened the door and my eyes took sight of a magnificent office with leather couches and reading chairs, a mahogany desk, chair, and bookshelves. My eyes started to scan the books even before I greeted the Priest. The shelves were lined with hundreds of theological, metaphysical, and philosophical books. It was the first time my eyes set sight on the names of Plato, Aristotle, Epictetus, Aurelius, Augustine, Aquinas, Averroes, Avicenna, Bacon, Rousseau, Machiavelli, Eckhart, St. John of the Cross, St. Theresa, St. Francis De Sales, Merton, Pieper, Maritain, *Upanishads*, *Bhagavad Gita*, *Koran*, *Lotus Sutra*, *Heart Sutra*, *Diamond Sutra*…on, and on, and on, the books went like eternity. When my eyes set sight on these books, the eternity of my soul awakened and made its presence known. It seemed as though I had entered another world, had been transported to another dimension. Wisdom's eternal light marked my soul. It was a kind of brand, marking me as its property. And I have belonged to Wisdom ever since. Life has never been the same. The Priest noticed my amazement.

Priest: How can I help you?

In a mixture of anguish, amazement, and rage I began to speak.

Guardian: I don't understand how there can be an all-powerful being that allows us weak beings to create and wage such violent destruction and death on earth. I don't understand how an all-loving being allows us weak beings, when we fail in virtue on earth, to enter an eternal hell at death? I don't understand how "sinning" is even possible when a perfect being created us in his image? I don't understand how "original sin" is even possible at the dawn of humanity. We are creatures. We are conditioned and temporal existence. We suffer disease. We suffer the harshness of nature. We are dependent upon water, food, shelter, just to survive. We need so much just to care for the body, let alone care for the soul. I don't understand, if I'm born in body to conditioned existence, and this birth of conditioned existence sentences me to death, and if in between I suffer vice and sin, even if I commit them again and again for a hundred years, at the time of death, at the time of judgment, I'm then cast into eternal damnation, why would I even accept the gift of life? No thanks. I'd rather not exist if that's the divine law. Those laws and those ideas are hell to me, the ideas themselves. Are we not in hell now? Nature is beautiful. The ways of men are ugly and sick and depraved. None of this makes logical sense to me. If those were the

90

conditions before birth, I'd not have chosen to accept them So why am I here? If this is the truth, if there is a heaven and a hell, I'm not waiting till death to know it. I'm going to seek heaven and hell now. If I enter hell, I am going to figure out how to get out of it. If there is a Heaven, I'm going to seek God and truth now and enter it. So that when I die I'm already there—I'm already there by being. Death will simply be a release from this physical body, a release from the temporal prison. I'm going to seek heaven now. I'm going to seek God now. I'm going to seek direct experience so that I know the truth.

This is what lived and still lives in me. My soul has been wrestling with truth ever since. That is why the ways of the world of men seem so depraved and insane to me. If you aim for truth, you see non-truth. You see the deception and the distortion. We have no respect for Nature. We exploit the Earth. We exploit one another. I hate it.

After a long pause of reflection, the priest spoke.

Priest: I do not have any words or answers to help this dark night of your soul. I do know we are sinners. I do know that we cannot know and see God, here on Earth. This is why we need Faith and Prayer. I do know that you cannot experience Heaven here and now; all you can do is hope to see God face to face, in the beatific vision. What you must do is God's Will and hope you will enter heaven at death. I suggest you go to mass daily, read scripture daily and pray the rosary daily.

His response infuriated me. I was enraged.

Guardian: Maybe you don't have the heart and soul and will to seek and know God now, but I do. I don't know how, but I'll make it my mission to make contact with God now. To know God, now. To see God, now. To experience Heaven, now. To transcend the temporal, now. To know the truth instead of believing in the truth, now. I don't discount what the Gospels say for they light the way. I do think it's unconscionable that the Catholic Church has produced so few saints and that Christian nations have waged such horrific wars.

Years later, I read the first *Yoga Sutra*–

Now commences the exposition of Yoga[26]

At that time, the presence of "now" initiated the journey.

---

[26] *The Yoga-Sutra of Patanjali: A New Translation and Commentary*, Feuerstein translation.

Warrior: I would have loved to have been there. I wrestled with the same existential crises, only I had combat to focus my mind away from the "Now" that grasped your soul. The combat has ended, and now is the time to wrestle with this.

Guardian: The rage of not knowing truth set on fire my awakening. The rage is divine madness flowing through me. I've opened my soul to its Madness. I cannot understand why no one has the courage to speak of our essence and nature. I trust in the power of one's true nature to realize its potential, and that's been my saving grace.

Potency awakens when we ask–

> Where did we come from?
> Why we are here?
> What are we to fulfill?
> Where will we go afterwards?

I learned to experience Grace and Freedom and Growth in asking questions I could not answer. I felt beinghood, here on earth. Right here. Where I could see it and smell it. Where it entered into the wavelengths my senses could detect. I needed to enter into the joy of existence itself, and the mystery of existence itself. But to enter that joy, I desired truth and the not knowing terrified me instead of inspiring joy in me. It still does. I don't know. I dance with this terror and fear daily and let it inspire courage and fortitude in me. I can tell you, I know my soul's displacement. Even back then, I knew I was lost.

Warrior: How beautiful.

Guardian: What?

Warrior: That is how we grow in the virtue of courage, my good man. We need fear. We need uncertainty. We need not to know but to seek knowing. The seeking is the journey. How did the conversation end?

Guardian: I looked at the books and then spoke.

> Guardian: Do you *know* these books?
>
> Priest: Yes, I've studied them and I teach them.
>
> Guardian: That's not what I asked. I asked do you *know* them?
>
> Priest: I don't follow.
>
> Guardian: You don't follow because you don't know them. You only 'know about' them. The truth has not awakened in you. The truth does not live in you. Only the 'knowledge about the truth' has presented itself to you.

Overcome with rage, I felt done and I turned to leave.

> Priest: Where are you going?

> Guardian: To enter the deep waters of the masters of truth. To awaken the truth within. To become the essence of what these books declare is our purpose—to become a living being of truth and wisdom.

Warrior: I am beginning to see why training for war and training for truth is similar to you.

Guardian: I set this aim twenty years ago and I'm still not awakened in truth and wisdom. I learned that this is not the point. The point is to get into these deep and living waters of truth and let them grow you and transform you and lead you into eternity, no matter how long it takes. That each day can be used to grow the soul or weaken the soul. That truth uses the fertile soil of everyday living as spiritual nourishment. So, where are we, now? Why did I even remember this experience? Why is self-introspection important during the tests?

As we described Gate 4, "THE TESTS," I remembered the experience of a test to lead me further towards my purpose even when I hardly knew the purpose. The test, the frustration, is what awakened a deeper part of my being. The experience served to test and fortify my commitment to an aim I felt most important. I could have easily given up or turned back. I kept moving forward. I think I shared that experience to describe what tests actually do; they serve to strengthen and to lead our soul on the emergent journey of living.

Warrior: You are still living these tests. The challenges lead us as we live in both the known and the unknown. I easily followed where you were going. We live this concept called the "Hero's Journey." In our existence, we live simultaneously in the known and the unknown.

To summarize, on the Hero's Journey, you have covered 4 gates: The Call, The Mentor, The Threshold, and The Tests. You set the demarcation from the preparation phase to the initiation phase, when we go from the known to the unknown, and our aim is to enter the unknown and learn to see in the depths by taking on the tests, the trials, and the temptations.

Guardian: Speaking of depths, Gate 5 is titled, "INTO THE DEPTHS."

Warrior: Of course, it is. The belly of the beast. That is where we learn to flourish. That is where the change happens. What others cringe at we must relish with every instinct. Every moment. Every ache and pain.

Guardian: This is the most challenging experience of the journey. We must be prepared for it. This is where, by design, all of our hidden and subtle fears, doubts, weaknesses, triggers and deficiencies reveal themselves. They reveal themselves so we can prove mastery and maturity by taking them on, by overcoming them, by bringing them into submission, by surmounting them, all in order to prove one's faith, intelligence, heart, and will.

Warrior: The fighting spirit comes to life in the deed.

Guardian: In *The Iliad*, Achilles' mentor is Phoenix, and Phoenix aimed to educate Achilles–

> To be both a speaker of words and a doer of deeds.[27]

And this ability follows from the investment in training and tests to become a person who is powerful in speech and forceful in action.

Warrior: This is all too familiar. It reminds me of combat training. Patton mentors–

> To be a successful soldier you must know history. Read it objectively—dates and even minute details of tactics are useless. What you must know is how man reacts. Weapons change, but man, who uses them, changes not at all. To win battles you do not beat weapons—you beat the soul of man of the enemy man....[28]

There is always a key moment in the warrior's development when his mind, emotions, body, and will break. It's not hitting rock bottom; it's when the temporal and conditioned aspect of our nature runs empty. It's the moment when there is no more strength. The strength of body is gone. It's the moment when there's no more emotional energy. The feeling, the emotions are stripped of all energy. The intelligence is numbed. You can't think. You can't make sense of what is going on. And yet the instructors demand that you keep going. You're not dead. You can still quit but you are instructed not to quit. It seems the training takes you to the place where there's nothing left for you to give, as though all sources of energy have been emptied. Then you are at the critical moment. It's not war, it's training, and you are being tested. You could quit; you don't. How do you keep going? For those who don't quit, something magnificent and marvelous and miraculous takes place. At that precise moment, when those sources reach empty, and your being decides to endure, I am almost afraid to say this, but the soul asserts herself and her power. A well-spring of energy and spirit awakens, and that spirit leads the will, the body, and the emotions. Now, this is not something that goes without limits, but it is something that gets you through the trial.

Guardian: Do you realize what you just said? We are documenting this. You are saying that the spirit of the man awakens, and only the spirit can get the warrior through the training because the training crushes the ego, the personality, the temporality of the being. This is what you are saying, correct?

Warrior: Yes.

---

[27] Homer, *The Iliad*. Translated by Stanley Lombardo.
[28] Patton, in a letter to his son.

Guardian: And you said you are agnostic. You are describing exactly the conditions required for spirit to awaken the soul. Now, in absence of warrior training, how does life awaken the soul?

Warrior: By enduring the hardships of living.

Guardian: Yes. Are we seeing truth? Is it revealing itself in the depths of our exploring?

Warrior: I hesitantly say yes.

Guardian: This is why, to develop the soul of a leader, we must take an indirect approach, not physically, but mentally and spiritually, to silence the ego in fatigue so the soul can awaken and release her powers to see light and truth.

Warrior: To be light and truth.

Guardian: To become the living light of the wisdom literature. It now seems more possible, after we have explored the path.

Warrior: As warriors love to crush the enemy, as we are trained to crush the enemy physically and psychologically, so you mean to train leaders to crush the only enemy that lives within, that fictitious fabrication that we call the ego.

Guardian: Yes. Because through that crushing our true nature and spirit awakens. Does it make sense? It's *the* divine cosmic test. No one escapes it.

Warrior: Yes, this makes sense to me. We are creatures and we are created and tested by living itself. Instead of focusing on this real test and awakening the powers of spirit, we create self-deceiving devices and structures that keep us in bondage.

Guardian: That is why I hunt for leadership genius in the souls of warriors. My experience has been that warriors, especially warriors who have been in combat, understand this and can sense it, because it's already been awakened. I also hunt for leadership genius in the souls of spiritual warriors. They do sense what I'm doing because they've undergone similar, yet different, training.

Warrior: Let's return to Musashi's passage on *crushing*.

> Smashing your opponent completely, even if he seems weak and you are strong, is called Crushing. This mentality is important. In martial arts situations… once you have confused them and found their weakness, you crush them. In other words, from the very beginning, you are intent on intimidating them and crushing them completely.[29]

---

[29] Miyamoto Musashi, *The Book of Five Rings*.

And if we use this as a principle of development–

We seek to crush and smash error, ignorance, falsehood, deceit, deception, delusion, pride, vanity, cowardice, betrayal, narcissism, etc. We crush the ego to awaken and free the soul. And only the soul can do this. We can't force this on another being. We can't command it or control it, but only set the conditions to liberate it. This is powerful.

Guardian: Which is the whole aim of education—to liberate—to lead out the moral and intellectual faculties—the spiritual faculties.

Warrior: We don't crush or oppress the spirit. We crush the negative energies and thoughts that seem to keep the soul in prison.

Guardian: That is why this is a war. It's a war for character, a war for truth, a war for goodness. Our aim is, through training, to be on guard against those tendencies within us that keep us in bondage and darkness and ignorance. The wise never war with the wise. If we had a planet of self-governing, truth-seeking beings, we would experience a temporal heavenly setting.

Warrior: We are secretly in love with the ego—we suffer vanity, greed and lust. The sins of self-love.

Guardian: Which is why narcissism, above all else, is the most treacherous—to be in love with your own image instead of loving truth. Erich Fromm writes that in the art of truth, there can be no truth-seeking without a transformation from this narcissistic tendency to a love of reality expressed as harmony and union.

Warrior: The saints don't seem so foreign to me anymore, now that I've examined them in light of their transformative path: the path of purification, illumination and union. We need to be on guard against those seeking affection, seeking attention, seeking to be 'seen,' to 'be known,' who suffer vainglory in their pursuit of wealth, status, achievement, recognition, and honors.

Guardian: That is why humility and detachment are key virtues. I found a powerful prayer called the NOVENA OF HUMILITY.

Warrior: What is a novena?

Guardian: It's a special kind of devotion, to bring about a change in character.

> NOVENA OF HUMILITY
>
> O Christ! meek and humble of heart, Hear me.
> From the desire of being esteemed,
> Deliver me, Christ. (repeat after each line)
> From the desire of being loved,
> From the desire of being extolled,

From the desire of being honored,
From the desire of being praised,
From the desire of being preferred to others,
From the desire of being consulted,
From the desire of being approved,
From the fear of being humiliated,
From the fear of being despised,
From the fear of suffering rebukes,
From the fear of being calumniated,
From the fear of being forgotten,
From the fear of being ridiculed,
From the fear of being wronged,
From the fear of being suspected,
That others may be loved more than I,
Christ, grant me the grace to desire it. (repeat after each line)
That others may be esteemed more than I,
That, in the opinion of the world, others may increase and I may decrease,
That others may be chosen and I set aside,
That others may be praised and I unnoticed,
That others may be preferred to me in everything,
That others may become holier than I, provided that I may become as holy
as I should…

Warrior: Wait. I'm not religious. I don't follow a specific religion. I am a man of spirit and truth. If I struggled with arrogance and wanted a method to practice humility, I could meditate on this NOVENA, only I'd remove the religious language, correct?

Guardian: Yes. Test it. See what happens.

Warrior: All of us, not just leaders, need this practice. Now I have a method. And I know what it is doing—it is silencing the ego and making room for the soul to awaken her powers. That is divine.

Guardian: Now we are getting clearer on the adversaries, which are qualities. That is why I don't judge human beings. I judge the qualities that I'm seeing. I speak to the qualities. We must be on guard against attention-seekers and image-seekers. Those qualities keep the truth veiled. We need to be on guard against "what seems so" and discover "what is so."

Warrior: This reminds me of Maslow's Self-Realization Theory.

What a man can be, he must be.[30]

---

[30] Maslow, *Motivation and Personality*.

Guardian: I resonate with his theory. How are you seeing the connection?

Warrior: I'll be brief. We can cover this in more detail downstream.

The most important point I see is the difference between self-esteem and self-realization. When you said to be on guard against attention-seekers and image-seekers, Maslow would highlight that these beings need recognition from others to establish a quality of inner self-esteem. He said, most never transcend this level of self-esteem; it comes from the outside in. When you speak of developing leaders to be independent and free of the will and judgment of others, I take that to mean that you also aim to grow a leader's self-esteem, so that it comes from within; that is the higher-order esteem of a mature person. She doesn't need external validation from others to generate her esteem. Her worth and value comes from within. This made even more sense when we covered how the soul awakens. The soul is worth and value in and of itself. I share this because most people's sense of self and worth and value comes from other beings.

To make this more concrete—

> Lower self-esteem is a drive and desire to be respected, accepted, and valued by others. This means a need for respect that comes from others and that is recognized by awards, achievement, fame, prestige and attention.[31]

> Higher self-esteem is self-respect, a drive and desire for strength, competence, mastery and maturity. It is a quality that comes from one's own being, from one's own self, independent of others, and leads to self-confidence, independence, and freedom.[32]

Guardian: That is terrifying. Most of us are paralyzed by the need for others to validate our worth.

Warrior: That is why I think many leaders fail once they assume command. Instead of being commanding they still look to others for validation, and this creates a paralyzing psychological fear. It's estimated that less than one percent of people in any field self-actualize. You are seeking to self-actualize leaders and this is a Herculean task because it's so rare.

Guardian: How do you define self-actualizing?

Warrior: The realization of one's talents and potencies. You are after those who are driven to self-actualize both professionally and personally, and I dare say spiritually. Your aim is to hunt for human beings driven to realize their potential. Or, to leap from Aristotle, to live as potency being realized by exercising power centers, the faculties of the human being.[33]

---

[31] Maslow, *Motivation and Personality*.
[32] Maslow, *Motivation and Personality*.
[33] Aristotle, *Nicomachean Ethics*, Sachs Translation.

Guardian: Yes, that is what I'm driving at.

Warrior: Then forget about almost everyone and develop yourself.

Guardian: I can't do that. I've tested monastic living. I need to live both the active life and the contemplative life, and the active life involves teaching and leading. I know there are beings searching for this. I need to hunt and find them.

Warrior: Then you must find a way to attract, assess, train, and select as we do in combat units. You don't have the enterprise capacity to do this.

Guardian: I don't have the transferable knowledge to teach. This is primary. The enterprise comes later. What we are discovering is the greatest problem of truth-seeking—to build true self-worth before we leap into the darkness of the truth-seeking that leads to transcendence.

Without transcendence—meaning, purpose, and true identity—we rage, become careless, and die like one who the tribe leaves behind in the wilderness.

Warrior: Yes, my good man. That's the threshold holding most people in chains. They can't let go of the need for attention from others. Attention is a source of energy and fuel for them. They are powered by it. Their self-worth and self-value come from others. This is why taking a stand is a definitive leadership act.

Guardian: Wait, how does this tie in to making leaders "independent of the wills and judgments of others" instead of "dependent upon the wills and judgments of others"? Is this the dialectical staring point we have been hunting for?

Warrior: I don't follow.

Guardian: If our aim is to take an indirect approach to transcending the ego and awakening the soul, instead of a direct approach, we can think of Hegel's Thesis, Antithesis, and Synthesis style of discovery to overcome this obstacle.

What I mean–

Our first aim is to develop a leader (forget the words ego and soul) to become strong enough to take a stand. The test of taking a stand is to develop the strength of self-worth to be "independent of the will and judgments of others." That is the first goal. If we fail to do this, all other skills will be rendered useless when the moment strikes. We can think of the antithesis of this self-worth as "dependence on the wills and judgments of others." That is what we are on guard against. This is the antithesis of our first goal.

What I mean–

There is a psychological tendency to equate competence with freedom, and when we feel incompetent we feel threatened and fear failure. Where does this fear of failure come from?

Does it come from the actual failure or incompetence of not being good at something, or does it come from the fear of being judged by the wills of others? We need to get to the depths of this. I never cared if I was incompetent. But I did care about getting the best training to build competence. And soon I discovered my leaders did not know how to provide the best training. They were not skilled at teaching.

I used to get frustrated when leaders would say,

> You need to become a critical thinker. You need to become creative. You need to develop command presence.

And yet they would not teach me how to become competent in these abilities. That is what compels me to the library to study and research any competency I need to develop.

What I am attempting to explain–

No one should feel good about being incompetent. But, they should know if it's from a lack of training. And we need to point out that it's not competency that builds self-worth; it's self-esteem that builds self-worth as a state of being, as a state of character. And we need to teach students not to create internal stress for 'letting down' their leaders, or for fear of how they look or how they will be judged. They need to learn to demand excellence of themselves and also learn how to learn new skills without guidance, because most leaders do not have time to teach and most times they are not skilled in the skills that the worker needs to become skilled at. Only then is there true forgiveness. True forgiveness is the ability to forgive oneself and live and learn from the pains of growth.

What I am attempting to explain–

We must become strong in character and in skill, if we are going to develop the strength required to take a stand when we receive the blasts coming from the wills and judgments of other beings.

Warrior: So, what is the synthesis then?

Guardian: I don't know. I don't see it yet.

Warrior: Let me take a shot.

1. The thesis is independence from the wills and judgments of others.
2. The antithesis is dependence on the wills and judgments of others.
3. The synthesis is interdependence with the wills and judgments of others.

I mean true friendships are the synthesis—friendships that produce harmony with the wills and judgments of others.

Guardian: There it is—what we hunted for, the significance of true friendships in our art. Character-driven friendships, honoring the dignity of the soul, never projecting their will and judgments onto their friends, but serving as guides and mentors to help their friends become better in virtue, excellence and wisdom. Friends as the bearers of true feedback.

Warrior: Yes. I don't mean to make this sound simple. But most organizations are not built around friendship. They treat human beings as capital and resources. There is no true trust. That is why I had to stay in the brotherhood of warriors. Nonetheless, this domain of warfighting still got mechanized. And if you could not adapt to the machine, you'd get ejected. But, I did discover and experience souls who became interdependent with the wills and judgments of others, because we had to purse excellence and perfection in warfighting. And seeking perfection means the most intense performance feedback.

Guardian: You are describing how, in the absence of ego, true friendship is built. True friendship tends to silence the ego because of the care and concern for the friend. That is why I think Aristotle, in his ethics, wrote extensively on the virtue of friendship.

Warrior: That is why on the hero's journey the mentor is more like an older brother, a true friend, a family member seeking to help guide his brother.

Guardian: How different the world would be with true mentors and true friends and true communities. You are describing the opposite of selfishness. You are describing selfless devotion.

Warrior: It is clear. True selfishness, true egotism, is the adversary.

Guardian: To transcend the ego is the burden placed on each soul. It makes sense now. The ego as the obstacle to the soul's powers.

Warrior: This is why you focus on our inner nature. That is what we must transform.

Guardian: So, the real task is to build self-esteem and then get the soul to understand its self-worth by knowing what it is, independent of anything external.

Warrior: Indeed. If we are to become true teachers.

Guardian: I had hoped to train souls who already possessed high self-esteem.

Warrior: You can hope all you want, but it's not reality that you have hoped for. This is ugly business, this business of educating and forming leaders. We need to plant ourselves at the threshold where most get halted and guide them through. Most do not cross this threshold of high self-worth, and instead they become arrogant and narcissistic. We need to get to them before this corruption and deformation takes place.

Guardian: I cannot work with arrogant and narcissistic beings. A leader once asked, "how to lead the soul-less?" I had to grin at the genius of the question. I can't lead the soul-less. I either war with them or manipulate them. What he was saying was, when people don't know they are souls, when they won't even contemplate if they are soul, when they are controlled by the ego, there's nothing you can do from a leadership perspective other than dominate.

Warrior: Maybe this is why things are the way they are with mankind. Aldous Huxley mentors–

> Reality is not clearly and immediately apprehended, except by those who have made themselves loving, pure in heart and poor in spirit.[34]

> Instead of this we have–

> Man's obsessive consciousness of, and insistence on being, a separate self is the final and most formidable obstacle to the unitive knowledge of God. To be a self is, for them, the original sin, and to die to self, in feeling, will, and intellect, is the final and most all-inclusive virtue.[35]

[35]Guardian: Then we must make ourselves worthy to ferry souls across the chasm between the abyss of the ego and the abyss of the spirit.

Warrior: And to do this, with an indirect approach in mind, we use the hero's journey because it resonates both with the ego (the self), and the soul (the spirit), because both love adventure, epics, and heroes. The former love the titans of industry and wealth; the latter, the wisdom of the saints and sages.

Guardian: Have we entered the unknown almost by chance, by practicing the indirect approach?

Warrior: We seem very far from the surface of worldly activity.

Guardian: Good. Let's continue in the deeper depths. It may be challenging to enter and to see, but, at the bottom, is it still, peaceful, illuminated, and true—at bottom is the divine ground.

Warrior: One teachable point we need to document, to avoid the habit of sophomoric arrogance. The danger of teaching with frameworks and models and theories, is, just as you experienced in your conversation with the priest that, in the beginning, students will only have "knowledge about", but, they won't have experience putting the knowledge and techniques into practice, to enter the state of "knowing."

Guardian: The art is essentially like Olympic gymnastics. It may be one thing to be able to perform a few gymnastics moves, but to compete as an Olympian is a completely different endeavor. And we aim to train like spiritual and intellectual Olympians. We will stress decades of daily training and experience to awaken the "knowing" in their being.

---

[34] Huxley, *The Perennial Philosophy.*
[35] Huxley, *The Perennial Philosophy.*

Warrior: Virtuosity in Knowledge and Skill. This is going to be one of the most challenging aspects of development–

> The transformation from knowledge to knowing.

This is why I suspect you focus so much on self-knowledge and dialogue, the kind we are having now—constantly to sharpen the intellect.

Guardian: Dialogue is the intellect wrestling. It's how I know the intellect is active and not passive. One's thinking seems clear in the mind until it is forced to speak in dialogue and write in reflection.

Warrior: And most avoid this because they realize just how weak their thinking is.

Guardian: Which is why they need to train the intellect like the Olympian trains the body. We are now at GATE 6, "THE RESOLUTION." This is the gate where the tests and trials have been overcome and we now have insights and clarity on the mission, skills, and actions that will be demanded of us if we continue to follow the *calling*. This is where our experiences, skills, and knowledge are fused into an integrated self where conflicts and contradictions are resolved. This is where there is a reconciliation of the inner and outer nature, and there is a new sense of freedom. This is experienced like the "fly-wheel effect" that Collins wrote of in *Good to Great*. Mathematically, this is called "the law of sensitive-dependence", commonly known as the "butterfly effect." It is the law that states that small variations over time result in major transformations in growth and ability.

Warrior: It seems to express how a decade of daily training for the Olympian is realized in the competition. But this rests on the initial conditions, that the Olympian had the mind and body to complete. Initial conditions are critical. This is why leadership training for executives is a futile endeavor, and why coaches focus on behaviors instead of virtues. This seems like the gate where we'll see leaders transform into beings of high self-esteem and self-worth, able to take a stand against the wills and judgments of others.

Guardian: And finally, GATE 7, "THE PURPOSE." This is where the hero returns from the unknown to the known. This is when the hero, after being tested and vetted, returns to help others by his mission and purpose.

Warrior: Beautiful. It seems that only 2 of the 7 gates are critical. The "Tests" and the "Depths," and this is where we need to focus. To summarize, if I had to explain the hero's journey, in the context of leadership development, I'd simply describe it in the following way–

> The Call–A deep drive to become one's potential.
> The Mentor–A friend and teacher who guides the way.
> The Threshold–Leaving the known for the unknown.

The Tests–methods to fortify virtue and excellence.

The Depths–Awakening the soul; tempering the ego.

The Resolution–Reconciling inner conflicts; integrity of authentic self; true freedom.

The Purpose–The return, knowing purpose and expertise in fulfilling purpose.

Guardian: Clear and concise. Difficult to realize.

Based upon the Hero's Journey, I sketched out a battle plan with the initial terrain mapping. I know it will change once we engage reality, but this is what I'm seeing.

1. The Call–We are called to discover the essence of leadership development and use that discovery to guide and develop new leaders.

2. The Mentor–We will use the writings of the Saints, Sages, Philosophers and Warriors as teachers and as thoughtful friends to guide the way. When facing obstacles, we will use their perspectives, discoveries, and principles as gear, and as footholds, and as protection to surmount the obstacles. We will do our best to transform "knowing about" into "knowing." We will also be mentors and friends to one another. We are both on this journey. This is both an individual journey and a knowledge journey. We will both be changed in essence and knowledge. We will both undergo the purification necessary for transformation.

3. The Threshold–We are embarking on a metaphysical and a spiritual quest. Its external form is a mountaineering expedition to discover the essence of leadership. Its internal form is a wilderness hunt to discover genius in the depths of the soul. This is a two-fold process, simultaneously leading to the depths of our being and leading to the heights of our knowledge. Our aim is truth revealing itself. Once revealed, our hope is to document what has become unhidden.

4. The Test–The greatest tests will be the transformation of "knowing about" leadership to "knowing and being" the essence of leadership. We must become a living example. We will fail if this is not realized.

What I mean–

When knowledge awakens in our being, it becomes an extension of our being. When this knowledge-as-extension-of-being is realized, we become the essence of leadership and can speak from "what we are" instead of "what it is". A good metaphor is alchemy. Our nature and essence will transform by practicing the principles and techniques of character-leadership-knowledge, when our powers of will, intelligence and spiritedness take command of them as extensions of these faculties. We are after potencies. This, if it takes place, will release serotonin instead of adrenaline. We will know when what we know is grounded in what we are.

5. The Depths–This is where, if we pass the test of knowledge-as-extension, a mysterious tacit and intuitive knowledge will awaken in us. We will be able to disclose truth, and this truth will be ignited from what is living in the depths of our being. In the depths, we will pass this gate if we generate concepts to build a domain of knowledge capable of being transferred in language.

What I mean–

We will be able to bring light and truth into transferable methods of teaching, training, and practicing. We will be able to demystify the art. We will be able to prepare future generations. We will be able to take what is metaphysical and spiritual and bring it into concrete and physical expression, in special terms, techniques, frameworks, and models. This is what Joseph Campbell did when he abstracted the Hero's Journey. All the myths were there. He discerned the intelligible pattern in the depths and shared those depths with us. We are better human beings with the knowledge he earned and shared.

6. The Resolution–We will build artifacts (books of knowledge) and we will be worthy to educate and develop leaders. We will also teach followers the markings of trustworthy leaders, those to whom they can turn and trust to lead.

7. The Purpose–To devote the teaching art to forming self-actualized and wise leaders of light and truth, who we would happily and willingly follow. Why? Because they have awakened their light and truth to exercise practical judgment and truth-disclosing and truth-seeing.

Now, I think I see the essence of leadership living in you, so I need you on this journey. In studying thousands of leaders, I've rarely witnessed this essence actualized in a living being. Because I can see it in you *(and dear reader, I can see it in you too)* it helps me abstract the knowledge. Just as Joseph Campbell needed as material, the actual myths, so with leadership, I need actual human beings who practice the art. And because I've conditioned myself to see the soul, I think I can give language to what I'm seeing.

Warrior: You know, that is why Plato and Aristotle needed one another—wholeness and union resulted from the two of them colliding and documenting their thinking. The philosophers say we need one another because we don't mirror one another—we help light one another.

Guardian: You mean, we need one another to help awaken the light and truth.

Warrior: Yes. That is why all pressure is on the mentor, on the teacher.

Guardian: And this is what I hope we can impart. When I pray, I pray for more leaders to become more like you.

Warrior: You know flattery is a sin.

Guardian: Truth is not flattery. I need living embodiments to study this domain. You devoted yourself to this art. You devoted yourself to leading men in combat. I've read the books. But I don't find leaders in books; I find leaders in the blood and spirit of beings.

Warrior: Wait, are you pulling Socrates' move of acting like a midwife, for souls?

Guardian: Sssshhh. Don't say that aloud. Don't whisper it. Since we are friends, yes, I confess, I serve as midwife for wisdom and truth to be born in the souls of leaders. I don't have wisdom and truth myself but I do have the ability to awaken it in others. A divine comedy. I'm reminded of Plato's *Theaetetus*. Maybe this will help us understand with a firmer hold on what we are doing. He speaks of his art in the following way–

> And the greatest thing in my art is this: to be able to test, by every means, whether it's an imitation and a falsehood that the young man's intellect is giving birth to, or something genuine and true.[36]

What we glean from this is that practical judgment is a truth-disclosing ability. We aim to develop a discerning mind and we need to be on guard against images, ignorance, lies and falsehood. We need to get away from image-seeking and head into truth-seeking. We need to test our thinking and we need to exercise intellectual humility.

Warrior: This means we also need to exercise intellectual patience. Plato's *Theaetetus* also speaks of the primacy of patience, and not being in a hurry to catch and grasp truth, but to let it reveal itself and let it lead. Truth is like water, and we follow it as a river, not knowing where it leads or when it will end.

Guardian: You are that rare combination of intellectual superiority and intellectual humility. That combined with the calling to be a warrior makes you the ideal spirit to take on this challenge.

Warrior: Are you sure you're not using 'flattery' to sell me on this adventure?

Guardian: Good God no! I know you're agnostic and I've been speaking about my Love of God and the Saints. I'm actually trying to find every reason why you would not want to go on this journey. But, I need help. Look at what I just quoted from Plato—I need help to eradicate my own ignorance and I need help from a highly qualified soul.

Warrior: Let me guess—I'm your last resort. You actually don't have anyone else.

Guardian: I know great mystics and yogis, but they are not called to endure the intellectual hardships of this adventure. They are on their own adventures, adventures that I intend to write about too. That comes later. My calling and my aim is to make leaders virtuous. And this is what is at stake.

---

[36] Plato, *Theaetetus*, Sachs Translation.

Burns, in his seminal text *Leadership*, he hits us in the gut with the crisis–

> The crisis of leadership today is the mediocrity or irresponsibility of so many men and women in power, but, leadership rarely rises to the full need for it. The fundamental crisis underlying mediocrity is intellectual. If we know all too much about our leaders, we know far too little about leadership. We fail to grasp the essence of leadership that is relevant to the modern age and hence we cannot agree even on the standards by which to measure, recruit, and reject it.[37]

We are after the essence, the standards, and the techniques. To uncover the essence of leadership, we need to become the essence, and then transform from a "who" to a "what."

Warrior: Ah ha. From "ego" as the "who" and the "I and me", to "soul" as the "what" and the "essence."

Guardian: Yes. Leadership is not a "who" but a "what." That *whatness* lives in us, waiting to be awakened. With your help, we may reach the summit of this noble adventure. I have no constraints keeping me from undertaking this journey. I see this as a deployment to a combat zone, only we are not going abroad to fight a combatant. No—we are going into the essence of spirit where our ego and desires are the adversaries keeping us, and others, from seeing the truth and leading from the truth. Are you in?

Warrior: I'm in.

Guardian: Good. Let's start preparing for the climb. I now think we are ready to journey into the unknown. To get our mind right, I see us as alpine climbers. We need very little gear. We need to travel light. Our intelligence will lead the way. I believe we are skilled enough to take on this Everest of leadership, without oxygen, in an alpine style with very little equipment and help, travelling and climbing light. I know you love science and I think science can help, but we must have the courage to leap into the unknown, to what science has not yet covered, to leap past the edge of knowledge. What does this mean? It means we won't know the holds, patterns, and paths until hidden truths light our way.

Warrior: Agreed. As I said earlier, let's take off our blinders of the known, enter the unknown, and learn to see when we reach those sublime heights. For a strategy, the indirect approach is best. We'll move with the least possible resistance. We need to treat this domain with awe, reverence, and respect. How do you want to climb—with what kind of pace and tempo?

Guardian: I climb with the courage to follow the truth wherever it leads. I climb with patience. I climb with a lucid and leisurely mindset. Being in a hurry kills truth-disclosing. We are both

---

[37] Burns, *Leadership*.

hunters and climbers. We must move slowly. We must find harmony; we must be still. We must observe. We must disclose new instruments and models to serve as gear and protection, and to make new foot- and hand-holds on the climb when there is nothing but sheer emptiness.

Warrior: Truth-seeking as the art of mountaineering in the abyss of emptiness...

Guardian: Yes. The beauty of spirit transforming being...when the mind is most at rest, its intelligence awakens most powerfully.... It has the ability to see and move and know in the abyss.

Now we cross the threshold into the darkness of the unknown.

CHAPTER FIVE
CROSSING THE THRESHOLD

Guardian: We are embarking on a metaphysical and spiritual quest. Our quest is, in reality, an intellectual mountaineering expedition to discover the essence of what makes a leader. As we go higher we simultaneously go deeper.

Our mission is to hunt after the truth, and if we are pure enough and patient enough, to give it permission to reveal itself. We cannot consume it. We cannot force it. We have to learn to see it. Although we are hunting to save our very souls, prudence will be paramount.

Our quest is a two-fold process–

> One requirement is to enter into the deepest depths of our being, to awaken our intelligence so that we can see what can only be seen by discernment.

> The other requirement is to leap out past the edge of our knowledge, to reach into the heights of unknowing, the knowable unknown.

Nietzsche would commend our efforts to stretch out in this manner. He described seeking to know, as the search for "immaculate perception." He writes, essentially, of this two-fold process, when he expresses the beauty of this "going to the deepest depths" and "being lifted to the highest heights," when he poetically says of this "immaculate perception"–

> It wants to be kissed and sucked by the thirst of the sun; it wants to become air and height and a footpath of light, and itself light. Verily, like the sun I love life and all deep seas. And this is what perceptive knowledge means to me: all that is deep shall rise up to my heights.[1]

He is speaking about giving birth to the light that is potency in our souls. He is speaking of pure desire. He is reminding us not to force or suppress, but to realize and to know. He is reminding us that each individual is a destiny unto herself, a light unto herself, and that to realize this destiny, the individual must awaken, must overcome, must become, must know, and must speak only of things that she knows in the fibers of her being.

Warrior: Maybe Nietzsche will be waiting for us at the summit.

Guardian: I hope so. Maybe Christ and Buddha and Socrates will too. All four spoke of light. Nietzsche's light as *übermensch*, Christ's light as divine light, Buddha's light as inner

---

[1] Nietzsche, *Thus Spoke Zarathustra*.

light, and Socrates' light as wisdom. And note that the light leads the truth; truth does not lead the light. Our intelligence, on this ascent, needs to awaken this light to see truth. The Yogis call this divine light. The yogis speculated that the core of the living principles that give us life is the light of the soul that forms the matter of the body. The aim of yoga, of meditation, of contemplation, is to awaken this light. *The Bhagavad Gita* summed up the entire 700-verse poem in one verse–

> The *buddhi*-yoked leaves behind here in this world both well-done and ill-done actions. Hence yoke yourself to Yoga. Yoga is skill in the performance of actions.[2]

The term *buddhi* is translated as wisdom and wisdom-faculty. The aim of yoga is to awaken and perfect the wisdom faculty to be skillful in thoughts, words, feelings and actions by moving from a sure-footed place of knowing. Just as the Latin root of "leadership" means to show the light, to show the way.

Warrior: I've defined leadership as "disciplined action."

Guardian: As a working definition, we can define leadership as–

> Disciplined skill in the performance of actions, to become virtuous, excellent, and wise.

Warrior: I like it.

Guardian: How do we teach it?

Warrior: That is what we are here to figure out.

Guardian: Does it not concern you that in the study of leadership, there are too many examples of leaders making the wrong judgment call or having a fall from grace in their character, or both: a combination of deficient-character and incompetence?

Warrior: It's what drove me to this study. I could not understand why, with my training and experience, I still made poor judgments professionally and personally.

Guardian: I do too. Training in "functional skills" seemed to restrict, instead of freeing, me in that act of leading. I needed training in discernment, to be free-thinking in the performance of actions, as an interactive movement, a dance, a harmony between *being, reality* and *knowing*. I'm getting tripped up with my expression.

What I mean–

---

[2] *The Bhagavad Gita*, Feuerstein translation.

It seems that being alive is a non-stop interaction with living itself, with existence itself. I think that the only way to come into harmony with existence itself is by training our inner nature in the dynamics that can respond to the "outer nature," the "environment" we engage with in the act of living. I think a better way to explain this is–

In my early professional years, I was successful but I did not know why. As though by only sheer force of will, I hit the targets senior leaders demanded of me. But, I did not "know".

Warrior: You did not have "disciplined skills." You learned, on the fly, Napoleon's early approach to strategy, "engage the enemy and see what happens." You engaged your work and you adapted and responded, but you did not have skill as expertise. You became experienced by necessity but you did not have the knowledge to understand what the experiences were building in you. You had the base of tacit and intuitive knowledge—you 'knew' what to do, but you did not 'know.'

Guardian: And not knowing infuriated me. Then I'd ask senior leaders for guidance, and they did not 'know,' they just 'acted.' That may be fine for expertise, but, not for leading. This is why we are going to use the two-fold process of going to the depths (to learn to see the tacit/intuitive knowledge) and going to the heights (to activate the known knowledge as an extension of our being).

Warrior: As above, so below.

Guardian: Spoken like a true wizard.

Warrior: A Freudian slip, you meant warrior.

Guardian: I meant wizard. Since you shy away from "mystic", I chose wizard.

Warrior: I'm no Merlin.

Guardian: Merlin was more mystic than wizard.

Warrior: Are you aiming at drawing out the call of the mystic in me?

Guardian: What if that's the only way? What if our essence and nature is only truth and light?

Warrior: What if we are only firing neural networks?

Guardian: I'm an idealist: Spirit into matter.

Warrior: I'm a realist.

Guardian: Not a materialist?

Warrior: I'm partial to science. Aristotle's epistemological realism holds.

Guardian: I am partial to spirit.

Warrior: You're leading this expedition. I'll do my best to follow the thinking and the logic.

Guardian: Speaking of logic, *Socratic logic* is the reason we use dialogue to disclose the truth. Now, what do I mean by truth? I follow Aristotle's lead in his definition of truth–

> For to say that what is is not or that what is not is, is false, but to say that what is is and what is not is not, is true, so that the one who says that something is or is not is either right or wrong.[3]

> Or

> If a man says of what is that it is, or of what is not that it is not, he speaks the truth, but if he says of what is not that it is, or of what is that it is not, he does not speak the truth.[4]

One way to do this is to speak our minds freely, to study what we are thinking and identify what is true. More commonly, truth simply means don't lie.

Warrior: I follow. But, I need to learn ancient Greek. My mind is spinning with the different translations.

Guardian: Now is not the time to lament a deficient education. We should have learned Latin, Greek, and logic in grammar school.

The way we can approach this climb is to understand that the challenge and the struggle is to see truth. Plato reminds us, our quest is to enter what is hidden and unknown and make it unhidden and known–to disclose truth. He writes that the way we are climbing involves both a struggle of ideas and our own psychological struggles. He says that the challenge is to eradicate our ignorance, and in doing so, to discover truth. A process of *via negativa*, not *via positiva*. Not to acquire, but to remove the blinders and see. A metaphor is that truth is sunlight to the soul. [5]

If we move in this way, moment to moment, we'll reach the summit. He invites us to seek the source of truth and light. And what is the benefit? To experience what it is to become "just" and "wise."

Warrior: Not wealthy and powerful?

Guardian: No. I follow St. Aquinas' lead–

> There is no greater act of charity one can do to his neighbor that to lead him to the truth.[6]

---

[3] Aristotle, *Metaphysics*, Book IV. Sachs translation.
[4] Peter Kreeft, *Socratic Logic*. Aristotle quoted.
[5] Plato, *The Republic*. Allan Bloom translation.
[6] Peter Kreeft, *Socratic Logic*. Aquinas quoted.

Do you follow these ideas about truth?

Warrior: I follow. You and I are seekers of truth. We first seek truth by eradicating our ignorance. We seek to be agonistic, not antagonistic. We seek spirited dialogue, not mean-spirited debate. We are not here to prove one another wrong, to get the upper hand, but to use our intelligence to see what is hidden. This is worthy of our efforts as it seeks to produce truth and wisdom. Distilled to its essence, you see this activity as an act of virtue…virtuous actions if you will.

Guardian: Indeed. Instead of taking the direct approach in seeking truth, we take the indirect approach, *via negativa*, removing the obstacles and obstructions keeping the truth veiled. One does not acquire truth, one does not prove truth, one does not possess truth; one sees it, and one realizes it. Does this not follow our concept of leading, disciplined skill in the performance of actions?

Warrior: Yes. We are practicing leadership development in this activity.

Guardian: In the process of our individual being and becoming, truth reveals itself. She's always there, waiting for us to turn to her. Now is the time to cross the threshold.

Warrior: How do you propose we leave the known for the unknown?

Guardian: With this first question–

> If you were deprived of authority and power, would your men select you to lead them?

The questions lead us into the unknown. The questions silence the ego. The questions awaken the intelligence. King Attila silenced his ego after his only defeat at the Battle of the Catalaunian Plains. He followed the question; he became a slave to the question, if you will. He retreated to the Danube and scuttled centuries of Hunnish culture and strategy. The question rendered everything naked. He had to remake everything and swallow his pride to ever face another enemy again. The ego was drowned. And the question was the point at which he then changed history.

Warrior: God, it seems so simple.

Guardian: It is simple. But what virtue does it take to enter the unknown?

Warrior: Ah. Moral courage. Fortitude. Endurance.

Guardian: With the questions, we can declare, "I don't know." When we declare, "I don't know" something mysterious happens; our soul, our intelligence awakens and enters the "unknown" of the question itself. Declaring, "I don't know but I want to know" opens up the gate to cross the threshold into the unknown. We are let in and invited to enter the unknown.

Warrior: The sublime simplicity of truth, once it reveals itself...

Guardian: You said it, not me. The question again–

> If you were deprived of authority and power, would your men select you to lead them?

Warrior: Have you asked this question of others?

Guardian: Hundreds of others.

Warrior: And?

Guardian: For the warriors, the gate opened. For the executives, the gate remained closed.

Warrior: Why?

Guardian: Warriors wanted to earn it. Warriors wanted mastery. Executives wanted control. Executives wanted to manipulate. The DNA of a warrior is courage. The DNA of an executive is wealth. They are different beings. Executives tend to be superficial in all things except calculation (to determine profit and gain) and image (to sell what is not necessary). Warriors are deep in their craft and studies. They are skilled (mastery in warfighting) and have character (strength of will and courage).

Warrior: What happened with the Executives?

Guardian: I crushed them with five days of PowerPoints. They could only "talk about leadership" but would never become "leaders." The process is too difficult and painful.

Warrior: The cardinal sin of leadership–

> Acting like you know, when you have no idea.

Guardian: Knowing about instead of knowing.

Warrior: What about the warriors?

Guardian: Five days of deep work, from one question to another. A method of both contemplation and meditation.

Warrior: And?

Guardian: By the end of the week, they dropped into the unknown. They were able to see and discern and awaken, and when they spoke from their soul we experienced their light and truth. As Nietzsche would say, because of their experiences, when they entered the depths, they spoke from immaculate perception. They spoke from being and knowing. Truly marvelous. I went into this work because I hunted for the genius in leaders. I had read all the books. I needed to meet living expressions. And I found it in these warriors once they made time to awaken and give voice to the light and truth of their depths.

Warrior: It is beginning to dawn on me why "intellectual training" is the missing activity and the key aim of what you're doing on this hunt. We are practicing what it is to "intellectually train."

Guardian: It seems to be the necessary way and the indirect way instead of the direct way. Liddell Hart, the sage of strategists, can mentor us here. These are his perspectives on the necessity of intellectual training in historical studies, which I have extracted for leadership studies–

> Truth is a spiral staircase. What looks true at one level may not be true on the next higher level…. To face life with clear eyes, desirous to see the truth… it is strange how people assume that no training is needed in the pursuit of truth…. We should recognize that for this pursuit anyone requires at least as much training as a boxer for a fight or a runner for a marathon. He has to learn how to detach his thinking from every desire and interest, from every sympathy and antipathy—like ridding oneself of the superfluous tissue, the "tissue" of untruth which all human beings tend to accumulate for their own comfort and protection. And he must keep fit, to become fitter. In other words, he must be true to the light he has seen.[7]

Now is not the time to meditate and contemplate this passage. That comes later. We use statements like these as triggers, as leaping points, which call us deeper into the unknown so that we grow in self-knowledge and discernment.

Warrior: Wait, Liddell Hart, the great British military strategist wrote this?

Guardian: Yes indeed.

Warrior: Did he leave a method to train this way?

Guardian: No. But his method on historical writing illuminates the way. Same with Burkhardt. That is what is driving me, to discover the training methods. To demystify. To make it a matter of work even if it's still cloaked in mystery. We must continually ask, with all our "know-how", why are we not trained this way, in this pursuit of truth? I look to Plato and Aristotle, the gospels and *The Bhagavad Gita*, in meditation and contemplation, for the insights to light the way.

Warrior: It is strange how elusive it is, to find teachers in the pursuit of truth. What is everyone doing?

---

[7] B.H. Liddell Hart, *Why Don't We Learn From History?*

Guardian: Avoiding the interior journey and the painfulness of that journey, I suppose.

Warrior: Hart's writings sound eerily similar to what you are doing and what we are seeking. His writings lead with heart and soul.

Guardian: When I discovered his gem *Why Don't We Learn from History?* I finally realized I'm not insane, though I do suffer divine madness.

Warrior: The compassion of the divine as the guide.

Guardian: Great leaders have reflected on what we need to know and become, but have failed to show how to bring this about. That is why the way of the saints and sages, their training methods, resonate with me. They focus on light and truth. And leaders need both. We are learning this art.

Warrior: And this art is eerily similar to the art of truth-seeking, to the art of light-seeking, to the way of the saints and sages? I had no idea how close the actual methods are, even if the ends are different, it seems to me the means are similar?

Guardian: Indeed. The means to light and the means to truth are called the contemplative art, regardless of the ends, be it sage, saint, warrior or leader. They train the same way. Only they train with different ends, knowledge and skillsets.

Warrior: No wonder executives and professors don't train this way. It's the most demanding endeavor a human being can undergo, similar to the training of the warrior.

Guardian: Yes...I don't see any difference except one.

Warrior: That being the warrior uses tools of violence...

Guardian: And the contemplative uses tools of light and truth.

Warrior: Then the weapons of truth need to be mastered like the weapons of war.

Guardian: That is our challenge: To discover the weapons of truth; to practice them; and only then can we teach them.

Warrior: Is this where we begin the initiation?

Guardian: It appears so to me. How do we condition our soul to be ready for the weapons of truth?

Warrior: In training for war, we begin by preparing the body.

Guardian: In training for truth, we begin by preparing the body.

The body needs to be full of vitality and vigor. Before we turn to the training, I want to go back to the central question–

> If you were deprived of authority and power, would your men select you to lead them?

The primacy of this question is to trigger the virtue of intellectual humility—to teach students the courage to act with intellectual humility. The primacy of this question is to trigger the virtue of detachment—to teach students to go beyond the ego to begin to awaken their intelligence. There is no winning in this art. There is no payment. There is no reward. There is only worth, merit and excellence.

Plato mentors–

> For it is likely that if a city of good men came to be, there would be a fight over not ruling, just as there is now over ruling; and there it would become manifest that a true ruler really does not naturally consider his own advantage but rather that of the one who is ruled.[8]

I never wanted to lead—I am called to lead because of the injustice and incompetence of so many men and women in power.

Warrior: That is why I am called to lead as well.

Guardian: It is a duty; it is not a prize. I hope we find better men and women to serve and let them lead.

Warrior: That is why we are called to teach leaders. Did Gandhi produce a better leader than himself? Did Lincoln? Did Marin Luther King, Jr.? Did Patton? Did Eisenhower? Did Jobs? Did Gates?

Guardian: No.

Warrior: Why?

Guardian: Their call to lead is different than our call to lead.

Warrior: Yes.

Guardian: The way we produce great souls is to develop two cardinal virtues: the virtue of humility and the virtue of detachment. Everything rests on leaders awakening the power of these virtues in their soul.

Warrior: Why?

Guardian: Without humility and detachment, truth will not reveal itself.

Warrior: Ah. If this is true, this is the reason why so many leaders fail. They are in the darkness and they think they see the light.

---

[8] Plato. *The Republic*. Allan Bloom translation.

Guardian: This is another question I ask–

What leads the leader?

Warrior: And?

Guardian: Vacant stares. Then I hear, "I lead."

"No. Truth leads the leaders." I command.

Then they respond arrogantly and obstinately, "No. Truth is relative."

"No. Truth is a spiral staircase. You are in darkness and ignorance. You don't see. You don't know the truth. You don't follow its lead." I command.

Warrior: Then?

Guardian: The egotists leave. I knocked them out of their beehive. They don't realize that they are a feckless threat. They don't realize they are impotent. They don't realize they don't have power. They are powerless outside of their organization. They have no stingers. Truth is the sting. They realize coercive power holds no dominance over truth. I use the question "what leads the leader" as an explosive to rid the egotists in the room. Truth demands humility and detachment. We need humility and detachment, because they are the core muscles of virtue. The muscles of virtue condition and strengthen the character and the intelligence to seek light and truth. I declare that truth will not reveal itself to those who do not fulfill these virtuous conditions. I must pull from the lessons of the Saints, where they declare that the soul cannot see God, unless it fulfills three conditions[9]–

1. Become unconditionally loving.
2. Become poor in spirit.
3. Become pure in heart.

Defined as–

1. Giving and serving as the antidote to lust and greed.
2. Humility as the antidote to pride, arrogance, and obstinacy.
3. Purity and chastity as the antidote to inordinate desire and covetousness.

In order to fulfill this condition, the soul undergoes three phases of transformation[10]–

1. Purification
2. Illumination
3. Union

---

[9] Huxley, *The Perennial Philosophy*.
[10] Ralph Martin, *The Fulfillment of All Desire*.

Defined as–

1. Beginning the spiritual path; initiated into the practices of prayer, meditation, scripture, and worship.

2. Continued spiritual growth in virtue, prayer, and a deepening love for God and neighbor; greater detachment from all that is not Holy and a desire for union with God.

3. A state of deep union with God; the soul experiences joy, humility, and freedom from fears, trials, and hardships.

I share this, because, I know, we are not seeking God, but we are seeking truth, and the conditioning seems to me to be very similar, only the object is different. The Saints seek the being of God. Leaders seek the being of truth. Both need the light and the truth of the soul to undergo a metaphysical transformation so that they can see light and truth.

Warrior: I caution you in the claims you make, the reasoning you make, and the ability to transfer the conditioning of the saints to the conditioning of the leader.

Guardian: What if I declare that it's the same with the conditioning of the warriors. Look at your own training. Look at it.

Warrior: My God. We call it differently, but we have three phases of conditioning, essentially strength, skills, and tactics. It's essentially the same condition, to create a freedom of being in which the skills become an extension of the being.

Guardian: Did the conditioning and the training transform you? Are you different because of the training?

Warrior: Yes.

Guardian: Then, from your perspective, what can we learn from this way of producing saints, this way of producing warriors, that will help us understand the way of producing leaders?

Warrior: What I've discerned from this example is that we, as potential leaders, must undergo a developmental process that transforms our inner nature, the way we think, the way we feel, the way we express, and the way we act. I declare this to be true. This transformation begins and ends with the virtues of humility and detachment. By practicing these virtues, we take an indirect approach to bypass the vice of the ego and awaken the soul to bring out her powers of will, intelligence and spirit into virtue (of character) and excellence (of skills). I declare this to be true.

We then take the power of these virtues and use it as the cause, the source, that energizes our nature, our character, and our expertise in the burden and demand of leading. And the apex is when we display disciplined skill in action, and this skill is an extension of our being, like an organ, like the heart or the lungs, working in perfect form with little conscious effort—even in the discernment of practical judgment. I declare this to be true.

This means leaders may have innate talents, but they are not born ready-made. They need to be trained like the warrior or like the Olympian. This training needs to be guided by a trainer who knows how to awaken these potencies. The leader then needs to learn the virtue of self-cultivating skill development. This art is a non-stop process of awakening these potencies. I declare this to be true. This way of being, this way of leading, is continuous, just like the heart beating and the lungs breathing. I declare all of this to be in the nature and the power of the human being, without supernatural aid.

Guardian: I follow. This is why our art is transferred from teacher to student. This is why the mentor is the prime element—the leader as teacher.

We need guides to demystify this process of awakening potencies. We need guides to carry the burden and ensure each generation of leaders is prepared. We cannot place the burden on enterprise leaders; they are not teachers and they do not have the time and space to devote all their efforts to leadership development. It is a war of development. In this war, the warriors are the intellectual and the moral teachers. Our scientists and creators have proven their worth to meet the material needs of the body; our professors and psychologists have failed in proving their worth to meet the needs of the soul. One wonders how the universities became dens of depravity instead of dens of truth. This is where our war rages. We must create educational dens of truth.

Warrior: Who makes you judge and jury?

Guardian: I'm speaking to what I see. Eighteen years of formal education and what did it produce? Darkness and debt instead of light and freedom. Am I in error? I will continually ask, am I in error? I don't want to be right. I want to know what is right and then have the courage to act accordingly. I'm speaking to what I've experienced. I'm speaking to what I've witnessed. I'm speaking to what I needed in those formative years and did not receive. I've taken it upon myself to discover how to create dens of truth and how to be of service to the formation of leaders. Service as an act of will. Service as an act of love. I dare anyone to prove they can awaken potencies without love as an act of will. As a Marine Lieutenant, at the Basic School, I gave a lecture to my peers, titled, "Love and Leadership." My peers could barely sit there when I declared, if you don't love your Marines, you won't be able to inspire and lead them though you'll be able to command them. I got roasted during the lecture. Decades later, a few peers would call and say, "you were right."

It still enrages me when an elder (a manager, a counselor, a leader) asks a young soul (I say soul because the soul is androgynous and we can rise above gender terms in our dialogue–That is why I use human being, soul, guardian, warrior, leader) between 18–26 years of age–

"What is your life plan?" or "What are your goals?"

They are not seasoned. They are without experience. They need guidance to lead out the truth of their calling and vocation and way of being. They need teachers and mentors who study their inner nature, who see their potency in skills, calling, and vocation, and who guide them moment to moment as their natural abilities take shape and form. That is the purpose of a guide, especially for those who may never have the union of calling as vocation and will be split between the means of economy (the job) and the means of experience (the joys of living).

Can we agree with the studies on human development, that the ages of 18–26 are the most uncertain and the most uncomfortable because the child is becoming an adult. These years are critical; our character is malleable and not fully formed, it's open to the confluence of ideas, people, and situations that form it during this period. I don't know about you, but this critical range of development is when I created and experienced the most wreckage, the most falls from grace, and at the time I did not even know the pain of wreckage and the anguish of disgrace. This wreckage drove me to seek understanding.

Warrior: Which is a good thing. It drove you in this direction.

Guardian: When I studied human nature, I learned that this phase of development is when our character is most unsound and most fragile, regardless of the way we were raised. This is the time when we need the most and not the least guidance. What do we do after high school? We essentially let students fend for themselves. I learned that our teachers and our parents are too unskilled and undisciplined to take on this responsibility. Even if they had the desire, they don't have the skill. They don't know how to study the soul, how to awaken the soul, how to develop the soul. And this is what is needed most to form a leader.

The divine justice—had I not struggled as a leader, I doubt I would have headed in this direction. There would not have been enough suffering and pain to trigger the search.

Warrior: Further compounding the issues, what do our leaders do? They expect young professionals and young warriors to come into the enterprise ready-made in their character and their maturity. When in fact they are most vulnerable.

Guardian: This is why we need leadership masters equal to music masters, to guide students during these vulnerable and critical years so that they don't grow corrupt and deformed, but grow straight and as sharp as a steel blade. This means we can't rush mastery, especially our own. We are not masters, my good man.

Warrior: God knows we are not. We are reminded–

If you meet the Buddha, kill him.[11]

_____

[11] Zen Master Linji, quote attributed him.

Guardian: That's why masters know they are not Gods. The jesting of the guide–

> The Tao that can be told is not the eternal Tao.[12]

Do you know the essence of that zen koan and this verse?

Warrior: I do, but I don't think we should comment, to force readers into contemplation.

Guardian: Can you give an anchor point?

Warrior: Kill ignorance. Kill image. Be truth.

Guardian: My blessed friend. They and we must rid ourselves of non-essentials and focus on the basic necessities to learn this beautiful craft that leads souls.

Warrior: That is what this journey is teaching me. It's not good enough to "know" or "to know about"; we must become the essence, it must be awakened inside of us.

Guardian: I have always taken to soul Lamennais' sage wisdom–

> Everyone looks at what I am looking at, but no one sees what I see.[13]

Warrior: We must, and our leaders must, learn to see by awakening what sees the unseen.

Guardian: I'm reminded of a conversation I had with an executive from ExxonMobil. We were at a dinner with real decision-makers, the ones who control wealth and by proxy control government policy. I felt a bit out of sorts, because I could not connect nor relate to the beings I met. These sorts possessed power by coercive means—ownership and economics—based on quantitative measurements, none of which I had. While I live a rich intellectual and spiritual life, I have virtually no assets. I live a Spartan existence, I wear simple clothes, and I have no wealth.

The conversation–

> Executive: Young man, what do you do?

> Guardian: I develop and train leaders.

Had I said, I develop the souls of leaders, I would have bypassed the following exchange. At the time, I feared telling executives what I actually did because I thought they'd run to the door once I began speaking. I had a policy of self-censorship back then.

> Executive: What makes you qualified to train leaders?

---

[12] Lao Tzu, *Tao Te Ching*. Translated by Gia-Fu Feng
[13] Félicité Robert de Lamennais. *Words of a Believer*. Translated by Grace Elizabeth King

He had a tone of contempt. He was old and weak in mind and spirit but wealthy and powerful.

Rage took over—I lost compassion—and I took a head shot at his ego–

> Guardian: Imagine, tomorrow you wake up to find yourself in the following state of existence: First, you've been fired from your executive position at ExxonMobil after 25 years of service. Second, your identity has been stolen and your finances have been wiped clean to a balance of zero. Third, your wife left you upon hearing the news of your misfortune, and sought comfort with another wealthy benefactor whom she met at an event like this a decade ago, and with whom she had been in correspondence because of her need for affection. Affection you never provide to her. Fourth, because you have no finances, foreclosure has taken place on your home. Your entire belongings have been auctioned off. Fifth, you find yourself with only a suitcase of belongings. Sixth, being stripped naked of the comforts and sources of power and authority, you find yourself standing before men like me. Seventh, and this is the point, in this state of nakedness, standing before men like me, what do you say to inspire and to lead us? What do you say? What can you possible say or do to inspire us to follow you?

I let a long pause bring the man into silence. Then I continued.

> Guardian: You don't have an answer. You can't answer. Why? Because you are nothing. Why? Because you're insignificant without coercive power. Why? Because you have no inner power. Why? Because you are a hollow man instead of a hallowed man. You know nothing of the hallowed ground. There's no light of truth in you. You're an empty shell. You're a company man. There's nothing in your soul worthy of admiration. You are a soul-less man walking.

He looked shell-shocked when I finished. He had vacant eyes. A longer silence ensued. I just stared at him. I both pitied and held contempt for him. He finally spoke.

> Executive: What kind of watch is that?

I looked at my watch. I looked in his eyes. Yes, he is a hollow man. He is a vacant man. And he is making decisions over thousands of people's lives and over the nature of earth.

> Guardian: I pray for your soul.

I left the conversation and I left the dinner. Obviously, I did not end up working with ExxonMobil. But, a strange thing took place a few years later. I received a call from him, introducing me to his son, who had just been commissioned a Marine Officer, asking if I would mentor his son.

Warrior: Wow. You wielded the tomahawk of truth.

Guardian: I share this story because it's too late by the time you're an executive to recover from growing corruptly. That is why we need to focus on the coming-of-age years. We need to work with human beings in their formative years. Even this Executive, upon reflection, steered his son toward me for guidance. And I am finding, this happens to be the case all the time.

Warrior: And yet, businesses tend to focus on their executives.

Guardian: Yes. See how it's all upside down instead of right side up? I share this as an example of how to use the tools of truth and the tools of spirit.

Warrior: I don't follow.

Guardian: How did I even learn to think that way? How did I know how to respond to this executive to bring the light of truth? I went to the dinner with the hope of working with executives. My hope did not match reality. Truth means meeting reality and coming into harmony with it. My hope is subjective. Truth is objective. The spirit of truth is objective. It does not bend to what it subjective. What is subjective bends to it.

Warrior: Ah. Then a great injustice is when souls, no, the ego, aims to bend the truth and light to its will, instead of turning its will to the light and truth it receives?

Guardian: Yes. When I looked deeply into the executive's soul, into his inner nature, his essence revealed itself. There is no hiding from truth. Where I failed, and I am ashamed to admit this, but because it's between you and me I will speak truly, is that when truth revealed itself my ego asserted itself and jumped out to strike the guy in a combative, antagonistic way. I should have worked with him to steer both him and me towards the truth. I regret that lapse and it still serves as a lesson to guide me.

Warrior: You created an injustice. You took the beauty of light and truth and distorted and corrupted it.

Guardian: I know. Painful.

Warrior: Then, how do we begin to uncover the tools of truth in the context of developing leaders?

Guardian: I think now is the time to bring in a few key concepts from Aristotle. These concepts will help us pave the way and structure the methods, the means and the ends. This is now a training period for us. We need to learn these concepts. We need to embed them in our beings.

Warrior: Go on. I love training. The more intense, the better. As you say, crush the ego and awaken the soul.

Guardian: We need to learn knowledge in such a way that it becomes an extension of our being, so that it expands and deepens our nature. We need this so that we can respond to life and challenges with grace, finesse and harmony. Before we cover theoretical frameworks, we need to understand how to use our intelligence to take command and become the actualization of these theories. We need to understand how to make sense of the theories in order to wield this knowledge as reality unfolds itself.

Warrior: We need to learn how to wield this knowledge as metaphysical tomahawks, hand-wielding mallets, and swords.

Guardian: That is what I hope for. In Aristotle's *Nicomachean Ethics*, he aimed to describe how the human being is led and transformed into a flourishing state. This flourishing state is when the potencies actualize and respond to life with vigorous and powerful activity. He is concerned with excellence, not rule-sets, that spontaneously respond accurately between right and wrong opinions, and good and bad actions. To give our intelligence command of this excellence, there are four concepts we must know and practice. He said these concepts, when actualized, anchor our thinking to live and act in a flourishing state. This state, he makes clear, is complete freedom of being in which this is no control, no restriction and no repression of the soul's knowing, willing, and acting.

The concepts–

> Active condition (*hexis*)
> Being-at-work (*energeia*)
> Contemplation (*theoria*)
> Practical judgment (*phronesis*)

Warrior: Are these the weapons of an awakened-intelligence?

Guardian: I think so. This is what is considered our "second nature"

Here are the definitions.

> Active Condition (*Hexis*)
>
> Any way in which one deliberately holds oneself in relation to feelings and desires, once it becomes a constant part of oneself. For example, fear is a feeling, and lack of confidence is a pre-disposition to feel fear; both are passive conditions. Cowardice or courage are active conditions one may develop towards them. One's character is made up of active conditions. Hence this is one of the most important words in *Nicomachean Ethics*, and the foundation of Aristotle's understanding of human responsibility.[14]

---

[14] Aristotle, *Nicomachean Ethics*, Sachs Translation. Sachs definition.

It still enrages me, with righteous flames of indignation, when I reflect that as a young leader I was told by superiors to become virtuous, but none taught me *how* to become virtuous—that virtues are the result of an active conditioning of the powers of soul that aim to strengthen our character. I still feel that rage every time a manager demands abilities in their teams that they themselves do not know nor understand—creativity, critical thinking, strategy, performance.

Warrior: We call them the bubble-head class, the figureheads of bureaucracies, ones with authority and no influence.

Guardian: These ignorant ones ignited in me a desperate search for understanding. I wanted to lead, not command, and to lead I needed to make myself trustworthy.

Warrior: You are an idealist.

Guardian: An old friend described me as what he called a purist in any art—one who seeks the purity of his art and seeks existence as unalloyed, unadulterated, and pure essence, in his being and in his technique.

Warrior: Maslow would call this self-actualization, characterized as beauty, completeness, effortlessness—unique, essential and necessary.

Guardian: Ah, yes—the notions of *Shibumi,* effortless perfection from training in simplicity, subtleness and beauty, and of *Satori,* deep awakening. We are after their yoked union.[15]

Warrior: And yet you live in the ugliness of human nature.

Guardian: That is the fertile and rich soil my blessed friend. The soil (the dirt) to plant seeds and begin the gardener's art. I don't see it as ugly; I see it as the material to grow the soul. And the soul has the choice to say yes or no to developing her powers. I see the soul as a crystal-light simply surrounded by obstructions. My job is to locate the light of the soul and let her wield her inherent powers. Indeed, the soul can be trained like an Olympian. The soul can be trained like a warrior. But, the soul needs to know how to train. The not-knowing is what is dangerous.

Taking Aristotle's concept, we need to make it our own. LEADERSHIP HEXIS is an aim. We will actively condition the character and knowledge of leaders. We are one movement closer to demystifying the art.

Being-at-work (*Energeia*)

The central notion in all of Aristotle's philosophy, the activity by which anything is what it is. To understand any of Aristotle's inquiries is to grasp the centrality in it of being-at-work. In the *Metaphysics*, everything is derived

---

[15] Trevanian, *Shibumi*.

from and depends upon the things that have their being only by constant activity. In the *Physics*, nature is not explained by material but only by the formative activities always at-work in material. In *On the Soul*, a soul is not a detachable being but the being-at-work-staying-itself of an organized body. In the *Nicomachean Ethics*, everything depends upon the idea of an active condition (*hexis*) that can be formed by a deliberately repeated way of being-at-work, and that can in turn set free the being-at-work of all the human powers for the act of choice. For example, actions that belong to courage must be performed before one can become courageous; after the active condition is formed, actions that belong to courage spring from it, not as a dead habit but from the full and unimpeded presence of active thinking and desiring.[16]

LEADERSHIP ENERGEIA is an aim. Were you taught leadership habits and actions before leading? So that they could flourish once leading?

Warrior: No. Just like bad strategy, bad leadership was preached. How did you extract these concepts and bring meaning to them in this endeavor?

Guardian: When I discovered these concepts, I was on the hunt for them. Everything my intelligence rests its sight on is observed with the question in mind: does this help to develop leaders? Because I observe from this perspective, when I read and studied the concepts, their light illuminated my understanding. That is how I knew what to extract and what to remove.

Warrior: It just occurred to me—you wanted to be developed as a leader, and you were not, so you went in search. Your desire ignited from your own underdevelopment. With me, what you are drawing out is the understanding that I know, intuitively and instinctually, but did not know how to teach other than by my example. And I am ashamed to admit this, but I was more concerned with warfighting than developing leaders. I never served as an instructor in the schoolhouse. In warrior cultures, you teach by example; it is essentially development by osmosis. And it works for warrior cultures, especially at the tactical level because the work is physically intense and visually engaging. But when I have failed as a warrior is when we stopped going to combat and needed to learn to lead in non-martial settings, especially in enterprise environments. This is where I'm finding this exploring meaningful. It's the whole-man concept we speak about but have not been able to teach.

Guardian: I'm not sure we will be able to teach this. It's one thing to know the concepts, it's another thing to practice them, and it's yet another thing to incorporate them into our being, so that they leap into action, with a freedom of unrestrained thinking and desiring.

Warrior: That is no easy task.

---

[16] Aristotle, *Nicomachean Ethics*, Sachs Translation. Sachs definition.

Guardian: No, it is not. We must live it. We must become it. Living is active and fluid and we can fall from grace at any moment. We know the falls have lessons, but without having a guide in the formative years, too many vices instead of virtues are created. As you know, eradicating vices could take decades and we need to prevent them from taking root.

Warrior: Have at it. Booz. Sex. Feasts. They are part of the culture of the warrior.

Guardian: Maybe that is why we failed. The culture of leadership must be noble and graceful. Our aim is not training warriors for war; our aim is training leaders to lead. I do think warriors are meant to lead this way, once they understand and accept the burden.

> Contemplation (*theoria*).
>
> The being-at-work of the intellect, a thinking that is like seeing, complete at every instance. In contemplation, a human being is most fully active, in that power underlying all thinking and perceiving has emerged, but also most at rest in what is knowable. Contemplation is discussed in detail in the *Metaphysics* and in *On the Soul*; in the *Nicomachean Ethics*, it is painstakingly uncovered as the most complete human happiness. The relation between contemplation and the virtues of character is best explained in the *Physics*, to come to rest in contemplation, a human being must overcome the disorder of the soul native to it from childhood.[17]

LEADERSHIP THEORIA is an aim.

Warrior: Hold on. Contemplative Wisdom as the Highest Happiness?

Guardian: Yes.

Warrior: Is contemplation what Clausewitz actually described in the concept of *coup d'oeil*, when he used the descriptions "inward eye," "quick recognition of a truth" and most penetratingly "an intellect that, even in the darkest hour, retains some glimmerings of the inner light which leads to truth"?

Guardian: I have to wonder if Clausewitz studied Aristotle.

Warrior: He studied Hegel, and Hegel studied Aristotle. Clausewitz used Hegelian dialectics to pen "*On War*". The essence of this method is Thesis, Antithesis and Synthesis.

Guardian: Colliding ideas, smashing them together, and seeing what is revealed…

Warrior: Clausewitz reminds us that we need to build strong and tough minds, not brilliant minds, as the nature most suited to endure the burden of leading.

---

[17] Aristotle, *Nicomachean Ethics*, Sachs Translation. Sachs definition.

Guardian: We can speculate on the historical threads? Clausewitz studied war, and he studied the genius of Napoleon. Napoleon studied the genius of Alexander the Great. The genius of Alexander the Great was developed as a student of Aristotle. The concepts of Aristotle could be one line of continuity that remains unbroken and alive to this day.

Practical Judgment (*phronesis*)

The active condition by which someone discerns the right means to the right end in particular circumstances. Hence the intellectual virtue of practical judgment and the whole virtue of character are mutually dependent and must develop together, since the right end is apparent only to someone of good character, while the formation of good character requires the repeated choice of right action, which is impossible without practical judgment. Apart from virtue of character, the capacity to reason from ends to means is mere cleverness; practical judgment involves skill in making distinctions and seeing connections, but if one does not recognize that such thinking imposes upon oneself an obligation to act, that skill is merely astuteness. Practical judgment is acquired primarily by particulars, but also involves a knowledge of things that are universal and unvarying within those particulars, the things studied by Aristotle in his inquiries into politics and ethics. The translation "practical judgment" is chosen here as the best way of conveying Aristotle's central understanding that ethical choices can never be deductions from any rules, principles, or general duties, but always require a weighing of particular circumstances and balancing of conflicting principles in a direct recognition of the mean.[18]

Thus established, we begin with four development aims–

LEADERSHIP HEXIS

LEADERSHIP ENERGEIA

LEADERSHIP THEORIA

LEADERSHIP PHRONESIS

Warrior: Is our task to create new concepts? A new lexicon?

Guardian: No, not create. But discover, or in this case rediscover, what has been lost or obscured or hidden in this art. More than that, we must become the reality of the concepts. We are after the "what" not the "who." What we are doing is not new. The human nature and human physiology have not changed in 70,000 years. We are discovering the way to igniting

---

[18] Aristotle, *Nicomachean Ethics*, Sachs Translation. Sachs definition.

all the potencies of human nature and we are documenting the process. Then it is up to the next generation to take on this challenge of development and to engage in the beautiful burden of leading.

Warrior: But we are creating new methods and language and frameworks to transfer in knowledge what we discover?

Guardian: Yes indeed. But, only at the summit, when looking back, will we see what we have produced. The hope is that we will have produced an integrated structure to build leaders.

Now we must take command of these foundational concepts (*hexis, energeia, theoria,* and *phronesis*) and learn them as leadership techniques.

Warrior: How do we take command of these concepts? How do you mean to use these concepts as techniques on our expedition?

Guardian: God knows, I'm not clear and do not yet know how to respond. Act one of command is observing. Let's observe these concepts and see what they reveal. I hope by observing them they will light the way. It's a gut feeling, an instinct that I have, that if we observe the concepts, they will light and they will teach and they will guide.

Warrior: Wait, the concepts themselves will guide and teach? Are they alive?

Guardian: They are alive and active and acting on our intelligence.

Warrior: Ah. Now, I'm seeing a causal link between Clausewitz's *coup d'oeil* and *coup d'esprit*. It is spirit. It is light. It is truth.

Guardian: If we search deep enough into history, I think we will find this causal link of spirit, light, and truth, by extracting the speculations of Pythagoras.

Warrior: What?

Guardian: Let me explain. Pythagoras is known for mathematics and music. Where did he acquire this knowledge?

Warrior: From study and observation?

Guardian: When he created the mathematical scales of music, what did he study, to make this discovery?

Warrior: Hold on. Did he invent or did he discover?

Guardian: Legend is he discovered.

Warrior: How?

Guardian: His intelligence leaped into the eternal, into the heavens, and when his intelligence glimpsed the heavens, he saw and he heard and he recorded what he saw and heard.

Warrior: And you believe this?

Guardian: Not necessarily, but, the idea that this is possible captivated my intelligence, so I began to investigate what has been recorded of him. For context, to guide you in what I'm seeing, I'd like to share what I've documented and its application to our work.

Warrior: Go on.

Guardian: He invented and coined the concept of "philosophy." He is known as the first philosopher. He is known as the first pursuer of wisdom. He is known as the first to admit his not knowing. Because he admitted to himself his not knowing, he knew his ignorance. Because he knew his ignorance, he knew he could not be called a sage. When others called him a wise sage, he rejected it. Legend is, he declared: I'm no sage, I am a lover of wisdom and a pursuer of wisdom. His declaration, I declare, is what awakened his intelligence to leap past the edge of human knowledge. What I gleaned from this is that we must engage the same leap, we must admit our not knowing, or ignorance, and hope this opens our intelligence to leap past the edge of human knowledge.

Santana said that when he witnessed Hendrix playing the guitar, it seemed Hendrix would reach up, take lightning from the sky, and send it to his guitar so he could wield lightning into his music. That is genius. Hendrix played from the discoveries of the Father of Music, 2,500 years later.

Pythagoras discovered harmonic ratios and gave music its true divine meaning—to nurture and heal the soul—HARMONIA as the divine principle of order into and out of chaos. We aim to do the same, to reach, to stretch our spirit to the Heavens and bring it down and wield it through the leaders. It's not the absence of chaos or disorder; it's our ability to wield order and beauty and harmony in and out of it, creation and destruction, engaged in non-stop dynamic exchanges. I declare, if there is no chaos there is no need for leaders. Because there is chaos, there is a need for leadership.

Further, I am not interested in what we know about Pythagoras or any great sage, but rather what we must learn and become, to develop the same capacities for virtuous-being and truth-discovering. I don't want knowledge and stories and facts; I want the ability to leap from the known into the unknown and experience the joy of discovery and the joy of ability.

I now turn to Socrates, for he used the same art of deflection to turn others away from him and to the truth. He knew he was no savior. He knew he was not wise. He rejected it when others called him a sage. His sharpest response to silent onlookers, is "I do not know. I only know that I don't know." He meant this ignorance of truth is the path to truth's discovery, not only in his own soul, but in his friends. Do you see? Do you see what happens to our intelligence when we are brought into a situation that has never been imagined before nor has been lived, and we declare, "I don't know, but I want to know"?

Warrior: I do now. It makes us prepared to handle any situation.

Guardian: What did both Pythagoras and Socrates possess? What is their greatest possession?

Warrior: Ah. The virtues of detachment and humility. They knew they did not possess the full and unabridged truth. They spent their lives devoted to its pursuit. I am beginning to see how, for the leader's development, the pursuit of truth is a noble endeavor. How do you reckon we pursue it?

Guardian: My good man, by taking a leap of faith.

Warrior: I have faith in science.

Guardian: Any time a scientist creates a hypothesis, he is in the realm of faith, the faith to discover. In war, did you have faith in science or faith in the spirit and skills of yourself and your men?

Warrior: Yes, I must declare, I had faith in our spirit and skills.

Guardian: In truth, I must declare, I have faith in our spirit and its powers to leap. Pursuing the truth requires faith both in spirit and in skills. Do we have the skills? Or must we leap with faith and hope truth reveals these skills? We have the spirit and we are in search of the skills, the tools of truth, the tools of light, the tools of leadership. What do you see?

We started this pitch seeking a foundation to leap from, in the human powers of *hexis, energeia, theoria,* and *phronesis.* And what are the powers that produced these abilities? Are they not effects of some inner cause of our powers?

Warrior: Wait. At our core, spirit and intelligence, which you call light and truth, are the causes of the effects of the concepts Aristotle calls active-condition, being-at-work, contemplation, and practical-judgment? Those are the ends we seek to become skilled at, correct? But, the source, the cause, is the faculties of our soul?

Guardian: I think so. That is what I'm driving towards. I am declaring that what we condition is our body, is our will, is our intelligence, is our spirit, and when we condition these faculties, then their potency begins to be realized, and this actualization process of our faculties is something that is dynamic and non-stop when developed regularly and rigorously in acts of living.

Warrior: To summarize this, I think it's necessary to map out the human being's faculties. All of them. And then point to the ones you are focusing on and why. Since you are focusing on the metaphysics of philosophy, I will speak in those terms. Here is the list I gathered for the faculties[19] (the power centers of the human being)–

1. Nutritive
2. Reproductive
3. Perceptive
4. Being-at-work (action)
5. Being Acted Upon (passion)
6. Intellect
7. Contemplative Intellect

I added contemplative, in addition to intellect (our ability to think), to include the aim of contemplation. I mean by intellect, our ability to think, to reason, and to understand.

Guardian: Ah ha. You've studied Aristotle and Plato.

Warrior: Sussshhh. Don't tell anyone. I use my love of science as a deflection. I'm not ready to be martyred—Christ, Pythagoras and Socrates—killed for their love of truth. I learned from Aristotle, and his relationship with Alexander, to lead with science, lest I create enemies I'm not interested in fighting.

Guardian: I'm willing to be martyred for truth.

Warrior: I know. But, you mean a martyrdom of reputation and achievement, not death.

Guardian: No, I include death. Death of body, death of reputation, and death of achievement, I know are means to freedom. Let me ask, you went to war for a decade. How is *that* fighting any different from *this* fighting?

Warrior: I went with the most advanced equipment and technology, with the most intense training, with the best tacticians, operating in the darkness, and engaged in special missions. It's very different from storming the beaches of Normandy or what you're doing, storming the beaches of darkness with the fire of truth.

Guardian: And yet, here we are. You knew glimpses of truth, and you've acted on its calling, just as Clausewitz pointed to the commanders who with light and courage made decisions in war. We are at war. We are in combat. We are storming darkness with the fire of truth. Only, we've removed other human beings from the war, for now.

Warrior: But this is not martial war. This is not combat. We have no real enemy. There is no real danger.

---

[19] Aristotle, *On the Soul*, Sachs Translation.

Guardian: That is why you are not seeing what I am seeing. Our battle is with intelligence and spirit, not body and spirit. We are fighting in the darkness with light and truth to eradicate bondage, delusion, deception, illusion, lies and falsehood that keep the soul enslaved in darkness and ignorance. Many human beings do not realize they are an eternal being having a temporal experience.

Warrior: Can you prove this?

Guardian: Can we realize this truth by the light of the soul? Can we realize and not prove?

Warrior: Okay, let me make sense of this on my own terms.

Guardian: Have at it. I don't want to control. I don't want to force. I don't want to prove. I want to realize. I want to experience truth.

Warrior: Understood. Let me make sense of this from developing warriors.

I need to return to Clausewitz and his two core concepts.

> The first concept is *coup d'oeil*.

> The second concept is *coup d'esprit*.

When you covered contemplation, my intelligence awakened deeper and I immediately went back to observing these two concepts. Even when you were speaking and I was listening, my intelligence was wrestling with these two concepts. I see what you mean by the deep waters of intelligence. I could be conversing with you, and still my intelligence could be wrestling with something in a deeper place. It's fascinating now to see this, the beauty of our intelligence.

The concepts were teaching me something and I knew how to pay attention, not to control, but to let the intelligence engage without interference.

Guardian: Is that not the intelligence that awakens by the soul's humility and detachment?

Warrior: Maybe. I now see a connection, a thread, that integrates these concepts with your concepts of light and truth.

Let me explain my understanding–

> *Coup d'oeil* is defined as "the inner light which leads to truth" and as an ability, "the quick recognition of truth."[20]

> *Coup d'esprit* is defined as "determination" and as an ability, "the courage to accept responsibility, the courage to face a moral danger." It is clarified "that

---

[20] Clausewitz, *On War*.

determination proceeds from a special type of mind, from a strong rather that brilliant one," and "employs the fear of wavering and hesitating to suppress all other fears."[21]

This seems to me to be a union, a marriage, a harmony of intelligence, will, and spirit to ward off the fears and doubts of our mortal nature. It seems that when we "rise above" our conditioned existence—what is mortal—we awaken to what is our immortal nature. Am I seeing this correctly, at least conceptually?

Guardian: Yes.

Warrior: What I'm taking from this, as a foundation, is that we need to develop the will, the intelligence, the spirit and spiritedness to rise above what is very real—conditioned and mortal existence—to enter into our nature that is immortal and spiritual.

Guardian: I think a good distinction, to mark, is the shift from 'subject and objective' to 'observer and observed.' We know we've made this shift when we transcend "self-consciousness." This is when our "feeling nature" or "emotions" that are unique to me and unique to you have calmed and lose their power. Then we can observe what we are observing.

Warrior: By making this shift, we'll be able to see in the darkness. And these concepts and terms will help us to see and to know and to take command by knowing.

Guardian: Indeed. That is why we study this domain—to learn to see. Let's look at what Aristotle saw as faculties of soul and provide the definitions[22]-

1. Nutritive Power: This is the need of the body for food and water to sustain itself and live in a state of health.
2. Reproductive Power: This is the need for the species to procreate.
3. Perceptive Power: This is the ability of the five senses to come into contact with physical phenomena.
4. Being-at-work: This is the ability to act, to make, to know, to produce. In the categories of being, this is defined as "action."
5. Being-acted-upon: This is the ability to be acted upon, to be moved. In the categories of being, this is defined as "passion."

Warrior: And our focus is action and passion, correct?

Guardian: Correct. Perception is not reality. I first heard that statement during military training. It is a material fallacy. Perception is one thing. Reality is another. The aim is to get souls to transform from perception of reality to knowing reality.

---

[21] Clausewitz, *On War*.
[22] Aristotle, *On the Soul*, Sachs translation.

Warrior: I take it you're referencing Plato's *Theaetetus*.

Guardian: I'm not smart enough to understand the depths of that dialogue. I'm just interested in the power to teach and to lead. What is critical is to increase the depth and breadth of our abilities of seeing, acting and moving. We can draw from martial arts. The power to act is the "giver" and the power to be acted upon is the "receiver". Leaders and followers must develop the ability to give and receive in the dynamic interplay of soulful contact. Leadership is a contact sport.

Warrior: Now I'm thinking of the power of persuasion as contact in the three-fold interplay of ethos (the character), pathos (the passion), and logos (the knowledge).

Guardian: Yes indeed. We're seeing the connections correctly.

Warrior: What about will, spirit, intelligence. How would we define those faculties and how would we use them?

Guardian: Let's call these the prime movers that are moved in giving and receiving, in the interplay of the ethos, pathos, and logos. These are the most powerful essences in our nature, more than perception, action, and passion.

> We need to become unmoved movers of these prime movers.

We need to be on guard so that we are not moved by the passions and actions of others. We need to learn to rest in the deep waters and become unmoved movers. We need to become deliberate and responsive when we move from the depths. As unmoved movers, we are the counter-weights to expediency and reactiveness when physical and emotional storms erupt on the surface.

Warrior: Ah. I see it—what it is to be an unmoved mover.

Guardian: Just like the Spartans and their terms for war, we need terms for leadership, to stay clear of our own susceptibility to the passions acting upon and clouding the vision of the soul. To do this, we must come to terms with our nature. And why? So we can move with compassion, as the Acts of the Apostles remind us–

> But now, my brethren, I know that you did this through ignorance just as your leaders did it.[23]

We need to get clear on "what" a human being is. Are we not more than flesh and blood? Our art depends on this as fact. Is not our intelligence and our will something non-moving, non-mortal, which knows no fatigue, no sorrow, and no harm? I declare this must be true. And I must act on good faith that this is true. Are not our body and our emotions the weakest aspect

---

[23] The Holy Bible, *Book of Acts*. Lamsa translation.

of the composite human being? The body is needy; the emotions are needy. We must rise above neediness. And when we rise above, what do we find?

Warrior: Because it's just you and I, I will allow that when we rise above, we discover will and intelligence, which are more than physical and perishable. I allow these concepts, even though you cannot prove them to be true. I allow these concepts because if we can realize this truth, it would be a wondrous and divine experience.

Guardian: We need to identify the true source of our energy, the wellspring that leaders will need. We need to identify the source of powers that are latent, the forces that leaders will need to act. We need to locate where the deep potencies of our being live and awaken them. Where do we begin the hunt?

Warrior: By the movement inward, to our inner nature. By the movement to make contact with our will, with our intelligence, and with our spiritedness, which make us an unmoved mover.

Guardian: What must we do to define these concepts and then take hold of the reality that they define?

Warrior: We first study—we study the definition of the concept. Then we leap.

Guardian: And?

Warrior: The definitions[24] are–

> WILL is defined as "the faculty by which a person decides on and initiates action."

> REASON is defined as "1: the power of the intellect to think, to understand, and to form judgments by a process of logic; 2: the capacity for consciously making sense of things; 3: the capacity to understand" and "the capacity to create knowledge."

> SPIRITED is defined as "full of spirit, full of vigor, lively and energetic."

> SPIRIT is defined as "the life-giving principle in humans."

Guardian: Then these are the roots of being that we must tend to and cultivate.

Warrior: When these roots bloom, we'll see human beings whose physical, moral, intellectual, and spiritual faculties are sharp, discerning, and developed.

Guardian: And how do we grow these roots?

---

[24] O.E.D. definitions for will, reason, spirited, and spirit.

Warrior: By nourishing and strengthening them with exercise.

Guardian: And how do we exercise them?

Warrior: By rigorous intellectual and moral training. Is it this simple?

Guardian: To know, yes. To actualize, no. Have we received such rigorous training?

Warrior: Only by the hardships of living, not by training.

Guardian: Would you go into the octagon and fight a MMA professional without MMA training?

Warrior: Absolutely not.

Guardian: Would you go into combat with the best gear but without training?

Warrior: Absolutely not.

Guardian: Would you lead without training in leadership?

Warrior: Until now, I would have said yes, but now I know it seems like suicide to lead without training.

Guardian: This is why we've accepted responsibility and taken on the burden to map this training.

Warrior: And now, I dare say, you'll explain why you've chosen to start not from Socrates' lead but from Pythagoras' lead. And why? Because we've been preparing to receive the gifts of light and truth?

Guardian: Yes, giving and receiving. The receiver needs to be ready and open to receive what the giver gives. It is with reason, with the demands and challenges of living, that we have our armor on, that we are guarded, that we are cautious, as receivers, not to be acted upon (the passions) by the actions of other human beings who do not have our best interests in mind. It is good to be guarded. Few have developed their character enough to be trustworthy for the action of their soul to act upon the passion of ours. No. We live in manipulative and exploitative times. But our challenge now, our call now, is to let our guard down, to take off the weight of the armor, and let the passion of our soul be acted upon, to receive from the source the gift of light and truth. And if we are blessed enough to receive this light and truth, we should let it acted upon the light and truth of our soul.

This is the challenge. To be receivers of light and truth.

Warrior: How is this even possible? How are we even able to have this dialogue?

Guardian: I can only speculate for now until we realize it. We are beings with a nature and a body, who can both receive truth and light, and produce truth and light into our faculties once we receive them. I speculate, our nature is the substance of truth. I speculate, our spirit is the substance of light.

Warrior: How did you arrive at those two statements? Let me guess, Pythagoras.

Guardian: A decade ago, I discovered these two statements attributed to Pythagoras.

> God, the nature of, declared by Pythagoras, to be the substance of truth.[25]

> God, the body of, declared by Pythagoras, to be the substance of light.[26]

The first time I read these statements, my being trembled to the core. I thought, are we really more than a physical being? Is there something immortal and immaterial in our nature? At the time, I was agnostic. Now I've had too many dark nights to rest in that freedom of not knowing. I know, when powers of light and truth, from meditation and contemplation, act upon my will and intelligence. I dare say that is how I see what others do not see. I use my faculties differently. I do not claim to know God as a "being" that can be known like a "human being," I do claim that a light and truth not my own lights my being. Not to share this and how it informs my discovery process would be deceptive. This I cannot do. The conclusion of these statements will change the way we think about leadership development. For we are tasked to train the nature and body of the soul—a nature and body which, at its core, is truth and light. These two substances, truth and light, are what activates the soul's faculties of will, intelligence and spiritedness. What we develop in a leader, what we develop in the soul, is nourished, sustained, and powered by truth and light.

I fear you'll turn away and reject the direction of our movements. Do you follow?

Warrior: I admire your courage. I admire your faith. The skeptic in me will remain silent for now. The judgments will come after our adventure. Instead of judgments I'll use my imagination, which is lively and active right now.

Do I follow? Yes, I follow your line of thinking–

Light is that aspect of being, which you call God, that breathes, that activates, living life into the physical body. Truth is that aspect of being, which you call God, that breathes, that activates living intelligence into the intellectual body.

Guardian: Then our challenge, again, is becoming receptive, to come to know intimately, not God, but truth and light, as sources of being. We need to learn to wield truth and light in the darkness. We need to learn to see in the darkness and make judgments that light the way for our fellow beings.

---

[25] Many P. Hall, *Secret Teachings of All the Ages.*
[26] Many P. Hall, *Secret Teachings of All the Ages.*

Warrior: How do we begin to come to know this source intimately?

Guardian: To begin?

> We begin with meditation.
> We begin with yoga.
> We begin with contemplation.
> We begin with wisdom literature.
> We begin with sacred dialogue.

Warrior: What we've been doing?

Guardian: Yes.

Warrior: To what end?

Guardian: We end where we begin, in these activities. They are the means, the ends, and the ways of leading. This is how we train, and training is continuous. The activities lead to the *buddhi*, the "wisdom faculty," awakening and flourishing. These activities, known as ways, practices, and techniques, lead to a state of contemplative wisdom, which Aristotle declared is our state of highest happiness. Did your leaders teach you this?

Warrior: No.

Guardian: Do you think leaders would become stronger if they made time to practice these activities?

Warrior: Yes.

Guardian: Why?

Warrior: They strengthen the faculties of the human being and the faculties are what are put to the test in the act of leading.

Guardian: Then when leaders ask–

> What to practice?
> What to learn?
> What to know?

We will instruct them in these activities. And when they ask why?

We'll respond, these activities lead to–

> Virtuous character
> Virtuous deeds

Practical judgment

Knowledge and skill as extension of our being

We'll respond that without these practices, a leader is dangerous because he can only point to "knowledge about," not "knowing." We'll respond that without these practices, knowledge remains foreign, external, insentient, inanimate and without life. We'll respond that the goal of training is to awaken the living knowledge in our being to become internal, sentient, animate, as an extension of our being. We'll respond that the goal of the training is to ignite the wisdom writings in our being, to become a living light of wisdom. This is why we focus on these methods—they increase and strengthen the inner light and truth of the soul. That is why this is rigorous training; it aims to pursue and catch truth; it aims to crush the ego and awaken the soul.

Warrior: I again caution you that these methods, though I am intrigued, seem too metaphysical and too spiritual for practical men and women to undertake.

Guardian: This is why we fail. Did we not agree, at the beginning of this endeavor, that we failed to teach leadership, to transfer it to others, to create self-actualized and wise leaders? How else do we hit the mark of wisdom and actualization? You've lived a warrior's life. But you have also lived the intellectual life, which, when it reaches a flourishing state, we call a contemplative life. If we know our aim, why is this too much? Should we change the aim so it's not too much?

Warrior: No. We are not changing the aim. As I stated when we began, this aim, and the means to the aim, will only be suited to a specific type of nature, a specific type of character.

Guardian: That is who Plato wrote for too. Nothing has changed in two millennia. What we are coming to terms with, this aim, and these methods, are only for a kind of leader, who has a kind of character and nature. I am fine with this truth. I'm not aiming at winning or acquiring; I'm aiming at finding those kinds of beings and devoting my energy to their growth.

Warrior: And you mean to put us through the training, to provide an example to leaders who might be interested in training and living and leading this way?

Guardian: Yes. And I mean to do it through the practice of contemplation. We will simply train and practice and study frameworks, theories, and techniques, in a leisurely and unhurried way.

Warrior: I see you've taken to Aristotle's way of contemplation–

> This way of being-at-work is a blessedness which results in a way of being
> that is self-sufficient, leisured, and unwearied.[27]

Guardian: Indeed, but the pattern I've modeled from Plato–

---

[27] Aristotle, *Nicomachean Ethics*, Sachs translation.

disposed towards philosophy and leadership...the ways of life and the pattern of the god.[28]

And while I aim for a pattern of learning and teaching, in a leisurely and divine way, I demand that our work be grounded in the rigorousness and seriousness needed for the act of leading. And here Liddell Hart, the great thinker on military strategy, provides us the call and the courage to reach up into the light and truth–

> The best of men have been conscious of being no more than windows through which comes a light that is not of their own making but like spiritual sunshine. Or to put it another way, they are merely receiving sets tuned in to the wavelength of a spiritual "radio" transmission. They can dust their window panes. They can improve their receptivity. But they are aware that the Source is outside far beyond their ken.[29]

This is why I focused on the practices as the way and the means, to be receivers and conduits of truth and light in the acts of leading.

Warrior: This is why you hunt for human beings with humility and detachment, ones that will become receptive to light and truth, and ones who will have the fortitude to act on the guidance of that light and truth.

Guardian: We have crossed the threshold. It will be an experience of beauty to serve leaders with the call to be receivers, givers, and conduits of the light and truth.

---

[28] Plato, *Phaedrus.*

[29] B.H. Liddell Hart, *Why Don't We Learn From History?*

CHAPTER SIX
BEING AND BECOMING

Guardian: This is the noble aim–

    To become receivers, givers, and conduits of light and truth.

How do we actualize this aim?

Warrior: Since you do not leverage science—which comprises theories that stand only until a scholar can disprove them—I am not sure how to respond. If we were slaves to scientific theories as if they were fact, we would still assume the earth to be both flat and at the middle of the universe.

Guardian: I leverage a different kind of science—a scientific method that we test with our own abilities, without the aid of precision instruments and without the aid of the scientists. We are after a shift in our nature. And that shift is produced by the way we train.

We have soul in the game as we test our soul. I love science for what science is best at studying, the perceptible and the material. But I am not on a scientific quest. If anything, the scientific method is only one tool in my arsenal for this journey—because even current scientific methods will be usurped by other methods as they have been time and again. I am an explorer. I am an artist. I have techniques and tactics that I rely on to aid us in our quest.

Warrior: I am a scientist.

Guardian: Good. I am a seeker. Can we be honest about the parameters and limitations of science and the social sciences (of which psychology is one...a social science, not a science as many people believe). The physical sciences and social sciences are all about finding inconsistent evidence to disprove hypotheses. The hypothesis with the least inconsistent evidence then becomes a theory. A theory is just a working hypothesis that has yet to be disproved. The history of science and the social sciences is the history of abandoning theses/theories for new theses/theories. Science and the social sciences are by definition transient. But what stays the same is the call for each human being to create purpose and understanding to live a meaningful life. Wisdom literature is a good guide into the study of ourselves and the world, and what actually matters and impacts us once our physical needs are assured. The wisdom literature leads to insights into what it is to be, and what being is remains important whether written millennia ago or yesterday. We are looking into wisdom that stands the test of time. What this means is we are not looking for quantified understanding, but qualified (the quality) understanding that takes place in the spirit and soul of the human being.

Warrior: Now, I caution you. These techniques are the techniques you've declared leaders must learn? Who gives you the authority?

Guardian: No one. I seek a higher authority, and when I seek a higher authority, concepts and structures are revealed. When they are revealed, I document them, study them, practice them, and then teach them from direct experience. I live in the realm of what is real in the sense that it is practical.

Warrior: Then why not bring in psychology or neuroscience?

Guardian: Who is to say I won't? We seek to know the powers of soul by direct experience. We can use knowledge as guides, but those domains never made me virtuous, they never changed my interior nature just by knowing of their knowledge. They only helped in broadening my conceptual understanding. Training for war, training as a yogi, training as a saint taught me how important it is to seek direct experience. I don't follow scientists and experts. They are our helpers—or I should say people who want to help—they are not leaders. They don't live in the chaos and madness of human emotion, energy, wants, and needs and undergo the pressure of making judgement calls, calls that are based on probabilities not certainties, that affect the lives of human beings.

What drives me is not to master what is known about nature and biology and cosmos. I don't want to lead in a way that manipulates what we know about the brain, so we can control it from the outside in. I do not tinker with the latest refereed conditional finding, nor with the mass-media over-simplification of said finding. I deal with what can be dealt with—the practical. I don't use tricks, unwanted influence, or pernicious persuasion. I want to explore from the inside out. What always holds is the basic structure. The basic structure of logic holds. The basic structure of math holds. The basic structure of human nature holds. These constants are fortifications we use in our climb, as footholds and handholds. I'm hesitant to use anything I've not tested or trained with. It's similar to sports. An athlete may excel at football but that does not translate to him excelling at distance running if he does not have the training. I need the courage to speak from what I know and I'll be hesitant to bring in other concepts that I do not have full command of. I am not hesitant about the models and techniques we're employing. I know firsthand of their ability to increase knowledge and strengthen the whole human being. Early in my studies, I began with psychology, because most leadership books were written by industrial psychologists. But when I studied them they did not resonate with the core of my being. It seemed these explainers, the explaining class, did not have any experience with transcendence of being. And most were simply making a niche for themselves to sell books. Certainly not all these authors could be correct—many contradicting or butting up against themselves. Why would I trust writers who I would never follow in their descriptions of leadership? I met true leaders, and I studied them even when I was the teacher. You don't hunt for leadership genius in a book; you hunt for leadership genius in the spirit of the person.

What we are doing is hunting for that spirit and documenting in writing what we discover. The observing class and explaining class did not write from their spirits; they only wrote what they observed. They missed the mark. We are here to correct their mistakes.

I did not resonate with these writers in part because they focused on the study of business leadership. I do not resonate with business leaders. They are glorified service workers. They are slaves to their shareholders, their products, and their profits. They work in order to make wealthy people just a little bit wealthier. While I'd like to think that wealth—based largely off credit and a belief in the stability of future institutional capacity—equals public good or translates into transcendence of the person, it never has.

That is not freedom to me. Freedom is beyond non-living-things. Money is inanimate. Things are inanimate. I am no slave to inanimate things. These business leaders were slaves to dead and inanimate things. I cannot learn from them. They don't see their bondage. It's funny to me that business leaders even see themselves as leaders—the English language fails us here in providing a broad umbrella for what leadership is—as they are the ones most enslaved in the business world, to investors and shareholders. They do not need greatness of soul to thrive. I also abhorred the structure of the modern business enterprises, and I hated the office experience. The office is a prison. I would break out into a sweat every time I entered an office building.

Warrior: Clearly, business as a way of life is not your calling.

Guardian: No. Clearly, leadership development is a business. Clearly, beauty is of primacy to me. Beautiful cathedrals, libraries, universities, chapels, and monasteries are places of deep work. My way of life is to serve all beings, especially ones of average ability. Most of us are what some might call average, and we get neglected because of focus on the extremes—those that are weakest, and those that are strongest at certain fashionable abilities in any given era.

Warrior: That is because you are a man of average ability—by the current trendy standards of your average media consumer—but you do have a strong heart and a strong mind.

Guardian: That is why I turned to the saints and sages; their writings resonated deeply in me. They made it clear that you do not need exceptional abilities to engage in the true practices. Their practices lead to inner strength and human flourishing. Average souls are the most equipped for happiness because they do not suffer abject poverty and they do not suffer vainglory. They rely on sources of potable water and the few other necessities of life, and they don't try continuously and fruitlessly to make more, more, more. Yes. I am average, and I needed methods that resonate with all human beings, independent of profession, as I see leadership development as independent of profession. This led me to understand the noble aim of pursing truth for its own sake. Truth is unconditional; it bestows its power on anyone who aims for it. My aim is to develop good souls, with good character, who can be relied upon in hardships and difficult situations.

145

Warrior: That is how we train.

Guardian: By letting go of conventional wisdom and what is sellable and popular, the mystics and sages pointed me to a deeper mystery of being than the observing class and the explaining class. They seemed to call us to use courage and faith to seek the source of our being, a divine nature, in the form of light and truth. That resonates deeply with me because it seemed to be the opposite of external control and power, the kind we see on display in our governments and institutions. It seemed to me that the call of the sages, the techniques of the sages, which are meant for all persons, lead to an inner freedom and knowing that is wondrous, marvelous, flourishing and fulfilling. Of most significance, this metaphysical freedom is independent of external sources for happiness. I seek the courage to look, in a state of truth, at evil and declare–

> You can kill me but you cannot harm me.

Warrior: The sages resonate with you because your nature is existential. You ask the perennial questions and you seek the answers to those questions–

> Why are we on earth?

> Where did we come from, before life on earth?

> Where do we go after life on earth?

Guardian: I live in these questions and go where their currents lead. I also turned from the scientists to the strategists in my studies. Here I found that, like the sages, the true strategists spoke of spirit and soul. They spoke of a higher nature and illumination. It is here where I started to make the connection and integrate these deep thinkers, because I learned that, because their souls were deep, they were able to write with depth, power and wisdom.

Warrior: Again, for my understanding, why not science and psychology?

Guardian: I am after different aims. I am not after achievement in conditioned existence. I am after eternal and immortal understanding. I aim to become the wisdom that is written in the wisdom literature. We are called to become what the writing reminds us of as our highest aim. I am after methods that aim for this awakening of wisdom and understanding in the soul.

> Leading will be simple after training in these methods. We do not take a direct strike at teaching leadership; we use an indirect strike, to awaken potencies.

I seek the highest realms of light and truth. I seek to stretch beyond the limits of my being. I seek to reach upward beyond the limits of my finite intelligence.

Warrior: Where did you look for methods to aim at this understanding?

Guardian: I contemplate the wisdom and sacred literature. This contemplation aims to unite the idea of wisdom with the fact of wisdom once it touches the substance and nature of the soul. In the absence of a true teacher, the wisdom writers were living teachers to me. Their writings are eternal and living. They teach meditation and contemplation. They teach how to enter into deep states of being. These states transcend time and absorb one into timelessness, into eternity. The experience of timelessness, of banishing time, is a condition that our training will seek. I also learned from these writings that the best way to defeat the adversary and transcend the ego is to devote one's being to an idea greater than oneself.

Now, this is the perennial challenge before us. We must always keep our minds on the objectives–

How do we make contact with light and truth?

How do we increase in light and truth?

How do we become receivers, givers, and conduits of light and truth in the act of leading?

I delayed diving into these questions until we were ready.

Warrior: We have been ready. How to do you define truth and light?

Guardian: Do you think I'm skilled enough to know how to answer? I consider it a great blessing that I can even ask the question. Good God, no, I do not have the wisdom to answer. That is why I study the wisdom literature that guides and mentors us. I'm not trying to define the concepts of light and truth. I'm trying to penetrate through these concepts for a direct experience at what they point to. We would be hopelessly lost without studying the ancient texts. But time and time again, these texts make you pay with the energy of your soul. If you are not ready, they do not let you in. I remember the first time that, after years of wrestling with one of these texts, it finally let me in. I can't prove what 'letting me in' is in some biological or even philosophical way; I can only share the experience.

It seemed that light as awareness and truth as understanding bathed my soul.

A baptism. A true baptism.

Warrior: How did you have the courage to press on, without understanding, when you wrestled with these texts, without knowing that 'the letting in' is possible?

Guardian: I read Gandhi's *My Experiments with Truth*. Out of the whole book, one section hit my core. He reflected, during the deepest darkness and sorrows of his calling, he would read *The Bhagavad Gita*, and it would bathe his soul with light as divine comfort, energy, and nourishment.

I thought: how is this possible? So, I too, experimented with truth.[1] To experiment with truth we can leverage the ancient writers as guides and mentors.

Warrior: Let us return to the central definitions–

> Light is that aspect of Being, which you call God, that breathes, that activates, living life into the physical body.

> Truth is that aspect of Being, which you call God, that breathes, that activates living intelligence into the intellectual body.

Guardian: The aim of light and truth–

> *Omne ens est verum*–all that is real is true.[2]

> *Omne ens est bonum*–all that is, is good.[3]

Let us claim the soul, as inner light, produces the beinghood, the person. Let us claim the soul, as intelligence, has the potency to know truth, to know what is. Let us claim, to be a receiver, to be a giver, to be a conduit of light and truth, the following *first principles* initiate us and lead us into the abyss and depths of being–

> "God, the nature of, declared by Pythagoras, to be the substance of truth."

> "God, the body of, declared by Pythagoras, to be the substance of light."

Warrior: These definitions seem awkward. Keep it simple–

> God's body is light, and his soul is truth.[4]

Guardian: Simple it may be. But, if we cannot agree on these as *first principles*, there is no point in going further. We will not be able leap from here into the unknown without these first principles. We would not have the nature and tools to seek an authority and source higher than our own nature, that could guide us and lead us in the depths.

Warrior: Can you clarify, what do you mean by first principles?

---

[1] Dear Reader, some of you may want me to declare God is truth, God is light, based upon the teachings of the gospels and other sacred texts. But this dialogue is a work of philosophical inquiry aimed at making the intelligence stronger, to then be able to explore these truths for oneself and speak from a place of knowing. It is not a place of believing, nor of copying, nor of repeating another's account. We're here to seek knowing by direct contact with the object that gives us knowing. I'm not knowledgeable enough, so I write in this way, as a philosopher, as a seeker of truth.

[2] Josef Pieper, *Living in the Truth*.

[3] Josef Pieper, *Living in the Truth*.

[4] Pythagoras, quote attributed to him.

Guardian: I mean to set down these two statements of Pythagoras as general first principles. These principles serve as our primary theoretical propositions to lead us to the source of light and truth.

As first principles, I am speculating that our nature is the substance of truth and that our body is the substance of light. As such, we did not create this light and truth; it is from a source beyond ourselves. And I aim to connect to and know that source. To learn about this nature and substance, we need to leap from our consciousness and stretch our being upward in an act that beholds the light, and travels in the light to where it leads.

Warrior: If it were not for my imagination, I might have trouble right now agreeing to these first principles as the catapult to send us further into the unknown. **But, because my mind can see the concepts, I'll agree to these first principles. I will use my imagination to ride the light and travel wherever it leads.**

Guardian: Riding light is a beautiful metaphor. I seek to ride light as fact. Can we lay down these first principles and build from here?

Warrior: Yes. I will accept them as a hypothesis, for the purposes of exploring deeper. I will use my imagination to run and wrestle with these principles.

Guardian: So be it. Light and truth are impersonal and immaterial. By themselves they do not solve anything. But we can reach into them to laterally and vertically reach out to the Source, to transcend the grip of the ego and the grip of ignorance. **To wrestle our way out of this adversarial grip, we need to discover light, in order, then, to see truth.** This light as truth-disclosing is an activity we must learn. Then, if we learn to teach this to leaders, and then they learn practical judgment as truth-disclosing, this exploring of ours will not be in vain. **If we succeed, our leaders will be given the greatest gift—methods to transcend the ego and ignorance.** I am not aiming at the proof of 'deductive certainty.' I aim to 'realize' these first principles in our souls. Then, with 'inductive probability,' we can transfer these truths as educational methods to make better leaders.

Warrior: Go on. It won't be in vain. You are demonstrating the powers of creative intelligence.

Liddell Hart mentors us here–

> Creative intelligence is and always has been the supreme requirement in the commander.[5]

The critical intelligence, or insurgent intelligence if you will, anchors creative intelligence.

Guardian: We have been in the unknown, correct?

---

[5] Roger H. Nye, *The Challenge of Command: Reading for Military Excellence*. Hart quoted.

Warrior: Yes. For quite some time.

Guardian: Can we dive deeper into the unknown?

Warrior: Yes. The unknown seems to be an infinite abyss.

Guardian: Then, is this another leaping point, to go deeper into the unknown?

Warrior: Yes.

Guardian: Let us leap. Now, look around, what do you see?

Warrior: I don't see anything.

Guardian: What do you hear?

Warrior: I don't hear anything.

Guardian: What is your consciousness witnessing?

Warrior: Hold on. I see and hear the concepts. Is this awareness as light? Intelligence as truth? Is this what is immaterial and intangible?

Guardian: I hope so. In these depths, all we have is our nature of truth and our substance of light. We've let go of everything else. We've let go of the sense-perceptions and physical phenomena. We are seeking to awaken intellectual and spiritual powers. Do you notice how still it is here? Do you notice how uneventful it is here? Do you notice how quiet it is here?

Warrior: I notice the sense-perceptions wrestling with boredom.

Guardian: Is this not what Aristotle meant, when the intellect comes most at rest, it awakens?

Warrior: It's a strange and freeing experience.

Guardian: Seeking the depths, is it worthy of the effort?

Warrior: Yes.

Guardian: We must learn to see in the depths of the darkness, the essence of our being, and go deeper and deeper until we can move like light in consciousness. Look closely. What am I?

Warrior: A teacher? A thinker?

Guardian: Look closer. You are the teacher. You are the thinker. You are the warrior.

Warrior: I can't see. What are you?

Guardian: Because we are friends, I'll speak truthfully. I've often wondered why I am on earth.

Warrior: Clearly, a lost soul par excellence.

Guardian: Being in body seems somewhat like bondage. It seems that being on earth, I'm in exile. Because Plato left his truths in writing, I learned I might be suffering divine madness.[6]

Warrior: Clearly, a madman par excellence.

Guardian: Let me explain to the best of my ability.

Warrior: I'll lend you my ears.

Guardian: I remember seeing a psychologist in my formative years. I told her, my blood is on fire. The fire and energy of my being could not rest; I experienced non-stop restlessness. The only time I felt free of this restlessness was when my body was in motion. In motion, when physically moving the body, I felt at rest. This meant I could not be still. I could not study. I could not read. I felt trapped in the body. I said, I wanted my wings back. My spirit and mind moved with great lucidity—I could see what others could not. Spirit in body. Spirit all around. My soul wanting to burst free. I felt the frustration of my teachers, parents and coaches. I could not listen. I heard static anytime an elder spoke. I found solace in movement. The doctor suspected I suffered from immaturity, indiscipline, and a wandering mind, commonly called ADD. I spoke to her concern–

> Guardian: Does this seem like an undisciplined mind? Before every practice and competitive event, which means every day, I go down in my basement and for an hour I prepare my gear. I then go to the locker room an hour before practice or game day. I sit in the stands and visualize for 30 minutes. Then I go to the locker room and methodically unpack my gear, and then don the gear. I then train and compete. I love this rhythm of training and competing. **I don't experience this rhythm in education. I need a rhythm of intellectual training similar to gymnastic training. I need more coaching and guidance. I need a mentor.** I do not resonate with the subjects and methods being taught. I know the love of knowledge has not awakened in me. Schooling is a very foreign and imprisoning experience. I'm not made to sit at a desk for 8 hours a day. I'm tired. I get bored. I can't keep my eyes open. This is hell. What I am being taught does not make sense. I am not interested in anything being taught. I don't see the significance. I feel outer forces trying to control me. It's all being forced. This forcing of my will and energy and mind seems like complete bondage. I hate it.

I went to a private school, one of the best in the nation, and felt it did nothing to help me prepare to deal with the reality of living. **All I heard was static. A painful static**. Like finger

---

[6] Plato, *Phaedrus*.

nails on a chalk board all the time. I had headphones on all the time to drown it out. Now, I have earplugs in all the time. I love the silence. The silence speaks. I heard it speak. At a young age, I learned to listen to the **inner voice**. Jim Harrison mentors us here–

> Some people hear their own inner voices with great clearness and they live by what they hear. Such people become crazy, or they become legends.[7]

I live and speak and write from this inner voice–I leap from it. The doctor acknowledged that I was disciplined in one activity and undisciplined in another.

> Psychologist: Just be patient in your maturity and you'll be fine.

Thank God she did not write a prescription. She knew it would not help. **Medicine could not help**. Medicine is to heal your body. But I did not need healing. There was nothing 'wrong' with me. I won't dull my natural senses and sanity to deal with the greyness of this world and its prisons. I'll instead harness what I have—something that was never broken—to achieve the most human thing of all: to transcend. I needed to be taught how to **master this non-stop energy**. My energy was like a dynamo—a riot in my soul and in my brain, driven by millennia of survival necessities finding a muted thud in today's world—and I had to learn to convert its energy wisely. What I needed to learn when I was young was meditation and contemplation. No one I knew taught these methods in high school or college. I felt rushed and forced in my formative years. I wanted a guide. I wanted a mentor. I had no business being in a school environment; I needed adventure. Life seemed too manufactured. Human beings have millions of ways of learning. Most school systems offer just one—or maybe a dozen if you're very wealthy and very lucky. So a lucky few will pass through unharmed. The rest rot. I did not realize I sought wisdom. The formative years were non-stop struggling, pain, doubt, and anxiety. This pathetic inner state killed my ability to learn.

Warrior: You had this awareness back then?

Guardian: To some degree. But, in reflection, the memories and the experiences poured in. Now, why do I share this? When I read Plato's *Phaedrus* and he spoke of divine madness, it hit my soul, and I had to reflect, do I suffer this? Then the experiences poured in to signify this truth.

Warrior: Do you have an example?

Guardian: In high school, when we would banter with one another. When I would hit my peers with banter, they would stop and look at me, in terror, and say, why are you so mean? I could not understand why they looked at me and not themselves, because they were doing the same thing.

Only they weren't.

---

[7] Jim Harrison, *Legends of the Fall*.

Back then, I did not know that I saw into their being, into their souls, and I would press what was deep within them, to what was secret in their hearts, and they had no idea how I would know that. Not the particulars, but the nature, the essence. In confusion, I started to suppress this seeing. This suppression led to repression, which led to rage. I'm still recovering from suppressing the gifts given to me.

Warrior: I see why the way of the contemplative resonates with you.

Guardian: Now, why do I share this? My being, just my being, if leaders are open to it, will help trigger spiritual growth and awaken the fires of light and truth in them. That is what I think I'm here to do. That is the calling. It's the most natural way I know. I'm no sage. I'm no saint. I'm no philosopher. I am a fiery spirit. I suffer divine madness. And I want to put this madness to work. I learned, when I started leading, that this divine madness is what gave me the power to see what was hidden from others. At the time I did not know the term "divine madness." Being raised Catholic, in a secular society, did not help. It led to more confusion and contradictions. No one could help. Teachers, coaches, leaders, priests and psychologists (who very often act as modern priests—it's not a cliché if it's true) claimed I was unstable and unreliable. This led to a rejection of secular and religious authority. They had no powers to heal and guide my soul. They did not know how to doctor to the soul.

Warrior: You seem to reject all manufactured authority—CEO, Bishop, Provost, Politician, Chancellor, Celebrity.... Fromm's wise words ring true, I paraphrase his meaning–

Why do you want to be adjusted, to be made to feel normal, in an insane society?[8]

Guardian: Which is why the way of the saints, warriors, and sages resonated deeply with me. Kreeft's wise words ring true as well–

The Saints are the only sane ones.[9]

Now, I share this so you know what I am and what I'm searching for in the unknown. This will help you understand what I'm actually doing and what is actually informing my will and intelligence.

Warrior: This authenticity makes you trustworthy to develop leaders. You are called to help in their formation. You want them to be free and powerful. In reflection, when did you first experience this concept—*divine madness*?

Guardian: For twenty years I've listened to the call, the call to develop leaders. I did not know where this call came from and I did not know why I listened to it. It seemed to me that the call came from the Heavens, from Eternity, and it used light and truth to brand my consciousness.

---

[8] Erich Fromm, *The Sane Society*.
[9] Peter Kreeft, *How to become Holy*.

I mean, I can see this call. It's just there, leading and directing all the time. It's the strangest thing to speak about. It seems the calling and the madness came from the same source, the divine Essence. The divine madness came earlier; the divine call came later. It seems the madness paved the way to listen to the call. If I had a normal existence, if I fit the normalcy, I would not have listened. The pain, the suffering, the madness made me listen. I wanted out of the suffering. I did not fit in. I hated the idea of fitting into a normal job, be it lawyer, financier, marketer, professor, or doctor. I wanted no part in the professions staring me down. My peers went in those directions. I wanted no part of that life. I wanted adventure. I wanted purpose. I wanted meaning. I wanted love and devotion to be expressed in the work. I did not want a job. I wanted a mission. I wanted an activity that I was called to do. The wanting for things to be otherwise opened the door for divine madness.

Warrior: What a wild place for a youngster to be in.

Guardian: Then, in college, I discovered the military officer path—the path of leading. I found it *via negativa*, the last option, when I turned from all the others. The path of leading served as an escape plan to get me out of the hell of modern business, economic, and domestic life. I needed a way out. Those who claim that hell is eternal do not know what they're talking about. Hell, Purgatory, Heaven are on full display, here on earth. Go into any office building in your nearest city, and you'll find some in hell. Go into any home in your nearest suburb, and you'll likely find some in purgatory.

People free of fear? Free of debt? Free of the things they own that begin to own them? Free of the effects of judgment by others? Free of judgment by yourself? No. You will not find this. You will find suffering. You will find people living in the past and in the future to a degree that causes pain and unnecessary anxiety. You will find people seeking outlets: booze, drugs, sex, television, phones, social media, anything to dull the pain, anything to make the present slightly less hurtful.

When the leadership path opened up, I realized that here I could bring to bear all my suppressed gifts in the act of leading the souls of human beings. The purgative phase toward liberation had been initiated. I started reading Bildungsroman books, coming of age books, of journeys into the formation of character and spirit—these writings hit me deep in the core.

A spiritual awakening? Is this possible?

I reflected, why does it seem fictional characters are leading more adventurous lives than me? That reflection infuriated me. I am the living being. On the leadership path, life began to lead me on a course of adventure. I've never looked back, even though I've found myself in management positions. I've never fit in with the normal, the common, and the comfortable.

Warrior: I appreciate you setting the context. I needed to understand the concepts of divine madness and divine calling. It seems if there is truth to this, one of our duties as teachers is to help students awaken to the calling and guide them in the direction of the calling. We need to learn how to listen for it and then how to have the courage to act on it. Please describe the experience.

Guardian: Let me ask, were you called to be a warrior, not just a soldier?

Warrior: After 30 years, looking back, yes—it appears so.

Guardian: Then, I declare these to be the first two leadership development challenges–

> First, the leader-to-be must patiently listen for the call (*coup d'oiel*).

> Second, once heard, the leader-to-be needs the courage to act on the call (*coup d'esprit*).

This is where we can guide the leader-to-be to train with courage, faith, endurance and effort to realize the call. This is how the leader-to-be can become aware of the divine, of the eternal and of the immortal. The call serves to unshackle the conditioned being from the mortal fear of death and the immortal fear of ignorance. How can we fear death when for hundreds of millennia, human beings have been born with a death sentence? The moment we are conceived, we are already on a certain crash course towards death of the body. How can we be free if we are ignorant? The calling leads to a freedom of being that is in harmony with the divine and the immortal. It is here that the soul experiences a direct contact with light and truth. This is when faith begins to transform into wisdom. The soul knows the calling. The ego is terrified and wants to hide and resist the calling. It is a great injustice not to listen to the call; it is a turning away from truth instead of towards truth. Only those who have the courage to listen to their call will suffer the rigor of the training we employ to realize inner potencies.

> Writer: Dear Reader, I am at the edge of my understanding. Please be patient with me. I seek to understand. I feel myself censoring my thinking and I'm afraid to speak truthfully. I am not attempting to prove to you, dear reader, anything. I am attempting to see if it's possible in writing to express how the soul awakens to its calling. Because the writer has listened to the call, this is what the writer writes from. The call leads out the light and truth of the soul. The call is the first sign of light and truth as metaphysical facts. The call receives light and truth from beyond itself and becomes receptive to light and truth—a sunlight for the soul. This is what leads to wholeness and freedom amidst limited knowledge of being. It's the one known thing that sets the soul free in the mystery of being. This is why the calling is of primacy. It awakens. We are in the depths now. Now, we need to endure. We need to learn how to listen to the call and act on it, continually in the act of living. We need to listen to the call's promptings as directives for action. It takes faith to act on truth's directives. The warrior and the guardian are

expressing what it might be like. The call is a truth; the light delivers this truth. The call is a sign that we live in a deep mystery. The soul's call is how to share in this deep mystery. The call is the anchor that guides actions and decisions. It helps the individual soul disclose the truth it needs to live its purpose. Our hope is that the guardian and the warrior inspire us to be open and receptive to this call as a first awakening. This is one way to have a direct experience with light and truth, to listen and hear the call, and let the call guide us.

Dear God, please guide this writer. We are about to explore how to reach the soul's light and truth upward into the divine light and truth. Please guide me to express how truth is received in the soul to hear the call. What I am writing, though cloaked in concepts, is how the soul makes contact and has a direct experience with the truth of its existence. I am writing as a path to make contact with the divine and the eternal, and bring it into the mortal and temporal. I am hopeful the reader will become open and receptive to light and truth, and learn to be a receiver and a giver of light and truth in the act of leading. The hope is the reader will be patient in the soul's quest to hear the call, and then once received, the hope is for the soul to have the courage to act on its divine guidance, and learn to be in communion with God as the source of light and truth. We are after direct experience and understanding, not beliefs. This is a beautiful way to guide the reader to "know" light and truth. Courageous writing is needed to break through the layers of consciousness that darken the soul. This is what I am about to attempt, to describe the layers of consciousness that need to be traversed to open the doors to truth. To do this, I need to allow the streams of consciousness to lead to deep insights that need to be made known. We aim for a state of soul that is beautiful and heightened. The writing needs to be led by the contemplative intellect and its powers. **My ego needs to be far way, as though asleep, because it does not have the power to comprehend these depths.** The hope is for the reader to experience light and truth taking flight with each word. Thank you for guiding us, the writer, the guardian, the warrior, and the reader.

Guardian: Warrior, you are interested to know the story of how I came to know of divine madness, not just the divine call?

Warrior: Yes.

Guardian: I describe the divine call as an experience in which the divine nature tattooed the call on the deepest realm of knowing in my consciousness.

Warrior: It sounds more like a divine branding.

Guardian: Indeed it is. The divine branding of the divine call. For twenty years, any time I started to waiver from the calling and its direction, I experienced a spiritual anguish and discomfort as though I were going insane. And when we met, I was not sure whether or not I was sane.

You said–

> You seem like a philosopher.

And I reacted–

> I'm not a philosopher; I'm called to develop leaders.

And you responded–

> No, not a modern professor of philosophy, but you remind me of the ancient ones. Please tell me you've read Plato and Aristotle? I thought you had because you called your training the light of leadership and focused on the pursuit of wisdom and the development of virtues.

And I responded–

> I've never read them.

And you said–

> You should, I think you'll understand why after you've read them.

And so I did. I read. And I read. I then stumbled upon Plato's *Phaedrus*. What I read shined like beams of illumination into my soul. I experienced a deeper interior freedom when I read–

> That would be rightly said if it were a simple truth that madness is a bad thing; but as it is, the greatest of goods comes to us through madness, provided that it is bestowed by divine gift.
>
> …madness is a fine thing when it comes by divine dispensation.
>
> …god-sent madness is a finer thing than man-made sanity.
>
> …we must comprehend the truth about the nature of the soul, both divine and human.
>
> …such madness is given by gods to allow us to achieve the greatest good fortune

...disposed towards philosophy and leadership...the way of life and the pattern of the god.[10]

Warrior: I see now. You are called to comprehend the truth about the soul, both the human and the divine truth. And you *"know about."* But you don't *"know"* yet, which is why you trust the practices. Courageous spirit, go on.

Guardian: I ask that we receive guidance and move in the ways of divine madness and see what is revealed.

Warrior: Go on.

Guardian: We are headed into an examination of a difficult model and two difficult techniques that we must get command of, if we are to awaken truth-disclosing and teach truth-disclosing. The easiest thing is to teach leadership tactics, but that comes later. The hardest thing is to teach the leadership framework and techniques that become extensions of our being, that we then lead into tactics. The metaphor to use–

Being asked to race a race car, but having no experience as a *race car driver*.

Warrior: Understood. Just like being asked to go to war with the best gear, but no experience as a warrior. We give people gear they don't know how to handle. This is evidently clear in the act of leading. We try to change everything but the human being. We try to change the systems, the technology, the structure, but not the human being who leads these elements. Where did you discover the model and techniques?

Guardian: First, as Campbell said, the hero must follow his bliss. The hero, when he listens to the inner voice, becomes divine madness, and this madness fuels the courage to act. I've listened to the inner voice and listened to the call. This means I've spent my life devoted to one aim—developing leaders. To do this, I asked one question–

What does it take to develop leaders?

And this question led me to plumb the depths, deeper and deeper, as time when on. The call led to a comparative study of the saints, sages, and warriors. Then, as with Campbell, patterns began to emerge. This pattern, this cycle that I am about to share, revealed itself early on as a consolation. I do not share it publicly.

Warrior: Do share. I'll listen.

Guardian: To begin, this is a theoretical framework. It serves to guide us in our ability to make contact with light and truth. Even if until now we never knew this, it's taking place all the time, independent of our knowing or our ignorance. Souls are being deceived and they do not even know it. We need to give this knowledge to our leaders.

---

[10] Plato, *Phaedrus*.

Proverbs mentors us–

> A wise man will listen and will increase in learning; and a man of understanding
> shall attain to leadership.[11]

Warrior: When did you discover this pattern?

Guardian: Fifteen years ago. I hit an impasse in realizing the call. At the time, I hired an executive coach to guide me out of it. What I needed, but did not know of, was a doctor of souls, a spiritual counselor, not a coach. She asked three basic questions–

> Where do you want to live?
> What do you want to study?
> What kind of work do you find rewarding?

The answers were easy–

> Move from the Midwest to West.
> Study for a Master's degree in Leadership.
> Work for a leadership firm.

Once she asked those questions and I answered, I thanked her and our work ended. Within a month, I moved west; within a year, I entered a Master's program; and within two years, I landed a job at a leadership consulting firm.

Warrior: Impressive and bold actions.

Guardian: No. What I needed, but did not know of, was a deeper purification of the soul. It would have been better to enter a monastery for two years. I needed spiritual training. I did not need to hit goals that will not "echo in eternity." My actions led to a deeper and deeper anguish and misery. I knew the restlessness to be from the soul's underdevelopment. I feared the promptings of the soul; I did not listen. That's when I learned the bitter truth that achievement does not make one free. I felt like a racehorse competing in races, not knowing why I was racing to begin with. Or I was a greyhound running after that fuzz ball, released into the wild and finally capturing an actual rabbit without any idea of what to do with it, or what to do next except to chase more rabbits. I suffered because I still moved on the surface instead of in the depths. Those decisions were superficial and conventional. I was still in bondage to modern life (the university, the organization, and the city). I had to take another deep look within. I battled this period of despondency by creating solo weekend retreats. I had no spiritual director. I only had silence and solitude as the guide. I continually asked–

---

[11] The Holy Bible, *Book of Proverbs*. Lamsa translation.

> What am I not seeing?
> What am I not listening too?
> What am I hiding from?

The silent retreats kept me still and silent to learn to listen and see again. I had become lost again, even though I knew the calling. I had closed myself off from wisdom.

Proverbs mentors us–

> Wisdom is the principle thing; therefore get wisdom; and with all your substance get understanding.[12]

Warrior: And what did you see and hear?

Guardian: Nothing. I hit an impasse. Life essentially said–

> Stop, be still, be patient, and observe.

Warrior: Then?

Guardian: Then Wisdom spoke–

> Stop running. You cannot run your way to freedom. You need to prepare to see.

I listened. I stopped. I observed. I quit running. I started walking.

Warrior: Seems insightful to me.

Guardian: During the period of this impasse, I spent every weekend in a self-directed meditative retreat. Even though I lived a stone's throw from the ocean, each weekend, instead of "doing something," I would turn my room into a silent retreat. I did this weekly for over a year. My memory has faded, but it seemed I did this for a number of years.

Warrior: What did you do during the retreats?

Guardian: From Friday night to Sunday night I would practice fasting with a yogic tea (black chai tea with honey and goat milk), I would practice silence and stillness, I would practice meditation, and I would practice contemplation. I would not just read; I would contemplate what I was reading. I would read slowly, initially out loud, to let the words resonate in my being. I practiced contemplating the wisdom literature, seeing if the light of the literature could hit the light of the soul. In time, I began to notice a healing that increased my interior freedom and joy. This seemed more like *via negativa*. Proportionately, the more I distanced myself from the non-essential and the non-necessary, external phenomena, the more joy I experienced.

---

[12] The Holy Bible, *Book of Proverbs*. Lamsa translation

Warrior: You mean, you distanced yourself from work and social life?

Guardian: Yes. I spiritually kept the surface of things far away, in my retreats. I remember the experience as a time of beautiful and graceful spiritual healing. I learned that healing needs to occur before the rigor of action. I had not known the purpose of balance and harmony. I learned I had a broken and fractured soul. In my sad shape, I needed to heal the soul from the corruption that resulted from my social activities. I learned that the social life, as it is practiced in the modern world, is dangerous and shrouded in distortion, delusion and wickedness. I never go to night clubs now. They are dens of wickedness that corrupt the soul. During this period of heightened awareness, I went with a priest to a bar. I drove so he could relax. He lived in Africa, engaged in non-stop missionary work. I rarely went to bars sober, and being sober, I saw it. I saw the wickedness. I could see beyond the veil. Its truth terrified me. How could this be real?

Warrior: You indeed are insane.

Guardian: Don't misunderstand, I love pubs. Remember anything can be a virtue or a vice.

That said, as I healed, I started to get restless. I learned that restlessness as the spirit grows in strength is a good thing. I regained my center. I learned observation and contemplation. I needed to learn how to live in this state in the chaos of living, not just in the silence of a sanctuary.

Here Pieper mentors us–

> The more embracing the power with which to relate oneself to objective being, the more deeply that power needs to be anchored in the inner self of the subject so as to counterbalance the step it takes outside. And where this step attains a world that is in principle complete (with totality as its aim) the reflective self, characteristic of spirit, is also reached. The two together constitute spirit: not only the capacity to relate oneself to the whole of reality, but an unlimited capacity of living in oneself, the gift of self-reliance and independence that, in the philosophical tradition of Europe, have always been regarded as the attributes of the human person, of being a person.[13]

I learned to rest and become aware in the depths of being. It is here that I found peace, joy, illumination, and understanding. When I left the inner sanctuary, I experienced intense turbulence and frustration. With the eyes of truth, I experienced turbulence when I engaged society. The incessant swirling of ignorant and unconscious human interactions assaulted my being. I felt weaker as a man as I grew stronger in spirit. I still needed to develop more strength. I needed to learn to remain undisturbed anywhere. It is here that I needed the warrior's art

---

[13] Josef Pieper, *Leisure: The Basis of Culture.*

most, to armor the soul against the onslaught of human madness that acted as if it were sane. This I when I learned first-hand the power of detachment and humility by meditation and contemplation. I had to learn to contemplate, to observe, what swirled around me and not get injured. This meant rarely taking action. I learned that very little, aside from one's work, demands our actions. Out of necessity I practiced meditation and contemplation. Out of necessity I armed myself with the virtues of detachment and humility. In our art, unless our leaders become skilled in meditation and contemplation and become armed with detachment and humility, they will fail. Truth will only disclose itself to the conditioned soul; the soul is conditioned by the exercises of meditation and contemplation. Again–

Truth, and God, cannot be mocked.

Warrior: Again, Emerson mentors–

God will not have his work made manifest by cowards.[14]

Guardian: In our art, achievement is not sought; wealth is not sought; honor is not sought; and happiness is not sought. In our art, the truth-seeking activity is sought. In this activity, the disciplined skills are put to the test. When the seduction of achievement and honor tempts our leaders, they will be instructed to turn away and head into the one activity that tests. In our art, our leaders know salvation is only found in the activities. Aristotle reminds us that contemplative wisdom is the highest happiness, and contemplative wisdom is not an acquisition or a possession but an activity. The activity is what matters most. The being-at-work (*energeia*) in an active-condition (*hexis*) is what matters most. In our art, we seek self-reliance and independence by being what we are and moving from what we are. This is why the calling is the holy grail. It sets us free from mortality, from affection and from recognition by external sources. The calling leads to wisdom, truth, and light. All else follows its lead. Living the calling is a living activity.

Our leaders must become independent of the adversary's wills and judgments. They don't need awards. They don't need to be special. They need to rise above and transcend the temptations of human idols. This is what is learned in the depths of silence and stillness. This is where our leaders will break free from the bondage of man-made madness cloaked as sanity.

Warrior: What did you see in the depths? How did it heal and make you stronger?

Guardian: I'm not sure if I saw anything. I did learn that when the soul is compromised, when it is weakened, its essence must be healed. How does this healing occur? For me, it's the activities of silence and stillness, prayer and reflection, being instead of doing. These activities exercise the soul. This is how the soul regains composure and strength. This is where I experienced the self-correcting nature of the soul without human guidance. How the soul

---

[14] Ralph Waldo Emerson, "Self-Reliance".

could experience this in silence and solitude I do not know. I am not skilled and wise enough to know "why," I only know the experience; I only know the what-ness. As I healed and strengthened, I began to experience a deepening restlessness. I wanted to act, but I did not see or know the next step. I had to sit still in this restlessness, without running, without acting, until the guidance revealed itself.

The questions kept shifting. They danced around, and I did not know which question to follow–

> What am I not seeing?
> Why am I so restless?
> What do I need to create?

I learned to be in the restlessness and to be in the boredom without moving. I saw the questions leaping around and I remained patient until one question remained. Then, like spiritual alchemy, a pattern revealed itself through the question. I could see.

Warrior: What did you see?

Guardian: How did I prepare to see? The restlessness started to increase, not decrease, the suffering. I wanted to move. I wanted to run. I stayed in silence and stillness. It seemed that healing increased the suffering. That paradox still perplexes me. Having no guide, I had to will my own development. To prepare to see, in restlessness and boredom, I spent two days staring at a map of the earth on my wall. I gazed for hours. Then it happened. A gift of inspiration took over my being.

Warrior: Restlessness transformed into stillness, as the key to insights and inspiration?

Guardian: Is that what you are seeing?

Warrior: Yes. When inspiration struck, what did you do?

Guardian: **I took hold of a marker and started writing and diagramming on the map what I saw in the mind. My consciousness disappeared in the work,** I experienced a Zen-like *satori* state. When I finished, as an artist, I took a step back and looked at what I discovered. I had mapped out a different kind of leadership training. I had mapped out a different kind of education. I had mapped out an education for a soul that is to lead in any endeavor. What I mapped out is what I needed, the kind of education I needed. Before I could teach leaders, I needed this education first. Distilled to its essence, this education, what we are doing now, is the way of freedom, the way of self-reliance. At the time, I did not study the Greek philosophers, but I did study the Indian sages and the Catholic mystics. Once I discovered the framework, the restlessness subsided. I entered into exquisite peace. In peace, I set out to study the depths of the framework. This began a 10-year period of autodidactic, self-taught learning. I had no mentors, so the ancient sacred texts continued to be my teachers.

Warrior: So, this is yours? You mean, I won't find this in another book?

Guardian: I've not seen this elsewhere. Please go easy on me—it's the first time I've spoken of it to another. I'm not sure I can explain it.

Warrior: Again, just speak simply by describing what you see.

Guardian: First, I need to declare the purpose of this model. The purpose is to demonstrate how we intend to lead out, to draw out, what lives in the souls of our leaders. We must be on guard against the tendency to live from the outside in, instead of from the inside out. Self-actualization and awakening is a process by which the soul ignites its potencies and leads them out.

What I hope to explain is how to lead one–

> From the depths of the soul's light and truth, into the soul's powers of will, intelligence and spiritedness, into domain knowledge and skills, and to unite them all for action in the arenas and activities of embodied living. Thereby, we make virtue, knowledge, and expertise extensions of being.

This is the keystone aim. This is the target. This is what we orient ourselves towards.

Warrior: Quite a significant task you've demanded of yourself.

Guardian: That is the key point of living a calling—it is guided by the divine but demands self-responsibility and self-accountability because it frees you from the authority of others, be it the institution or a person. We aim at true freedom. We see on earth souls escaping from the burden of true freedom. The modern business environment is bondage and prison par excellence. Only the owners, creators, and investors are free. Workers are not free.

Warrior: You are a harsh judge of modern life. It's strange how you seek independence from the judgment of others but you judge harshly the way of life of most people.

Guardian: It is true. I am sure I would hate any human setup where we allow staggering wealth and staggering poverty. I do hate rule by wealth—monarchy, aristocracy and plutocracy. I hate all that is not devoted to the noble ideal of all souls flourishing. I cannot verify the source of this statement, but it's attributed to Napoleon–

> In this life, we are either kings or pawns, emperors or fools.

I share this because I have no calling to rule or to wealth, and mankind is governed by ruling and wealth. I'll play the fool. I've taken myself off the board. I act as though I am already dead—the way of death of the Hagakure. I act as if I'm already released from the physical body. If I were released from the physical body, I ask what would I do? What actions? And not being in body, I focus on spiritual and intellectual activities. This mindset helps free me from the bondage and prison I see on earth.

Warrior: You are strange. You are radical.

Guardian: How else do we become free? Give in to wealth, power and indulgence? I always felt uncomfortable when I used my will in leading to make people submit out of coercive power. That is bondage. That is injustice. I want no part of it. I want people to choose to do good and important work. The purpose of this framework is to teach how to lead out the powers of spirit, to lead out what is tacit and intuitive and give it life in concepts, structure and activity. That is why I am sharing this with you. Think about the absurdity of modern warfare and how much gear you need. You are dependent on weapons systems and lasers. All this to combat a physical enemy, when the real enemy is intangible and immortal. You don't see it. You are still ensnared on the surface.

Warrior: Are you judging the warfighter now?

Guardian: No. I am judging the incompetent men that dominate high command in the military. Do you judge them?

Warrior: Yes. I judge their incompetency. They use the wrong strategies and tactics in the wars we fight because they are not strategists, and they are not leaders.

> They are limited, weak, and institutional men.

> They are rewarded for failure and mediocrity.

> They will redefine victory to make up for their failure before admitting to
> their failure.

Guardian: Then, you, as I, must lead the way of freedom in our endeavor. There are only a few thousand warriors who know this truth. The rest of the two million military personnel are servants of advanced weapons systems that are the source of the greatest manmade misery and menace on earth. This science has created weapons and technology that ignorant human beings are entrusted to employ to fight wars. Is there not a better way?

Warrior: Are you saying to halt progress?

Guardian: No, my good man. I'm saying we need better human beings to manage these weapons and technologies. What wisdom does Zuckerberg possess? He's a boy with staggering wealth who would get reduced to nothingness in our training. He's ego par excellence. It's atrocious what we are doing on earth. We've defiled the garden. And we need to educate leaders to make earth a garden again.

Warrior: So you are the optimistic pessimist.

Guardian: I am neither. I know until all beings are awakened, there is a raging spiritual war in every human heart. The ego runs from it instead of engaging it. I ran from it until I understood what is actually taking place. Our aim is to engage it, not run. The eternal fight is within. The last enemy is within. We will face this adversary soon enough. We will unite the archetypes of the warrior and guardian to face and conquer this adversary. We experience victory every time a soul awakens to light and truth and conquers this adversary.

To begin–

We seek freedom. We seek freedom in being, in knowing, and in seeing. We do not seek the freedom of wealth. We seek the freedom of skilled excellence. We see freedom as self-reliance, interdependence and sentience on earth.

How did I know I was in bondage? I did not know the answers to the most basic questions of living–

> What am I?
> How am I here?
> What is the purpose of being here?
> Where was I before earth?
> Where am I going after earth?

These questions are the vital drivers of freedom. The questioning of human beings is what distinguishes our species from all others. We seek to know. Knowing leads to freedom.

> We seek freedom as knowing. Nothing more, nothing less.

What led me? I have no interest in the survival and achievement methods of modern man. City life is corrupting and disconnected from nature. The body may survive in comfort, but the being and soul of the man is in bondage. Rousseau[15] can mentor us–

> The solitary man is good. The social man is wicked.

Warrior: How so?

Guardian: The wicked man needs men to manipulate. The solitary man needs none. The solitary man is self-reliant. This is the contemplative man, who rests inwardly, even though he moves outwardly to share in the common good. It is the interior state we seek to know.

These wicked ways, the pain of bondage, in spite of material luxury and professional success, led me to seek a way to freedom. I wanted release from the metaphysical prison I found myself in. The drive to inner freedom led me to turn to the substance and nature of being, to light and truth.

Warrior: The pain, not the pleasure, led the awakening?

---

[15] Rousseau, *Emile, or On Education*.

Guardian: Yes. The pain of bondage. We head into pain instead of heading into pleasure.

Our aim is true freedom–

We aim to see and know the soul. We aim to see and know the soul's light and truth and the source of this light and truth. The metaphysical fact is that we did not create our being, we did not create light and truth, we did not create the cosmos. A simple speculative inquiry leads to the idea that there are greater beings and intelligences in the cosmos. When we study our leaders, we need to see if the soul is diminished in light or illuminated in light, ignorant of truth or awakened in truth. So, what pattern have I seen?

Warrior: I've been patiently waiting to hear.

Guardian: I've seen more light in a grocery clerk than I have in an executive. External achievement is no measure. **Good God, human success is no measure of truth**. We need to know how to seek goodness and beauty in our nature. We need compassion for souls who suffer darkness, ignorance, and bondage. To serve as a guide, we must earn their trust to lead them out of this deceptive and deluded state.

Warrior: Which means, we share with them our own state of darkness, ignorance, and bondage. Which is always true, to a lesser or greater degree, as we are imperfect beings, in the cycle of being and becoming.

Guardian: Yes. We simply share methods to awaken light and truth. But, as teachers, we must see the structure of light in the soul. We need to learn not only to see, but to hear when the soul speaks truthfully or falsely. To listen and see, we need to heighten our own powers of perception.

What I mean–

When a soul is darkened or lightened in truth, when it speaks, when it gives voice to its thinking, we can learn to hear it, to receive it as a frenetic, static or harmonious frequency akin to a clear or unclear radio transmission. That is why we ask our leaders to speak from their core, so we can tune in to them. So we can train them to be sharp and discerning when they speak.

We will suffer with souls who are not awakened. We are not separate from their suffering. In suffering, we will guide them through the layers of their consciousness to reach the exquisite states in the depth of their being. Then, instead of suffering they, and we, will experience joy.

Warrior: We will lead with compassion—suffering with and seeing the light.

Guardian: Yes. Do you want to know why this is even possible?

Warrior: Yes.

Guardian: Do you want to know why most souls on earth are not free and illuminated?

Warrior: Yes.

Guardian: Then I share the following observations and metaphysical framework.

Warrior: Speak simply and I'll follow the thinking. Be fearless when you speak about these matters of truth.

Guardian: If every soul is created in the substance of light and in the nature of truth, how can the soul act counter to its substance and its nature?

Warrior: Based upon your keystone aim, **this can occur when the conditioned being does not know it is made of light and truth**. If the conditioned being does not know it is both soul and body, then the being is dominated by temporal drives of thirst, hunger, sex, and protection (fear of death of self and seed). If this is the case, then the soul's powers are not driven from the inside out, but from the outside in. The soul's powers are acted upon by these drives. This means that the drives of thirst, hunger, sex, health, and protection dominate and control the soul's powers of will, intelligence and spiritedness. You aim to strip the temporal drives of their powers. You aim to turn the soul's powers away from the bodily senses, inward, to gaze upon the soul. Once that inwardness of being is discovered, then the senses and the powers will be ordered by the direction of the soul's light and truth.

Guardian: Beautiful. The essence and nature of the soul is pure, perfect, whole, eternal, immortal and free. How did we, as a species, become corrupted and deceived on earth?

Warrior: When the ruling classes, monarchy and plutocracy, aimed to dominate instead of liberate.

Guardian: Saint Augustine provides an insight–

> Therefore, if a people is well-ordered and serious-minded, and carefully watches over the common good, and everyone in it values private affairs less than the public interest…but suppose that the same people becomes gradually depraved. They come to prefer private interest to the public good. Votes are bought and sold…[16]

Warrior: Have you considered we are just intelligent animals? And as animals, some are powerful and some are weak and some are average? And the strong dominate by their strength, intelligence and cunning?

Guardian: At one time, when agnostic, I contemplated this idea. But I have had too many direct experiences to have faith in the idea of humans as only intelligent animals. Self-awareness, in

---

[16] Saint Augustine, *On Free Choice of the Will.*

fact, appears to have little to no correlation with intelligence. In some respects, machines are the most intelligent things in this world, but they are yet to be self-aware. While some non-human animals may be somewhat self-aware, Boethius can mentor us here–

In other living creatures ignorance of self is nature; in man it is vice.[17]

Warrior: And you are saying, with contemplation and meditation, man becomes self-knowledgeable, and that self-knowledge leads to knowledge of what we are, and what we are is a composite-conditioned being, of both body and soul?

Guardian: That is what I am saying. We are creators and discoverers in heart and mind. There seems to be more of a godlike quality to us than an animal-like quality. That is why we need techniques of realizing truths, progressively, by awakening our potencies of intelligence and spirit, which result in increased inner freedom. Now, we must exercise courage and inquire into the immortality and eternal nature of the soul. Can we inquire to see what we might learn if the soul is, in fact, on earth as part of its education?

Can we speculate that there is an immortal aspect to our being?
Can we speculate that this aspect of being is eternal in truth?

Warrior: We've come this far. To quit is not an option. Keep going.

Guardian: We need a method to reach the light and truth, to be free, not seem free. Follow my line of thinking. Make me give an accurate account.

This is what I see. I see multi-dimensional, geometric spheres and shapes. I see first, a sphere that represents the soul. I see second, a cube, which represents physical phenomena. I see third, a sphere that represents the universe (all immaterial and material phenomena) as infinite. Let us look at each shape to deepen our understanding.

First, I see the soul-sphere. I see the soul as a perfect sphere made of only light and truth. I see perfect, free, immortal, immaterial, indescribable and indestructible essence. I see the soul as the infinite potency of illumination and awakening. When the Buddha awakened, what is it that awakened? His body? His brain? His emotions? His intelligence? His being? His spirit? His soul? What awakened?

Warrior: The immortal spirit, from the depths of his being, awakened into his mortal existence.

Guardian: The spirit of the soul is what awakens?

Warrior: Yes.

Guardian: The spirit of the soul that awakens to its potency of light and truth?

---

[17] Huxley, *The Perennial Philosophy.*

Warrior: Yes.

Guardian: Is our quest to awaken and realize this idea as fact?

Warrior: Yes.

Guardian: Then I see, in the center of this soul-sphere, the concepts of spirit, love, light, truth and potency. If this is so, I now ask, how is it possible for the soul to be defiled and corrupted? How is it possible for the soul to be darkened? How is it possible for the soul to be ignorant?

Warrior: The soul's essence is not darkened; its light and truth are not darkened. Its powers are darkened and corrupted.

Guardian: Yes. The essence of the soul, its spirit, knows no pain, sorrow, fatigue, frustration or corruption. But its powers do know this, be it physical or spiritual. My powers of soul have experienced both the darkness of the physical and the spiritual. The will, intelligence, and spiritedness are extensions of the soul's beinghood. When these powers become potent and active by the drives of thirst, hunger, and sex, the soul's sight becomes corrupted, distorted, and deceived.

Wait, did you just see the flash?

Warrior: No.

Guardian: It just flashed before me, a fourth geometric shape, which now comes second, that of the body-octagon. This has been hidden. I only saw the physical body before. Let me take a deeper look and reshape what I'm seeing. If the soul's essence is not corruptible, we agree, its potencies and powers are.

Warrior: Correct.

Guardian: How do we explain this possibility? First, we have the soul-sphere, as the essence of spirit, love, light, truth and potency, which activate the soul's powers of will, spiritedness, and intelligence. Now, do we see that it is possible for the soul's powers to be hijacked by the temporal essence and drives of thirst, hunger, protection and sex? Is this what we are seeing?

Warrior: Yes. This is the outside in, of the physical and temporal essences fueling the soul's powers and directing them. In this manner, the soul is rendered powerless, as in war we render the enemy powerless.

Guardian: If this is possible, we may have found the key to freedom. To the soul-sphere and the soul-powers I now add the body-octagon, not as a sphere, but as some sort of temporal prison or vehicle that we inhabit on earth. Think of it as the avatar suit the soul inhabits.

Warrior: And the challenge is to integrate the two, being led by soul, instead of being led by body?

Guardian: Yes.

The body-octagon can be thought of as how the soul comes to know her powers and how to wield them in a physical experience. The soul's experience on earth is visceral and physical. The soul via the body experiences pains it would never have without connection to the body. The body is the material; the soul is the form. The bodily potencies are inherently good, necessary, and essential. We could view the body as having these faculties which are similar to the soul–

> The body as the faculty of physical power.
> The emotions as the faculty of spiritedness.
> The mind as the faculty of intelligence.
> The will as the faculty of volition.

From this view, the soul-sphere is greater in circumference and envelops the body-octagon. Combined and ordered, it is essentially a dual-integrated-system. We are simply reordering the guidance systems.

Warrior: Wait. I see how the ego emerges.

Guardian: How?

Warrior: On earth, the education of the soul is to learn to wield her powers into the will, the spiritedness, and the intelligence. When this is done beautifully, light and truth guide and order the activities and actions of the temporal body's will, intelligence, spiritedness.

Guardian: Yes. I follow.

Warrior: It's a dual system. One is to meet the demands of Living (which is mortal), the other is to meet the demands of Spirit (which is eternal). The human being lives in the abyss between these two demands.

> Canfield guides us here, in his wisdom–
>
> One must live continuously in the abyss of the divine Essence and in the nothingness of things…[18]

Guardian: Now we can see what gets darkened, corrupted, deceived and defiled. It's not the soul's essence. The soul's powers can get darkened, veiled, and manipulated by the body-octagon when it thinks its primal drives are what's most real, when in fact they are only the material.

Warrior: And this is where the fiction of the ego is created. This is the fiction that claims false authority and imprisons the soul by taking command of the soul's powers. Our aim is to turn

---

[18] Huxley, *The Perennial Philosophy*. Canfield quoted.

these powers away from the ego and towards the soul, so the soul's powers make contact with the soul's essence.

Guardian: Good God, yes. Knowing is not enough. The ego can be viewed as a brutish defense mechanism. But how can what is weaker control what is stronger?

Warrior: When the will of the human being as soul refuses to acknowledge that it may be created from a divine, eternal, and immortal nature.

Guardian: This is why the saints say there is a spiritual war raging in every human heart and mind. How do we proceed?

Warrior: There is no escaping the demands of the body.

Guardian: As composite-conditioned-existent-beings, we must act with sensitivity and gentleness towards the body-octagon, not with malice, because it is designed to survive in the harshness and ruthlessness of nature. It is designed to protect itself and survive at all costs. That is the way it's designed. And we must treat it as such.

Warrior: Ah, this is what makes transcendence possible.

Guardian: The soul's awakening in its powers and its leadership of the body is the experience of transcendence. That is what we are called to achieve. All of us.

Warrior: And why is this possible?

Guardian: Because we were created with powers that transcend temporal and mortal existence. It's easy now to discuss conceptually. It is difficult to prove and realize.

Warrior: What are the operating dynamics? What is being activated to do this?

Guardian: I am seeing that if the human being practices meditation and contemplation, the light and truth of the soul is activated. When this is activated, it reaches beyond the individual-conditioned-mortal-temporal-experience and connects with the eternal-immortal-light-truth all around.

This can be described as the experience when the soul-sphere reaches upward and beyond the limitations of the ego-body-octagon to the source of light and truth. When this happens, the beinghood of the soul-sphere experiences a transcendence as though it unites with the very fiber and fabric of sentience, existence, and awareness. Are you seeing these two metaphysical shapes, the soul-sphere and the ego-body-octagon?

Warrior: Yes.

Guardian: Now, a third shape comes into view. **I see a massive cube, a granite-black cube that surrounds the soul-sphere and the ego-body-octagon**.

Warrior: Is this the prison you realized you were in?

Guardian: Yes. Do you see it?

Warrior: Yes.

Guardian: And this cube, what shall we call it?

Warrior: What is it? How do we know what to call it if we don't know what it is?

Guardian: Do you see it?

Warrior: I lost sight of it. Go on, I'll follow by listening.

Guardian: Now, see this cube as man-made. This cube absorbs all cultures, all governments, all religions, all institutions and all systems. The earth is not included. The earth is a sphere that orbits in the heavens. Only the creations of us surface dwellers are included. Let's call it the leviathan-cube. Do you see it?

Warrior: Not yet.

Guardian: Look deeper. This leviathan-cube can be seen with the sense-perception. We think it is real because we see it with sense-perception. This all-encompassing web, that envelops our soul-sphere and ego-body-octagon, assaults our being insensately. There is no break from it unless we turn away and enter the depths. We are born into it without our will.

It is as though each soul is placed in a raft already moving in the currents of a violent river. The river's banks are the blinders. The soul can only see the river and spends her existence adapting and surviving to the river's currents and flows. But all this devotion to mastering the river keeps her from mastering her own potential. The soul needs to leap from the raft and make her way to the still and stable banks. Only the soul can't see it yet as a possibility. She's heard legends that this might be the case, but she refuses to leap into the unknown. She's made an existence adapting to the river. This is the outside-in effect of the leviathan-cube. We think we have no control over it because we cannot see the source of its pressure and control. This is what keeps the soul in darkness, bondage, and ignorance. This man-made bondage keeps the soul from knowing light, freedom and wisdom.

Warrior: I am beginning to see. The leviathan-cube is the fusion of ideas, laws, standards, sourced from culture, religion, and government. From our earliest age, these cognitive sets assault the soul, in this case for bad, instead of for good. We become locked up in an invisible prison without our knowing, and this keeps the soul's light and power suppressed. This can be considered a cultural conditioning that ensnares instead of frees. What do you see as the elements of this cube that envelopes the soul-sphere and the ego-body-octagon, and makes us submissive and obedient without our knowing?

Guardian: The wise never go to war with the wise. Education is not a liberation; it is mass socialization to fit the system. The ego, not the spirit, manages this system. The spirit is designed for freedom; the ego is designed for control. I see a double-veiled-structure ensnaring the soul. Since the ego-body-octagon is designed to survive, I see it conforming, adapting and competing against others in this leviathan-cube, thinking the leviathan-cube is real, that it's something to master and control, instead of something to detach from and break free from. Because I study leadership, I know that being a CEO or a president is actually the greatest increase in bondage that a soul can experience, but the ego thinks it is the most freedom. Why would the sages turn away from power, wealth and control?

Plato mentors us here–

> The greatest of penalties is being ruled by a worse man if one is not willing to rule oneself... For it is likely that if a city of good men came to be, there would be a fight over not ruling, just as there is now over ruling; and there it would become manifest that a true ruler really does not naturally consider his own advantage but rather that of the one who is ruled.[19]

What we have is a society of wicked men fighting to rule. We vote wicked men into office and appoint them to be CEOs. None of them have been prepared to lead souls.

Warrior: These wicked ones sought freedom by dependence on coercive sources of power. The lust for power led them straight into bondage.

Guardian: Boethius teaches us that only the soul that contemplates truth is free.[20]

The ego-body-octagon, because it does not know its source of power is within the soul-sphere, turns away from the leadership of the soul-sphere, and engages the leviathan-cube in a non-stop combative fight for dominance over other ego-body-octagons. In fact, now we can see the pattern of how the ego-body-octagon, in competition with other ego-body-octagons in the leviathan-cube, led to development of nations with standing armies. Both nations and standing armies are manifestations of the blindness and veiling nature of the ego-body-octagon and the leviathan-cube. All this is man-made and an abomination of truth, spirit, and freedom.

Warrior: Now you have proven you are insane.

Guardian: I look at the soul as a sun. The universe is infinite with stars. Stars do not compete with other stars unless gravity and the higher nature draws them toward a collision. Souls as suns, as self-reliant beings, need spacing and distance from one another. The ego-body-

---

[19] Plato, *Republic*, Bloom translation.
[20] Boethius, *The Consolation of Philosophy*.

octagon is dependent on other beings because that is where it derives its power. It needs to dominate another. The soul-sphere does not. What do nature and distance cultivate?

Warrior: Harmony, balance and peace.

Guardian: Cities are dens of injustice. We send young men to the death mills of war and to what end? To return future young men to the death mills? The adversary, which we will confront soon enough, has been hidden for too long. We aim to see the web it created to remain hidden.

Warrior: What concepts are in the leviathan cube?

Guardian: Let me lead into it–

> The soul-sphere is light, truth, love, spirit, and potency.
>
> The connections of soul-to-ego are will, intelligence, and spiritedness.
>
> The ego-body-octagon is comprised of primal drives—survival, protection, thirst, hunger, and sex.
>
> Now–
>
> The leviathan-cube is the composition of coercive sources of power—culture, government, religion, industry, education and information.

The leviathan-cube is designed to make the soul obedient and submissive, just as the ego aims to make the soul obedient and submissive to its desires. And when the ego-body-octagon engages the leviathan-cube, what do we see?

Warrior: My Lord, the source of all suffering.

Guardian: Yes. What else? What second-order effects would you place in this cube?

Warrior: I see pain. I see threats. I see competition. I see disease. I see ego. I see fears. I see loneliness. I see beliefs. I see distortions. I see pride. I see vices. I see toxic emotions. I see injustice. I see indolence. I see intemperance. I see desires. I see weakness. I see fragility. I see illusions. I see mortality. I see scarcity. I see rigidness. I see obstacles. I see untrustworthiness. I see isolation. I see unjust laws. I see addiction. I see wantonness. I see craving. I see longing. I see pain that cannot be dulled with the strongest opioid or the most colorful app.

In summary, I see bondage, darkness, and ignorance.

Guardian: I see man-made hell. Can we state that this is the result, the second order effect, of the domination of the ego-body-octagon's primal drives over the soul's powers?

Warrior: Yes. Wild to contemplate. The dual threat of the micro and the macro, the ego-body-octagon and the leviathan-cube. I see a self-reinforcing closed system instead of an open system. I see a self-reinforcing destructive system that continually leads to war, poverty, injustice, and suffering on a massive scale. What I am seeing is the ego-body-octagon in a perpetual state of groundlessness and powerlessness. I see the ego-body-octagon in a constant state of deprivation. I see it in non-stop acts of desperation to gain and hold power in the leviathan-cube.

Thoreau mentors us–

> The mass of men lead lives of quiet desperation.[21]

In this deprivation and desperation, the ego-body-octagon, even if it gets power, is ensnared and rendered powerless because it becomes bonded instead of liberated. It is the illusion of strength and power. It is not self-reliant, a being unto itself.

Case in point–

> Any general or CEO who retires realizes how insignificant he is. Life throttles forward just fine without him.

Guardian: A well-educated and well-loved child does not suffer this desperation in her formative years, even though she undergoes the rigors necessary and essential to her growth. After this beautiful growth, the child becomes an adult and must adjust to the systems and ways in place. And then what happens?

Warrior: We start to see the breaking down of goodness into darkness—compromise, adjustment, settling, atrophy, spectating, voyeurism, numbness, anxiety, fear, adultery, addiction, depression, violent extremism, self-harm, and suicide. We see bondage instead of liberation. We see adults, underdeveloped, becoming weaker instead of stronger. Why?

Guardian: They cannot ward off the temptations, the cravings, the lusts and the desires. The leviathan-cube, created by the ego-body-octagon, created a self-closed system designed to assault the primal drives instead of liberating people from those drives.

Warrior: You imply that the ego's drives created a system designed to turn those drives into passions and to feed those passions?

Guardian: Yes. Everywhere you turn the primal drives are being assaulted. The ego-body-octagon is not designed to free itself from these primal drives. It's designed to live by them.

Only the soul, when she asserts her authority and wields her powers, can reduce these passions. Rousseau can mentor us here–

---

[21] Henry David Thoreau, *Walden*.

> From where does man's weakness come? From the inequality between his strength and his desires. It is our passions that make us weak, because to satisfy them we would need more strength than nature gives us. Therefore, diminish desires, and you will increase in strength. He who is capable of more than he desires has strength left over; he is certainly a very strong being.[22]

Guardian: Then are we seeing our state correctly?

Warrior: Because we are seeing in the depths, I would say we are beginning to see things correctly.

Guardian: The ego-body-octagon—because its primal drives are survival, thirst, hunger, and sex—knows no satiation. Once these drives become passions, they transform into appetites that lead the human being into a state of deprivation and desperation instead of freedom and flourishing.

> The passions take command of the will, intelligence, and spirit.
> This is how the soul is set into bondage, ignorance and darkness.

This is why we need the soul's powers to take command of the primal drives. When the soul takes command of the drives, the result is a flourishing and virtuous state. This is why we focus on bringing the soul into the powers, into the drives, into the knowledge, into the skills, and into the living. Now, can you see the kinetic chain that makes the soul powerful?

Warrior: Yes.

Guardian: The soul-sphere, not the ego-body-octagon, is the true source of power to combat the leviathan-cube.

Warrior: And you are telling me, most do not even know they are a soul in body?

Guardian: Yes.

Warrior: Are you telling me most think they are a mortal ego-body?

Guardian: Yes.

Warrior: And does it therefore follow that left to their own accord, these ego-body-primal-drives, in fact, are turned into insatiable passions that become the leviathan-drives needed to create and sustain the leviathan-cube?

Guardian: Yes. A man-made system designed for bondage instead of freedom. Man has created a structure that thrives from manipulating and unleashing these drives of survival,

---

[22] Rousseau, *Emile, or On Education.*

hunger, thirst, sex, and protection. In doing so, they created a desire to dominate instead of liberate.

Why do we keep trying to change the leviathan-cube (the structure) instead of changing the ego-body-octagon (the creator) by the powers of the soul-sphere (light and truth)? What if we allowed the soul to create the structures?

Warrior: These structures would be created by light and truth instead of the primal drives.

Guardian: The result?

Warrior: A city of truth. A city of light—Not utopian ideals, but realized powers of spirit demanding each generation to make them manifest, again and again.

Guardian: Just as one soul awakens, so too the fibers of society, its cultures, governments, industries, and religions, can be designed to awaken by the powers of light and truth we put into them by our leadership and management.

Warrior: The wise leading technology instead of technology leading the unwise.

Guardian: The leviathan-cube is the prison, not just the ego-body.

Warrior: What is the way to freedom?

Guardian: Let the sages and saints lead the way. The weapons they wield most are meditation and contemplation. Soon we will learn these weapons.

Warrior: You know what this means.

Guardian: Yes.

Warrior: Everyone must change. Everyone must awaken. Living is a contact sport. There are no spectators.

Guardian: Do we see correctly?

Until all souls, each generation, are educated and initiated into the path of truth, the manmade leviathan-cube simply reflects the state of our interior corruption and delusion. The leaders we elect, though we may not admire them, reflect the state of our interior nature.

What I mean—

All we create reflects the state of our interior nature. If it's created from soul, it's divine; if it's created from ego, it's wicked. The ego cannot create goodness and beauty. The ego is not designed with creative powers. It tries to dominate intelligence and creates distortions. The soul is designed to create beauty with intelligence. Do you see?

Warrior: I see. The insatiable leviathan-ego-body-octagon is fueled by unbridled desires.

Guardian: And what does this lead too?

Warrior: The source of all suffering and misery. We create it all.

Guardian: And how do you strike a dagger into the heart of this source of suffering?

Warrior: Good God. Strike the desires. Strike the passions. Practice mortification.

Guardian: The saints seem wise from this lens, do they not? Are they not interested in true freedom as liberation from this source? This is why wisdom makes the soul surrender all except virtuous living. Wisdom is the kinetic chain that leads to self-governing and self-cultivating souls, which then leads to self-governing and self-cultivating institutions, and ends in freedom.

What do we have instead of this kinetic chain?

Warrior: We have a kinetic chain of avaricious egos which lead avaricious institutions, and end in tyranny if successful.

Guardian: Our institutions have become dens of tyranny.

Warrior: What is the way out? What is the last geometric pattern you see?

Guardian: If there is a source of light and truth that educates and leads the soul, we need to know how to make contact.

Warrior: This is where you will explain how the soul becomes a giver, receiver and conduit of light and truth.

Guardian: Yes. Pay attention. This is the most important. The forth structure I see is an oval-sphere that represents the entire universe. It is infinite and eternal in dimension and essence.

We can call this the eternal-sphere.

This sphere is the fiber and fabric of all, the physical and the spiritual. The wise say that love is the source that binds the universe together. Now, let us return to Pythagoras.

> God, the **nature** of, declared by Pythagoras, to be the substance of truth.
> God, the **body** of, declared by Pythagoras, to be the substance of light.

We cannot claim to know what God is, and we will not call God a "Person" as we call a being a soul or a person in the anthropomorphic sense. We cannot create that injustice with our searching.

We can, instead, use the concept of being and the universe as a being, as cosmic light (as awareness) and cosmic truth (as intelligence).

In this sense, I see our concept of God as being the source that nourishes the light and truth of the soul. Where else can the soul go? Nothing on Earth can educate its eternal and immortal nature. This is why at night we gaze at the heavens. What if what we gaze at is Intelligence? How can we make contact with it? What is actually taking place in meditation and contemplation?

Warrior: I've never pondered these ideas. My existence has been rooted in warfighting and victory, not philosophy. I need the hard sciences to create systems, weapons, and gear.

Guardian: Except for those decisions in battle when *coup d'oeil* and *coup d'esprit* revealed the inner light and the inner courage needed for action. And you had to act in chaos by trusting your training and the light being revealed to you.

Warrior: Yes.

Guardian: Then you have direct experience with the mystical and the mysterious.

Warrior: Yes.

Guardian: Good. Saint Matthew mentors–

> But let your words be yes, yes, and no, no; for anything which adds to these is a deception.[23]

Now, what concepts would you place in this eternal-sphere?

Warrior: I see light. I see truth. I see actuality. I see energy. I see planets. I see solar systems. I see stars. I see sun. I see creation. I see timelessness. I see spirit. I see divinity. I see eternity. I see will. I see infinity. I see unity. I see peace. I see power. I see beauty. I see goodness. I see harmony. I see order. I see wonder. I see the unfathomable.

Guardian: We need to see the love that binds it all. Now, look at these four geometric structures when we arrange them in the following way. Do we see a path that leads to freedom?

Warrior: Yes.

Guardian: This is what we see–

> The soul-sphere envelops the ego-body-octagon.
> The leviathan-cube envelops the soul-sphere and the ego-body-octagon.
> The eternal-sphere envelops all three geometric shapes.

Warrior: I see.

Guardian: Do you see what this means?

---

[23] Holy Bible, *Book of Matthew*. Lamsa Translation.

Warrior: I see the soul-sphere placed within the body-octagon. I see the soul-sphere and the body-octagon placed within the leviathan-cube. I see the soul-sphere, the body-octagon, and the leviathan-cube placed within the eternal-sphere.

Guardian: Yes. Is the eternal-sphere a realm of freedom of being?

Warrior: Yes.

Guardian: Is the leviathan-cube in a realm of freedom of being?

Warrior: Yes.

Guardian: Is the body-octagon in a realm of freedom of being?

Warrior: Yes.

Guardian: Is the soul sphere in a realm of freedom of being?

Warrior: Yes. Because all that is, is within the essence of the eternal-sphere, the universe.

Guardian: If this is the case, then why are we not free?

Warrior: Because our species, in our methods and practices, rejects living from the soul-sphere and the eternal-sphere. We live in the deception of *samsara*, the endless cycle of birth and death in which life in the material and physical world is bound.

Guardian: You mean, each generation which is not taught what we are is by ignorance continuing this endless cycle of birth and death?

Warrior: Yes.

Guardian: Is this freedom of being?

Warrior: No.

Guardian: If we know the material of the physical body is destined for mortality, why does most human energy go to serving its physical needs instead of its spiritual needs?

Warrior: Our species has deceived itself that it is not immortal, that all it has is the experience of this one life.

Guardian: Is this freedom of being?

Warrior: No.

Guardian: Is freedom of being possible, here and now?

Warrior: By your speculations and the writings of the wisdom and sacred canons, yes.

Guardian: And what is actually seeking freedom on earth? The physical nature of the human being or the divine nature of the human being?

Warrior: You've finally wrestled it out of me. Don't tell anyone what I'm about to say. If it is possible, I dare say the soul-sphere or the divine nature of the human being is what seeks freedom—not physical, but metaphysical, freedom.

Guardian: Yes. We are hunting for nothing less than metaphysical freedom.

Warrior: Now I understand why Aristotle called the first philosophy, the divine philosophy, the being of beings, the metaphysics. I now see. I can see it. Many human beings are free in their human nature—powerful wills, emotions, bodies, intelligences, wealth, and talents—but, they are still not free. And they are not free because their soul, the divine nature, has not awakened its potencies.

Now I understand why decision-making can paralyze these kinds of people. When the calculative abilities fail them, they become gripped in fear. They cannot disclose the truth. They lack the moral courage to make a true judgment call, a courage that only comes to the conditioned soul that has been prepared to see truth as it reveals itself. This is why wealth generation attracts these weaker beings; it's essentially a calculative endeavor, quantitative instead of qualitative. And our art is essentially a contemplative and qualitative endeavor.

Guardian: Do you see the way out by the use of meditation and contemplation?

Warrior: You stated you hunt for leadership genius in the souls of the human beings before you. Your focus is to teach the leadership techniques of dialogue, inquiry, feedback, listening, discernment, meditation and contemplation.

Guardian: Yes.

Warrior: This is what I see–

You use these techniques to awaken and strengthen the light and truth of the soul. You use these techniques to awaken the soul's powers of will, intelligence, and spirit with light and truth. You use these techniques to move from the soul's light and truth, into the soul's powers of will, intelligence, and spiritedness, and then into the primal drives of protection, survival, thirst, hunger and sex.

Continuing this movement, I see the soul-sphere being ignited like a sun that dissolves the illusions of the ego-body-octagon and the leviathan-cube. I see this reaching the pinnacle when there is a union between the soul-sphere and the eternal sphere.

For a metaphor, I now see the ego-body-octagon and the leviathan-cube, when ordered properly, as a thin layer of clothing that the soul dons in mortal existence, yet at its pinnacle it's the least significant thing it knows, because it's been united with the light and truth of the eternal-sphere. This is what you mean when you say the soul learns to be a giver, receiver, and conduit of light and truth on earth.

Until just now, I did not see what you were doing. You were aiming for the soul to reach and stretch her powers through those layers, to make contact with the fabric and fiber of the eternal-sphere, which, for simplicity of language, you align with the concepts of light and truth.

When a soul stretches her light and truth to make contact with the source of light and truth, then the soul receives guidance, and can hear the call, and can be a co-creator with divine essence.

Now I see why meditation and contemplation are the core techniques to awaken and strengthen the soul. That is how the soul becomes aware of itself, and once aware, it's how the soul makes contact with light and truth. Then the soul needs to learn to trust the guidance it receives when it makes contact.

Guardian: Beautifully stated. Is this not a beautiful adventure?

Warrior: I wonder where all the spiritual teachers are?

Guardian: Don't you see, they are guiding us. Wisdom is the shepherd.

Warrior: Are we called to be living shepherds?

Guardian: Yes. We are the shepherds leading souls to light and truth. And aren't we also sheepdogs keeping the wolves of avarice and ego at bay?

Warrior: Yes. Then this is how I would describe the adventure–

There are two obstacles to transcend. **First, we need to transcend the ego-body-octagon. Second, we need to transcend the leviathan-cube, which is a macro-manifestation of the ego-body-octagon.** We transcend these obstacles by the practices of listening, dialogue, feedback, meditation, contemplation, discipline, wisdom literature and exercises. We make the ego-body-octagon, by exercise, a garment that we wear on earth. Then we bring in meditation and contemplation to expand the soul-sphere, to dissolve the power and effects of the leviathan-cube. We need to become free of its ensnaring. Its force cannot reach the depths of soul. This is why we live deep. In this war, we use the indirect approach. Taking it head-on, we would lose.

What I am seeing–

The soul-sphere, as it transcends, grows in dimension and magnitude. Its metaphysical power presses into the ego-body-octagon and the leviathan-cube. Visualize the soul-sphere's circumference in a state of continued expansion. In time, the soul experiences an infinite inward freedom and this freedom makes the ego-body-octagon and the leviathan-cube seem like a thin layer worn as an iridescent sheath that surrounds the soul-sphere in its mortal experience.

The soul-sphere continues its expansion and it then seems like there is no separation between the soul-sphere and the eternal-sphere. When this happens, that is what is called *enlightenment*. Meditation and contemplation are how the soul grows in power, expansion, transcendence, freedom and joy.

At this point, if we take a step back and look at the image of the model, it seems that the soul-sphere has merged with the eternal-sphere, except for a thin layer of the ego-body-octagon and the leviathan-cube. From this vantage point we see the harmony of the mortal and the immortal. We see the soul-sphere and the eternal-sphere united in light and truth, working with physical materials to give them form, both animate and inanimate.

And the purpose of conditioning the soul is not to obtain godlike powers, but to use light and truth to eradicate bondage, darkness, and ignorance.

Guardian: Yes.

Warrior: Then you declare that the light and truth expand the soul-sphere as sun-light illuminates our mornings, expanding true power. This is similar to the warrior's art, when we make contact and have to respond to that contact.

Guardian: Yes.

Warrior: Only in this art, this contact empowers but does not threaten the soul's movements.

Guardian: Yes. This is how dialogue awakens, when it is led with meditation and contemplation. Now we can see the importance of meditation and contemplation, to transcend these hidden obstacles. To make these obstacles unhidden. This is how we remove blindness; this is how we are given true sight. Even atheists can practice these techniques.

Warrior: That is a stretch. I don't know atheists who would follow your lead. They will follow mindfulness and neuroscience and psychology.

Guardian: Compassion for the great explainers. The great talkers. Saint Thomas warned of them when he said, to enter the mystic wine-cellar–

> Be slower still in frequenting places of talk.[24]

Warrior: But, not our dialogue?

---

[24] Saint Thomas Aquinas, "16 Precepts".

Guardian: Good God no. We are speaking soul to soul, light to light, truth to truth.

Warrior: You mean, we must take visual and hearing fasts, not just fasts from food, but from the media, the pundits, the politicians, the taking-heads, and social media?

Guardian: Good God yes. They poison the soul. They are the roots of the virus that attacks the mind. They are the ego-body-octagon and they suffer foolishness, acting like they know but they have no idea.

Go ahead, ask the babbling-class–

> Do you speak from the soul's light and truth?

> Do you know how to be conduits, receivers and givers of the light and truth?

They are the babble-class and they are venomous creatures suffering the pretense of importance. We must discipline our intelligence to focus on what is necessary and essential, what is timeless, eternal and everlasting. In this age, with hand-held computers that connect with satellites, why do people struggle with reading and comprehending a single passage of a sacred text?

Warrior: Why?

Guardian: The graphic revolution—the screen—the image. We must turn from the screen and let the intelligence awaken itself to strive for perfection. Our art demands the ability to think for one's self. To investigate for one's self. To meditate. To contemplate. To know. Our art places the leadership burden on each soul, each person, to practice, to experiment, to explore and hope to come into knowing as contemplative seeing. We are not after beliefs. We are after direct experience and methods that disclose truth to help guide leaders.

As Pressfield[25] warned, our enemy is the resistance of our ego-body-octagon. Our enemy is within. Our enemy does not want to conform its will and mind and spirit to the good and the true and the beautiful. The ego-body-octagon is going to resist this work. Once this work begins, the ego-body-octagon will be thrown into boredom. Its wants are insatiable and with boredom we plan to starve the wants and kill off the wants. The ego-body-octagon is not designed to study *thyself*.

For our art, the knowledge of thyself (Not *your*self. Not *your* personality. Not *your* predilections.) is the first study. This study of thyself is not only necessary, but is essential.

> If you know thyself, the soul, you know the thyself of all souls.

Warrior: Can you speak of your experience with Thyself?

---

[25] Steven Pressfield, *The War of Art*. Concept of *resistance*.

Guardian: The inspiration that created this spiritual framework is not mine. I don't claim it. I don't own it. There is nothing new to what we are doing. We are returning to simple and basic practices that are ageless. Wisdom is ancient. We are promised that insights reveal themselves through purification.

We need to understand what is taking place in meditation and contemplation. This framework is a helpful aid. All it is, is an aid. It claims no proof. It invites the explorer to seek a direct experience, and the direct experience with light and truth is beyond concepts and language.

Warrior: Does this mean, if every soul practiced these two techniques daily, it would revolutionize their being and experience on earth?

Guardian: Yes, once they become skilled, that is what I'm declaring, if it's done correctly and with rigor and with a trusted teacher. This has been my experience. When done correctly, there is purification and there is inspiration.

Warrior: Do your best to describe a direct experience.

Guardian: I return to the weekend retreats. Months of fasting, meditation, contemplation and detachment led to a release from the domination of my ego. It seemed as though my soul was released from the shackles of a metaphysical straightjacket. The freedom of release is otherworldly.

I experienced–

> An awareness of what might happen when we depart from this conditioned existence. I felt whole, complete, eternal and free. Timeless. Deathless. Immortal.

I remember during the experience thinking, in this weightless and spiritual ground, that this is what happens at death. It felt as though I had left my body but was still in my body. I was young, 27, when it happened.

After that experience, I felt marked, I felt branded, I felt I now lived a different type of existence.

> I found beauty.

> I also found it practical in the art of teaching leadership, because I was looking for what led to light and truth, humility and detachment, freedom and discernment.

Warrior: Then what?

Guardian: Then–

A decade of divine madness. A period of aridity, of uninspired and laborious work, to create development methods that were simple, non-religious and non-dogmatic.

Then, one aim–

Teach the soul to awaken and lead out her light and truth.

Then, two techniques–

Meditation to know light

Contemplation to know truth

Warrior: It is that simple?

Guardian: Many know the basics of chess. There are few chess masters. Many know the basics of religion. There are few saints.

Warrior: To learn our art, to be wielders of light and truth, to make knowledge, experiences and character an extension of the soul's being, we must learn how to train the basics to mastery?

Guardian: Yes. Now, we turn to examine meditation and contemplation. We need to come to know these two techniques intimately. We need to build a relationship with them. These are the two weapons, the two metaphysical swords, we need most for our art. And it is an art. There is no six-step program. There is no medication. There is no rote-memorization program. The more we wield these weapons, the freer we will be. The more we wield these weapons, the more knowledge and skill become extensions of our being.

Warrior: Onward to weapons training.

CHAPTER SEVEN
THE WEAPONS OF CONTEMPLATION AND MEDITATION

Writer: Dear Reader, our explorers do not realize, in their eagerness to learn the two techniques of light and truth, that they have entered into the deepest depths—the knowable unknown. This is their first attempt to venture past the edge of their knowing. As you may have noticed, they have been practicing, through dialogue, how to awaken the intelligence and how to awaken the wisdom-faculty in order to make contact with light and truth. This method is a mixture of meditation and contemplation. To be sure, they may be experiencing light and truth, but they do not know light and truth. They know the practice of dialogue. They know the practice of meditation and contemplation. But they do not know its source. Most importantly, they will soon find out, they do not know how to teach these techniques, even though they are skilled practitioners. They will become aware of the greatest source of their frustration—the inability to teach what they know; the inability to lead out their tacit and intuitive knowledge. As they attempt to summit and reach past their edge, they will enter the unknown. This unknown they will experience as darkness—not the darkness of the ego, but instead the darkness of their ignorance. Be patient and observe how they wrestle with difficult concepts, methods and techniques, to learn to see in the darkness as they transcend their ignorance. As Aristotle points out, contemplation is not acquisitive or possessive; it's an activity independent of one's command of it, and this fact should inspire all of us to pursue this activity of highest happiness. This is where we will see humility, detachment, and acceptance being brought to bear on these two souls. You may think these two souls are worthy of admiration, but they are nothing in the abyss of consciousness. This section of the dialogue serves to inspire the moral and intellectual courage needed to enter the unknown, again and again, when journeys reach a never-ending sea of impasses that must be continually traversed and overcome.

What we will see is that the best way to learn something or to know that you know something is to teach it. Not being able to teach something hints at not fully understanding it in the first place. The techniques will serve as the tools of this learning-to-teach method. This means once you read something or hear something, the next action is to break down the knowledge and concept for yourself in your own way. This is what John Boyd calls "unstructuring and uncoupling" and "destructive deduction" and "creative induction."[1] The next action is then to turn around and teach it to somebody else. As you're teaching the knowledge, you may find that some of the parts you thought you understood, you actually misunderstood from the beginning. This requires you then to go back and reread a section and break it down for yourself again, and then teach it to yourself once more. This is called the Feynman technique. The technique is ancient and the

---

[1] Frans P.B. Osinga, *Science, Strategy, and War: The strategic theory of John Boyd.*

Socratic method aims at the same end, understanding. In other words, knowledge is only truly gained when you are able to break it down in your own way and then teach it. If you can't teach it, do you really understand it? Is there something to the fact that if you can't teach it you haven't internalized and wrestled with it enough? The guardian and warrior know how to lead, but do they understand how to teach leaders? This is their goal—the understanding necessary to teach leaders. This is how the knowledge becomes unitive. It is our hope that they will discover this understanding and make this knowledge intuitive in their being.

Live in the light, The Writer

Guardian: The primacy of meditation and contemplation. Why?

Warrior: To know and wield light and truth.

Guardian: You mean, first to conform, to obey the light and truth. Then, second, to wield it.

Warrior: Conform? Obey?

Guardian: Yes. That is where I have erred for twenty years. That is how the ego, the personality, can keep us in darkness. To know is not enough. Our will needs to conform to the truth of being.

What is the greatest injustice the soul can commit after it receives the blessing of light and truth?

Warrior: I don't follow.

Guardian: The greatest injustice is when the ego, not the soul, bends and shapes the light and truth to its own ends. It is the greatest injustice as it directly harms ourselves and any gifts we might otherwise have to offer—to breed isolation, loss of true identity, and feckless searches for meaning. It is also the greatest injustice because it will ultimately harm others. As faux leaders, egotists breed human bondage, suffering, and even more ego-driven leaders following false gods.

Warrior: When the ego hijacks the soul's powers and controls and bends the light and truth to its will?

Guardian: Yes. We must become the light and truth bearers. We must become the pure ones. We must become custodians of the light and truth we receive, and give it as directed by the guidance we receive from it. We must continually be on guard against the temptation to use it for our own ends and our own gain.

Our adversaries use it for their own ends. They are the black magicians—the tricksters and grifters. They are the ones who strike the ego and the irrational desires and control the masses of humanity. They are our adversaries.

Do you follow?

Warrior: Yes. Grudgingly so. The ego is being triggered.

Guardian: That is the test, to come into correspondence with reality, objective reality, and adapt our being to it. Aristotle calls this "formal identity theory."

To help in our understanding, I turn to Kreeft's description–

> The very same identical 'form' or essences (appleness) that exists in reality
> (in the apple) materially and individually and concretely, is abstracted by the
> mind and exists in the mind immaterially and universally, and abstractly.[2]

Warrior: Ah. I see. This is humility. This is detachment. This is freedom. This is how knowledge becomes an extension of being. This is how we know—the knower becomes one with the known.

Guardian: Indeed. Merton mentors–

> We must know the truth and we must love the truth we know, and we must act
> according to the measure of our love.[3]

To learn to be conduits, we need to go deeper into consciousness. I am being let into a deeper realm.

Warrior: What are you seeing?

Guardian: It's a blinding darkness. I am blind.

Warrior: What? How so?

Guardian: I'm not pure enough to see here. I am not holy enough to see here. I've heard about this. The light, this light, because I don't know it, is experienced by my soul as darkness. Maybe we've entered the dark night. The light, its powers, render our sense-perceptions powerless. I do not perceive or see anything. The imaginative-faculty seems powerless too.

Warrior: Let your being come into contact with the darkness. See if an imageless image reveals itself.

Guardian: Seriously, it's imageless down here. It's peaceful. It's serene. It's, I dare say, freeing—in the darkness of this unknown as though something is tending to the soul, though I cannot see what it is or where it comes from.

Warrior: Ah. I think this is what Canfield said of the search for truth–

---

[2] Peter Kreeft, *Socratic Logic*.
[3] Thomas Merton, *The Ascent to Truth*.

one must live continuously in the abyss of the divine essence and in the nothingness of things...[4]

Guardian: Ah. Is this ego-shedding? The destruction of "I-ness" to merge into "is-ness"?

Here, the sense-perception and primal drives have been silenced in energy and desire. I don't experience the pressure to act here. I don't experience the pressure to know here. It's a strange peacefulness. Maybe the soul is returning home, and the peace is from anchoring into the flowing abyss of being. This is where contemplation leads, to help the soul regain its powers.

I remember reading about this, when Huxley wrote on contemplation–

> It is in imageless contemplation that the soul comes to unitive knowledge of reality...the fewer distracting symbols, the better.[5]

> The divine ground of all being, reveals itself to those in whom there is no ego-centeredness (nor even any alter-ego-centeredness) either of will, imagination, feeling, or intellect.[6]

God, I'm not pure enough. My ego, my will, my selfness are the obstacles now. The relentless struggle does not end.

Warrior: Guardian, no wonder you cannot "see." You are conditioned to see with physical sight; now you are being conditioned to see with inner sight. And physical sight does not really exist, so there is only truly inner sight. A very small width of wave length enters our eyes and ears. Then our brain must actively hallucinate the world, trying to make best guesses on what is going on, using our own history to fill in gaps and provide meaning. Once we accept that the wavelengths that enter into our many senses play a very minute role in understanding the world—that our minds are telling most of the story actively with very little outside data and no objective absolute data—we will understand the importance of inner sight. In the most literal sense, though it is not exactly what we are discussing here, we find that people who could see and later become blind realize this importance of inner sight almost immediately. They again and again explain how our brains are actively hallucinating the world, especially when we have working eyes. But I digress. Back to inner light in a deeper and less literal sense. This kind of contemplation is not for describing and documenting; it is for the soul alone to realize. Now, I see the difference between proving and realizing. We will use the highest height of contemplation as an art to learn practical judgment as a truth-disclosing activity. It seems simple to understand now.

---

[4] Huxley, *The Perennial Philosophy*. Canfield quoted.
[5] Huxley, *The Perennial Philosophy*.
[6] Huxley, *The Perennial Philosophy*.

Guardian: There is a drive igniting to go deeper.

Warrior: But you can't. We can't. And you want to know why?

Guardian: I know why. We still suffer the ego's bondage.

Warrior: Indeed. We are not purified.

Guardian: I cannot return. I need to be freed from this bondage.

Warrior: I think we've come far enough. We know enough to teach meditation and contemplation.

Guardian: This is why we fail. We know how to practice; we do not know how to teach.

Warrior: How so?

Guardian: I am still blind. I am lost and free in the abyss. I do not see the source that emanates light and truth, but I am experiencing its power and beauty. Why leave here and speak of it to others? No. I am not leaving here. I need to learn to see, here. This is where we practice the teaching art. This is where we will learn. This where we will cross another threshold.

Warrior: Wait. Are you saying that right here we need to heal our blindness with the sight of light and truth as it educates our souls?

Guardian: Yes. I am lost again, and I've learned that when lost, I wait to be found. The light and truth will find me and guide me. I hope to discover the source of what I seek. I cannot teach the truth about our art yet, even if I can practice it. We need an education.

Warrior: Guardian, you are not lost. You are underdeveloped and unskilled in this teaching art.

Remember, we are after *teaching disciplined leadership skill in the performance of actions*. This is what makes us trustworthy. Turn your intelligence from seeing in the abyss to seeing in the mind. What do you see?

Guardian: Ah. Okay. Self-reflection. Introspection. Self-discovery. A method to take an indirect approach instead of the direct approach to the apex of contemplative light and truth?

Warrior: Yes. What are you seeing?

Guardian: My intelligence is in knots, and it's wrestling to get free. I know meditation and contemplation. I know light and truth. I've practiced for twenty years. I live in a constant state of seeking, as objects, light and truth, both in the inner nature (the soul-sphere) and the outer nature (the eternal-sphere). Before I learned these techniques and sought these objects, I experienced great loneliness and isolation and exile as a human being on earth. I felt lost. Did not everyone know their lost-ness, I thought? Through these techniques, I experienced great oneness, great spiritedness and great friendship with, I dare say, existence itself, being itself, and by proxy, all beings themselves. Glorious—beings within being. What can I prove? Nothing. What have I mastered? Nothing. What have I achieved? Nothing. I'm no saint. I'm no sage. I've met these holy ones. What have I realized? I have experienced numerous moments of contemplative happiness and discernment. I've listened to an eternal call for decades. I have experienced moments of Joy. I have experienced grace. None of it was lasting, as I'm not pure enough in the realm of sacred truths. Nonetheless, I have experienced numerous blessings and graces in the activities of meditation and contemplation. I would be miserable without these sacred practices.

What path has been leading me? Socrates expressed it best, from the wisdom of Diotima–

> Anyone who wants to pursue this goal correctly must begin by turning to physical beauty, and then if he gets the right guidance fall in love with a particular individual and with her produce thoughts of beauty. He must then perceive that the beauty of one individual is similar to that in another, and that if beauty of form is what he is pursuing it is stupid not to recognize that the beauty exhibited by all individuals is the same. With that recognition, he becomes the lover of all physical beauty, and his passion for a single individual slackens as something of small account. The next stage is for him to reckon beauty of mind more valuable than beauty of body, and if he meets someone who has an attractive mind but little body charm, to be content to love and care for her and produce thoughts which improve the young; this again will compel him to look for the beauty in habits of life and customs and to recognize that here again all beauty is akin, and that bodily beauty is a poor thing in comparison. From ways of life he must proceed to forms of knowledge and see their beauty too, and look to the fullness of beauty as a whole, giving up slavish and small-minded devotion to individual examples, whether a woman, or way of life, and turning instead to the great sea of beauty now before his eyes. He can then in his generous philosophic love beget great and beautiful words and thoughts, and be strengthened to glimpse the one supreme form of knowledge, whose object is the beauty of which I will now speak…. For anyone who has been guided so far in his pursuit of love, and surveyed these beauties in right and due order, will at this final stage of love suddenly have revealed to him a beauty whose nature is marvelous indeed, which is the culmination of all his efforts.[7]

I cannot claim mastery of the art of contemplation and meditation; I can only claim regular practice and direct experiences with truth. Diotima simply expressed the upward path to where contemplation ends. I follow this upward path. I fail, fall, and get lost daily, but, I, each day,

---

[7] Plato, *Symposium*, Bloom translation.

endeavor to head back onto the upward path, to where it leads, no matter how long it takes. I would be hopelessly lost without the guidance of the sacred wisdom literature.

Warrior: This is similar to Socrates' call to perfect oneself to seek the source of the good and use it as a pattern for leading.

Let us return to his mentoring again–

> And when they are fifty years old, those who have preserved throughout and are in every way best at everything, both in deed and in knowledge, must at last be led to the end. And, lifting up the brilliant beams of their souls, they must be compelled to look toward that which provides light for everything. Once they see the good itself, they must be compelled, each in his turn, to use it as a pattern for ordering city, private men, and themselves for the rest of their lives. For the most part, each one spends his time in philosophy, but when his turn comes, he drudges in politics and rules for the city's sake, not as though he were doing a thing that is fine, but, one that is necessary. And thus always educating other like men and leaving them behind in their place as guardians of the city, they go off to the Isles of the Blessed and dwell…And ruling women too… Don't suppose that what I have said applies any more to men than to women, all those who are born among them with adequate natures.[8]

While we cannot claim to know light and truth, we have the aim. Knowing the aim is the critical piece. It is our X factor. The adventure leads us to this X and calls out for our subsequent actions. This is a blessing. We can claim to our students that to seek the X factor and to make the training more visceral, we use the techniques of meditation and contemplation, as activities to discover what *is* truth, what *is* beauty, and what *is* good. We will claim to use meditation and contemplation as acts of courage—to see if we are in truth, in light, in goodness and in beauty. This is our method of accountability. And this is true accountability. This is the deepest and most difficult part of integrity. This is how we will learn discernment as the technique to disclose the truth to make judgment calls. We can test the veracity of these techniques to see what is disclosed, with or without them, in these critical moments. We will claim to use meditation and contemplation as methods to ask courageous questions and see if through those questions, truth discloses itself. This is how we will make it practical. Can our students disclose truth in contemplation as a next action? This is how we will create daily tests and build disciplined skill in the act of practical judgment.

Guardian: We are discovering a beautiful and noble way of developing our leaders.

---

[8] Plato, *The Republic*, Bloom translation.

Warrior: Are you now seeing in the abyss?

Guardian: I don't feel as lost now.

Warrior: Go on. What are you seeing?

Guardian: In war, you set objectives, targets, and you seek to achieve those objectives by hitting those targets. And in war, based on strategy, the objectives and the targets can change. Correct?

Warrior: Correct.

Guardian: I am wrestling with a pull to change our objectives. This is what I set as our objectives–

> Teach leaders to give and receive light and truth.
>
> Teach leaders to make light and truth, as virtue and knowledge, an extension of their being.
>
> Teach leaders to lead out their tactical and intuitive knowledge in order to teach what they know.

I've used these objectives to lead us into the unknown. Now I am experiencing doubt. Are these objectives possible? Or am I simply chasing a ghost? I fear I've led us into a hunt for a ghost, a fiction, an image, not a teachable domain with teachable methods. As in war, should we change the objectives to simple human development and strategic thinking?

Warrior: Good God no, Guardian. Remember, don't quit. We are progressing every moment.

Guardian: It doesn't feel like progress. It seems the further we get the more we are sucked into the ground. It seems like, sometimes, the further we go, the farther from any goal we actually are. It's like a war in which the more resources we pour in, the further from victory we are. The questions we ask open up from questions and so on.

Warrior: Anything worth doing, any type of training, and any journey always seems this way while one is on the path. You never said this would be easy. Remember, we set out on a course where we will either discover these truths or perish on the summit.

Know this—your will and intelligence and spiritedness are being tested. On this journey, you are in a constant state of fatigue and weakness. This journey is a constant revelation of your imperfections and short-comings, no matter your past achievements and victories. You must act, knowing you are not self-realized nor God-realized. That is why we are to be trusted as teachers. We are servants. We are midwives. We are handmaidens. Our students know, regardless of our imperfections, we know how to awaken their depth and lead out their faculties, to learn this art. All you have to do is continually strike your will and intelligence in these depths. This is as it should be. You must rise above the fatigue and weakness and follow the light's lead. As you stated, light and truth know no fatigue, your will knows no fatigue, your intelligence knows no fatigue, and your spirit knows no fatigue. You know it is at this point when your humanness is at its weakest that the deeper potencies of the soul are awakened and realized. Draw in the light and truth and wield it in the darkness all around.

Guardian: Good God, the grip of self-will and ego-bondage! What is the drive of my conviction? Our objectives, our targets, are what enable one to lead with truth and excellence. My conviction is that we must learn to teach to our objectives, no matter how long it takes. Yes, I am willing to perish on this mountain. I will not turn back until leadership's truth reveals itself. I am at an impasse. Good. If this were easy, everyone would climb it and claim it. I conservatively estimated that I have 7,000 hours of practice in meditation and contemplation. Yet, I cannot teach? The cosmic joke is on me.

Warrior: A painful truth we both suffer. I suggest you describe what you actually do to get into meditation, to get into contemplation, to get into the light and truth. I think you are at an impasse because, in these depths, you need to speak of individual practices and experiences. You are experiencing the difficulty of leading out tacit and intuitive knowledge. Good.

In this realm, the realm of essence, the realm of beinghood, to transfer knowledge that you cannot find in a textbook, you have to transmit understanding almost as light and truth itself, form one soul to another. First describe the experiences. Then, we can draw out the teachable points, principles and actions. Our primary concern is how to make these principles come alive in the soul, to bring forth integrity in the soul. Now, I see why teaching this inner art is challenging—we must bring to life, to create in language, experiences that might not be within the grasp of words. Quite an impasse we've landed in.

Guardian: The knowable unknown.

Warrior: The unknown is not unknowable.

Guardian: Now, I see how effective transmission is from being to being, by the power of mentoring and apprenticing. Our art is classic apprenticing. We need our students to be along for the ride when they are in their formative years. We cannot just 'speak at' them.

Warrior: This is what we were not seeing. Our art is informal, occurring at all times and all the moments and spaces 'in between.' The liminal spaces. This is why we need the wisdom literature to mentor us. What you call peer mentoring is the blind leading the blind right now.

Guardian: Painful humor, my blessed friend. Yet we see, somehow, thanks to the literature.

Keep your patience. I must become still. I close my eyes. I sit in an easeful posture. I breathe deeply and rhythmically for 20 minutes to enter deeper into the abyss.

I'm observing the mind and the thinking. We cannot lie to ourselves. If we cannot teach this, we will have to lead by force of will and example, pulling the wills with us. We will be compromised and create superficial content with no depth, value, understanding or significance. We will be forced to say what we know is unknown and unknowable. And our students will have to trust us without demanding that we give an account. This is the root of blind obedience.

Warrior: We aim to teach, not to lead. We've led. It's time for others to rise.

Guardian: How do principles and techniques become an extension of being? How is this possible? How is this achieved? I keep seeing this as a relationship. The soul builds relationships with knowledge, and the soul and knowledge are activated in friendship. I see a living relationship, one of light and truth, awareness and knowing, and substance and nature.

I see love as a relationship that is formed when the soul's light and truth unites with knowledge's light and truth. I see this as a relationship that we must build. I see it as a friendship. That is how knowledge becomes an extension of our being.

I ask how to demonstrate what activates this knowing as a living relationship, through the techniques of meditation, contemplation and dialectics.

Warrior: You see the soul and knowledge, and the source of the soul and knowledge, as a relationship, as a friendship, as a beloved binding?

Guardian: Yes. That is what I am seeing. That is how it comes to be a living expression of our soul.

I am fearful that this is so. This is what sets the soul free from human bonds. This is how the soul is set free with a self-reliant bond to reality. It seems logically like a paradox. We let go of and transcend human bonding so the soul can awaken and bond with truth and light, and this is what leads to the inwardness and unconditional-ness of the sage.

The element of love, friendship, the beloved, to me are what is living when knowledge and soul fuse together.

Warrior: So the element of love, and by love you mean the act of will towards truth and goodness, is the missing element that makes this actualization possible?

Guardian: Good God, I don't know. This is what I am seeing light up before the sight of my mind.

A love of knowledge that leads the soul into knowingness—a oneness with the known.

A love that is beyond human belongingness and security. A love that is infinite spiritual potency. A love that is light's sunshine. A love that is the fiber and fabric of the living light and truth of the soul. I set this down as a speculative principle. I must be courageous and not let fear hold me back from what I'm seeing. This is how leaders remain strong, resilient and steadfast as they wrestle with chaos, conflict and disorder. They learn to move from the indefatigable powers of being.

Warrior: Do you see what the exploring is doing for you? How it is conditioning you? You are receiving a baptism in how to remain resilient when physical, emotional, and mental energies are weakening and fatiguing.

You are experiencing how to wield light and truth, in the practice of meditation and contemplation, you must practice selflessness and self-forgetfulness. You must aim for egolessness and desirelessness, so that light and truth can fuel, guide, and light the way for continued exertion and exploration. That is, I think, how we can say, "the soul learns to act beautifully."

Guardian: And love is an aspect of light? In addition to awareness and sentience?

Warrior: Love is the unlimited energy of metaphysical freedom. I'll allow it, if it helps you direct light into teaching these techniques.

Guardian: Again, cautiously, I am going to move deeper into the unknown.

Warrior: This is the first time I've seen you cautious. This means you are experiencing your weakness, your lack of command in the darkness of the knowable unknown light. Be courageous.

Guardian: I'm searching my intelligence. I must respect the sanctity of the autonomy of my intelligence. My mind is looking–

> What is the cause of this impasse?
>
> We have been practicing meditation and contemplation through dialogue. Do we need a different technique?
>
> What remains hidden? What aren't we seeing?
>
> Why can't we demonstrate the swordsmanship of these techniques?
>
> Why can't I see the source of light and truth?

Warrior: We may be too attached. We may be too close. Bring in this principle from Musashi–

> To see the faraway as nearby and the nearby as faraway is essential to martial arts.[9]

---

[9] Miyamoto Musashi, *The Book of Five Rings*.

Guardian: To keep what is far close and what is close far?

Warrior: Yes. Distance yourself from the impasse. Let it be far away. Study your methods with distance. What are you seeing?

Guardian: Wait. It does not matter if I see the source of light and truth; we are living in light and truth, the essence of the eternal-sphere, the universe, at all times. I don't see, but I do experience it. I am going to let what I cannot see act upon me. I am going to open to it. Is this the first step to receptivity?

Warrior: The quality of openness is now a guiding principle.

Guardian: This openness means we will be open, instead of closed, to a range of suffering and pain.

Warrior: This is how we can practice compassion.

Guardian: Not being afraid to suffer spiritual anguish, but welcome it, as a fire of purification.

I need the courage to define meditation and contemplation in my own words.

> Meditation is how the will distances itself from the mortal, the conditioned, the emotional, the primal nature (ego).

> Meditation is how the will becomes aware of the immortal, the eternal, the substance, the light.

> Meditation is how the will receives light, gives light and expresses light in goodwill, charity, and freedom.

> Meditation is how the will seeks freedom of being—independence from conditioned and mortal existence, independence from the will and judgments of other mortals.

> Meditation is how the will (inner reality, subjectivity) turns to reality (outer reality, objectivity).

> Meditation is how the will learns harmony by conforming itself to reality.

> Essentially, meditation is how the will builds the virtue of humility and the virtue of detachment.

> Contemplation is how the intelligence takes command of the mind's sea of thoughts.

> Contemplation is how the intelligence corresponds with truth.

Contemplation is how the intelligence responds to events with actions of detachment, humility and wisdom.

Contemplation is how the intelligence comes to knowing and understanding.

Contemplation is how the intelligence informs the will to act.

Contemplation is how the soul first learns truth-disclosing.

Essentially, contemplation is how the intelligence builds the virtues of practical judgment, discernment, and wisdom.

Warrior: Guardian, very good. Why light and truth? Why meditation and contemplation?

Guardian: They are the causes of the leadership effects of humility, detachment, practical judgment, discernment, and wisdom. We are after the cause that produces the leadership effects.

Leadership is a second order effect of the primary causes.

Warrior: Can you give this to another human being?

Guardian: No, each human being must fulfill the conditions necessary in the nature of their being for the effects of these virtues. The cause is found in each human being, in her inner nature. What I am seeing is that meditation conditions my interior being to be pure and free by receiving light, and contemplation makes my intelligence pure and free by receiving truth. I do not know how this is possible. I just know the experience. I know, when I did not practice these two techniques I felt confused and lost and made many mistakes. I know, by practicing these techniques, I experience clarity and unity and make fewer and less grave mistakes. My conscience becomes free and serene when I practice these techniques. I know that the effects are worth the effort of training the causes, as they lead to a life of simplicity, beauty, meaning, and purpose. I know, through these techniques, I become aware of a guidance that calls and challenges me to strive deeper and deeper into the mystery of being. I know, by these techniques, inner and outer suffering has been reduced to an insignificant degree. Now I am concerned with the welfare of all humankind. This is what I am seeing.

Warrior: Beautiful. I will continue in the direction of this movement.

What I am seeing–

These two techniques help leaders connect deeply with the human beings they lead. To use your language, it makes them trustworthy to lead souls engaged in challenging human endeavors.

What I am seeing–

In our art, what is essential and necessary is for our leaders to care about the inner development of the souls in their stewardship. In our art, we seek to guide the soul's liberation by encouraging it to make contact with light and truth. In our art, we guard against the easy way out—manipulation. Our adversary uses manipulation. Only free beings can withstand the stratagems of manipulation.

In our art, truth-seeking leads to liberation, leads to freedom of being, leads to the flourishing state of awakening potencies. This is our art. That is why we practice meditation and contemplation, because what guides the leader is truth.

Guardian: In our art, leaders are both shepherds and builders. In our art, this is where we learn to enter deep states of grace and serenity, to receive insights and guidance to strengthen the will to produce the moral courage that is necessary to act on higher guidance. This higher guidance always runs counter to the prevailing currents, the thinking and the passions, be they professional or personal.

I am experiencing a wave of grace descending upon my soul's will and intelligence. I need to be still.

Warrior: Let us be still.

Guardian: This is what I am seeing in the mind–

We used dialogue as a learning and teaching method. We explored two frameworks to take command of knowledge and transform it into an extension of our being. Are we now experiencing a transformation? Are we now changing? Is a transformation taking place simply by the activities which guided our exploring?

Warrior: A warrior is transformed differently from a soldier. A guardian is transformed differently from a professor. Are we being transformed to be educators of leaders?

Guardian: What does it do to the soul to establish light and truth as its aim, means, and end? We have been led by two techniques, the central methods to know, to receive, to give, and to wield light and truth. We use meditation and contemplation to learn how to awaken and actualize latent potencies of light and truth. Our essence and nature and powers have been constantly challenged and activated with each movement of exploring.

Warrior: Wait. We don't need to see light and truth to teach to seek light and truth. We don't need to be masters; we only need to know what to practice. We need to teach students what to practice. That's it. In our art, we are never separated from the students; we are with the students—a living river of light and truth by activity and being, not by possession or acquisition. Contemplation means we never acquire the whole truth. We disclose it movement by movement in the act of living.

Guardian: This is why humility is demanded of us. We never control or command truth.

Warrior: This means we never arrive. We never finish. Our art must be lived. This means we are in flux as both teacher and student. This means we will never have "full, complete, and unabridged" knowing. It's not a destination even if we know the aim; it's a journey, ultimately.

Guardian: That is why our art is a way of being, teaching and serving. This is how these techniques, in a dynamic and cyclical fashion, make knowledge, expertise, and character an extension of being. It's the dynamic cycle of being and becoming.

Warrior: Then, I see–

For leaders to take command of the known, temporal, and practical challenges, they must undergo training in making practical judgments (prudence, practical wisdom) by experiencing the knowable unknown in order to learn truth-disclosing activities.

Guardian: Good God, what are we seeing? We need to be with our students in the knowable unknown so we can confirm the truths they disclose.

Warrior: Yes. In our art, the training is more rigorous than the act of leading.

Guardian: Good. That is what I hoped.

Warrior: Our leaders must become virtuous first—I mean the practice of virtuous development which is non-stop. This is where they will undergo the most painful interior trials.

Guardian: I am still experiencing these painful interior trials.

Warrior: This is where they will learn they are insignificant.

Guardian: This insignificance they will learn by observing the fact that reality ejects every one of us. We have all been sentenced to death by being born in mortal bodies.

Warrior: They will learn of their interior weaknesses. This will be a period of non-stop humility-making.

Guardian: I am still made aware of my interior weaknesses.

Warrior: Then, once the character is set, we will teach truth-disclosing by leading them into the knowable unknown. Simple to state. Difficult to know, train, and teach.

Guardian: The light is still blinding when I turn to it. We might need a guide to show the way through this impasse.

Warrior: You mean, to ask for help?

Guardian: Yes. The vulnerability to ask for help. I've learned, when I get stuck at an impasse, and I've been circling for too long, I must seek out a master to help guide me through the impasse.

Warrior: Now is not the time. We are progressing and traversing.

Guardian: You mean we have not wrestled enough with this impasse.

Warrior: Guardian, we are in the depths of consciousness and the heights of knowledge, where do you suggest we turn for help?

Guardian: My good man, I don't mean quitting and turning around, I mean the teachers will find us, here and now, by the light and truth.

Warrior: Strange soul you are.

Guardian: Has it occurred to you where we are at, on this journey?

Warrior: Yes. We have entered the deepest depths.

Guardian: It's time to pull out the sledgehammer of introspection.

Warrior: Have you not already been doing this?

Guardian: Yes. You reminded me that a basic technique when at an impasse is introspection. I aim to see. I aim to heal this blindness. The sledgehammer of introspection can sometimes be violent. The clarity of new vision can burn.

Warrior: Strike away. Blast away.

Guardian: Ah, I see the stream of thinking. What you and I know is of little significance. What you and I have experienced is of little significance. As beings, you and I are of little significance. Leading—in the main—is easy. Achievement is easy. Leading souls is hardship. Shepherding is burdensome. Removing ignorance is relentless and provides no harbor. We have failed as educators. Our leaders and each generation have failed.

Ranke mentors us–

> Each generation is equidistant from God.[10]

Who can comprehend and teach the way to reality, soul, spirit, light, truth, meditation, contemplation, leadership, and wisdom? The path is vague, ambiguous, abstract.

Where do these questions come from?

> How does the soul remember what it is, where it came from, and what it is here to do?

> How to teach souls to blast through the darkness by connecting to light and truth?

---

[10] Jacob Burkhardt, *Judgments on History and Historians*. Ranke quoted.

Why the resistance to these questions?

> There is no soul; there is no light; there is no truth; there is no reality; there is no free will; there is no eternal law; there is no natural law; The human being does what he wants; there are no consequences. Give up. Quit. No.

Trust *via negativa*, not *via positiva*. Reduce to the necessary. Reduce to the essential. Reduce to bare-boned essence. Fight from substance and essence.

> Practice no holds-barred intellectual development—bare-knuckle truth fights.

More questions–

> Is not being-hood infinitely more truthful than bone, blood, flesh, and survival?

Fight with faith to leap from the limits of human knowledge. Wait. Do you lack faith? Do you fail because you lack faith?

> Faith lives in the knowable unknown.

> Faith moves in the knowable unknown.

> Faith never runs counter to reason—Faith leaps from reason's soundness.

> Beware of anti-rationalism and anti-intellectualism. Beware of the anti-truthful. Beware of false-bearers.

Warrior: Now, in these depths, we bring to bear the virtue of faith. Faith is the weapon to blast the impasse of darkness and blindness, to disclose the light and truth in the knowable unknown. Our art is combat. Now I see its combative nature.

Guardian: What are you seeing?

Warrior: This is what I've captured–

The vision and understanding to know and to teach contemplation and meditation is combative. There is an adversary. We don't see the adversary. Contemplation and meditation are combative methods we use for fighting in the darkness. Light and truth will reveal themselves if we are virtuous enough; we only need our character to be 51-percent virtuous / 49-percent vicious on the scales of Justice.

Guardian: Good. That is where I've been. At any moment I can turn from light to darkness and I pay for it each time.

Warrior: I see–

In methods to transmit knowledge into ability we are seeing the importance of mentoring and apprenticing, to transfer the knowable unknown as a kinetic chain from teacher to student, then student to truth.

To demonstrate the swordsmanship of contemplation and meditation, the students first need light and truth to strengthen their will and intelligence. Then they'll be able to take their will and intelligence, and wrestle with knowledge and insights on one side, and opinions and deceptions on the other. This will keep them on guard against being manipulated—teaching them to see in the darkness.

Guardian: Are we also seeing that the human being, left to his own faculties, without the aid and guide of mentors, will not even know this is possible?

Warrior: That is what we are seeing. Let me ask, who taught you this?

Guardian: Ancient wisdom.

Warrior: Then, you did not have a teacher who taught you how to meditate and contemplate and seek light and truth?

Guardian: No. There are very few true teachers. They exist, but I did not meet them until decades after my formative years. I've been cleaning up the wreckage ever since.

Warrior: So you had no mentor who spent hundreds of hours teaching you.

Guardian: No.

Warrior: But you became aware of these possibilities when you read the ancient texts.

Guardian: Yes.

Warrior: Then this is the challenge: we must teach students these techniques, and we must teach students how to approach these wisdom texts as living teachers who can guide in the absence of true living teachers.

Guardian: Yes.

Warrior: This is why our art, I think, right now, is too overwhelming for most souls on earth. They are wholly underdeveloped. The spark of light and truth has been veiled. And you hope to gently lift the veil for the students of our art, and let in the light.

Guardian: Yes. That is why education and guidance is critical for our leaders. Our art, a teaching art, leads to a flourishing state of the soul's being-at-work. Our art, a teaching art, leads the soul to awaken her inward potencies, in order to realize and actualize her full powers.

Again and again, let the questions lead us–

How are the powers of the soul activated?

How are inner light and truth awakened?

How do inner light and truth reach upward to outer light and truth?

In our art, we must have the courage to asking these questions. In our art, we live in the depths of these questions. I imagine the soul, strengthened by meditation and contemplation, transforms into a torch bearer, to blaze like a radiant sun and dissolve the darkness, the ignorance and the bondage, and reveal the light, the truth, and the freedom in the being of each soul.

Sachs mentors us here–

> Etymologically, the Greek word for truth means something like 'what emerges from hiddenness.'[11]

By unhiddenness, the soul will see and know that the conditioned existence of the body is simply a garment, a piece of material being, to be worn like an iridescent cloak until it's necessary to depart at the time of death and let the cloak fall away. That, I imagine, is beauty and freedom.

Warrior: Beauty, freedom, truth, are the values you hold dearest.

Guardian: Yes. To achieve this and these values, I imagine, the soul needs to become skilled in techniques that wield her powers. I declare, the soul cannot be manipulated; only the ego can be manipulated. Our students will learn to wield the courage of the soul to counter and transcend the survival drives of the ego-body.

Warrior: And that is what we seek to take command of, the primal drives, by the techniques of meditation and contemplation.

Guardian: Yes.

Warrior: Now I see how your experiences shaped your thinking. Now I see how these techniques lead from the abstract to the concrete experience. Now I see the nature of the soul is to reach up, and extend into light and truth to free herself from the darkness and the ignorance that has veiled her and kept her in bondage—in a metaphysical prison. Can we describe this as consciousness expanding? I have had similar experiences.

Guardian: What did you do to expand consciousness?

Warrior: I practiced mindfulness and ego-shedding. But I never thought of what it was, that was shedding its ego.

---

[11] Plato, *Theaetetus*, Sachs translation.

Guardian: You blessed fellow. You mean the soul is the ego-shedder? You never thought you were a soul?

Warrior: No. I thought, I am a human being with consciousness and I have desires that I need to wrestle into submission, to keep me in a free state of mind when leading.

Guardian: Wait. Do you reject the idea of soul? Our art is to come to know the soul, first by exercising her perennial and primordial powers, then by her virtues of humility and detachment to transcend the ego's primal drives and desires.

Warrior: Initially I did reject your idea of soul, light and truth. In my mind, when you used those concepts I replaced soul with consciousness, I replaced light with awareness, and I replaced truth with intelligence. I did not contest your concepts and methods because I aimed to be a good advisor and let the dialogue flow, and explore the adventure of what you are seeing, even though it is quite different from what I see.

Guardian: Wait. Is not the essence of our concepts the same in being? Am I in error? If so, should we replace–

> Consciousness for soul
> Awareness for light
> Intelligence for truth
> Mindfulness and ego-shedding for meditation and contemplation
> Expanding consciousness for illuminated awakening?

Warrior: My courageous and truth-seeking friend, not now. I am seeing your concepts differently now. I am building a relationship to your concepts and letting their essence act upon my consciousness, my soul. For now, let these other concepts hover around in a holding pattern. We can return to them and reach up to them, if we need them.

Guardian: I am reminded of Hunter S. Thompson's waxing lyrical perspective no matter how fueled by mind-altering chemicals–

> No sympathy for the devil; keep that in mind. Buy the ticket, take the ride...
> and if it occasionally gets a little heavier than what you had in mind, well...
> maybe chalk it up to forced consciousness expansion: Tune in, freak out, get
> beaten.[12]

HST reminds me of a person experiencing divine madness and not accepting it. In our art, we are interested in knowing the purpose of leading consciousness expansion—the transcendence of the conditioned existence.

---

[12] Hunter S. Thompson, *Fear and Loathing in Las Vegas*.

Warrior: On divine madness—how else could he create gonzo journalism, as being-in-it, not separate from the events he reported on. He was not only aware that his own observation of unfolding events changed those events, but also wore this phenomenon with open glee. Ah, now I see—suffering from divine madness and not knowing it, lost souls turn to mind-altering substances to slay the internal pressures of ego-body-octagon to experience the soaring light of the true free spirit—the sage, the yogi, the mystic.

Guardian: And, by forcing, instead of leading, consciousness-expanding, HST got crushed by the ego-body-octagon. Same with Hemingway—geniuses in their art, corrupted in their souls. The prison of the soul can be opened by the substances. But this openness is not from true power. The openness does not last. The internal pressures return and are heightened. The soul is still in a metaphysical prison. It only knows freedom with the aid of an altering substance to silence the ego. This is why, in our art, we train, we expand, we become powerful from the inside out.

You shared two practices–

> Mindfulness
> Ego-shedding

Warrior: My take on how to achieve the same ends of meditation and contemplation–

> The will to true knowledge
> The will to true and good action

Guardian: How do you practice mindfulness and ego-shedding?

Warrior: That is no small task you are asking of me. I thought I was here to support you? Now you are making me sweat with this challenge to give an account.

Guardian: Just do as you recommended me to do. Speak simply. What are the movements of your thinking? What are you seeing?

Warrior: For context, I witnessed first-hand the human madness of the ego and its horrific acts after not being held in check and not being restrained, but being let loose unbridled and unrestrained in war and violence.

Guardian: The absence of self-restraint and self-denial—I bet no one taught those leaders how to shed the ego. I bet non-stop unrestrained freedom was valued and rewarded in their performance and achievement.

Warrior: Point 1: No, never. Point 2: Yes. It seems to me the ends of actions, the rewards of performance and achievement, fuel, rather than strip, the ego's thirst for power, glory, and honor. We reward the ego-body-octagon because the system of measurement and achievement is created by the ego-body-octagon, not the soul-sphere.

Guardian: Good God! Human Madness veiled as sanity—we have discovered the roots again.

Now, I understand. Now, it makes sense. Generals (men of rank), executives, marketers, and politicians thrive from ego, and the ego is rewarded for its thirsting and thriving in the ends of advancement, achievement, and adoration.

Warriors not generals, stewards not executives, sustainers not marketers, statesmen not politicians, shepherds not governors: this is what is needed. These former beings are created from the soul-sphere; these latter beings are created from the ego-body-octagon.

Warrior: Selfish-focused instead of purpose-focused.

Guardian: Are we seeing the roots that lead to power and domination instead of freedom and liberation? Is this why egotists and narcissists are at the helm of our institutions? They are built to find and reward these self-centered natures. Souls have no desire and drive to dominate. They know those drives are weak, immature and brutish, with nothing to show for them but pain.

Warrior: My good man. I think we are seeing truthfully—finally, some light. I think we are seeing a way through this impasse to the beauty and freedom of true understanding, an understanding that does not need to be omniscient. The route is through understanding what we are seeing in the act of living, and then responding accordingly with truth and goodness.

I see the ego as the primal self, the brutish self, and its nature is a beastly wildness with no interest in seeking and conforming itself to light and truth. Its only interest is unbridled physical power and dominance of nature and beings.

I learned as I matured as a leader that the ego's drive for power and dominance blinds the leader to the higher leadership arts—operational and strategic, command and management–because these high arts need practical judgment, discernment, and wisdom.

Because I saw this blindness in my superiors, I wanted to know its cause. Being a scientist—an observer questioning everything—at heart, I sought knowledge in psychology, psychiatry, and neurobiology. This search led to a serious study of cognitive biases and a practice of ego-shedding. The two main practices I've used that most leaders who are blinded do not are the daily practices of self-reflection and mindfulness. It's made all the difference. I do not fail as often because of this practice.

Guardian: Ah. I think I see another practice—self-reflection, not just introspection. What does ego-shedding aim at?

Warrior: Removing the blind-spots. Removing blindness. Seeing past the tiny few wavelengths that crash against our irises.

Guardian: A key cycle, in our art, is beginning to reveal itself. The intellectual activities of this cycle are self-reflection, introspection, discernment (to identify blind-spots), and self-knowledge (to remove blind-spots). It's a cycle designed to generate new insights and understanding. This is a practical, self-corrective method of being and becoming. Professionally, what do we call this cycle, this practice?

Warrior: The AAR cycle, the after-action report, a performance feedback technique. And what you mean, and what we have just drawn out, is the critical need to create a character feedback technique.

Guardian: Dialogue. Meditation. Contemplation. They are self-correcting feedback techniques to disclose truth and Insights. And to increase knowing and understanding.

Warrior: All this leads to truth-based freedom of movement.

Guardian: So, when we teach leaders these techniques, the purpose, when they ask, is to create a built-in feedback mechanism to help them grow in character and excellence, and to increase their capacity for freedom of movement in a non-egotistical and truth-centered way.

Warrior: Yes. Now we can, with command, bring in the spiritual cycling model and reconfigure it for performance cycling. I am starting to see the patterns and how it's becoming integrated between person, skill, relationship, organization, and purpose. I am seeing the wholeness and union of all these concepts.

Guardian: That is contemplation—seeing the whole in an instant.

Warrior: Now I see it. Now, when you describe the technique of meditation, this is what I mean by mindfulness.

By mindfulness, I mean self-reflection–

Being in silence and alone with my mind, and observing the thoughts swirling around in my mind. I practice by a dual method of seated silence and self-reflective journaling. Each night, after the chaos of the day, I make a list of what went well and what did not. Based on frustrations and challenges, I assess what I read accurately, what I misread, and what needs to be corrected. Then I let the subconscious mind go to work when I sleep. I use sleep as a great method to work out problem sets.

I must stress, self-reflection is anchored by putting pen to paper. Putting pen to paper makes the mind clarify its thinking and strengthen its thinking—its intellectual powers. It invites questions. It sharpens thoughts. It shows cognitive weakness—naked on the page without passion or prejudice. It shows the things that once were solid to be weak. It exposes things that perhaps once seemed weak to be well substantiated. By writing, we produce deeper thinking, and by deeper thinking we produce more insights—we learn to disclose the truth.

When I speak of mindfulness, I adhere to the Samurai swordsmanship principle.

Takuan Soho mentors us here–

> Never let mind rest in one place, let it gaze in the whole field of perception.[13]

This is, I think, how contemplation awakens the soul's powers—to see the whole in an instant, beyond discursive thinking—to see intuitively. This gazing reveals insights. Writing is a way to practice this insight-revealing ability. We gaze meditatively at what we are writing, using the full powers of the intellect.

Guardian: Is this not an example of how to practice practical judgment as a truth-disclosing activity? You used "insights" and I could easily interchange "truth-disclosing" and "insight-generating." Both concepts hold the meaning we seek. For a scientist, your practices sound more intuitive than based in symbolic logic and deductive analysis, as you plumb the depths of consciousness.

Warrior: That is why I am intrigued with your perspective.

I am most intrigued by how knowledge, character, and expertise become an extension of one's being, which leads to an effortless and intuitive ability to respond. I am beginning to see that our art may not take place in the brain, in the ego-body-octagon, where I always thought it did. I am beginning to see that in our art, if this soul-sphere is real, this is what is exercised, trained, and freed.

Let me explain what I am seeing–

Training for combat is a deliberate, regimented and logical process of the non-stop repetition of tactics, to prepare for war. However, there is a crucial moment in development, when the warrior is freed from the step-by-step regimented process, and this moment tends to reveal itself on the battlefield.

What I mean–

The demands and intensity of combat trigger a heightened state, as though, even in the violence, a calm and still and fluid ability unites the unit and the warrior into an integrated and intuitive nature, which moves and responds with harmony, rhythm, coherence and resonance.

Guardian: It seems you mean, instead of moving as a system, you move as a living and self-correcting organism?

Warrior: Indeed. You extracted the concept that I know well, from first-hand experience, in John Boyd's strategic thinking.

---

[13] Takuan Soho, *The Unfettered Mind.*

Organisms must also cooperate and harmonize their activities in their endeavors to survive as an organic synthesis.[14]

The experience in Zen is *satori*, a state of heightened awareness and ability. It is strange that it reveals itself in combat.

Guardian: It reveals itself to beings who train for mastery—the one-pointedness of focus, letting go of all else but the activity.

Warrior: Yes. The intensity, the demand, the focus, the training, the one-pointedness of endeavor seems to reveal the spiritual fabric of inner harmony and intuitive perception. And, I dare say, the moment reveals the actual experience of oneness and transcendence in violence, not in spite of it.

Yes, it is an experience of transcendence, of rising above one's self. While we do not practice meditation and contemplation as individual skills, the way we train is essentially contemplative and meditative, if you mean the power to move with mastery and freedom against an adversary.

I am seeing the connecting threads now. Training for combat, if I look at it from a different angle, requires operations of mind that seem akin to the operations at play in contemplation and meditation. If I substitute the physical contact for intellectual contact, it seems the mind is working in a similar way.

Guardian: Then just as you master techniques that become an extension of your being in combat, we aim to master techniques that become an extension of our being in leading.

Warrior: How do we teach this?

Guardian: By taking each leader on metaphysical journeys, as we are doing now, for years of sustained development. There's no bypassing this preparatory training. Can we speculate that our art demands that the soul become lucid and intuitive?

Warrior: Yes.

Guardian: Can we speculate that the only way to realize this is for the soul to awaken the depths of its being?

Warrior: Yes.

Guardian: Can we speculate that when the soul awakens its light and truth, it will experience true freedom, harmony, and rhythm?

Warrior: Yes.

---

[14] Frans P.B. Osinga, *Science, Strategy, and War: The strategic theory of John Boyd.*

Guardian: Then we must set down meditation and contemplation as the techniques to awaken this lucidness and intuitiveness. These qualities of soul, when fused with rigorous training and skill acquisition, makes one's leadership ability an extension of one's being.

Have we found the route through this impasse?

Warrior: Yes.

Guardian: We learned we do not need to be omniscient. We learned we need understanding to be flexible and adaptive in constantly changing environments.

Warrior: Yes. I know first-hand, this takes place in warrior cultures. Now that I've reflected on it, true warriors are a mystical-kind-of-being. Without this mystical aspect I cannot call someone a warrior. He is a fighter, a soldier, a killer, not a warrior.

Guardian: I have seen this mystical-kind-of-being with my own eyes too. Are we seeing more clearly what we are hunting for, when we say we hunt for leadership genius in the soul of the human being?

Warrior: Yes. We are seeing truth with increased understanding. The spirit of the man, the spirit of the woman, is what we hunt for.

Guardian: Then, meditation and contemplation aims to get to the spirit of the human being?

Warrior: Yes.

Guardian: Leadership genius strikes from the spirit of the human being?

Warrior: Yes.

Guardian: Now, what happens if we do not reconfigure the abstract, intelligible, nature of light and truth into concrete, tangible and teachable frameworks and methods?

Warrior: We will fail. Our aim will be rejected. Our aim with not be measurable. Our aim will be without substance. If we cannot measure it, we cannot give an account. If we cannot give an account, leaders will not be able to measure their progress.

Guardian: This is why I failed in the past. I knew the techniques but I did not know how to measure them in sustained efforts. This is why we will take an indirect approach in the beginning, and why we will focus on tangible domains and theories. Students can build strength by studying these domains, and they can practice building a relationship to them. The study of Aristotelian logic would crush them. At least, it crushed me. But our aim is to produce virtuous beings who have been conditioned to seek truth, and to know truth and to act on the truth they know.

Warrior: This is how I make sense of what we are conceiving–

Our aim, through training, awakens the light and truth, the spirit of a leader. We declare that the composite and conditioned human being is more than a conscious, mortal body with thoughts, feelings, and desires. We declare that the human being is a composite-conditioned-being, made of both physical and spiritual elements, simply delineated as body and soul. We declare that to produce abilities in our art, it is critical to get to the spiritual elements of the being, to awaken the soul's powers. We declare that the process of igniting light and truth serves a two-fold purpose–

> First, it acts as a purifier to lift the veil of darkness and ignorance, thereby receiving and knowing light and truth.

> Second, this knowing light and truth is what does the heavy lifting in the art of practical judgment, or truth-disclosing and insight-generation.

We declare, to do this we need a set of concepts and techniques that form the basics of workable and repeatable practices, which can produce and sustain skilled leaders. I return to the martial arts—our art is the art of the Giver and the Receiver. We declare that the techniques we set down produce this ability. We declare, when leaders mature, they will have the skill to reveal what is hidden and the courage to act on what is revealed.

> Truth-disclosing as what emerges from hiddenness

We declare, when they mature in this ability, they are the ones who will deserve to be followed.

Guardian: Beautifully stated.

Warrior: Now, in the leadership arts, we need to master the weapons to fight this battle, to engage in combat, to slay darkness and ignorance by the powers of light and truth. This is a war, a war that is fought by non-martial violent means. We, and our leaders, need to master the art of striking the soul to awaken its light and truth. Then, when awakened, darkness, ignorance and deception lose their hold. This is the transformation from metaphysical bondage to metaphysical freedom.

Guardian: If we take a look back and practice self-reflection, what weapons have we discovered and what have we been practicing this entire expedition?

Warrior: Now that I have the concepts, now that my intelligence is being informed by these concepts, when I look back, this is what I see–

We have been practicing moral and intellectual virtues—patience, detachment, listening, humility, faith and fortitude. And, most strikingly, without realizing it, we have been practicing meditation and contemplation.

Guardian: Now do you see how similar are the mind-sets and characters of the warrior and the leader? But only that the methods and aims are different?

Warrior: It's a stretch, but yes, if you mean the dedication and devotion and singleness of mind to learn an art. You are seeing a specific kind of leader, one who embodies the virtues of a warrior as defender and the virtues of a guardian as protector. I see you looking to build a leadership archetype based on these two archetypes. I see you doing this to establish a pattern of what-ness for leaders to aim at realizing. I see in all three archetypes the same essence, nature, and character, independent of the domain-specific skills.

Guardian: Then do we need to discover the leadership archetype?

Warrior: Yes.

Guardian: This is no small task, to discover the archetype to serve as a pattern for the yet-to-be-leaders to model themselves after. I fear that to do this we must first study and come to know the archetype of the warrior and the archetype of the guardian. I hope that by comparing these two archetypes, we will discover a deeper archetype and pattern that is still hidden. Once it is unhidden, we will use that archetype and unite it with the knowledge and skill. Then we may be able to teach this art.

Warrior: You know what this implies?

Guardian: Yes.

Warrior: The death of the individual self and the transformative birth into the 'what-ness' of the archetype.

Guardian: Yes.

This is what I'm seeing–

> Leading in war-combat, we use weapons to make our opponent powerless in mind, body, and spirit.

> Leading in truth-combat, we use weapons to make individuals powerful in mind, body, and spirit.

When we engage in the art of truth-combat, let us imagine, if we are of true worth, we lead as though our hands are handcuffed behind our backs. In this restriction, all we have is our light and truth, moving through our will, intelligence, and spirit, using language as the medium, to send that light and truth to another soul and inspire the light and truth that reside there.

Warrior: You declare this is possible?

Guardian: Yes.

This is how we learn to lead from soul to soul. The mind can be manipulated, but the soul cannot. We must have courage to look through the eyes into the soul and speak to it. And if we truly do this, we will be able to inspire the soul freely and consciously to take actions that demand what is best in itself, in the form of virtue, discernment, and excellence. We will use no manipulation of wills, feelings, and desires, if we are truly to lead souls to pursue noble deeds.

Warrior: Go on.

Guardian: This why we have set it upon ourselves to study the techniques of contemplation and meditation. They are the metaphysical swords to engage in the battle of truth-combat.

Warrior: Now the teacher training begins for us?

Guardian: Maybe. We learned that we need to study these concepts further. We learned that we need to awaken deeper in our spirit the source that wields contemplation and meditation.

Warrior: Do we not already know this? That the soul as light wields meditation and the soul as truth wields contemplation?

Guardian: No, we do not "know" this. We "know about." We are not skilled enough to teach.

I've never beheld the source of the light and truth, the nature and the substance. Be that as it may, being an imperfect being, I do have an idea of how we can learn to teach this art, without waiting to behold the source of the light and truth.

Warrior: How?

Guardian: We are to ask the source to act upon us. We can be the receivers and givers without being the cause, nor knowing and seeing the cause.

The way we can practice these metaphysical swords is to use them as we turn our study to the development domains of our art. Let us set these as placeholders and return to them once we have finished this quest and have yet-to-be-leaders to guide.

> Heroic Development (Archetypes)
> Character Development (Virtue)
> Identity Development (Know Thyself)
> Ethical Development (Justice)
> Intellectual Development (Discernment)
> Leadership Development (Wisdom)
> Spiritual Development (Awakening)

Warrior: Wait, after this quest, we have to turn to these domains and master them?

Guardian: I am afraid so. But, at least when we study them, we will know how to make their knowledge an extension of being.

We have just been let through this impasse with our increased understanding.

As we move upward, put these principles to memory.

Meditation–

> How the will distances itself from the mortal, the conditioned, the emotional, the primal nature (ego).
>
> How the will becomes aware of the immortal, the eternal, the substance, the light.
>
> How the will receives light, gives light and expresses light in goodwill, charity, and freedom.
>
> How the will seeks freedom of being—independence from conditioned and mortal existence, independence from the will and judgments of other mortals.
>
> How the will (interior reality, subjectivity) turns to reality (exterior reality, objectivity).
>
> How the will turns from subjectivity to objectivity.
>
> How the will learns freedom and harmony by conforming itself to reality.
>
> Essentially, meditation is how the will builds the virtue of humility and the virtue of detachment, to perceive and correspond to objective reality.

Contemplation–

> How the intelligence takes command of the mind's sea of thoughts.
>
> How the intelligence corresponds with truth.
>
> How the intelligence responds to events with actions of detachment, humility and wisdom.
>
> How the intelligence comes to knowing and understanding.
>
> How the intelligence informs the will to act.
>
> How the soul first learns truth-disclosing.

Essentially, contemplation is how the intelligence builds the virtues of practical judgment, discernment, and wisdom.

Warrior: Let us also put to memory the known definitions.

Contemplation

The being-at-work of the intellect, a thinking like seeing (lucid—shines light), complete at every moment and instant. In contemplation, a human being is most fully active, in that the power underlying all thinking and perceiving has emerged, but also most at rest in what is knowable. It is the most complete human happiness. To come to rest in contemplation, a human being must overcome the disorder of the soul native to it from childhood.[15]

Defined as the ability to penetrate through surface observation to discover essence, hidden relationships and deeper meanings.

Activities–

Awaken the wisdom-faculty.

Strive to be "devoid-of-longing for all objects of desire, then yoked to truth, then wisdom-faculty awakens."[16]

Search for ways to ascend the depths and heights of truth.

Reach into depth and essence (knowing, not knowing about).

Go past the mere perception of something (truth-disclosing).

Make detailed judgments about situations.

Develop insights by going below the surface and exploring the depth of a situation and challenge (practical judgment).

Know, understand, and relate one's self to persons and things by comprehending them (To let in their truth, nature, essence).

Discover the soul's light and truth.

Meditation

Defined as the ability to think deeply or to focus one's mind in silence, for a period of time, to cultivate depth of thought and intellectual discipline.

---

[15] Aristotle, *Nicomachean Ethics*, Sachs translation.
[16] *The Bhagavad Gita*, Feuerstein translation.

Activities–

Conquer fear, through purification, gazing at light.

Practice "disunion of the union with suffering."[17]

Purify through one-pointedness of mind.

Renounce worldly passion and develop self-restraint.

Practice "indifference to sense-objects, pain and pleasure, honor and dishonor, victory and defeat, success and failure, wealth and poverty, health and sickness."[18]

Detach from sense-objects that create unstable emotions and insatiable desires.

Conquer ego through purification.

Practice self-denial to remove selfish motives.

Practice methods to season the mind to cultivate depth, breadth, clarity, and precision of thought.

Teach self-management by building strength of character and increasing self-discipline.

Increase concentration and energy.

Increase creativity by visualization and nonlinear methods.

Guardian: Now we turn to discover the archetype of the warrior.

Warrior: Onward—upward in transcendence and downward into the deepest nerve centers of light.

---

[17] *The Bhagavad Gita*, Feuerstein translation.
[18] *The Bhagavad Gita*, Feuerstein translation.

CHAPTER EIGHT
WARRIOR ARCHETYPE

Writer: Dear Reader, our journeymen have made progress in the depths and the heights. They are now embarking on the climb towards understanding the archetypes of leadership. The writer admires those who will be waiting in the heights—the sages, the saints, the mystics, the Buddha, the Krishna, the Christ. What this teaching aims for is the wisdom and discernment of those enlightened beings there near the summit. But those we admire on this journey upwards are the teachers, the guides, the warriors, the guardians—the leaders. I share this because leaders are imperfect, caught in a cyclical dynamic of being and becoming, and must not wait until perfection to lead. No, it is in their imperfection where they must have the courage to lead, leading from what they are, not just what they hope to become. They must make each movement of living take on a meaning that is geared towards growing and perfecting their being. We must not wait until we are perfect to act. We must strike our essence, our will and intelligence, at every moment of choice, to learn to command rightly and act with integrity. We develop strength by overcoming obstacles and adversity. We will fail daily, because we are not perfect beings, yet. We learn from the failures. We learn from the imperfections. That is why courage is the most essential characteristic. The guardians and the warriors embody courage: the courage to seek truth, the courage to face an opponent. Leaders live in the knowable unknown: the Buddha, the Christ, is awakened with knowing-the-wisdom that we pursue. Pursuing wisdom is the journey of the human being, whether he knows it or not. We are the sons and the daughters of truth, of wisdom, of light. The warrior and the guardian are androgynous archetypes that each man and woman dons as the "what-ness" of leading. Our leaders pursue noble goals of the highest meaning and use their inner determination, their *coup d'esprit*, to do what is right, not what is expedient or acquisitive. The wise do not war with the wise. When all beings devote their mind and energy to the pursuit of truth and wisdom, we will return to a spiritual garden ripening into the deepest potencies of the spirit, the daemon, the god-within. That is why for the wise, not courage but compassion and benevolence are the most essential characteristics. A teacher of leaders, we will learn, must be a union of the warrior and the guardian who serve as ferryman, crossing the chasm from ignorance to truth and from darkness to light. We need to understand what a warrior is and what a guardian is, and why we should select them as patterns to develop our character in our formative years. Why? To willingly engage in the dynamics of one's calling and vocation, of one's potential and purpose, of one's virtues and talents.

Lead in the light, The Writer

Warrior: I am in wonder at how demanding it is to return to the depths. Now, once here, I do not want to return to the surface of being. There is freedom in the depths.

Guardian: That is why on the journey we have the choice to make the return, to fulfill our purpose and potential. The challenge is to remain in the depths as we engage the surface—to rest inwardly in the depths of being as we engage the reality we see.

Warrior: You mean to stay in the deep waters of being as we engage a humanity ensnared in *samsara*?

Guardian: Yes. If you mean *samsara* as–

> The endless cycle of death and rebirth to which life in the material world is bound.[1]

Warrior: Yes. It took tremendous energy and patience, on my part, to stay with you as you found the words to describe what you've experienced.

I learned, just by being a good listener, that true listening is a powerful method for ego-shedding. What I see you doing, on this journey, is a continual shedding of the ego by turning away from it and turning to light and truth.

Guardian: And what happens when we distance and detach ourselves from this fiction called the ego?

Warrior: We increase our ability to see and know. We increase the chances that we will make contact with light and truth in the knowable unknown.

Guardian: But, this is not enough for us. I know holy souls who I would never want in leadership positions, even though they are great and true doctors of the soul. They are divine in their counseling and healing and revelatory abilities, but they are quite worthless when it comes to leading in the chaos and conflict of *samsara*.

Warrior: It makes you wonder what would happen if we practiced the virtue of justice and let managers lead the religious institutions, and let the holy ones focus solely on holy activities. We create continued injustices by spreading human beings across too many domains. Justice is doing one thing to contribute to the all, and doing that one thing to the best of one's ability.

Guardian: Yes. I hated as a young officer hearing the popular rhetoric—officers are jacks of all trades, master of none. That is deadly. That is like an athlete also being an owner, an agent, a general manager, and a coach. There are too many demands.

Warrior: Undisciplined souls run from the singular focus of calling and purpose.

---

[1] O.E.D. definition of samsara.

Guardian: Pieper[2] mentors us here—

> These souls suffer 'self-deception and empty busywork.'

Warrior: I see the same injustices in the profession of arms. Warriors are tasked with essentially business administration functions. It's madness. Not divine madness, but human madness. That is why warriors do not have time to study and be scholars of the art of warfighting in the operational and strategic setting. It's not valued enough. There should be a clear distinction between administrative functions and warfighting functions.

Guardian: We are seeing the tyranny of the bureaucracy in full light. That is why, in our art, we need to live outside of any institution as we focus on human beings and their powers, not the institutional powers.

Instead of making our leaders servants to the pattern of the institutions, we focus on making our leaders become the interior pattern of an archetype. This is how we develop the soul; this is how we set free our interior nature in this conditioned existence. Then, we adapt the archetype to the demands of institutional activities. Then our leaders will be free, in any setting, as they move and contribute by what they are, not only by what they do.

In this light, our leaders will not lose their footing, but will learn to move from an inward and centered state of being as they focus their efforts on the critical, the necessary, and the essential activities that institutions aim at manifesting.

Warrior: Unmoved movers.

Then in our art, we need to create an archetype, a baseline minimum viable ability, to serve as an ideal for our developmental aims. I am not sure how to do this for our art. I know how to do it for warriors.

Guardian: I am leaning towards the pattern of the philosophers—the lovers of wisdom, the seekers of truth—as the archetype[3]

I do not share this publicly, but because we're friends, I'll share my thinking with you.

What do you think would happen if I opened up a training with this command—

> We are here to crush the ego and awaken the soul's light and truth by wielding the swords of contemplation and meditation. We do this to release

---

[2] Josef Pieper, *Living The Truth*.

[3] O.E.D. definition of archetype–The original pattern or model from which copies are made; a prototype; a typical specimen. In Jungian psychoanalysis, a primordial mental concept inherited by all from the collective unconscious. A pervasive or recurrent idea or symbol in legend, etc.

you from the veil of darkness now blinding you. We will lead you into the depths of the knowable unknown, and in these depths, the genius of your soul will awaken and reveal the truth and light that must guide you. Then, you will have command to disclose the truth, from hiddenness, and make it unhidden. This is how you learn to wrestle free the light from the darkness and the truth from the ignorance. We do this so you can fulfill your purpose, reach your potential and achieve the highest aims of mankind.

Warrior: You'd have no one to train. Most are gripped by the ego's fiction and they would run for the door. They'd call you a madman.

But, I love it—it's ego-shedding par excellence.

Guardian: This is why we do not act as torch bearers but as awakeners. The direct approach as torch bearer has resulted in many failures to lead and inspire souls. This is why we need the indirect approach, the subtle art. We can do the work with subtlety by focusing on the study of an archetype and the study of knowledge.

We need to make the training less abstract and esoteric, and more concrete and exoteric. What if we made it simple, like math or accounting, so it's not threatening to the ego, to the personality, to the sense of self, and seems to the student the equivalent of studying and learning the techniques of an art?

This means our training is gentle and not violent, and does not rupture one's sense of self, even if one suffers delusion.

Warrior: I am reminded of Kierkegaard and we must take in his sage advice–

> If real success is to attend the effort to bring a man to a definite position, one must first of all take all the pains to find him where he is and begin there. This is the secret art of helping others.
>
> All true effort to help begins with self-humiliation: the helper must humble himself under him he would help, and therewith must understand that to help does not mean to be a sovereign but to be a servant.
>
> Be the amazed listener who sits and hears what the other finds the more delight in telling you because you listen with amazement.
>
> No, to be a teacher in the right sense is to be a learner. Instruction begins when you, the teacher, learn from the learner, put yourself in his place so that you may understand what he understands in the way he understands it.[4]

---

[4] Peter Kreeft, *Socratic Logic*. Kierkegaard quoted.

Guardian: Our art in essence is a teaching art, a true teaching art, where our aim is the student's growth in knowledge, character, skill and ability. And to do this, we must become one-pointed and let go of all other aims. Am I seeing correctly?

Warrior: Yes. I served you by being the amazed listener.

How often have we failed to do this?

It is, in my estimation, the most time-consuming and energy-demanding art in which one can have no control over the outcome, as the student controls the outcome. This is where we must place faith and trust in our students and be devoted to their growth. We want them to be free and powerful, not obedient and submissive to authority.

Guardian: In our art, the teachers we seek are also of a different substance and quality than most academic teachers, correct?

Warrior: That is what we are seeing. Is this asking too much of both the teacher and the student? What if this is not possible?

You stated, early on, that you created something that you needed, and what you created lived inside of your spirit, seeking actualization. What if this is not scalable, repeatable and teachable? What if it's a singular calling and that you are tasked to be a solo mountaineer, and only sometimes, as with me, invite others along for a part of your journey? What if you are a contemplative and your work lives in silence and solitude?

Guardian: Then I have failed. Then there is no point in going further. We need noble, good, and just leaders who do not bend to mass opinion and emotions, but lead others out of opinions and emotions and into the light of truth. This calls for leadership, not pandering. Pandering, not truth, wins elections.

Aristotle is speaking to me, in his *Rhetoric*, on the art of influence. It can be a vice or virtue–

> The vice of: mastery over speeches and mastery over people, witchcraft, a hypnotic art that molds false but potent speeches, pandering, manipulation of crowds in a servile rather than masterful way.

> The virtue of: the study of all things that make an opinion persuasive, a dialectical inquiry applied to non-dialectical subjects, those that do not admit of knowledge, but do admit of opinions that can be shown to rest on better or worse evidence.[5]

---

[5] Aristotle, *Rhetoric*.

Now, we must bring to bear the virtues of hope and faith that our art is teachable, and that we will find students who have the drive to undergo rigorous training. That our teaching and their learning will produce sagacious leaders. I must wield faith. I must wield hope. We only need 10 such beings to make an impact.

Burkhardt writes of the founding of the Jesuits–

> Regarding the power of the Jesuits: It is not so hard for firmly united, clever, and courageous men to do great things in the world. Ten such men affect 100,000 because the great mass of people have only acquisition, enjoyment, vanity, and the like in their heads, while those ten men always work together.[6]

I must believe there are 500 souls on Earth called to train in our art. They will find us. I will never allow myself to be despondent again.

Warrior: What kind of beings are needed for our art?

Guardian: I am wrestling with an archetype that binds together the concepts of guardian, warrior, iconoclast, and hero. I am not clear. What I'm seeing is vague.

Not only must we define what our art is; we must define the type of nature that will resonate most with our art. And we must learn to hunt for that nature, knowing its potential, by finding it lying in wait in the soul.

I say art because knowledge is not enough. Our art demands skill. And skill begins and ends with mastering and uniting basic knowledge and techniques.

It is beginning to seem simple and elegant, the training, at least in my mind.

Warrior: If I remain still and look from where we started, yes, it's beginning to take shape, but still it's a harrowing teaching and training activity.

Guardian: Ah. Now, I understand why monks do not allow their initiates to contact or see family members during the first two years of training. The distance and detachment are required to break from *samsara*, to break from the surface imprints of culture, government, and religion, and to slowly enter into the depths.

Warrior: Does our art demand total devotion and dedication?

Guardian: Yes.

Warrior: Then, if we had students in a monastery setting, our task would seem simple and basic. That is why we have failed. We never created the baseline to demand two years of

---

[6] Jacob Burkhardt, *Judgments on History and Historians*.

concentration, to create the interior foundation. What if we created a training center in the mountains and led two-year training cycles?

Guardian: We would not fail, if we could discover students with the right natures and the right potential. Then, without the distractions of non-necessities and non-essentials, the students of our art would come to experience for themselves the inner joy and freedom of the practices, once they learned the basic techniques.

Warrior: How could they not experience freedom when they learned to make contact and obey and wield light and truth?

Guardian: Then we have a new task ahead of us. We need to discover the nature of what we hunt for, and define a specific kind of leader-as-guide and leader-as-student that are interchangeable.

We need to trust the nature of the students (the potencies) as much as the nature of the guides (the realized). What I am seeing is that the student and the teacher are one and the same, only one has been awakened and the other is being awakened.

It is hellish when the wrong natures for our art find their way into our training.

First, some preliminaries to define what we are seeking–

Our art is not meant for most human beings.

Our art makes our students better human beings.

Our art makes our students trustworthy.

Our art makes our students embody true esteem.

Our art makes our students truly skilled.

Our art makes our students discover their calling and purpose.

Our art makes our students grow vertically (character and potential) and horizontally (knowledge and skill).

Our art makes our students secure in their being and in their art.

Our art makes our students independent of the wills and judgments of others.

Our art makes our students and teachers interdependent in wills and judgments.

Our art makes our students know how to give and receive light and truth.

Our art values our students as unmoved movers.

Second, with these ends in mind–

We need to discover an ideal archetype and pattern that our students can aim for. This means that the burden is on our teachers-as-guides to have actualized that pattern and to embody it, so the students can have both an abstract understanding and a concrete example of the archetype they must become. To be led by one who is actualized will encourage them, for they will know that the journey is possible.

Warrior: This is why most educators fail. They have only acquired "knowledge about" but have not liberated their potencies. They do not possess the character to liberate the soul of their students. Modern education is mass socialization. We need to return to the roots of education as the way of liberating the soul.

Guardian: Terrifying. That is why the military academies fail. They create yes-men, highly prized conformists, instead of free persons.

Third–

We must provide the basic knowledge and training methods that are means to hit this ideal, this end.

Students need to know what they are aiming for and why it is worth their efforts to commit to realizing this ideal in their being.

Fourth, with this task–

We can practice meditation and contemplation as a method for concept and insight generation. These practices, when combined, create an insight generation model by colliding creative induction with destructive deduction.[7]

Warrior: That last statement packed a punch, and I can tell you've been influenced by John Boyd. What do you have in mind?

Guardian: How do we know what we are? How do we learn to hunt for a specific kind of nature?

Warrior: First, by examining our own nature? By a practice of self-examination to see if we have actualized the ideal in our being? So we don't suffer the sin of acting like we 'know' when we only 'know about'?

Guardian: Yes. To do this subtly, I plan to take another indirect approach into the depths.

Warrior: Deeper still? The depths as a never-ending abyss.

---

[7] Frans Osinga, *Science, Strategy, and War: The Strategic Theory of John Boyd.*

Guardian: Yes. We must be tested to learn to see in these depths.

We must take a hard look within and conduct an examination of our nature.

Warrior: By now, I know you mean not an examination of our emotions, nor our personality, nor our predilections, tastes, and preferences, but of our core being.

Guardian: Yes. Our core being is as deep as true self-knowledge can go.

Once we know the core, then we can lead it into knowledge and skill acquisition.

And then, with knowledge and skill acquisition, we can transform and unite it with our being.

Finally, we will know how knowledge and skill become an extension of our being.

Warrior: Then what I need to know is how to discover the core of being, the core of knowing, to transcend knowing-about.

Guardian: We do this by learning and teaching this concept–

Knowing as an extension of being

Warrior: And, are you suggesting that we begin this understanding by an examination of what we are? And if we see what we are, we can know what we are, and that knowledge can transform what we are by awakening deeper potentials?

Guardian: That is exactly what I'm suggesting.

Warrior: How do we begin?

Guardian: By studying what we are, not who we are.

Warrior: Go on.

Guardian: We need to describe the nature of a warrior. We need to know what that nature *is*. To do this, I need to hunt for that nature in your being, as the warrior nature lives in the being.

Warrior: Go on.

Guardian: Then we need to describe the nature of a guardian.

Warrior: You suggest that I hunt for that nature in your being?

Guardian: Yes and no.

Warrior: I don't follow?

Guardian: What am I?

Warrior: You are a guardian.

Guardian: No. I've donned the guardian archetype. What am I?

Warrior: I don't know.

Guardian: What is the nature before you that understood how to enter the depths of beinghood?

Is the guardian archetype designed to do this?

Warrior: Not necessarily.

Guardian: What am I at the core?

Warrior: Ah. The core of you is divine madness. The guardian is a cloak you wear, and you know this cloak well.

Guardian: Do you know what that *is*, divine madness?

Warrior: No. And you imply that I do not need to know. You imply that we need to know the warrior and guardian archetypes, and you are making sure that I do not lead out divine madness as the pattern of the guardian.

Guardian: Correct. This is why we need two intelligences to wrestle out the truth. You hunt for the guardian archetype and I hunt for the warrior archetype.

This is where we learn how to make what is tacit and intuitive, explicit. This is one of the tests.

It's easier to see who we are than what we are. That is why we misread the beings before us.

What we are is not a personality. What we are is our true nature and our true character. What we are is the true dynamic of calling, virtues, and abilities.

What we are is what we trust.

Now, before we had the understanding of what we are, there were periods of confusion and uncertainty, but once we knew, we became prime movers—or unmoved movers. We learned to rest in our being and move from our being, whether we realized it or not, because it is what we are. We learned freedom from resting in being, from resting in reality. By this inwardness and centeredness, we became unmoved movers because our nature cannot be moved nor taken away; it is what we are.

> It's as though events and beings orbit around us instead of us being moved by events and beings.

Warrior: Dear God, I never thought about this, but it is resonating! That is why what we are remains calm and cool in chaos and turbulence. In fact, the more chaos and turbulence there is, the calmer a warrior becomes. At least for the true warriors.

Guardian: And we are after the true ones—like the true master swordsman who takes on a dozen opponents and moves in an effortless and graceful and unmoved way.

Warrior: Can we teach this *"effortless unmoving way"* in our art?

Guardian: Good God, I hope so.

Look at how you and I approach one another as beings. We do not even use our given names, as a counter measure to avoid the cult of personality and the cult of ego, *the who*.

We use *the what*, the nature and the essence—the Guardian and the Warrior.

Warrior: These are subtle ways to shed the ego.

Guardian: We are after the *what*, the *essence*, the *is-ness* of our art.

There is no room for the *person* and the *ego*; both must remain at home, locked in a vault.

Warrior: I bet you hear that you are too impersonal.

Guardian: That is a good sign, my friend. This creates detachment and distance from human weakness, from distracted minds, and from unstable emotions.

We now must even distance ourselves from our nature, the nature of the warrior and the nature of the guardian, so we can see it clearly, so we can let it reveal itself.

Warrior: How do we do this?

Guardian: These archetypes are not our true nature; they are the second order effects of the soul's powers. The archetypes reflect how we have directed those powers. The soul is what we are, so we penetrate to the soul's substance, nature and powers and direct them to our temporal nature on earth, as warrior and guardian. From this depth of being, we will be able to see the nature of both. From this seeing, we will learn how to lead the soul's substance, nature and powers to produce the archetypes of warrior and guardian in living beings.

Warrior: Good God, it seems simple with this understanding.

Guardian: In this way, we will move from the deepest and most powerful ground of our being. The soul is the artist that creates, forms, and commands the archetype. The archetype does not shape and control the soul. Do you see?

Warrior: Yes. Now I see the freedom and creativity and power of our art. I also see that our students may not be ready to hear these truths, but I think they will be ready to trust the guidance and selflessness of the warrior and the guardian as their guides and teachers.

Guardian: And why is that?

Warrior: I'm not sure.

Guardian: When we meet our students, they will be living from ego and not know it. They live from the ego-body-octagon's drives of comfort, protection and security. Our student's egos will be set at ease by the commanding presence of guardians and warriors. The psychological straightjacket of the ego will be loosened by the comfort, protection and security of our guides.

Warrior: Powerful. You are using the guardian and warrior as the guides to meet the person, the ego, the who, and to subtly disarm the mechanisms and drives of the ego. Beautiful. The ego's primal drives are inherently designed to admire the natures of the guardian and warrior because they are the essence of–

Security and protection; power and strength.

Guardian: Yes. The suits of armor around students' souls have been hardened, to shield them from the self-absorbed authority figures who attempted and failed to dominate and control their being—their will and their intelligence. Our students, rightfully so, will come to us psychologically armored against teachers. Their experience has been that teachers are insecure and weak. Their experience has been that teachers, instead of educating, tried to dominate by demanding obedience and submission, as if they were gods of the intellect.

Warrior: I think the archetypes of the warrior and the guardian, keeping the indirect approach in mind, will resonate deeply with most students, because most human beings want to protect and defend their loved ones from adversaries and threats.

Guardian: Yes. I am speculating here, but I think in the depths of each being that we train, we will find an admiration for guardians as protectors and warriors as defenders. Our teachers will be the example and will inspire our students to train because of these admirable qualities.

Through this trust and admiration, our students will find strength to train with fearlessness as they seek the ideal, knowing we will guide the way. Meaning that we will be able to simultaneously calm the ego and strike the soul. This will be the genius of the training methods.

But I am struggling here, because what I am seeing is that the soul's nature and essence is created to admire and trust guardians and warriors too, not just the ego. I am struggling because the highest aim is the pattern of a philosopher-saint-sage, but a young soul has the spirit to resonate more deeply with the guardian-warrior-leader pattern.

Warrior: As Kierkegaard recommended, this is how we meet students where they are, not where we want them to be.

Guardian: Yes. We know our training leads to freedom and wisdom.

But, we will strike their spirited nature in their formative years by focusing on the guardian-warrior-leader ideals so that they can train with intensity, courage, and vigor.

Then, as if by nature itself, by being-what-they-are, the training ends in the transformation of the soul from the archetype of the guardian-warrior-leader into the archetype of the philosopher-saint-sage, the enlightened.

All this movement is seamless, like a natural progression of spirit.

Warrior: You are hunting for what is called Sagacious Leadership.

We now see the disparate threads of guardian-warrior-leader-philosopher-saint-sage originating in one and the same source—the soul. This is why the interior training remains the same, correct?

Guardian: Yes. Because at all times we are striking the soul's nature, essence, and powers.

I see a lifelong mosaic of integrated development. Our responsibility as teachers is to weave the threads of the soul into bulletproof fabrics of being.

The way we train in the basics engages the same powers that make manifest any of those archetypes.

Because courage is the keystone to all of this, I selected the guardian-warrior archetypes. These archetypes hit deep in our psyche—look at all the myths, novels, plays and movies showcasing heroic qualities.

Warrior: Ah. I see what you are doing. If all souls are living an adventure, the guardian-warrior archetypes resonate with what is already taking place within them. Further, you are going to showcase how the guardian-warriors demonstrate heroic qualities in the way they train and live.

Guardian: This is what I am seeing. The core attributes of heroic leadership[8] are–

1. Physical and Moral Courage
2. Greatness of Soul
3. Extraordinary Achievement

Warrior: I see. This is why we fail. We have not trained students to act with courage, to act with soul, and to respond to noble challenges. To do this, our students need to know how to develop virtue by the powers of the soul. It seems that we bypass the conditioning of the soul and leap into great challenges unprepared. This is why our leaders fail. They have not been

---

[8] Peter Gibbon, *A Call To Heroism*.

conditioned. Because they have not conditioned their souls, they cannot see what needs to be done. In darkness and blindness, they make decisions that lead to ruin.

Guardian: This is why we need to strike the depths of our students. If they are called and driven to extraordinary achievement, we need to condition their being first so that achievement is the effect of the cause of their soul.

Twain mentors–

> It is better to deserve honors and not have them than to have them and not deserve them.[9]

This is why we need to identify the elements of a guardian and a warrior. Then our students can practice the powers of soul, by creating the archetype through training.

Our first task is to distinguish both archetypes. Then we can compare the patterns and see if we can conceive of a new archetype—the leader. I don't have a preconceived idea of what it will look like; I just know the value of smashing together powerful concepts to see if deeper truths reveal themselves.

Warrior: I see what you are doing. This is a good activity for practicing truth-disclosing, the forerunner of practical judgment.

Guardian: My wise warrior friend, you see it because it is your nature.

Let me begin with the examination of the warrior archetype–

> What is the means of the warrior?

Warrior: You don't want to hear this, but the means of the warrior is violence.

Guardian: Good God, did you not know that the means of turning the soul towards the primordial light is violence?[10]

In this turning to the light, the ego is killed. It is a metaphysical violence that is transformed by gentleness, but the ego does not experience this gentleness—only the soul does.

Warrior: The violence of the light has just hit me deeply. I, at this moment, am experiencing compassion for my former commanders who failed. I judged them harshly and unfairly—we did not train them to embody greatness of soul and moral courage. We trained them to win. We trained them to focus on the end state. They should have been trained on the primacy of the means that cause the end—on the end being the legacy of the means.

---

[9] Mark Twain, *Notebook, 1902–1903*.

[10] Martin Heidegger, *The Essence of Truth*.

The ends never justify the means if the means are unsound, unjust, immoral, wretched and wicked, especially in war, the exercise of violence. Just violence is not unjust violence.

Pieper mentors us–

Moral action is 'doing the truth,' *veritatem agere*.[11]

I see now, our training failed our Commanders. I failed them. They were trained for courage in the face of mortal danger; they were not trained for moral courage in the face of moral danger.

They don't even have the understanding of truth-disclosing as the art of turning the soul to primordial light to receive the light of truth.

Upon reflection, it now seems moral courage is every bit as demanding as bravery in combat. I had no idea. This truth remains hidden and we all suffer for that in the darkness.

Guardian: It seems our primary teaching virtue is compassion.

Warrior: Why?

Guardian: First, so we don't judge harshly and add intellectual and moral injustice to our list of vices. Second, so we don't force our will on a student and make her study compulsory out of fear.

Warrior: I take it you've suffered by delivering these injustices to students.

Guardian: Grown men and women who were leadership students, yes. I had not the wisdom of experience.

Warrior: What did you learn?

Guardian: Most managers and achievers display skills and abilities beautifully, yet are weak in their character.

I see this all the time. They refuse to do the introspective work of leadership development. It's too difficult for their egos, for their self-esteem, for their insecurities, to take a hard look within. They suffer self-deception. They are morally weak and yet we expect them to be morally strong.

I hate pusillanimity.

Warrior: What?

Guardian: I hate pusillanimity because I suffered it and did not even know what it was.

---

[11] Josef Pieper, *Living the Truth*.

Warrior: What is it?

Guardian: The opposite of courage. It is called by other names—cowardice, weak-mindedness, mean-spiritedness. It is the opposite of *eudaimonia*—good-spiritedness, gentleness of mind and spirit, grace, elegance, and fortitude.

I experienced rage when achievers refused to do the inner work. I had to learn to transform the rage into gentleness. This was one of the most important teaching lessons.

Our art demands a hard look within, to the depths, to reveal the stinging truths of our imperfections. There can be no true greatness of soul without this act of humility. When I look to my past, to my most serious failures, I had no awareness of what lurked in the depths, before I acted. I made the mistake of reading Ayn Rand in my unstable formative years. Its subjectivity cloaked as objectivity was made for a young egotist. I imbibed her idea of one's intelligence as the law, rather than correspondence and harmony with the natural and eternal laws.

Our intellect, when it comes into correspondence with truth, commands our will to act rightly. I always fail when I act on the irrational, unstable and primal drives of the ego-body-octagon.

But the blessing, as though truth rights all errors, comes to a reflective soul–

> By necessity, the pain of failures triggers introspection and examination, to evaluate the state of one's inner nature.

Warrior: Life has been your teacher. I now know what fires your rage.

Guardian: There are a few qualities that I hate.

Warrior: Which is why we need compassion.

Guardian: Yes. It's the antidote, the medicine, to transform the rage to gentleness and to keep the soul clear of the irrational fires. I hate weak beings of coercive power who exploit others. I hate when authority and force manipulate other beings. I hate conceited, arrogant, narcissistic and vain people—those who live by their ego instead of shedding it.

Warrior: Hate is a strong choice of words. I bet you've exhibited these egotistical qualities in your own being.

Guardian: Yes, I've suffered these same afflictions and I aimed to right myself first, before I guided others. I've suffered them all. Because of the rage, I had to learn the virtue of forgiveness. We will demand that our guides practice and embody forgiveness. We will not judge the egos and the persons; we will judge the qualities. The qualities can be changed through teaching and training, as the essence of the soul is without stain.

The guardian nature revealed itself early. I remember witnessing a high school kid bullying a friend of mine. We were 7 years old. I leaped at the aggressor and woke up in a hospital with a broken jaw.

The irony of the story was that the nurse asked what happened. I told her. She asked who was the bully.

I said, "your son."

Warrior: Then what?

Guardian: The bully stopped bullying and become a friend and a guardian of us underlings.

Warrior: Divine justice. All things made right.

Guardian: Indeed. I've learned that because we are conditioned and temporal beings on earth, it all ends in good. All is allowed; all is made right. It took me 40 years to learn this truth.

That said, when I witness qualities of manipulation, conceit, arrogance, vanity—the warrior, the deliverer of violence, seeks violently to put an end to their power over others. I want to make them powerless in a non-martial way.

It is wild that most injustices on Earth are the result of weak beings who wield emotional, intellectual, or economic control. That is what drove me to discover non-martial methods.

That is why our guides must have this warrior essence, to engage in combat, be it martial or non-martial.

Warrior: What you are highlighting is the object and aim of the warrior–

> To render the adversary powerless.

The means is violence.

Guardian: I already see the fusion of the guardian and the warrior. I'm wrestling with my intelligence to lead out what I see.

Our leaders need to unite the elements of warrior and guardian–

> By making friends powerful and by making adversaries powerless.

Warrior: What are you seeing?

Guardian: Dear God, the adversary of doubt is striking my being. Where does this adversary come from?

Warrior: What are you seeing?

Guardian: I'm seeing, once again, that I am not important.

Warrior: Good, that is ego-shedding.

Guardian: …And that the work is what is important.

Warrior: Good. Keep shedding the ego.

Guardian: That I am insignificant.

Warrior: Good.

Guardian: I am called to do this work. But I can say no. I have a choice.

Warrior: Good.

Guardian: That what I am is a contemplative, not a guardian.

Warrior: Even better. That's how divine madness reaches you. Allow the truth to reveal itself.

Guardian: That I'm most free in reflection, inquiry, dialogue, study, prayer, meditation, and sacred canons.

I now see the "call" from the ego's perspective as bondage. But, from the soul's perspective, I see the "call" as a spiritual bond, a true bond, a true purpose, that is not essentially "free from" but rather "free to." Freedom is my most valued value. Freedom of soul now seems to mean something very different from the ego's idea of freedom.

Warrior: Truth is an ascending staircase. It looks like the ego is striking you and the power of soul must vanquish it.

You are a contemplative, a truth-seeker, who knows divine madness, but your calling is to fulfill a purpose on earth. You heard the call and you listened to the call, and the call and the soul created a beautiful bond. You transcended the ego's vice of bondage, of seeking to sate inordinate desire. It was a form of spiritual marriage—the soul uniting with the call's light and truth.

Guardian: Good God, this is liberating. On the surface, I thought my nature was that of a freedom-seeker. This is not so. My nature is a truth-seeker, a contemplative. The ego used my love of freedom as a weapon of deception. I never saw the truth of this.

Freedom as a second order effect of truth, not a first order cause. A deeper veil has been lifted.

The effect of knowing truth is a true freedom, but it is not a freedom to do what one wills; it is the freedom of knowing that commands the will.

Warrior: We have had it backwards. We thought that willing came first. Now we see that knowing comes first. The kinetic chain has been ordered truthfully—knowing, willing, acting.

Guardian: This, the soul's correspondence with reality, is the means. The end is union of the soul and reality. Now I understand. This is metaphysical freedom—knowing and obeying the light and truth I see. The will follows this knowing; the knowing does not follow the will. The will to truth is the will to pursue the truth. The truth is the lead.[12]

Warrior: I see the value of dialogue. Even though you are leading by examining my nature, it also triggered a deeper awakening in you. You are demonstrating a learning mind-set, a growth-mindset, a self-knowledge that awakens. It's fascinating to witness.

Guardian: Ah ha. I see something that's been hiding. Freedom from bondage is not unbridled freedom. I see true freedom as bondage to truth. This is a paradox to the ego but a victory for the soul. I see true freedom as a bond to light and truth. A relationship. A lovingness. A friendship. I see this kind of freedom as the Holy Bond, the essence of *agape*, of charity.

Warrior: The Greek *agape* means brotherly love.

Guardian: Then I see this bond, this binding, occurs when the soul creates a living bond to truth and light. This bond, a form of Platonic Love, fulfills the purpose of free will as the bond to truth and the bond to light. This is how we connect from soul to soul. This binding is non-possessive, non-material, non-acquisitive, non-physical, and non-emotional. It's how the soul's light and truth create metaphysical freedom; It's freedom as a state of being.

As a metaphor, I see two images, one as the virtue of freedom, one as the vice of freedom.

I imagine the vice of freedom, the possessive kind, symbolized as the image of two hands in a palm-to-palm, locking fashion, with intertwined fingers creating a bonded vice effect.

I imagine the virtue of freedom, the non-possessive kind, symbolized as the image of two hands in fists, with the knuckles of each uniting in the grooves of the other. This is like our art. We are like tectonic plates, moving organically. Sometimes we're violent and explosive, sometimes dormant and silent, shoulder to shoulder, facing the challenges, leveraging one another as needed.

Where are we again?

Warrior: We are defining the elements of the warrior. This is so we can create standards and measure the students training and growth.

We have documented two elements of the warrior–

> The means is violence.

> The object is to make the adversary powerless.

---

[12] Augustine, *On Free Choice of the Will*.

Guardian: Wait. Do you see it?

Warrior: No.

Guardian: What this reflection disclosed–

> The essence of our art is a series of relationships.

Warrior: Relationships?

Guardian: Yes. The soul builds a relationship with the archetype of the warrior; the soul builds a relationship with the knowledge and skills of the warrior; the warrior-teacher builds a relationship with the warrior-student. The warrior builds a relationship with his unit. These relationships are living, not dead. Our art must be lived.

The concept of true binding leads to true relationships and leads to true friendships. This is how our art becomes an extension of being.

Warrior: How?

Guardian: By building relationships from the primordial essence of spirit, commonly called love. The concept of "love as bond" builds a relationship of true friendship between the soul and knowledge. We become friends to knowledge. We become friends to skills. And when we bond with them, they become an extension of our being.

I never understood Aristotle's concept until now–

> What is a friend? A single soul dwelling in two bodies.[13]

This is what I see–

In our art, the two bodies are the archetype and the knowledge. They both dwell in the soul and they unite as one in the soul.

Warrior: Is this the true art of spiritual alchemy?

Guardian: This is what I see–

In our art, the two bodies are student and teacher. The soul dwells in both.

This is how archetypes and knowledge and skill become an extension of one's being, one's soul.

We have discovered that friendships and relationships, true ones, are how we make archetypes, knowledge, and skill become living expressions of being, and how we transfer this living expression from teacher to student.

---

[13] Aristotle, *Nicomachean Ethics*.

Warrior: I do follow, but there's a depth of mystery and mysticism I'm seeing that I am not used to acknowledging as fact with merit and substance. But I see it. It seems we are getting more clarity on how to make knowledge and skill an extension of our being. The missing concepts were bonding, relationship and friendship.

Guardian: That is why in war we seek to destroy the moral bonds of the adversary. That is why, as teachers, self-humiliation is a necessity.

Warrior: And it's why we value the virtues of humility and detachment. We honor the dignity and nobility of the student's potential. This creates a bond of friendship and trust. It is a living relationship, and with it we lead the soul.

Guardian: I hated managers who attempted to dominate and control their subordinates. They made their own teammates weaker, not stronger. They lacked the courage and humility to build true relationships and friendships aimed at noble and good ends.

And we wonder why there is little trust in the modern corporation. There is no freedom; the corporation is a prison and we don't even see it.

True relationships are absent. No one is cultivating the cause of the effect of trust. We don't even study how to become a true friend.

Warrior: What you seek and what you are describing, when it's done correctly, is called a Brotherhood. The image of King Arthur and the Knights of the Round Table comes to mind. This is a rare kind of friendship and brotherhood. Most organizations are not set up for this kind of excellence, and this kind of relationship and this kind of friendship.

You and I maintain the motive of excellence, for ourselves and for others, so the image will hold.

Many organizations are set up to use human capital for an external end, and that external end is given more value and priority than the well-being of the human being.

That is what enrages you. That is what instills hatred. You suffer when you see the potencies in human beings remaining latent and dormant instead of being awakening and realized.

I am beginning to see how your nature as a guardian is a nature that suffers, when it observes the potential in others not being guided out, not being led to a flourishing and divine state. That suffering is a noble form of compassion. Because you see the poverty of soul, you suffer.

It seems as though you've come from another realm. Maybe you don't understand what a *human being* actually *is*. It seems you see human beings as some kind of God-created being with divine qualities of light and truth, who are holy and sacred and free, in and of themselves, regardless of their work, station, or class on earth. You see the human being as a conditioned and composite being learning about its divine and eternal nature.

Where others see what is human, you see what is divine.

Guardian: Am I not seeing truthfully? Am I speaking falsely?

Warrior: I think you'd be more peaceful and serene if you just resigned yourself to living a contemplative life and staying in the wilderness, away from cosmopolitan life.

Guardian: As a Noble Savage?

Warrior: Yes.

Guardian: I love humanity too much to be resigned. Maybe in future hardships and failures I'll be resigned, but I must listen to the daemon, the God-within, for it speaks, and I listen to what it says, and I act on its guidance. I follow its lead.

Warrior: You are a strange man, my blessed friend.

Guardian: We need to imagine what these same organizations would be like if nothing changed except the characters of their leaders.

Warrior: Go on.

Guardian: Imagine if our leaders led these enterprises. What would happen?

Warrior: When I search in my memory through all my experience, I am led to believe that everything would change, in virtue, in value, in culture, in excellence and achievement.

Guardian: Why is that? What has your experience been?

Warrior: One of the strangest experiences in the military, independent of command, control, authority, laws, and regulations, is this experience–

A new Commander is selected and takes command of the unit. Nothing changes in terms of training, deployments, and operations, and yet everyone under the Commander experiences an emotional negativity, a toxicity, even though nothing quantitatively has changed. You could call this kind of Commander a Tyrant, a Despot, a Coward, an Incompetent; it does not matter what you call the Commander, the experience under his command is nasty and ugly. And yet, everyone makes mission and achieves. I always thought these kinds of Commanders were simply incompetent and corrupt, in their skills and in their character, but I did not understand how they affected the Unit to such a degree simply by their being, by their presence, at the helm.

Guardian: The leader's essence, his spiritual DNA, for good or for bad, affects all human beings under his Command. This is what I meant about the relationships, for good or for bad, between leader and those being led. How is it possible that wicked and corrupt leaders ascend to pinnacle leadership positions? If we look truthfully, will we discover that corrupt leaders spin a cloak of goodness that veils their wickedness?

Warrior: Yes. And then, as in a sort of spiritual alchemy, a new Commander is selected and takes the helm. Nothing changes except that the leadership DNA of one human replaces that of another. Then, immediately, morale skyrockets—morale in the sense of harmony, freedom, inspiration, excellence and innovation. All this, simply due to the nature and essence, the DNA, of the leader.

Guardian: How is this possible? How does one person, taking the helm, have this ability and effect?

Warrior: The simple answer is Command Presence and Leadership Presence.

Guardian: Do we not aim to make sure our leaders have this presence? If we do, what is it, really? How does the soul of the leader create such goodness or badness simply by her character?

Warrior: I'm not sure. I never gave the spiritual implications serious thought until now.

Guardian: This is what I see–

The leader's DNA, her spirit, good or bad, becomes the energetic imprint that overlays the entire unit and cascades through the entire enterprise.

Because no one has created the standards and measures, as we intend to do, we live in a game of leadership chance–

> Where all we have are highly skilled achievers who are often underdeveloped
> in their character, and when they take command, things may get ugly and bad
> or beautiful and good.

We cannot leave this to chance. We need the measures and standards to smoke out and to refute cunning human beings who have ascended the chain of command, but who in truth do not have the greatness of soul to lead.

This is why we have the rampant abuse of power that we see today. We have no guardians at the gate. We have no true vetting of character. We have no method to refuse these character-deficient, talented beings, who have no idea how to lead the souls of human beings, nor how to disclose the truth and act accordingly to the truth that reveals itself. The corrupt lead by their will; the wise let their will be guided by the light of truth.

Again, "what leads the leader?"

Warrior: The truth leads.

Guardian: We are so afraid of judging others, with our desire to be accepted and our fear of being judged in kind. This immaturity of soul is averse to the commands of truth. We don't want to listen. We don't want the radical change of truth commanding our wills. We don't want the burden of the metaphysical freedom—the commands of truth. Instead, we suffer the pleasure of fiction. Look at the consumer and entertainment industries—love of inanimate things as idols, love of escapism instead of truth.

Warrior: I sense your rage. What do you do to temper the fire and fury directed at your adversaries, many whom exercise coercive power over much of humanity?

Guardian: I pray for the virtue of temperance. I practice the virtue of gentleness towards adversaries. They are simply weak and underdeveloped. It's the qualities I see in them that fuel the fire, not the souls exhibiting those qualities. The self-deception is terrifying; they suffer ignorance. We suffer self-knowledge and compassion. It seems we are always suffering.

Warrior: So, you transmute the anger into gentleness?

Guardian: I hope so, but I fail daily. Forgiveness, detachment and humility lead to the virtue of gentleness.

Aquinas mentors us here–

> Gentleness makes man a master of his being.[14]

Warrior: We are in the midst of self-examination and I must tell you what I am seeing. The anger in you, the rage, the madness—are you telling me that you're learning to use that spirit wisely by transforming it into gentleness of being?

Guardian: That is what I'm saying, and it's why I'm not living as a noble savage in the wilderness.

That is why I practice detachment and humility. The virtues reign in the soul's spirited-nature. The virtues make sure that the spirited-nature does not dominate the intellect and the will.

There is freedom in humility. I am of little importance. I am expendable. Life goes on just fine with or without me. I learned these bitter truths in the military. Independent of our nothingness, we learn freedom and fulfillment by living our purpose and our potential, by living our calling and our vocation. The calling is where we discover significance, seriousness, and importance.

---

[14] Josef Pieper, *The Cardinal Virtues*, commenting on Saint Thomas and the virtue of temperance.

When I started teaching leadership, I was brought face-to-face with executives I hated—snakes in the form of vanity, narcissism, conceitedness, and arrogance. They mesmerized and conned people. They achieved. I wanted to destroy them. But as a teacher, all I could do was observe and keep silent.

Warrior: I'm reminded of sacred scripture–

> Behold, I am sending you like lambs among wolves; therefore, be wise as serpents and pure as doves.[15]

Guardian: Silence is a mighty weapon with which to crush narcissists. They need someone to fight with. I sit in silence and observe.

Warrior: You do this to ensure you do not get ensnared.

Guardian: Indeed.

Warrior: What I see–

You are speaking of the challenge to become pure in heart. To love your enemies and your friends equally in spirit, to become invincible in the soul to endure your calling and purpose.

To do this, your calling is revealing all your blind-spots, all the darkness and imperfections within that must be cleansed and purified so that you can arrive at metaphysical freedom.

> I have learned here that for you to be my inquisitor, seeking to discover the elements of the warrior, is easy.

> What is not easy, I've learned, is the constant self-examination that you are willingly putting yourself through, using me to keep you accountable.

> I have learned, as a truth-seeker, that we must practice introspection, a method by which the virtues of detachment and humility and gentleness make the heart and mind pure and lucid, so that truth will reveal itself.

Guardian: I also pray to be unconditionally loving (charity/ *agape*) and I do my best to take the anger and transform it into a loving gentleness, so that I can connect with the souls of other human beings. To be like sunlight instead of a volcano.

Warrior: Now I'm seeing how we practice the shedding of the ego, of the outer nature, through meditation and contemplation, to reveal the inner nature.

---

[15] The Holy Bible, *Book of Matthew*, Lamsa translation.

Guardian: The principle of *via negativa*—this is not that—the way of denial. We do this by the constant removal of all non-essentials and non-necessities. In the absence of the emotions or the ego, what is left? What reveals itself? Light and truth as awareness and knowing?

I've been seeking to describe how meditation and contemplation wield light and truth. I think I've just hit on the right note. We lead light through meditation, to transmute the spirited nature from a violent expression to a gentle one. It's still fire; it's just that the way we wield it changes.

Now we must explore how to do this with all elements, with all learning, with all skills, and with all challenges.

Do you see?

Warrior: My blessed friend, I see.

> We seek to know how to become virtuous.

> We seek to know how to know truth.

> We seek to know how to make virtue, knowledge and skill an extension of our being, of the light and truth within.

Now I see the practical application. Light and truth, wielded through meditation and contemplation, are how we achieve the *hexis*, the active condition, by responding to the challenges of living.

Now I see the soul's constant *energeia*, the being-at-work, as the taking command of the faculties of our inner nature—the will, the intelligence, the spirit. The *energeia* coaxes out virtuous words, deeds, and feelings, as it builds a relationship with the outer nature and reality itself—with nature, living beings, human beings, purposeful work, knowledge and skills. By living, we are beings-at-work, knowing, willing, and acting. The soul and the knowledge are one and the same—one soul in multiple bodies.

I am seeing that we build, for good or for bad, a relationship with living itself. It's fascinating.

Guardian: I'm seeing with more clarity too. The relationship concept revealed a deeper understanding.

Now, when speaking of ego-shedding, what is it that we are shedding?

We are shedding qualities of will, spirit, and intelligence that have been molded into delusion and deception, manifesting as vanity, arrogance, narcissism and conceitedness. And this happens because the soul's powers have been taken over by the body's primal drives (security, protection, thirst, hunger and sex). It is as though these primal drives press upon the soul's faculties, instead of the soul pressing upon and leading the primal drives.

We tell people to be virtuous but we don't teach them how to be virtuous. Trying to become virtuous by the power of primal drives leads to bondage. This is what is occurring and no one knows it—they've become enslaved by the inordinate desires created by the primal drives. The only way to become virtuous is by the leadership of the primordial drives—the powers of soul.

In our art, we reclaim command of the soul's faculties. We take command of the primal drives. Our souls' primordial essence and drives know no suffering, pain, sorrow or fatigue. Primordial means what is ancient and oldest and eternal in us. The soul does know good from bad, right from wrong, and suffers when it's in error. The body knows sickness, pain, disease, but it does not know right from wrong. The primal drives do not know right or wrong, good or bad.

Are we seeing more clearly?

Warrior: Yes

Guardian: In our art, we turn away from the ego, from the limited, from the corrupted, and turn our faculties to the source, to light, to truth, and let these causes strengthen our faculties and lead us on the path to liberation. I see liberation as a bonding to light and truth, simply and completely, at all times.

In our art, we fail when the ego resists and turns away from this bonding.

Before our expedition I never thought much about our adversary the ego; I only thought about the knowledge and the techniques of the light and truth.

Warrior: Sun Tzu[16] mentors here–

> He who knows his opponent and knows himself will not be imperiled in a hundred battles.

Guardian: Until now, I could not see what it *is* that resists truth and goodness and beauty because I had not studied the enemy. We will have to confront this adversary once we discover our archetype, to test it and strengthen it in battle with the adversary.

Warrior: This is why you speculated that the warrior and guardian archetypes would be needed to fight the adversary. You knew that this is a war. You knew that there is an adversary. And you are seeking to clarify this adversary and our archetype.

Guardian: What led me this far is the concept that, until the soul bonds with light and truth, there is a spiritual war raging in the heart and mind of each soul.

---

[16] Sun Tzu, *The Art of War*, Mair Translation.

This is why we look to guardians and warriors. Both display the courage, the humility, the detachment, the sacrifice, the excellence, and the pursuit of mastery to engage in combat.

Both archetypes are expendable and will give their lives defending and protecting others.

As we ascend, I see a clearer reason for our work, and a more important mission.

Warrior: What?

Guardian: In free societies we are not only concerned with the education of leaders.

We are equally concerned with the education of followers.

Few are called to lead in our art. All are called to live the adventure and burden of freedom.

We need to make sure followers know who is trustworthy and worthy of admiration, and who is not. We need to teach followers to turn away from the masters of deception.

Now I'm seeing more clearly the archetype for our art. I'm seeing an indirect approach. Yes, we train the leaders, but we must simultaneously educate the souls of the followers. Our "followers" follow the truth, not the leader, just as the leader follows the truth, not her will.

And why is this dual-function critical?

Warrior: So the followers turn to our leaders and away from demagogues and tyrants.

Guardian: Followership is a beautiful activity. Followers should demand that leaders help and guide them to flourishing states. We are on guard against blind faith and blind obedience. Both the leader and the followers are reaching toward light and truth.

Warrior: This is another breakthrough, a deeper truth revealing itself. We've been focusing on training leaders, but the whole point of training leaders is the impact they have on free citizens.

Guardian: I happily follow human beings who I admire. I'm surrounded by them. I experience increased freedom around these admirable beings.

Warrior: So now we have another aim: to awaken an understanding in followers, so that they have the ability to discern between the true and the false leaders?

Guardian: Yes, indeed. I feared that I was presumptuous in saying that the first archetypes our leaders should emulate are the guardian and the warrior. When I initiated the examination into the warrior archetype, I kept going deeper into the depths because I did not want to prove foolish. With your help, I have been saved from this fear.

Warrior: Fear not, my wild friend. Your contemplative nature guards you from such foolishness. You listen to the inner guidance. This guidance, not you, made the judgment that warriors and guardians, the true ones, are the ideal beginning patterns. You use the warrior and the guardian because they seek truth and excellence, and they display courage and valor in their endeavors.

You want leaders who possess both physical and moral courage, both truth and excellence, both vigor and valor.

Keep diving, I will follow.

Guardian: Then, what I am seeing is–

We need to teach followers to display courage by turning from darkness to light. The relationship between leader and follower is one soul in two bodies. We need to seek that depth of unity, harmony, and resonance.

We need to prepare followers for when right choices require actions that are disorienting and uncomfortable. Followers, indeed, need truth and wisdom, to understand that change for the good is going to challenge their habits, appetites, passions, and beliefs.

Jefferson mentors us here–

> I know no safe depositary of the ultimate powers of the society but the people themselves; and if we think them not enlightened enough to exercise their control with a wholesome discretion, the remedy is not to take it from them, but to inform their discretion by education. This is the true corrective of abuses of constitutional power.[17]

Warrior: Citizens as one soul in two bodies, both the leader and the follower, one in light and truth. Leaders are the custodians of the citizens' basic governmental needs of security, protection and well-being of mind and body.

Thoreau mentors us here–

> That government is best which governs least.

> That government is best which governs not at all.[18]

And why is that? The soul is the source of power and does not need to be governed; it must govern itself. It is sovereign over its being. But the ego, the fiction, thrives on control and dominance. God does not control man; man must not control man. The only reason for government as such is because we, as a species, are still gripped by the ego and the primal drives.

Guardian: We need to teach followers that the panderers and demagogues play on their irrational nature, on their fears and desires and passions. They need to learn to see how the

---

[17] Thomas Jefferson, Thomas Jefferson to William Jarvis, 1820.
[18] Henry David Thoreau, *Walden*.

manipulators prey on their weaknesses and fears. We need to educate their reason to be sharp and discerning.

This is the bitter truth. Our leaders are not saviors. Our leaders are shepherds. Truth demands that all of us bond with the light that frees the soul. All of us, every last one.

Warrior: You are showing your Catholic heritage, the call to lead souls to God, or in our art, to lead souls to light and truth. Noble and good is this calling, but difficult and treacherous to make it manifest.

Guardian: This is how our citizens will create strong foundations and conditions for living more truthfully and purposefully. It is their choice. We trust in the power of choice.

We need to teach followers to be on guard, always, when a leader appears, so that they are not seduced by image-seekers, wealth-seekers, and control-seekers—all of whom are society's seductive snake charmers.

What would you call the opposite of warrior and guardian? Who is the adversary?

Warrior: Weasels, rats, scumbags, temptresses, vultures—predatory natures.

Guardian: How are these the adversaries of the warrior and the guardian?

Warrior: I'm searching my mind for the qualities so as not to judge the person–

> Tyrants and despots are the adversaries of the warrior and guardian.

I'm hunting for qualities to be on guard against–

> Weasel implies an intention to mislead. To lie. To manipulate.

> Rat implies what is contemptible and cowardly. Sycophant, flatterer and deceiver.

> Scumbag implies abusive, worthless, despicable, immoral, wretched.

> Temptress implies seductive, manipulative, alluring, attracting. To deceive away from truth.

> Vulture implies preying on and tormenting the mind and emotions. Rapacious, violent, greedy, grasping.

> Tyrant implies cruelty, violence, and wickedness.

> Despot implies absolute rule and oppression.

And let me add–

> Narcissist implies the worst kind of vanity, extreme self-love and self-admiration.

> Vampire implies preying ruthlessly on others.

Guardian: These are the wicked and wretched qualities that can be found in a human being?

Warrior: Yes, most certainly.

Guardian: What do we do to combat these qualities?

Warrior: If a soul is not willing to correct itself, we use coercive methods to render those human beings powerless.

If the soul is willing to rehabilitate itself, then we guide it through rigorous purification and cleansing techniques. These techniques reach the light and truth, activate the powers of will and intelligence, and transform the qualities from cowardice to courage, from abuse to kindness, from immoral to moral, from greed to generosity, and from vanity to humility.

By observing the nature of our adversary, we can determine how our archetypes will be the antidotes and counter-measures, the truth-serums and truth-knowing, that prepare our leaders to combat the adversary.

Our leaders must learn to see the energy, character, and spirit of the beings before them, with the ability to make the distinction between friend and adversary. When we see the adversarial qualities arise in our friends, we strike them down, unapologetically. Such is our allegiance to the truth.

Saint John mentors us here–

> But when the spirit of truth is come, he will guide you into all the truth.[19]

When we see the opposites, when we see the adversaries, we will be able to wield the antidotes, the weapons, and the techniques to engage in non-martial combat.

Warrior: What is the greatest weapon we have?

Guardian: Aside from light and truth themselves?

Warrior: No, I mean how best to use light and truth in non-martial combat?

Guardian: In the beginning, to practice detachment and humility, one of the greatest weapons we have is for our leaders and followers to use silence as they turn away from our adversaries, without needing a leader to shepherd and guide them.

The tactic is the dual threat of silence and distance. Our adversaries are rendered powerless when human beings turn away from them and rest in silence.

Warrior: You mean, the adversary's followers make it powerful?

---

[19] The Holy Bible, *Book of John*, Lamsa Translation.

Guardian: Yes. In free societies, all power is given to the individual. The individuals, when turning to a leader, give that leader power. When individuals turn away, the leader becomes powerless. Most individuals do not see this, and most, if they do, do not have the moral courage to break away, to turn the other way, to turn towards the good.

Warrior: Can you give an example?

Guardian: Competitive Sports, TV Shows, Movies, Musicians, Networks, Advertising—their source of power is their ability to take your attention and glue it to the screen, to the show, to the movie, to the event and to the news. All of this is non-essential, non-necessary, superficial and profitable. Truth is not profitable. Illusion is profitable.

Warrior: And how are we to combat it?

Guardian: What if, in mass, all people turned off social medial and turned off TV networks and Cable networks? What would happen?

Warrior: Ah. There would be no viewership. No viewership means no advertising dollars. No viewership means no ticket sales. Empty stadiums and empty arenas. The source that funnels money is halted.

Guardian: If we are rediscovering the perennial war against truth, there should be little room for entertainment because souls, instead of being passively entertained, are concentrated on awakening their potencies and fulfilling their purpose. This actualization of potencies is unlimited and unending.

I would love to see the political and organizational response to the collective action of a global 30-day fast from work, media, and print. Imagine what 30 days would do to recharge the truth and beauty of the human being, the human community, and the earth? A global strategic pause.

We would learn to enjoy the company of our neighbors by engaging in simple civic life.

We would realize how powerful and free we are, in free societies, by the practice of *via negativa*.

Do you not see, our adversaries are indeed vampires; they ruthlessly prey on the thoughts, feelings, desires, and actions of human attention, of human energy and of human potency.

They feed on our inordinate desires and appetites, which they call market share and growth, by fabricating and manufacturing, like some sort of magician, the idea that non-essentials are essential. This fabricating and manufacturing ability is the magic they employ to control and manipulate human beings by hijacking their minds and wills. Our will is most weak at night and what do we do at night? Passively watch the screen—hypnotism of the most dangerous kind.

These vampires lose all power when people reject them and turn away.

Warrior: Do you have experience in this, using silence and distance?

Guardian: My good man, the first thing I had to learn was my own emancipation from the bondage of the adversary.

I knew I was ensnared. But I had no idea how to free myself from the bondage.

Warrior: What did you do?

Guardian: I entered the background, where God is, where truth is, where light is. I became a silent witness, a contemplative. I learned to close my eyes and pray in stillness and silence and wait. In this state, I learned to work through the drives and desires that ensnared me.

Warrior: Ah. This is how you discovered the spiritual cyclical framework?

Guardian: Indeed. Nothing had to change. I had to change. I did not look for my career to change. I did not look for my relationships to change. I did not look for my finances to change.

I bypassed the means of acquiring external power.

Instead, I distanced and detached myself from all of it. I needed truth. I needed light. I needed understanding. Then I began to experience the subtle awakenings. I learned to move from this awakening back into life, back into work, back into relationships.

Warrior: You learned from Thoreau.

Guardian: Yes. I discovered that wherever I am is where the action is. I saw how the senses and the ego crave sensory-stimulation, resulting in insatiable drives that never lead to satiation, nor to freedom, but only to bondage. I noticed how the ego and the body and the senses get restless in the silence and stillness of a soul seeking truth. I learned how the restlessness of the senses could be eased into stillness by the silence and solitude of meditation.

Then the depths would send wisdom upward to my conscious mind, like a mysterious inner oracle of truth. The depths speak—truly, the god-within speaks. And its speech is very different from the swirling thoughts of the superficial mind. Show me a soul's desires and I will know what's swirling in her thinking. Our thoughts are a reflection of our state of being; change the state of being and watch how the thinking changes.

Warrior: Do you have an example?

Guardian: Why would I trust a century of nepotism at the Grey Lady, by the Sulzberger dynasty? Why would I trust twenty years of nepotism in the Oval Office, by the Bush dynasty?

Why would I trust the business and financial control of the American oligarchies and our taxation system?

Warrior: And why trust the monarchs and tyrants abroad?

Guardian: Indeed. I never trusted the generals, the entertainers, the politicians, the owners, the executives, the athletes, and the worst of them all, the pundits, the chattering class. Something is wrong in a society that pays a chatterer, a talking-head, the news and show anchor, twenty-million dollars. Something is wrong in a society that pays thespians, the acting class, millions of dollars. What do we value? Greed and lust or generosity and charity? Thespians strike our emotions, something that we are called to transcend and transform, not mull around in. Why would I want someone to strike my emotions for entertainment? It's a serious game we play now. Few are serious enough for our art. And yes, I too, love great films and music and athletics, as a medium for the expression of the soul.

Sach's mentors us here–

> Serious (spoudaios) – Deserving respect. This is the word that Aristotle reserves for people of the highest human excellence, who see things as they are and know which of them is worth taking seriously, thus providing, by their own judgment and choices, the standards for the rest of us to look to…a truly serious person takes few things seriously.[20]

> Strike my reason, strike my will, strike the light and truth.

> I take one thing seriously—the growth of the soul.

All our institutional and enterprise leaders have something to gain and something to lose. Unless you have nothing to gain or lose but the truth, you are not trustworthy. I do not trust *the takers* and *the gainers*.

What happened to the Constitutional Republic's aim of leading a strong Commonwealth?

Why would I take debt (which I did and suffered) for student loans, car loans, and a mortgage, when I had no trust, no command and no understanding of the "ways of the world?" I do not trust the principles of the "banking fractional system." I do not trust the leviathan-cube of the ego-body-octagon, that I found myself in.

I had to become free in being before I engaged the truth of mankind's creation. I learned about freedom not only from the sages, but, from the entrepreneurs–the boldness of creating something from nothing but an idea, and then making it manifest. Marvin Bower[21], a Founder of McKinsey, created the industry of management consulting. I learned from him–

---

[20] Aristotle, *Nicomachean Ethics*, Sachs Translation.
[21] Bower, *The Will to Manage*, inscription to a partner on an original 1966 edition.

Valued partner and outstanding contributor of new thinking to our exciting adventure of building McKinsey & Company into a world-wide force for strengthening the will to manage.

Warrior: The lesson of Plato's "Allegory of the Cave" still stands, in any human endeavor. The call to adventure leads one out of the cave, out of passivity, and demands the exercise of courage to cross the threshold and enter into the unknown sea.

Guardian: Yes. I learned from Bower. Virtuous executives make business a calling and an adventure. He helped ramp up the management functions of Eisenhower's White House.

The titans—Eisenhower, Marshall, Churchill, Bower, Drucker, Maslow, Geneen—I learned from them.

Independent of what I learned from them, I still did not trust and did not understand "the ways of the world." I detached myself and wrestled myself free from the insanity of "civilized society." I found solace in the ways of the transcendentalists, in the ways of self-reliance. Thoreau read not only the Bible, but the *Upanishads* and *The Bhagavad Gita*, Plato and Aristotle and Homer. He spoke of the true treasures of humanity. He led me to the ancient canons of the sacred and wisdom literature. I read, and the more I read, I asked, "why are we not taught how to become these truths?" These canons were what I searched for—they are the treasures I hunted for. They made the thoughts and writings of Eisenhower, Bower, Maslow, let alone the moderns, look childish. I can hardly read anything now, other than these writings, such is the power of their truth and wisdom. The writings helped wrestle my soul free from conditioned existence. I sought to enter the eternal seas.

I learned to trust only those who disclose truth and follow the truth. The true warriors, the true saints, the true sages, the true philosophers—I learned to trust, not them, but their ways of being, their techniques and practices. When I followed the pathless path, the truth, light penetrated the depths of my soul. I began to experience the first light of freedom.

I learned that wherever we find ourselves there is work to be done. I learned one-pointed concentration. I learned never to rush. I learned to move at a contemplative pace. I learned the beauty and freedom of minding my own business. I learned to hunt for important work and devote my being to it. I am still learning what I learned back then.

Warrior: This is how you learned the counter-measures to resist the tempters and the seducers, the tyrants and the manipulators?

Guardian: Yes. I learned that to do this I had to discover the true adversary, the one that lives within. The stinging truth of the adversary within is what awakened me from the fictions I lived. I lived in the fictions of personality, of success, of winning, and of wealth. I learned, in truth, that I am not important. I learned to trust, not in others, but to trust in the life that created me. The life that creates life—I listen to its guidance and commands.

Warrior: Faith in action?

Guardian: Yes. It is simple—our adversary rejects the truth. That rejection closes the door to truth-seeking. If the door to truth-seeking is closed, there is no transcending ignorance and darkness; it is a mirrored self-imprisonment that appears to be free.

Warrior: Narcissism.

Guardian: Yes, the most pernicious type of adversary. Early on, when I confronted our adversaries, who I learned are in metaphysical prison, I used the weapons of silence, distance and prayer to counter the fire in me, the wrath in me, the corruption in me, to crush them physically, mentally, and spiritually. As a guardian, when I see these predators, I must attack, but I must employ indirect tactics because of the non-mortal kind of combat our art demands.

Warrior: Good God, they are *real* vampires, takers instead of givers. They need the admiration, attention and energy of others in order to experience power, because they do not possess inner power.

Guardian: Yes. This is the benefit of the indirect approach—strip and starve them of their source of power, instead of engaging them and taking a direct shot.

Warrior: We are getting closer to our adversary's archetype. The villains—the Magicians, the Illusionists, the Image-seekers, the Takers.

Guardian: Now I'm ready to examine the archetypes of warrior and guardian. I have enough insight into our adversary. I needed the perspective to shift.

Thank you for your guidance as I wrestled through the intellectual impasse. We will study the adversary later. I needed these seeds planted to prepare me for what we will face further on.

This is the first time, I'm cautious to share, but I see the summit. I think I see the route. The vision has revealed itself.

Tell me again the means of the warrior?

Warrior: The means is violence to make the adversary powerless—morally, intellectually, physically, and economically.

Guardian: Good. I see how means and ends are united.

For a guardian, the means is truth, to make a friend powerful—morally, intellectual, physically, economically and spiritually.

Tell me, how do you define violence? I ask because we may need to employ non-martial violence against the adversary who is not a friend. And when we do this, we will be called aggressors.

Warrior: For violence, let us use the three-fold definition[22]

1. The exercise of physical force so as to cause injury or damage to a person or property.
2. The state or quality of being violent in action or effect; great force or strength in operation; vehemence, severity, intensity.
3. Strength or intensity of emotion; fervor, passion.

Guardian: Good. It is clear, in our art, that we will use this violent nature toward physical strength, intellectual might, moral steadfastness, and spiritual vigor.

But we will not use the term violence because our leaders will reject the need for violent capabilities if they are leading in light and truth. This is because they have not faced the adversary. We will prepare them to face the adversary.

We must seek and know the roots, the causes, and the qualities of great force, great strength, great intensity, and great passion. These great qualities will be the second-order effects emanating from the goodness of the soul's light and truth, which can appear blinding, forceful and violent. Yes. Our leaders will have violent capabilities.

Warrior: We'll think of violence as great force and great strength to wield moral courage.

Guardian: When you train warriors, you train them in skills, techniques, and tactics aimed to increase their lethalness in violence when they engage the enemy.

Warrior: Yes.

Guardian: This means the exercise of intense physical force and intense emotional force in action.

Warrior: Yes. We are killers. We hunt human beings who are our adversaries.

Guardian: Okay. That's what I'm looking for, beyond merely using violence as a means, you are hunters.

Warrior: Yes.

Guardians: That is a formidable skill. I am a hunter too.

Let me look at the concepts now–

---

[22] O.E.D. definition of violence.

Violence, Great Strength, Great Emotions, Great Force, Killers, Hunters, Formidable Skills.

I'm in the process of destructive deduction, to get to the essentials of the warrior's being.

Warrior: I am following.

Guardian: What is the central action of war?

Warrior: The battle.

Guardian: Battle means where the action is when there is contact?

Warrior: Yes. Distilled to the essence, the warrior is one who trains to flourish in battle.

Guardian: Distilled to its essence, how do you define battle?

Warrior: It's a duel, a battle of wills.

Guardian: Ah ha. It's the same with political battles, which are battles of wills, not of truth.

So, we add to the mix the concepts of duel, will and battle.

Warrior: Yes.

Guardian: How do you define duel?

Warrior: My pious friend, a duel is a gunfight. We are gunslingers.

I define duel as combat. In combat, no matter the plans, the enemy has a vote. He can choose to resist, defend, or attack.

Guardian: How do you define will?

Warrior: For will[23], let us use this two-fold definition–

1. The faculty by which a person exercises his or her capacity for initiating conscious and intentional action; power of choice in regard to action.
2. Intention or determination that what one wishes or ordains be done by another or others; force or energy of intention.

Guardian: Do you see what is being revealed?

Warrior: Yes. I see Clausewitz's *coup d'esprit* as determination, and determination lives in *will*.

---

[23] O.E.D. definition of will.

I am seeing *"strength of will"* as the most critical aim of our training, both for leaders and for followers.

> The will to courage
> The will to fight
> The will to skill
> The will to knowledge
> The will to learn
> The will to awaken
> The will to manage
> The will to command
> The will to lead
> The will to truth
> The will to act
> The will to be guided by truth

What I am seeing is that the will, once it receives light and truth, is the soul's indefatigable source of power. I see the will as the most important faculty of the soul. I see the will being instructed and energized with light to pursue truth.

Guardian: And if someone were to ask, why meditation?

Warrior: We respond that meditation is where the will receives light and is energized by light. With this light, the will takes command of truth and delivers it as right intentions and right actions.

Guardian: And if someone were to ask, why contemplation?

Warrior: We respond that is how the intelligence informs the will to act—in truth, in rightness, in beauty, in harmony. We respond, that is how the soul practices truth-disclosing. The highest art is when the soul, through decades of experience, can observe an impasse or a challenge or a battle and have the *coup d'oeil* to see the light of the situation, to disclose the truth of the situation and to act with vigor and intensity.

Guardian: That is what we were seeking to understand. We are making progress. One of two great spiritual powers is the human will. Our adversaries manipulate the wills of others; we bring dignity and truth and light to the wills of others.

Warrior: When the will turns away from light and truth and towards darkness and ignorance, that is what leads to the fiction of ego. It's a mirage. It's the result of the veil of darkness.

Huxley[24] now mentors–

---

[24] Huxley, *The Perennial Philosophy*.

Voluntas propria (The Takers) vs. Voluntas communis (The Givers)

Voluntas propria is the will to get and hold for oneself. It is the root of all sin.

Voluntas communis is the will to share, the will common to soul and source. The source of love is this will.

Guardian: That is the crux of the battle—

Using the will to dominate or using the will to liberate.

The fiction is the image resulting from a corrupt and deformed application of the soul's powers.

The truth is the known resulting from a purified and principled application of the soul's powers.

Our will knows no fatigue or suffering or injury; it is the driver of all our faculties.

The will acts, and the intelligence leads the will to act.

Our will for good wields light and truth, and we learn to do this with integrity by the methods of meditation and contemplation. Without these, the will is blind and does not even know it. Self-knowledge is not possible without tools of self-reflection.

When the will is underdeveloped, it cannot be expected to know what to do. That is how the primal drives take hold of the will—*Voluntas propria.*

Now we see the reason our students need guides—they need teachers to exercise and strengthen their power of will. The soul, as a being, needs the strength to take command of the will and the intelligence.

When the will is corrupted, it needs to be held accountable and corrected. Out of expediency, we often punish the will and neglect to correct it.

We now understand that when the will is corrupted and deformed, we see qualities of arrogance, vanity and conceitedness as active conditions. The *hexis*, or active condition, is vice instead of virtue.

Our whole aim is to set the will in harmony with light and truth. Yes, there will be temporal challenges that are complex and difficult to solve, but human beings need not add more chaos, distortion and deception because they are either underdeveloped or corrupted in their beings.

Warrior: What we are seeing is that many human beings are either underdeveloped or corrupt.

Guardian: Yes. And because more are underdeveloped than corrupted, they are carried away by passions and the body-octagon drives of security, protection, thirst, hunger and sex. They are easily manipulated by advertisers, politicians and executives—the coercive power brokers. I am seeing this terrain now with clarity; I see how to engage in the combat.

If our substance is light and our nature is truth, we have discovered what directs our action, for good or for bad—the consent of the will.

We now see how the will can either come into harmony with light and truth or manipulate light and truth. The former leads to goodness the latter to wickedness. We are not designed to wield light and truth to our own ends; we are designed to wield light and truth to true ends.

Warrior: Do you see the paradox? The will can wield light and truth correctly or incorrectly.

Guardian: In the difference between the mystics and the magicians the will is everything.

Warrior: That is why in training, most people do not fail; they quit.

Guardian: Good God, now I know what drives me and where it got started.

Warrior: What?

Guardian: In my formative years, my will got crushed and I did not even know it. I made decisions out of fear and external pressure and did not even realize the corruption taking place in my soul.

Warrior: Do you have an example?

I loved athletics and I had the opportunity, after high school, to compete in junior leagues before going to college, to prepare to play Division 1.

Warrior: And what did you do?

Guardian: I went to college.

Warrior: Why?

Guardian: Though I didn't know it at the time, out of fear of the future. I still tried out, knowing I would get cut from the team. The coach said to go play juniors for two years and then return. It was not a question of potential talent; it was a question of maturity and growth—actualizing the talent.

Warrior: Did you leave to play juniors?

Guardian: No.

Warrior: Why not?

Guardian: Though I didn't know it, fear of failure and fear of the unknown.

Warrior: What are you saying?

Guardian: I'm saying I quit.

Warrior: There it is. The bitter truth. You quit.

Guardian: Fear took hold of my will and I had no idea. I was in bondage, darkness and ignorance. It was hell.

My will had been rendered powerless by an internal fear I could not see, but one that shaped my decisions. I had a great fear of failure and did not even know it.

Warrior: The brutality of truth's self-knowledge.

Guardian: The sting of self-knowledge.

Why do I share this? We need the courage to look within and see our imperfections, our ignorance, our darkness and our bondage, so we can free ourselves of them.

We're highlighting the seriousness of striking the "power of will" towards the truth. I've had direct experiences of the will being assaulted and diverted from the truth.

Back then, in my formative years, I had no idea that the will of my being suffered the assaults of fear, the assaults of the ego, and the assaults of the primal drives.

Warrior: Now we add fear as an adversary?

Guardian: Indeed.

I had no idea what lurked in the depths of my being. I did not even know what "being" was. The moral reasoning process remained veiled; the motive remained hidden. I did not know how these hidden motives convert intentions to actions. The motive of fear hid inside me, and I did not act truthfully; I acted in cowardice.

Warrior: Painful.

Guardian: Pain, anger, and sorrow gripped my being. Truth remained hidden. Understanding remained hidden. Had I known, I would have pursued my goal until I failed or succeeded, but I would not have quit the pursuit. That fear of failure cursed me for a long time. The fear created a fog around my intelligence and I had no idea. I regret so many "acts" from my formative years.

Thank God for the power of self-examination. Introspection leads to understanding, understanding leads to truth, and truth leads to unhiddenness, so we can see what is and act accordingly.

That is why we practice self-examination, to see our deep motives and if necessary to change them by the power of will. The will, not intelligence, is the source of courage and fortitude.

Warrior: Now I understand why you're wild with divine madness in your pursuit of truth, light, and leadership.

You are all in. You've leaped into the abyss. You are willing to die on the ascent.

You'd rather die than quit again on what you know to be true and living in you.

It is good you experienced this bitter truth early on. The pain and suffering strengthened and awakened you.

Guardian: This is why dialogue is so important. To reveal what is hidden. To strike and lead it out.

Warrior: It's fascinating to witness how our dialogue keeps triggering self-awareness as we study knowledge and archetypes.

Guardian: That's why *telling* people what to do and what to know is dangerous.

Warrior: Why?

Guardian: It means we deny their intelligences and wills the chance to discover it themselves. We strip them of the burden to come to know, to understand and to act. We neuter them, we castrate them, we strip them of their potency, power, and vigor.

We need our leaders to heighten and deepen their awareness—to see and respond in an adaptable, non-premeditated way.

Warrior: This is what warriors are excellent at: responding, methodically and deliberately, instead of reacting.

The concepts we have for warrior are–

Violence, Great Strength, Great Emotion, Great Force, Killers, Hunters, Formidable Skills, Battler, Dueler, Willpower, and Combative.

This is the is-ness of the nature of the warrior.

Guardian: This is-ness is an extension of their being. That is what I am seeking to produce in our art—an is-ness.

Warrior: That is why the training is rigorous.

Guardian: What is the main obstacle in battle?

Warrior: The main obstacle, aside from preparing for the duel, is termed friction.

Friction, coined by Clausewitz, is that element in war that makes even the simplest action difficult. This is due to the indomitable physical pressures placed on a soldier.

To train for combat, to overcome friction, Clausewitz sets the aim–

> Perseverance in the chosen course is the essential counter-weight, provided that no compelling reasons intervene to the contrary. Moreover, there is hardly a worthwhile enterprise in war whose execution does not call for infinite effort, trouble, and privation; and as man under pressure tends to give in to physical and intellectual weakness, only great strength of will can lead to the objective. It is steadfastness of will that earns the admiration of the world and of posterity.[25]

Guardian: We, with Clausewitz as a guide, can lay down the principle that "great strength of will" is necessary and essential for any noble endeavor.

As you train warriors for indefatigable physical exertion, we will train the intelligence for indefatigable mental exertion in our art.

Warrior: This is how we can prevent moral cowardice and strengthen moral courage.

I need to add to your understanding of friction–

All plans, even the most complex, appear simple on paper until you engage in combat. In combat, all there is is friction. It's the nature of war that reveals the element of friction. In combat, we seek to reduce our friction and increase that of our enemy. This is where the art of war comes into view. Sun Tzu stated that to do this, you must know your enemy and you must know yourself.[26]

Guardian: Few know themselves and few know the enemy. How is this not the same as the Delphic Oracle's "Know Thyself"?[27]

Warrior: It is. That is why in our art, we aim to know ourselves and we aim to know the adversary. The more you know "thyself," the more you know what is in the "thyself" of every other soul, be she friend or adversary.

There are no short-cuts to accelerate this knowing—only time, energy, training, skill, and experience.

Guardian: Then, from the perspectives of economy of effort and the law of constraints, the warriors who thrive most adapt best to friction and see it as the main obstacle and main tactic to wield in their art?

---

[25] Clausewitz, *On War*.

[26] Sun Tzu, *The Art of War*, Mair Translation.

[27] Plato, *Apology*.

Warrior: You mean, learning to wield friction? Yes. The masters of war know how to wield friction against the enemy.

That is why we train with rigor and intensity. We make simple things tough in training to strengthen the will, body and mind to thrive in the nature of war.

Guardian: You highlighted another key element. Not just *will*, not just intelligence, but *mindset*. Strengthening the mind to develop the mindset to master its response to friction and adversity.

> Writer: Dear Reader, the writer lives in this friction as he writes. Writing is a non-stop creative battle with friction and resistance. The writer uses will, energy and time to produce victory, one thought at a time.

Warrior: This is what makes warriors great problem solvers. We have the mindset to overcome any obstacle we face.

Guardian: Warriors demonstrate lucid mindsets when they engage in combat?

Warrior: Yes. Lucidness as the ability to unite the light of intuition with reason, from deep expertise and experience.

Guardian: *Coup d'oeil* as the hallmark of enlightened warriors?

Warrior: Yes. Wait–

You had this in mind for the entire cross-examination? To wrestle this consent out of me? This whole time you have used yourself as an indirect method to lead this out of me.

Guardian: Yes.

Warriors: As for warriors, most of us are developed to a minimum viable product standard.

The ones who rise above this standard to the ideal, those who self-actualize, might hit the mark of "Enlightened Warriors."

Guardian: Have you met these warriors?

Warrior: Yes.

Guardian: These enlightened warriors–

> Do they see what others cannot see?
> Do they see in the darkness?
> Do they see what is hidden?
> Do they act on their inner sight?

> Do they act on their inner truth?
> Do they let this light and truth guide their actions?
> Do they wield friction?
> Do they wield violence against the enemy?

Warrior: Yes.

Guardian: Do you trust these ones?

Warrior: Yes.

Guardian: I have been hunting for this nature.

These are the ones who can learn and teach our art.

Warrior: Why?

Guardian: We need realized beings who can set the example for our students. These enlightened warriors are the nature and essence we seek to awaken the potencies of others. These warriors will be able to see the deep structures that need to be awakened and realized in students through knowledge, teaching and training.

In teaching, the grace of the warrior is the same as the grace of the sage.

Warrior: Since we are friends, I must be honest. These ones I speak of, ones you call enlightened warriors, are indeed a mystical kind of being. There is a shining light in them, and they inspire not only by their excellence and skill, but by their being.

I have been resisting this truth the entire time because I did not understand it nor how to teach it.

Guardian: You hunted adversaries; I hunted sages. I hunt for natures who know light and truth.

You can teach these warriors, these leaders, the art of using their mystical light as a teaching method to strike the light in our students. Do you understand?

Warrior: Yes. I admit this truth. It is good you are a contemplative. You learned to hunt for the daemon, the genius, the God-within, the light of truth.

Guardian: Yes.

Warrior: It seems the warrior and the guardian are the same in being but different in aim. A warrior seeks to make the adversary powerless, and the guardian seeks to make the student powerful. Both use power, force, vigor, and excellence.

Guardian: Does not the warrior seek to make other warriors powerful?

Warrior: Yes.

Guardian: Then we need both abilities to be realized in our leaders. We need to produce combative truth-seekers who make their friends powerful and their adversaries powerless. The difference is that we will train specifically in non-martial combative arts.

Warrior: Peck coined adversaries of truth "people of the lie."

Guardian: Peck also coined the definition of *agape* (love)–

> The will to nurture one's own or another's spiritual growth.[28]

The basic truths are simple, let us not lie nor deceive–

Saint Matthew again mentors here–

> But let your words be yes, yes, and no, no; for anything which adds to these is a deception.[29]

Unlike the warrior, the guardian does not face mortal danger. The guardian does not face time constraints. The guardian rises above the temporal and reaches into the eternal.

Warrior: What does this imply?

Guardian: The experience of the warrior is a rush of adrenaline. The experience of the guardian is a rush of endorphins. We will use meditation and contemplation to guide these warriors as they prepare for a different kind of combat. Our combat lives in a deep peace and tranquility. This is how truth presents itself.

Warrior: Instead of adrenaline, the guardian experiences endorphins?

Guardian: Yes.

Warrior: The ascent become serene and beautiful instead of arduous and rigorous?

Guardian: Yes. That's the beauty and grace of the soul's maturity. I pray we become lighter and can see in this light, as though the individual light were becoming the cosmic light.

But we are nowhere near this realm. We are still hammering away at the impasses impeding truth at each stage of discovery.

What is the game of the warrior? Of combat, of battle? What is it?

Warrior: It's a game of chance.

---

[28] Scott Peck, *The Road Less Travelled*.
[29] The Holy Bible, *The Book of Matthew*, Lamsa Translation.

Guardian: What do you mean by chance?

Warrior: There's no guarantee of victory. Chance means the element of luck is at play.

Chance means war is a game of uncertainty. The goddess Fortuna is at play. Combat takes its course; it's not predictable. It's a game and he who learns from the unexpected generally wins. It's a game where, when the unexpected happens, you must learn to exploit that unexpectedness. You have to respond to it. Those who respond best to the unexpected tend to be victorious.[30]

Guardian: Does this not describe truth-disclosing as well, as the unexpected discloses itself and you have to respond to it, in order to gain an advantage?

Warrior: Yes. It appears that leading in battle is a truth-disclosing art.

Guardian: How does one expect the unexpected?

Warrior: He has the mindset to observe and wait.

Guardian: Tactical patience?

Warrior: Yes.

For an analogy, in chess, you need mastery to get underneath the game, to see it from a different perspective, and that different perspective reveals something that an opponent can't see.

Guardian: Truth discloses itself.

Warrior: Something reveals itself. Something becomes unhidden.

Guardian: That something is truth. We are discovering the foundation of why we ground our being in light and truth, in meditation and contemplation.

Warrior: This is why we begin, with our students, with self-examination, because it leads to self-knowledge—the truth of one's being.

Guardian: There is no bypassing self-knowledge in our art.

Warrior: No.

Guardian: It is the simplest and most difficult way to study the depths of being.

When we learn to do this, we can study any domain with the same techniques, and make knowledge an extension of our being.

Warrior: For what you are seeing, we can call on John Boyd to mentor us.

---

[30] B.H. Liddell Hart, *Strategy*.

He said that in complex and uncertain environments, we need to assimilate the knowledge, to embed the knowledge intuitively in us. Not "knowledge about" but "knowing." This assimilation, the pain we endure by changing our way of being, is the price we pay to learn this art.

He highlights this aim in his writings–

> To flourish and grow in a many-sided uncertain and ever-changing world that surrounds us, suggests that we have to make intuitive within ourselves those many practices we need to meet the exigencies of that world…. The contents… that comprise this Discourse unfold observations and ideas that contribute toward achieving or thwarting such an aim or purpose.[31]

Guardian: Dear God, this scientific strategist ended up a philosopher because, to compete, he needed the highest and most abstract intelligible concepts, so that the concepts could be re-configured, as needed, to win in combat.

> He is writing about how we make virtue, knowledge and skill an extension
> of our being.

This great strategist, through his study of war and science, states that not only is this possible, but it is essential to lead and fight effectively, on our own terms, "to improve our capacity for independent action."[32] He learned scientifically what the philosophers, especially Sun Tzu, knew to be metaphysical facts.

The uninitiated should not be expected to know and understand what we are doing. They need to trust us by faith that rigorous training will result in this intuitive ability.

When we hunt for the light and truth within, once we strike it in our students, it is up to them to turn their will to see and wield this light and truth. We cannot give this to them. That is the beauty of our work. They must become it. We can simply guide the awakening.

Warrior: Now we see the scientific and philosophical integration. Faith never counters reason, but leaps from it, into the unknown.

Guardian: What this implies is that our students will have a pattern to aim at in order to awaken and realize their beings. But they, by their courage, must take the leap.

This transformation, this awakening into an archetype, is a second birth.

This second birth is essential and it is painful. This is why our students need the will and mindset to endure the rigors of the training.

---

[31] Frans Osinga, *Science, Strategy and War–The Strategic Theory of John Boyd.*
[32] Frans Osinga, *Science, Strategy and War–The Strategic Theory of John Boyd.*

Warrior: Don't quit. This is redemptive. Making sure that the students understand it is good and noble work. All they are required to do is train, trust, and not quit until they are transformed.

Guardian: And we must not quit on them. We are their guides over the long haul. We will not rush their development.

Again, what is the object of war?

Warrior: The object of war is to make the adversary powerless, to thwart his freedom of action and freedom of movements. To make him submit. The object of war is not destruction; it's to stop the adversary's actions from affecting others negatively.

Sun Tzu says–

> Causing the enemy forces to submit without battle is the most excellence approach.[33]

Even better is to force an enemy to submit before they are an enemy. Better still is when the history books cannot discern the influences that occurred to–

> Stop an enemy before becoming an enemy.

> Stop the inception of the idea of war before it even occurs.

As Kautilya claims-

> The arrow shot by an archer may or may not kill a single man; but skillful intrigue devised by wise men can kill even those who are in the womb.[34]

And as Liddell Hart reflects, centuries later-

> On a higher plane of warfare, the impression made on the mind of the opposing commander can nullify the whole fighting power that his troops possess.

> And on a still higher plane, psychological pressure on the government of a country may suffice to cancel all the resources at its command so that the sword drops from a paralyzed hand.[35]

Which calls back to Genghis Khan's understanding of victory—that there is no honor to be found on the battlefield itself, but only in achieving your aims (of course the Khan failed to live within moral or ethical boundaries):

---

[33] Sun Tzu, *The Art of War*, Mair Translation.
[34] Kautilya, *Arthashastra*.
[35] B.H. Liddell Hart, *Strategy*.

The Mongols did not find honor in fighting; they found honor in winning.[36]

Which then points to the way to achieve this 'war without warfare,' or 'defeating an enemy when there is no enemy.' This approach is known as transcendence. It's when not just deterrence but true fear and respect enters the very heart of would-be adversaries so that no one even considers warfare in this or in any age. As Kautilya explains-

> [A conqueror] should infuse enthusiastic spirit among his own men and frighten his enemy's people by giving publicity to his power...[37]

And as Giap expounds-

> Our strategic decision...became the common resolve of our entire Party, our entire people and our entire army from North to South and inspired our nation to unite as one man...

> People seek transcendence, so this is not as much a push of leadership but rather a pull to reflect the true nature of the human soul of a constituency.[38]

And as Eric Hoffer claims-

> Though they seem to be at opposite poles, fanatics of all kinds are actually crowded together at one end. It is the fanatic and the moderate who are poles apart and never meet.[39]

Guardian: Let me ask, if there is no adversary, is there no need for a warrior? Does a warrior need an enemy?

Warrior: Yes, a warrior needs an adversary, a threat, a menace to counter. A warrior needs a fight even if that fight is in the distant future, and not yet even an idea in the minds of potential adversaries.

Guardian: Can we claim that our ego is the final nemesis, the final adversary, the final menace to fight, as it hides in the will and in the mind and corrupts both?

Warrior: We can claim it is a possibility to be investigated further.

Guardian: One more question—what is the experience of war like?

Warrior: I could use hell as a metaphor, but I'll add that it's an experience of constant antagonism and menace.

---

[36] Jake Weatherford, *Genghis Khan and the Making of the Modern World*.
[37] Kautilya, *Arthashastra*.
[38] Võ Nguyên Giáp, *Military Art of People's War*.
[39] Eric Hoffer, *The True Believer: Thoughts on the Nature of Mass Movements*.

Guardian: How do you explain that experience?

Warrior: I mean that it's an experience of an adversary, of an opponent, in the form of an opposing force seeking to render you powerless. It's a collision of wills, using physical, psychological and mental forces.

Guardian: So the essence of war is a battle of wills, each projecting its will against another with the goal to render the opponent powerless.

Warrior: Correct.

Guardian: In our study of the power of will, do you think the wise ever go to war with the wise?

Warrior: No.

Guardian: What would happen if the wills of all beings reached upward to light and truth?

Warrior: War would be rendered obsolete.

Guardian: But, war, on Earth, will never be obsolete, because of the collision of different beliefs, values, ideals, wants, and pressures.

Warrior: Yes. There is evil. I've seen evil.

Guardian: Until the evil in each human heart of each generation is purified, there will be war and suffering.

Warrior: Yes.

Guardian: To make sure I've understood correctly, this is the summary of the warrior archetype.

> Warrior Archetype–The means is violence; it is a battle of wills; the obstacle is friction; it is a game of chance; and the object is to make the enemy powerless.

Warrior: Yes.

Guardian: The warrior uses violence as the means of warfighting. This means the warrior is trained in the art of violence. The warrior prepares for a battle by learning the tactics of combat to battle against the will of an opposing force. In combat, the essential element to overcome is friction, and friction thwarts freedom of movement and makes the simplest tasks arduous because of combat's nature. Might against might. Will against will. Mind against mind. Moral bond against moral bond. The battle is a game of chance. There is no certainty once the battle begins, and those who capitalize on the unexpected increase their odds of winning. The end or aim or object of war is to render the opposing force powerless. That is the end of the game, making the enemy submit because they've been rendered powerless to attack or defend. Finally, the overall experience of war is constant threat and menace experienced as antagonism.

Warrior: Yes. But the warriors at every level, who are seeking this end state, are shackled by means, by parameters, set by the moral, ethical, and physical constraints governing the laws of war.

As Liddell Hart observes:

> A strategist should think in terms of paralyzing, not of killing.
>
> Even on the lower plane of warfare, a man killed is merely one man less, whereas a man unnerved is a highly infectious carrier of fear, capable of spreading an epidemic of panic.[40]

A cautionary insight–

We should never allow the ego, bloodlust, or tools that we happen to have at our disposal to dictate how we act to achieve an interest or advantage.

As Lawrence Freedman writes (and it can be applied even to the squad leader):

> Strategy is the central political art.
>
> It is about getting more out of a situation than the starting balance would suggest.
>
> It is the art of creating power.[41]

Guardian: In other words, a warrior should think not only in terms of the violence at his disposal, but of all physical and psychological means to achieve a goal. There won't be awards and medals. You won't be found in the history books. But your victory will be assured.

Warrior: Yes. We are providing a simple and yet incomplete overview.

Guardian: Do I have enough understanding?

Warrior: Yes.

Guardian: Good. Let us now look at the concepts we have uncovered.

Warrior: The concepts–

---

[40] B.H. Liddell Hart, *Why We Don't Learn from History*.
[41] Lawrence Freedman, *Strategy: A History*.

Means–violence; Battle–wills; Obstacle–friction; Game–chance; Object–adversary–powerless; Experience–antagonistic

6 categories, 13 concepts

Guardian: The way of a warrior is to train and master these concepts in any configuration, to seek advantage and victory in the unexpected nature of war?

Warrior: Yes. Expect the unexpected. These concepts are the most abstract and furthest from the concrete elements of weapons, systems, tactics, support, alliances, etc.

To keep it simple, the way of the warrior is to use violence to destroy the enemy.

Guardian: So, war is putting the enemy in bondage—bondage being the opposite of freedom.

Warrior: Yes. Bondage as stripping their freedom to dominate and control and rule over others.

But this is not to strip their freedom to move freely in accordance with the rule of law respecting the inalienable rights of life, liberty, and the pursuit of happiness.

Guardian: You realized what you are saying?

Warrior: What?

Guardian: Are you defending Western values or truth?

Warrior: More precisely, the values written in the U.S. Declaration of Independence and the Constitution.

Guardian: Where do these values obtain their power? From a human being or from the Creator of human beings?

Warrior: Have you spent all this time to wrestle out of me that truth and light comes from what created us?

Guardian: What is the truth?

Warrior: I consent. The truth that I defend comes from our Creator, not the mind or will of a human being.

Guardian: The warrior aims to defend and protect the rights of the individual man and the community of free men. The warrior defends individual freedoms, the freedom of will, of choice, and of action.

Warrior: Yes.

Guardian: A defender of souls?

Warrior: Yes.

Guardian. What I am seeing is–

Our warriors crush those who do not honor the divine rights of the soul. Am I seeing correctly?

Warrior: From your perspective, you are seeing correctly.

Guardian: What I'm getting at is–

Our warriors defend individual freedoms from adversaries who seek to crush those freedoms that we claim are our rights from our Creator?

Warrior: That's an ideal. I'll concur.

Guardian: What I'm getting at–

How is this not a spiritual war, fighting for divine law and rights, against the evil assaulting those divine rights and freedoms?

We did not create the human species; we are creatures born by some act of creation. And this creator designed us with the intelligence and the will to discover these individual rights, by the power of light and truth in our substance and nature.

Is not the noblest purpose of the warrior to guard and defend these rights?

To guard, defend, and attack those who attempt to crush freedom of being?

Freedom as the highest ideal that leads the formation of our warrior archetype?

Warrior: Yes.

Guardian: Then, freedom comes by what?

Warrior: Knowing truth.

Guardian: Is the truth self-evident?

Warrior: The truth is often hidden until it becomes evident. It can be like seeing mirage after mirage in the desert before coming, desperate, to an oasis.

Guardian: This is why we now turn to examine the guardian archetype. The means of the guardian is truth. Without this means, there is no guardian. And what this means, we just realized, is that there is no true warrior without the truth acting as her guide.

Empires and Monarchs and Conquest—that is the leviathan-cube.

Have we examined the warrior archetype, its nature and essence, with enough thoroughness?

Warrior: Yes. We have investigated it thoroughly.

Guardian: Before we turn to the guardian archetype, let us close this examination by contemplating the nature of war–

The science of war stops short of the need for military judgment, the impact of moral forces, the influence of chance, and other similar forces. We thus conclude that the conduct of war is ultimately an art, an activity of human creation and intuition powered by the strength of the human will. The art requires the intuitive ability to grasp the essence of a unique battlefield situation, the creative ability to devise a practical solution, and the strength of purpose to execute the act.[42]

What do you see?

Warrior: Military judgment as practical judgment, and as a truth-disclosing active condition involving intuition and reason.

Guardian: Yes. This is why we now turn to the guardian archetype—to know how to develop practical judgment. This archetype seeks–

Truth as the end.

Truth-seeking principles as the means.

The integration of the kinetic chain of knowing, willing, and acting.

The union of means and ends.

The integration of being and becoming.

The ability to disclose truth from hiddenness.

Do you see the threads? The threads connecting it all?

Warrior: Yes. I see virtue, excellence, and wisdom as the connecting threads. Threads woven by the powers of soul.

Guardian: You see correctly.

[42] United States Marine Corps, *Warfighting–The U.S. Marine Corps Book of Strategy.*

CHAPTER NINE
GUARDIAN ARCHETYPE

Writer: Dear Reader, the courage to seek the truth, to receive insights from objective reality and to respond to those insights, is the drive that leads the guardian and the warrior to the summit. Their journey is leading them to where the truth of reality reveals itself. To teach their art, they need to see and know the truth as an objective reality, always at play and guiding their intelligence.

Here, the Angelic Doctor mentors us, via Joseph Pieper–

> 'Because of the leisure that goes with contemplation' the divine wisdom itself,
> Holy Scripture says, is 'always at play, playing through the whole world.'[1]

The aim is to see the truth as a living activity, and then to speak to it and learn from it and act on its guidance, in a state of freedom and divine Play. Seeking truth is not hard work; it is a gift to the receptive soul. No, receiving this gift is not difficult work. The difficulty comes from conditioning our being, by the exercise of our will and intelligence, to receive it. Yes, the conditioning is rigorous and arduous. Once conditioned, we take part in the divine play of truth and light. This is why the writer views leadership development as an athletic and artistic and intellectual pursuit—it is the playing of the soul's powers. The warrior's art is the most un-leisurely of activities; the guardian's art is the most leisurely of activities.[2] What could be more joyous than the soul who learns to play the true art? The art of leadership rests in the dynamic principle that there is an objective reality that guides both our subjective experiences and our response to those experiences in the act of living—a kinetic chain of knowing, willing, and acting.

Here the Angelic Doctor mentors–

> Knowledge is the offspring of truth.[3]

This is how our leaders learn to "live in the light" and "live in the truth," and then to "act on the light and the truth." If they can hunt down the truth, the discovery of leadership knowledge will be the offspring of their truth-disclosing abilities. If you have not already realized it, this art is the offspring of the nonstop, beautiful struggle of divine play at work in our souls—the way of being and becoming. Struggling and striving for truth is the way human beings awaken

---

[1] Josef Pieper, *Leisure, The Basis of Culture*.
[2] Aristotle, *Nicomachean Ethics*.
[3] Josef Pieper, *Living The Truth*. Saint Thomas quoted.

the unlimited potencies of the soul. This means we live in a dynamic, unending state of being and becoming. It is a struggle to make manifest the good, the truth, the noble, and the beautiful in our being, in our aims and in our actions. This struggle to come to know truth, no matter how far and remote it seems, is what leads leaders. The struggle itself is to manifest the good and true. This is how our leaders know they're becoming receptive to what truth will unveil—the process of knowing thyself, the constant self-examination, is what opens the door. To see truth, we need the warrior's determination, the *coup d'esprit*, and the guardian's inner light, the *coup d'oeil*. This is the crux of the expedition. If we learn to see the inner light, we can turn and use it to guide all willing, knowing, and acting. Now our journeymen commence to wrestle with the art of truth-seeking. They will use meditation and contemplation to seek truth as it reveals itself. The hope is that, because our explorers are following their own true natures, they will be led to the intelligible realm of truth. We hope to see a union, a continuity, from light and truth into their will, intelligence, and spirit. Then we hope to see, with continued contemplation and meditation, the union of the soul's light and truth with the domains of character, identity, ethics and leadership. The hope is that these domains, as external knowledge, will unite intuitively with the souls that study this knowledge. Once they are intuitively united, then, we hope to see for ourselves how virtue, knowledge, and skill become an extension of being. Once this union occurs, by the transformation of being, our journeymen will have crossed the threshold from "knowing about" to "knowing." And then our leaders will be able to teach this art and fight the adversary—the one who wields power to dominate instead of liberate.

Lead in the light, The Writer

Guardian: We now turn from the warrior archetype to the guardian archetype. We need to discover the hidden truth and reveal it in the depths of being. Our leaders must know how to act in truth and not suffer ignorance. Our understanding of what truth is will lead to an inner freedom instead of an inner tyranny. This means not just physical freedom, but, most critically, metaphysical freedom. Our leaders need to catch any distortions, deceptions and delusions as they occur. The guardian archetype is concerned with metaphysical, and not physical, protecting and defending. This is where we learn the true leadership art—how to awaken and actualize the powers of soul. Our art lives in the soul.

Warrior: Lives where?

Guardian: In the awareness. In the intelligible.

What kind of guardian am I? What kind of guardian are you?

Warrior: I'm no guardian.

Guardian: Really? Are you so sure? We've travelled a long way from the realm of physical combat. On this metaphysical quest, what archetype did you display by your conduct, character and skill?

Look again—what are you, in the core of your being?

Warrior: I'm not sure what you are asking.

Guardian: Did you not, in fact, serve as a guardian, watching over my movements, to make sure I did not get lost in the abyss of reality and the abyss of the soul?

Warrior: Wait, did you orchestrate this from the start? In order to verify what you suspected, that the core of my being is a guardian? Is this why you invited me on this journey? You knew you could have done this by yourself?

Guardian: Yes. I could have journeyed in silence and solitude. But guardians and warriors live in and move in human conflict and chaos, to bring order, peace, harmony and truth. Our metaphysical quest served a two-fold purpose–

> First, as a training method, to transmit the knowledge of this art to you.

> Second, to document the way of the warrior and the way of the guardian as the core archetypes of this art.

You are blessed to embody both—you lead in the way of the guardian, and the way of the warrior follows.

Warrior: I've rarely been shocked like this. My footing seems to have lost its centeredness.

Guardian: A Buddhist *Shockabuku*?

Warrior: Yes. A spiritual tomahawk to the jugular of the ego to awaken the depths of the soul.

Guardian: Now we must begin to learn this teaching art.

Are you not curious why the guardian is so critical for teaching leaders?

Warrior: I've never thought about it until this expedition.

Guardian: What is a guardian?

Warrior: A teacher. A guide. A guard. A watchman.

Guardian: In what way?

Warrior: To educate, train and develop leaders, to make sure they have the knowledge, expertise, experiences, and practical judgment to lead. To learn to lead by following the truth's light. To learn to be courageous when acting on the truth's light.

Guardian: And this truth we seek, is it subjective or objective?

Warrior: It must be objective, it must be something that our intelligence receives by contemplating reality—to bring order out of chaos, to bring certainty out of uncertainty, to bring simplicity out of complexity. Yet we never have complete certainty, complete order, nor complete simplicity.

Guardian: Is it not strange, we live in an age when people do not believe there is a truth. We live in an age when people think truth is subjective, not objective. We live in an age when most human beings have lost the ability to see reality as it is and to respond to the reality they see with courage and justice. Why is this?

Warrior: Without fluency in dialogue, meditation, and contemplation, as the means to turn the perceiving mind away from inordinate desires and towards objective reality, it's not possible to see truth. Instead, reality's light and truth has been firewalled by the delusion and darkness of the ego-body-octagon.

Guardian: Our art rests on this principle—there is a truth, there is a reality, and this truth, this reality, can be known and can be hidden.[4] Our art is to make truth known—truth as unhiddenness (*Unverborgenheit*), to see and respond to the beingness of reality.[5]

Warrior: Yes.

Guardian: Then can we declare our nature is such that when we contemplate reality, when we come into a relationship with reality, when we come to know reality as such, we in fact, become givers and receivers of this objective reality?

Warrior: Yes.

Guardian: Then what is the purpose of the human being in this infinite universe? Is it reality as such?

Warrior: The highest aim is not self-realization, but transcendence.

Guardian: This transcendence, is it ever fully realized in the human being?

Warrior: No. In the act of living, being and becoming are always at play.

Guardian: How does the human being begin to fulfill her purpose?

Warrior: Beyond survival on its own terms?[6]

Guardian: Yes.

---

[4] Carroll Quigley, *Tragedy and Hope*.
[5] Martin Heidegger, *The Essence of Truth*.
[6] Frans Osinga, *Science, Strategy, and War–The Strategic Theory of John Boyd*.

Warrior: Seeking to know thyself—the path of self-knowledge?

Guardian: And where does self-knowledge lead?

Warrior: To hear our calling and to become our calling.

Guardian: And our calling, where does it come from?

Warrior: Not from us, that is clear—we did not create our being, nor our existence, nor our purpose. Most of us resist the truth of the call. Most of us resist being still and silent, in meditation, because a voice other than ours speaks, and when it speaks, it directs and commands. We simply affirm or deny its commands—such is the power of will. Reality itself, the source of our being, is what speaks, and it speaks to guide the soul to fulfill its purpose.

Guardian: And what initiates the self-actualization of the call?

Warrior: The courage to act on the insights we know to be true—the inner promptings, the inner guidance that make its presence known to our intelligence.

Guardian: There it is—what we know to be true!

Therein lies the source that awakens our potencies and activates the good and true in our being–

> The kinetic chain of knowing, willing, and acting in accord with the truth we know.[7]

Warrior: The union of knowing, willing, and acting. Musashi[8] mentors–

> Pen and sword in accord.

Guardian: The sword of truth. The sword of light.

Edward Bulwer-Lytton coined the adage–

> The pen is mightier than the sword.

Command of language (the pen) is the truth (the metaphysical sword) of the guardian's spirit once he knows the light of wisdom.

Why do most fail to master this sword of spirit?

---

[7] Josef Pieper, *Living The Truth*.
[8] Miyamoto Musashi, *The Book of Five Rings*.

Warrior: They lack the courage to act on what they know to be true. They are afraid to act. Their *hexis*, their active-conditioning to fear, is a state of cowardice.[9]

Guardian: Then the foundation of our art is the soul's willingness to act courageously on the truths it knows to be true.

Warrior: Yes.

Fortitude, the *coup d'esprit*, the determination of the will, is essential. Here Saint Augustine mentors us–

> And isn't fortitude the disposition of the soul by which we have no fear of misfortune or of the loss of things that are not in our power?[10]

Guardian: Is this why we focus on the guardian archetype for our art?

Warrior: Yes. The guardian guides the soul to master and wield the kinetic chain of knowing, willing, and acting. Our art aims at true-ends by the path of true-means. The ends we seek command the soul to become virtuous by exercising her powers. The virtues are caused by the powers of the soul. Virtues are the means to our ends. The means cannot be bypassed. Achievement without virtue is hollow and empty. For our art, we undergo rigorous training to live in the conditioning cycle of "being and becoming."

Guardian: The virtues seek the good. How do we first learn to hear the call of the good?

Warrior: I do not know.

Guardian: The Angelic Doctor states it is in our nature to hear and to know the "voice of the primordial conscience."[11]

Warrior: There it is, my friend, the source of the soul's primordial drives—the conscience—to know good from evil and right from wrong.

Guardian: Wisdom declares that the voice of our primordial conscience is always right and never wrong in its understanding. What is prone to error is our practical judgment. When commanded rightly, practical judgment is displayed as the virtue of prudence—practical wisdom.[12] When commanded wrongly, practical judgment is displayed as imprudence—foolishness, indiscretion, and rashness.[13]

---

[9] Aristotle, *Nicomachean Ethics*.

[10] Augustine, *On Free Choice of The Will*.

[11] Josef Pieper, *Living The Truth*. Saint Thomas (the Angelic Doctor) quoted

[12] Josef Pieper, *Living The Truth*.

[13] O.E.D. definition of imprudence.

It is our actions that can be good or bad; it is our thinking that can be right or wrong. But the voice of primordial conscience is never wrong.[14]

Warrior: Do you believe this?

Guardian: Faith initiates; practical judgment tests and verifies.

Warrior: Trust and verify.

Guardian: Yes. Accountability and responsibility are placed on each being—the beings who will, think, and act. The primordial drives are caused by light as substance of being and truth as nature of being. The virtues are the means of light and truth. Truth and light never fail; only our judgments succeed or fail.

Warrior: What do you mean by "the voice of the primordial conscience"?

Guardian: Do you want to learn to disclose truth?

Warrior: Yes. I've suffered determined wills, obstinate leaders who lacked truth, who refused to listen, who committed wrongs and still won by the measures of achievement. They are hollow and empty souls. They are my adversary. They win in spite of being untruthful.

Guardian: Hart[15] mentors us here–

> It is strange how people assume that no training is needed in the pursuit of truth.

> Whoever habitually suppresses the truth…will produce a deformity from the womb of this thought.

Do you want to win or do you want to know truth? Do you want to build a relationship with truth?

Warrior: I've won enough. I've excelled enough. Now, I want to know truth, live truth and act in truth.

Guardian: The Angelic Doctor calls the voice of the primordial conscience *synderesis*.[16] The etymology is from the Greek word *sunteresis*. The concept implies that in the act of cognition, our intellect has a voice and that voice, as conscience, commands, guides, and guards the soul. The theological roots of the concept imply that the root of the intellect itself is a conscience that serves "as a guide for conduct in an innate moral sense."[17]

---

[14] Josef Pieper, *Living The Truth.*
[15] B.H. Liddell Hart, *Why Don't We Learn From History?*
[16] Josef Pieper, *Living The Truth.*
[17] Josef Pieper, *Living The Truth.*

We are created with this ability to know. What this implies is that when we run from the commands of the inner voice, we run straight into darkness, bondage, and ignorance. And when we listen to the commands, we run into light, freedom, and truth.

Warrior: Do you believe this?

Guardian: Are you willing to investigate these principles thoroughly?

Warrior: Yes.

Guardian: We are not after belief. The wise and the sacred have left their accounts of the truths they disclosed. Our purpose is to awaken those truths in the soul. Full stop, period.

This is the reason why our leaders need guardians. We must become trustworthy to guide our students. As guides, we will teach students how to actualize their potencies and disclose truth as the core techniques of leading.

Do you see now how truth-disclosing is possible?

Warrior: Is it a potency in our nature, to know truth?

Guardian: Yes.

Warrior: This means–

As with the body, so the soul must be exercised and conditioned to reach this excellent state of truth-disclosing?

Guardian: Yes. This is the most honest and the most difficult art to teach. We need to study the domain of the guardian—the essence of truth-seeking.

This is the domain. This is where we need to live and move from to teach this art. Our adversary will be easy to crush once we have awakened these abilities in our students.

Our war is not to end physical tyranny. That is for the warriors.

Our war is to end the inner tyranny, the metaphysical bondage, that most citizens do not realize they are in.

Why do they not know they are in bondage?

Warrior: Because they live in a sea of subjective wants, desires and appetites. They have not been trained to see, to know, and to act on truth. They do not know how to contemplate reality.

They possess "knowledge about" and acquire domains of knowledge as wearable ornaments. True knowing alludes them; they act without understanding. They are dominated by forces and energies that they do not see and do not think exist.

Guardian: The guardian's realm is the interior nature of consciousness. The guardian enters into consciousness and is the warrior of the interior light and truth in each being. The purpose of the guardian is to wage war–

Truth vs. Ignorance

Light vs. Darkness

Unhidden vs. Hidden

Freedom vs. Bondage

Wisdom vs. Tyranny

Only the awakened ones are liberated. And you and I, my blessed friend, seek a deeper awakening. You intuitively knew to shed the ego. Why? Why did you mention the ego as the final threat? Is the ego real or is it a fiction? If it is a fiction, how can it be a threat? How can we suffer from a fiction? What is the way out of this fictional living?

Warrior: Let me wrestle with this.

The soul in its essence is intellectual and spiritual power. In the dynamic play of being and becoming, the soul sharpens and strengthens her powers. The ego is simply a distorted view, a belief that the temporal-conditioned-human-being is all there is, that there is no higher realm of spirit nor soul. By this denial of higher realms of being and truth, the powers of the soul are enslaved to the ego-body-octagon's primal drives.

To set the soul free of this metaphysical prison, the soul must, on a leap of faith, seek to make contact with the eternal sphere of being, of light, and of truth. In this leap, only the primordial drives, not the primal drives, can make contact with the higher realm of being. This is how the soul's light and truth reach up into the divine's light and truth.

The ego is simply an "is-ness" or identity, one that suffers distortion and incomplete understanding. The ego thinks it is a law until itself. The soul, our true identify, knows it is not the law. It knows that the universal laws of creation bind it and lead it. The soul knows that, by the justice of the immortal and eternal laws, it will be liberated and self-actualized. The soul receives the sunlight (*sunteresis*) from light and truth; the ego-body-octagon receives sunlight from the sun. The soul knows there is a higher intelligence that guides it; the ego thinks it is the higher intelligence. The soul awakens from making contact with the fiber and fabric of reality; the ego thinks it is the force of reality, subjecting all to its will and desires.

The ego is not real. The individual being is real. The individual being needs to know what it is and the end for which it was created. Simply by turning the soul's powers to truth, the ego is rendered powerless; it is dissolved, and the individual being remains.

Guardian: Where does the ego live and hide?

Warrior: In our minds—as passions and prejudices and biases.

Guardians: But not in our spirit, intelligence or will?

Warrior: The ego cannot hide in a source of power. We need to be clear, the perceiving and thinking intelligence is different from the mind. The mind is a container, a vessel, of our living experiences. Our powers can clear the mind of all distortions and delusion, thereby awakening and freeing it, so that it can see, by the powers of spirit and intelligence.

Guardian: Let us consider, for now, that the mind and soul are the same. And that the soul can get darkened and deceived. Only by sharpening the soul's powers in light and truth does it reclaim its command and sight.

The guardian is an ego-slayer. The first ego he slays is his own. After this direct experience of slaying his own ego, he can see the ego at play in the minds, not the intelligence, of other beings.

Because of this sight, the guardian does not strike the mind, where the ego hides. No, the guardian strikes the powers of will and intelligence, to reach the primordial conscience, to get it to speak. When I say I speak from soul to soul, I mean that I'm seeking to speak to the soul's conscience and truth. Do you see?

Warrior: Yes. Guardians use light and truth to eradicate deception, illusion, falsehood, and delusion, and to inspire integrity, clarity, and illumination.

What are the weapons, the means, that the guardian wields to strike the soul of one who is distorted by ego?

Guardian: The means is truth. What we are seeking is not the means, but the necessary and essential conditions that must be established for the guardian to strike past the ego without resistance. And for this, the condition a guardian must establish first is friendship—a friendship based on trust, loyalty, respect, and admiration.[18] Without this condition, the ego will resist any truth-seeking light that counters its prevailing beliefs, aims, and desires. Without this condition, there is no awakening.

Warrior: And this is why the guardian is also a warrior. To slay the egos of adversaries who deny truth.

Guardian: Yes.

Warrior: With a friend, you seek to liberate the soul; with an adversary, you seek to slay the ego, to make the conditioned-being powerless.

---

[18] Transformational leadership values (trust, loyalty, respect, admiration).

Guardian: Yes.

Warrior: How do you define truth?

Guardian: Before we define truth for our purposes, Huxley[19] mentors us with three "distinct and very different senses" of how the term "truth" is understood–

> Truth "as a synonym for 'fact'."

> Truth as "direct apprehension of spiritual Fact, as opposed to second-hand knowledge *about* Reality."

> Truth as the judgment "to assert that the verbal symbols of which the statement is composed correspond to the facts to which it refers."

Warrior: If I understand correctly, "truth as judgment" refers to logical reasoning, "truth as fact" refers to any method of evidence and verification, and truth as "direct apprehension" is contemplation, a direct knowing of reality?

Guardian: Yes.

Warrior: And the truth we seek is this direct knowing, this expansion of ourselves into the true realms of leadership potential and its actualization—it's here that our leaders make their mark.

Guardian: Yes. To know and to love the truth we come to know by direct apprehension.

Warrior: When leaders fail, why do they fail?

Guardian: They fail to come to know truth as direct apprehension—they act in blindness and darkness. They fail to come into harmony with reality and with the truth of the challenges they were tasked to overcome.

For our purposes, we now define truth with a three-fold meaning–

> Truth as unhiddenness.

> Truth as correctness and correspondence with reality.

> Truth as identity of knower and known.

This first one is the aim of practical judgment.

Warrior: To guide us deeper, let us look again at Kreeft's[20] summary of Aristotle's formal identity theory–

---

[19] Aldous Huxley, *The Perennial Philosophy.*
[20] Peter Kreeft, *Socratic Logic.*

The very same identical 'form' or essence that exists in reality materially and individually and concretely is abstracted by the mind and exists in the mind immaterially and universally and abstractly.

This is how the perceiving mind comes into correspondence with objective reality. Truth, the most important concept in man's life, is the one concept the ego resists most. For we don't create truth, but rather we discover and receive truth.

Here Hart[21] mentors us–

The Fear of Truth. We learn too that that nothing has aided the persistence of falsehood, and the evils resulting from it, more than the unwillingness of good people to admit the truth when it was disturbing to their comfortable assurance.

The Evasion of Truth. I have come to see how many of our troubles arise from the habit, on all sides, of suppressing or distorting what we know quite well is the truth, out of devotion to a cause, an ambition, or an institution; at bottom, this devotion being inspired by our own interest.

Guardian: If practical judgment is a truth-disclosing active condition, it is here where we learn to wield moral courage, and to speak and to act guided by what we know to be true. It is here where our leaders make their mark.

Warrior: We must learn to take command of truth-disclosing. How do we learn to intuitively unite the essence of truth into our being?

Guardian: How did you prepare for war?

Warrior: How did you prepare for this art?

Guardian: I first learned, by second-hand knowledge, the way to know truth, by studying the wisdom and sacred canons. We will teach our leaders how to study these canons and use this study as an exercising technique. These canons are educational tools. Reading them is one of the best ways to silence the adversary. The adversary, the ego, like an algorithm, cannot detect the qualitative aspect of truth. Wisdom literature is a great way to crush arrogance and ignorance.

Our "babbling class" does not understand these texts; they are too superficial, the depths and significance of these canons, will not let them in. Truth does not reveal itself to the vicious and the deceived. They live in the dark. They are not prepared to see, to know, and to act on truth's guidance. They move from instinct and ego and are intellectually and spiritually weak.

---

[21] B.H. Liddell Hart, *Why Don't We Learn From History?*

Warrior: That is why our leaders must free themselves by the baptism of self-knowledge.

Guardian: Truth, to awaken in us, needs self-knowledge to unite with knowledge, expertise and experience.

Once these conditions are established, practical judgment happens as a second order effect. It is simple to state, but difficult to realize.

Warrior: Can you speak to truth from a simple perspective?

Guardian: Yes. I ask a simple question–

> Have you ever seen what needed to be done, but when you spoke to what you saw and what needed to be done, other people not only did not see what you saw—they thought that something else should be done. And when they said what they thought, it seemed to you that they had no idea, no grasp, of what was occurring in reality, and that they failed to see correctly what was occurring?

Warrior: I see this all the time. They are blind. They cannot see what is. They are too close. They are not detached enough. They are deceived.

Guardian: Why is that?

Why is it that what you see, you see as unhiddenness? And why can't others, equal in expertise and experience, see what you see? Why does truth remain hidden?

Why do you see what they cannot see?

Warrior: I'm not sure. I used to think they were blinded because they lacked intellectual humility, intellectual fortitude and intellectual curiosity.

Guardian: And even with expertise and experience, if a leader does not sharpen her intellectual virtues to be discerning, what happens?

Warrior: The truth of the particular situation does not reveal itself.

Guardian: And because you are intellectually virtuous, you demanded of yourself to hunt for deeper understanding, and this deeper understanding prepared you to see the hidden truth, when it revealed itself, when it became unhidden. Then, with practical judgment, you acted with decisiveness. This is why you always waited until the last moment to make a decision. You kept integrating new facts as they revealed themselves through the rigorousness of your thinking.

Warrior: It appears so.

Guardian: Unlike you, what do blinded leaders do when they act?

288

Warrior: They are intellectual cowards, hiding from the burdens of leading. They are hiding from their primordial conscience. They are intellectually lazy. They are intellectually vicious. They have bonded with self-deception to hide from the demands and rigors of practical judgment. They lack intellectual fortitude. They lack discernment. They refuse to engage in the non-stop struggle to see and reveal the truth that is hidden.

Guardian: Yes.

You learned to see the intelligible form in the reality you contemplated.

Warrior: Yes.

Guardian: We need to teach others to see this form, this intelligibility of truth. And to do this, we need to sharpen the intelligence of our students.

When you see what others do not, do you give an account to help them see? To lead them to see for themselves?

Warrior: Yes. If they practice detachment, humility and patience. This is why rank and authority are dangerous—leaders often lean on expediency instead of truth.[22]

Guardian: We lean on truth. Wisdom is the insight of truth disclosing itself to the soul, moment to moment, as life unfolds.

Warrior: Are we speaking of wisdom or truth?

Guardian: Truth as the knowing, wisdom as the willing and acting on the knowing–

> The right consideration, the right judgment and—above all—the right concrete command, these are the acts of the virtue of prudence.[23]

What is the relation of wisdom and truth?

Warrior: Truth leads wisdom.

Guardian: What is practical judgment's role in disclosing truth?

Warrior: Practical judgment is the activity of acting on truth. Once we see the end that truth aims at, then we must select the means to achieve that end.

In strategy, this is the dynamic between the object (the end) and the objectives (the means).[24]

Guardian: And wisdom?

---

[22] B.H. Liddell Hart, *Why Don't We Learn From History?*
[23] Josef Pieper, *Living the Truth.*
[24] B.H. Liddell Hart, *Strategy.*

Warrior: Wisdom is acting on the guidance of truth to make a decision on a course of action. Not the truth or the ends, but the choice of means is where leaders are most fallible, where they make right or wrong decisions and take good or bad actions.[25]

Guardian: Wisdom is that aspect of truth that points to the next move to take towards the end goal. We will never have command of the truth of all that is, yet we have the never-ending potential to receive truth's light and to act on the inner light we have received. One human being will never be all-knowing, and yet our nature can rest inwardly and contemplate the essence of the entire universe.[26]

Warrior: I still do not know what truth is or what wisdom is.

Guardian: Neither do I.

Warrior: It seems the guardians, the true ones, are the reflections of truth and wisdom. They have become living essences pointing to the fact that truth and wisdom are beings of reality. And they remind us that our nature seeks to know these beings and to become them.

Guardian: I'm at the edge of my understanding. Truth and wisdom appear to be an intelligible light and an intelligible truth. If we can take a speculative leap, it seems this is how the divine mind and the human mind move in the divine play.

To become secure and take firm hold of wisdom and truth, we must *live* wisdom and truth. We can grasp truth's insights as we respond to the demands of living. Our composite and conditioned being is the tool in which we learn to wield the guidance of light and truth.

Think of wisdom as the offspring of light and truth.

Warrior: Then how do we prepare our intelligence to see truth?

Guardian: Do you not see? We have been preparing the entire time to see truth as reality, and to see the truths of teaching leadership in this reality.

Have we not been strengthening our cognitive powers in the depths of these realms of inquiry?

Warrior: Do I fail to see, just as I said that others could not see?

Guardian: You would see if you learned to take in the truths you once refused. Do you have the courage really to see?

Warrior: Yes.

---

[25] Josef Pieper, *Living the Truth*.
[26] Joseph Pieper, *Leisure, the Basis of Culture*.

Guardian: Open your inner sight. See past the verbal symbols and penetrate now, with direct apprehension, the objects of those symbols.

We, as souls, as living beings, are tasked to contemplate and respond to objective reality.[27] Our intelligence interacts with reality from three different points of view. Pieper[28] describes these points of view as a relationship with reality–

> From the point of view of the mind, we have cognition, the ability to know.
>
> From the point of view of reality, its objects can be known. These beings that we observe have an intelligibility that can be known.
>
> From the point of view of both in harmony, the knower and known, we have truth.

You see truth. In the depths of your being you want certainty, you want proof, you want evidence—you want to be an omniscient being. But this is not the truth we seek. No man is omniscient and thank God for this. Do you see?

Warrior: Are you stating that our intelligence is equipped to grasp reality as it is and to respond to it, moment by moment, little by little, insight by insight, in the life-long act of being and becoming?

Guardian: Indeed I am. This is why we need both physical and moral courage. The way to free ourselves from our metaphysical prison is to turn from our subjective experience of the soul (the inner nature) and seek harmony with objective reality (the outer nature), thereby coming to know truth by objective experience of the known (reality) in the knower (ourselves).

This is difficult to understand and to practice. The reason why we practice detachment is to become objective in what we are observing, to see clearly.

The greatest sin occurs when a leader subjectively influences his perception of the truth instead of responding to the real truth of the situation.

I look to Pieper to describe this sin of subjectivity, ego, bias, and self-interest–

> If, then, any determination of the content by the will of the subject enters into knowledge, if the subject wishes one thing to be so, something else to be different and something else not to be at all; then, as far as this personal subjective influence extends there is actually no knowledge at all.[29]

---

[27] O.E.D. definition of reality–that which underlies and is the truth of appearances or phenomena.

[28] Josef Pieper, *Living the Truth*.

[29] Josef Pieper, *Living The Truth*.

Warrior: Which is why we need the virtues of detachment and humility. Without these virtues, we corrupt the truth of the situation by our subjective influence and our self-interest. What we have been calling "ego" is a state of soul not in harmony with the truth of reality. We see now how, because of the soul's wants and desires, it turns from the light of truth into the darkness of arrogance and ignorance.

Guardian: Yes. This is the cause of all human misery, corruption and wickedness, and it is how self-deception begins. We have had to study human nature and potentials, to get at the what-ness of the human being and the what-ness of the leader. The purpose is to open the leader up to the study of knowing, thinking, willing, and acting.

With strong and virtuous leaders, there is a harmony of knowing and willing towards the good, the true, and the beautiful. With weak and immoral leaders, there is a bondage of control, greed, and dominance. These weak leaders manipulate others to their ends instead of to true ends.

We focus on truth-seeking, so that when we study the domains of leadership we can become the knowledge—one and one, known and knower.

What this implies–

> The reason why knowledge can become an extension of being, an extension of the soul, is that our intelligence becomes one with the known.

The Angelic Doctor mentors us here–

> Truth is nothing else than the relation of identity between the mind and the reality.[30]

What this means–

Our leaders must study the domains of leadership and become one with that knowledge. This means they must build a friendship, a relationship with knowledge. In this light, practical judgment, prudence, is the knowing that guides willing and acting.

Warrior: Then the question "what is in it for me?" is a great leadership sin.

Guardian: Yes.

Warrior: Great questions of leadership, instead, are "what is the truth?" and "do we have the courage to act on the truth we know?"

---

[30] Josef Pieper, *Living The Truth*. Saint Thomas quoted.

Guardian: Yes. Our greatest teaching challenge is to make our students build a relationship with truth. There is a truth to leading; there is a truth to leadership development. And we need to observe this truth, study it, and teach it.

This truth is not found in organizational realities, and yet it informs leaders who live in these realities.

Warrior: By your estimation, most of us are suffering self-deception.

Guardian: Yes. How could it be otherwise? We live in an age of materialism[31], subjectivism[32] and relativism[33]. This has led to a culture of highly skilled, highly successful, and highly ignorant beings, who are manipulated by others and by greed, to engage in non-essential activities that increase wealth and comfort. We have lost sight of the true, the good, and the beautiful.

Warrior: This is why we must discover the truth about the guardian archetype and about truth-seeking principles?

Guardian: Yes. A necessary return to realism.[34] This is where we take a stand against all self-deception, specifically our own.

Quigley mentors us–

> To the West, in spite of all its aberrations, the greatest sin, from Lucifer to Hitler, has been pride, especially in the form of intellectual arrogance; and the greatest virtue has been humility, especially in the intellectual form which concedes that opinions are always subject to modification by new experiences, new evidence, and the opinions of our fellow men.[35]

Warrior: Then, the main adversary we face is intellectual arrogance. We must learn how to combat it. To prepare for this combat, we must learn to wield intellectual humility. We do this by turning the mind and will to objective reality—to what is real, to what is true.

---

[31] O.E.D. definition of materialism–The doctrine that nothing exists except matter and its movements and modifications. Also, the doctrine that consciousness and will are wholly due to the operation of material agencies.

[32] O.E.D. definition of subjectivism–The doctrine that knowledge, perception, morality, etc., is merely subjective and relative and that there is no objective truth.

[33] O.E.D. definition of relativism–The doctrine or theory that knowledge, truth, morality, etc., are relative and not absolute.

[34] O.E.D. definition of realism–The doctrine that universals have an objective or absolute existence. The doctrine that matter as the object of perception has real existence and is neither reducible to universal mind or spirit nor dependent on a perceiving agent. Also, the doctrine that the world has a reality that transcends the mind's analytical capacity, and that propositions are to be assessed in terms of their truth to reality rather than their verifiability.

[35] Carroll Quigley, *Tragedy and Hope*.

The will to truth and the will to self-actualize are founding principles in our art. Truth is never in error. But our judgments and decisions can err. What you are describing is the kinetic chain from truth-disclosing (knowing), to willing, to acting–

First, we observe the reality of the situation. Second, by our knowledge, by the theoretical reasoning abilities of our mind, truth discloses itself as insights between possible means and ends. Third, our practical reasoning abilities begin to unite knowing, willing and acting by deliberating, discerning and deciding on a way forward. Fourth, and lastly, once we decide, our will commands us into action. This is how we demonstrated the truth-discoing process by the kinetic chain of knowing, willing and acting.

Guardian: That is why truth is to be lived. That is why truth is a living and dynamic principle.

You described the process of practical wisdom, which Aristotle called practical judgment and which Saint Thomas called prudence.

The virtue of prudence, Pieper defined as–

> The art of considering, deciding, and commanding rightly.[36]

And this means–

> Consideration, choice, and command are by no means free from the possibility of error.[37]

Warrior: I clearly see the primacy of humility and detachment. This is how we learn to see and to know the inner sight, the *coup d'oeil*, the best possible way forward. This is how we learn determination, the *coup d'esprit*, the courage to act on the truths we know.

This is the aim of our art, and why our students must undergo rigorous training—to prepare for "commanding rightly."

Guardian: Twenty years ago, I wanted this knowledge and training and did not receive it. Now, to make amends for the sins of the past, we must demystify this art, teach it to others, and leave an enterprise in place with one aim—to transfer this art to posterity.

Warrior: To demystify, we must begin with the virtues of patience, humility and detachment and end with the union of tactical patience and practical judgment—to learn to wait until the last possible moment before we strike boldly in the decisive act. This is how we will learn to wait for truth to reveal itself. Undisciplined leaders act too hastily and too expediently; weak leaders do not act at all. Both undisciplined leaders and weak leaders lack command of the operating environment. Our leaders act in harmony and take command of the operating

---

[36] Josef Pieper, *Living The Truth*.
[37] Josef Pieper, *Living The Truth*.

environment. They learn to act, deliberately and decisively, by hitting the targets of their operating environment—the operational objectives that lead to their strategic object.

Guardian: Saint Thomas Aquinas prepares the ground for us–

> Revelation is not oracular… Propositions do not descend on us from heaven ready made, but are… more a draft of work in progress than a final and complete document, for faith itself, though rooted in the immutable is not crowning knowledge, and its elaboration in teaching, namely theology, is still more bound up with discourses progressively manifesting fresh truths or fresh aspects of the truth to the mind. So the individual Christian and the Christian community grow in understanding; indeed they must if, like other living organisms, they are to survive by adaptation to a changing environment of history, ideas, and social pressures.[38]

Warrior: To take this and make it practical to our art, I think–

> We need dialogue (discourse) with trusted teammates to continually manifest fresh truths to enlighten our minds. The aim is for all of us to grow in understanding and move like an organism, not an organization, in adapting and responding to our operating environment.

Further, we can integrate Boyd's Strategic Theory as the practical application of Aquinas's insights on truth–

> Aim–Improve fitness as an organic whole to shape and expand influence and power over the course of events in the world.[39]

And a leader does this by–

> 1. Insights–the ability to peer into and discern the inner nature or workings of things.
> 2. Initiative–Internal drive to think and take action without being urged.
> 3. Adaptability–Power to adjust or change in order to cope with new or unforeseen circumstances.
> 4. Harmony–Power to perceive the connections between apparently disconnected events or entities.[40]

And further, we will be wise to commit to memory the Angelic Doctor's insight on our true nature of being and becoming–

---

[38] Carroll Quigley, *Tragedy and Hope*, Saint Thomas Aquinas quoted (from Summa Theologica).

[39] Frans Osinga, *Science, Strategy, and War–The Strategic Theory of John Boyd*.

[40] Frans Osinga, *Science, Strategy, and War–The Strategic Theory of John Boyd*.

> Every being is perfect insofar as it is realized, and imperfection lies in this, that its potentiality is not realized.[41]

Guardian: This is why our art lives in the pursuit of truth and realization—the dynamic play of being and becoming. We are not gods. We need reality, we need truth, and we need courage to act on the truth we know. We are imperfect creatures seeking perfection; we are not born ready-made. We must be educated and trained to live fearlessly in this dynamic play of being and becoming. We do this by uniting our being to true aims, good ends, and virtuous means.

The only way I know to counter self-deception and egotism is to focus on challenges that make us better human beings, as we struggle to make manifest true aims and good ends. To devote ourselves to something beyond ourselves, worthy of all our effort. This implies that we are the means, just as virtues are the means, to the ends we seek.

Warrior: To sacrifice, to give of self, to a cause greater than one's self.[42]

Guardian: Yes. Let us begin our examination of truth-seeking principles and the guardian archetype.

Warrior: Go on, I will follow.

Guardian: We need to understand that the way of the guardian is the way of truth. We need to know how the mind learns truth as unhiddenness, as correspondence with reality, and as the union of the known and the knower—the kinetic chain of natural being and intelligible being.

Warrior: Is this beyond our reach?

Guardian: I'm not sure. For guidance we need to lean on the writers of the wisdom and sacred canon.

Warrior: You means the ones who have been our mentors on this journey?

Guardian: Yes.

We need to study the concepts of truth, and we need to test these concepts by undergoing rigorous training. We need to verify that the knowledge and the techniques we teach can transform the being of the soul into a self-correcting, truth-disclosing, freedom-seeking leader.

Warrior: How is this possible?

Guardian: Let us lean heavily on Saint Thomas.[43] Here are two core principles in knowing truth–

---

[41] Josef Pieper, *Living The Truth*. Saint Thomas Aquinas quoted.
[42] Transformational Leadership Principle–Sacrifice for A Cause.
[43] Josef Pieper, *Living In The Truth*. Saint Thomas Aquinas quoted.

- Principle 1: "Objects are the measure of our knowledge."

- Principle 2: "In knowledge the intellect and the known reality become one."

I leaped from these concepts with an end in mind. I needed to learn how to make knowledge and expertise an extension of being. What I had in mind was the vision of a leader who moves with grace and beauty and power and wisdom, as though his being had become truth itself, light itself, in the act of leading. Searching for this way of leading brought me only to dead-ends. Turning from dead-ends, I stumbled into what Thoreau called "the treasured wealth of the world," the sacred and wisdom canons. He pointed me in the true direction–

> To read well, that is, to read true books in a true spirit, is a noble exercise, and one that will task the reader more than any exercise which the customs of his day esteem. It requires training such as the athletes underwent, the steady intention almost of the whole life to this object. Books must be read as deliberately and reservedly as they were written.[44]

It was here, in these treasures, where I found the way of the true leaders—the sages, the warriors, the saints, the philosophers and the guardians. The exemplars of our art were standing there, eternally still, in the pages of these books Once they recognized us as courageous souls, they affectionately called to us, and invited us to journey to the last and final transformation of being—the realization of light itself, and the realization truth itself.

Here, Father Reville, commenting on the Saint Francis De Sales classic *The Devout Life*, sets the stage for the journey–

> It deals in truth and power with the vital questions that affect the lives of men, it enters into the sanctuary of the heart, it brings light, the sometimes blinding light of God's truth into the neglected shrines of inner consciousness and sends echoes of forgotten principles ringing through the awakened soul.[45]

Warrior: There it is, the insight of light and truth that penetrated your soul so long ago.

Guardian: Can we claim now that our art is of the most serious nature, and is worthy of all effort and devotion?

Warrior: Such lofty and idealistic aims—the noble, the good and the true—the transformation and transcendence of being. You lead in the opposite direction to the momentum of materialism.

Guardian: When it comes to building leaders, am I in error? Am I headed in the wrong direction?

---

[44] Henry David Thoreau, *Walden*.

[45] Saint Francis De Sales, *Philothea–An Introduction to the Devout Life*. Father Reville quoted.

Warrior: No. Your purity of intent is rare. You genuinely care for the good of all.

If we're fortunate enough to find students who trust us, how would you teach to awaken the potencies in our students to realize the way of true leading?

Guardian: We need to look at two core concepts of reality–

1. Natural being
2. Intelligible being

Natural beings are the beings (the things) we observe in reality—the terrain, the human, the animal, the vegetation, the food, the instruments, the situations, the environments, the gear, the vehicle, the knowledge. This is what we observe with the perceiving mind.

This perceiving mind has the ability to abstract, to reach in and to draw out the essence, the form, the intelligible image of the beings it contemplates and observes.

Intelligible being means there is truth to the natural beings, and that the perceiving mind has an innate ability to know, by abstracting from the beings it observes, an intelligible image of the natural thing.

Pieper anchors our understanding–

> The intelligible image is in a certain sense the essence and nature of reality itself, not according to natural being, but according to intelligible being.
>
> Natural being and intelligible being are two ways of being, so to speak, of the same reality.[46]

Warrior: But how did you even know to hunt for this, for light and truth, for reality and understanding, for the way that led to the truths of the wisdom and sacred literature?

Guardian: Remember when Burns[47] said that the crisis of leadership is intellectual mediocrity?

Warrior: Yes.

Guardian: I started hunting from that question, but from the positive assertion—that to solve the crisis of leadership, the goal of leadership must be to develop intellectual strength, discernment, and wisdom. I do not mean quantitative strength as in math or cunningness as in rhetoric. I meant qualitatively, the ability to come into contact with objective reality. I started searching for writings on truth, virtue, contemplation, and wisdom as core aims of development. This led to the discovery of techniques for truth-seeking and truth-knowing. I

---

[46] Josef Pieper, *Living The Truth*.
[47] James McGregor Burns, *Leadership*.

learned that the art live in seeking and struggling to know truth, and in seeking and struggling to transcend our ignorance and arrogance. I learned to understand the rhythm of being and becoming that every leader must face in every great challenge.

Warrior: How is this possible?

Guardian: Our nature as knowing, willing, and acting can be conditioned to know and wield our art.

Warrior: Ah. The kinetic chain–knowing, willing and acting.

Guardian: This means that we need to unite the kinetic chain to practical judgment—an action that unites means and ends in an unbreakable metaphysical and physical bond.

Warrior: Then what is the crux of our art?

Guardian: The two most powerful and spiritual potentials of the human being are the will and the intellect.[48] It is these that we must make sharp, discerning and developed.

Because we have a will and we have an intellect, we have the power to do good or evil. We have the power to know and not know. We have the power to be right or wrong.

Saint Thomas mentors, via Josef Pieper–

> The soul, however, possesses the power of knowledge and the power of will. Conformity of being and will, then, is called 'good'…. Conformity of being and knowledge is called 'true'.[49]

And if it is true, we become good to the degree that our wills conform to the being of reality, and we become true to the degree that our intellects conform to the being of reality. Then we can state that our ability to make practical judgments rests in making our wills good and our minds true. Further, if we are not both good and true, truth will not disclose itself, and we will fail in the act of leading.

Do you follow?

Warrior: I follow.

Guardian: Let me ask, can you be evil and dishonest, suffering from deception and delusion, and still be a brilliant manager, physicist, or mathematician?

Warrior: Yes.

---

[48] Thomas Merton, *The Ascent of Truth*.
[49] Josef Pieper, *Living The Truth*. Pieper's statement, with Saint Thomas quoted.

Guardian: Why?

Warrior: Because our calculative abilities do not require reality's truth; they only require reason's logic.

Guardian: Do you believe this?

Warrior: Maybe. We have few saints and sages; we have many managers and professors.

Guardian: Remember why this is true. The ways of the world are based on the ego-body-octagon, which lives in what is calculative and runs from that which is truthful.

Let me ask, can you win and achieve and still be evil and dishonest?

Warrior: Yes.

Guardian: Why is that?

Warrior: We only measure winning by what is calculative, not by what is qualitatively superior.

Guardian: Let me ask, what requires more wisdom, learning chess or learning a video game?

Warrior: Learning chess. Video games manipulate the senses, the emotions and the mind. Chess strips the senses, makes the emotions temperate, and awakens the intellect of the soul.

Guardian: Why is that?

Warrior: Emotions create a fog around the intelligence. In chess, if you are emotionally compromised, you will not be able to see the patterns; they will remain hidden instead of unhidden.

Guardian: Let me ask, where have we failed in leading others?

Warrior: We do not strengthen their intellects to correspond to reality. We do not strengthen their wills to correspond to reality. This means they don't actually know what is true or good. They are blind. They are lost. They do what they are told and they are rewarded for doing it—we have created automatons.

Guardian: What do we do to control their wills and minds?

Warrior: We bind them to static and meaningless values. We bind them to goals and activities that have nothing to do with what is best or what is noble. In essence, their professional lives become long, lucrative and blinding experiences of self-deception. In essence, their lives become pursuits of pleasure and entertainment.

Guardian: We are we seeing?

Warrior: Global self-deception. The tyranny of the nation-state. The tyranny of the organization. The tyranny of wealth. We see the highest forms of self-centeredness winning. The cost of this winning is the denial of truth itself. My God, the allegory of the cave,[50] is in fact a reality.

Guardian: We do not have the power to change the enterprises, be they nation-states or corporations. But we do have the power to change the leaders of the enterprises. What if nothing needs to change except the souls of the leaders? And if the leaders change, what if the second order effect is that the systems change in response to the leaders at the helm? That is what I see. Our systems are reflections of our inner nature. Change the inner nature and the outer nature will change. Do you see?

Warrior: I see.

Guardian: Where do we begin?

Warrior: We will hunt for the high-potential people being prepared to lead these enterprises. Once we find them, we'll lead them on a metaphysical journey to learn the ways of the guardian, the ways of truth-seeking and the ways of truth-disclosing.

Guardian: We need to teach leaders how to make their souls virtuous, true, and good, and to discover the essence of both their inner and outer natures. We'll teach them how to correct souls when they suffer non-virtuous, that is, vicious thinking, willing, and acting.

We can help leaders develop their intellects in order to reach into the intelligible essence of natural being and reveal what is hidden. The practice of revealing the hidden is the role of leaders, and it's possible when they lead from the soul, from within the knowable unknown.

Warrior: This means that we as teachers must first reach into the souls of our leaders, and activate their light and truth. And once we awaken them, we must lead their souls on a metaphysical journey that takes their being from the ego-body-octagon to the soul-sphere. When they cross this threshold, when they learn to see light and truth at play in reality, they will become givers, receivers, and conduits of light and truth in the enterprises they lead.

Guardian: Yes.

Warrior: And we will simultaneously combat the intellectual arrogance and ignorance that has been blinding them.

Guardian: Yes.

---

[50] Plato, *The Republic*, Bloom Translation.

Pieper describes what we must condition in the soul of our students–

> Two-fold power of soul: power to know (truth); power to love (goodness), one
> enables it to know all things, the other to love all things.[51]

All love is rooted in the act of willing, not the act of feeling. The lack of *agape*, loving as
being, is the cause of the blindness. Knowing is not enough. Uniting knowing with loving is
the way out of the arrogance, ignorance and darkness.

Warrior: How is this even possible?

Guardian: Because we are designed to know, to will, and to act. To will rightly is to love
rightly.

Warrior: How do we train to realize these abilities?

Guardian: Do you not see? We've been training all along.

We begin with principles that direct and command our knowing, willing, and acting. Principles
are essentially the musical notes of the soul. We need to know how to play these principles in
living, to become one with them, to master our art.

These principles of truth-seeking have led us on each step of this expedition. We would be
lost without them.

Warrior: You knew this all along?

Guardian: Yes. Just as I knew you were a guardian and I needed you to demonstrate this ability
on our expedition.

Now we turn to the art. But we must teach a student before we finish this quest, to prove that
we know our art well enough to teach it.

Let me ask a question–

> Do you think there is a truth, a reality, to the knowledge and art of leadership
> development?

Warrior: Yes. I've witnessed you hammering and chiseling out the form of this art, its intelligible
image. I think you've been able to do this because you did not restrict your quest to the study
of sacred canons. No, you turned to reality to hunt for leadership genius. These living beings,
these realities, you knew, cannot be found in the literature. You sought to awaken the truths of
the sacred canons in the souls of living beings. You learned to abstract the intelligible form of
leadership genius from the souls of true leaders who stood before you. You verified the truths of

---

[51] Josef Pieper, *Living The Truth*.

the sacred canons by contemplating their souls, and you did this by trusting and acting upon the principles of truth—by coming into correspondence with a leader's being and soul, by uniting him to yourself, into one soul, the known with the knower. You discovered a knowingness of leadership truths in your being; you were blessed with insights. Because you studied sacred and wisdom literature, you were prepared to see the intelligible patterns before you. This is how you learned to see what was hidden from others. You were able to penetrate to the core being of the leaders before you. This abstract, intelligible form then transformed into concrete knowledge when you integrated it with the domains of virtue, wisdom, excellence, and truth—a synthesis of leadership movements and motions of knowing, willing, and acting. You learned how knowing and being are united. Now you aim to transmit this knowledge—it is not enough for you simply to know. You're called to be with yet-to-be-leaders, to awaken their intelligence and strengthen their will through study, exercise, practice and mentoring. You watch over them, as sacred cargo, to guard them, to mentor them, and to teach them, and to free them by learning this art.

I never understood how you did this. Now I do. I can see the forms of the leaders before me; I see what has been hidden.

This is how you learned to detect non-leaders, the charlatans, the posers and image-seekers, because you can see the nature, the form of their character, living deep within, by the methods of meditation and contemplation. The truth of this art has let you in and now it has let me in. Nothing is hidden when a being is before us.

My God, if we can teach this to leaders and to followers they'll be able to detect the charlatans, the magicians, the manipulators. The purity of this art is that bad and evil people, even if we train them, cannot learn it. Truth does not reveal itself to the wicked.

Guardian: I've shouldered doubt my whole life, about whether I could teach this. Now I've been blessed with faith. We can teach this art, so long as we have students of goodwill. I have failed in the past. I once had a student to whom I taught these methods. He scheduled a meeting to give me feedback.

When we met, he started by saying–

> I feel bad. I am using the tools of truth you taught me against you.

I said–

> The tools of truth cannot be used against a truth-seeker. If I am in error, the truth will correct me. The tools of truth cannot be used by non-truthful beings. The truth will not disclose itself. The truth will not be mocked. What do you see? What feedback do you need to give me?

Every point he made he made in error. He suffered from narcissism, egotism, self-delusion and self-deception. He did not understand. He made judgments uninformed by objective reality. He suffered from the blindness of subjective thinking, wanting and desiring. It seemed a dark cloud enveloped his soul. He lacked experience, expertise, and knowledge. And he couldn't integrate knowledge, expertise and facts to read the situation accurately. To him, most of his leadership work was meaningless pick-and-shovel work—though this is the essence of digging out truth. This true leadership work, he felt, was beneath him. The work smoked him out. He sought glory; he sought fame; he sought idolatry. He did not seek truth.

Warrior: And then what?

Guardian: And then? I had to take a hard look within. How had I not seen the truth of his being? And then I saw the error in my judgment. The truth stings. I had seen a brilliant mind with unlimited talent. I'd failed to look deeper, but when I did, I saw a wicked heart and will lurking in the depths. It took me months of reflection to learn to see. I figured out that he was a narcissist. I'd never met one before, at close range, and I was in the dark until I realized his true nature.

Every action I take is to fight arrogance and ignorance, in the will and in the intelligence. This student did not want to lead; he wanted to dominate others. He had a tiny stature and constitution—a Napoleon complex. It's deadly to our art.

Warrior: And then what?

Guardian: He quit. He started a band. He started acting out the life of a rock star.

Truth always reveals itself. I could not see him clearly until the demands of work placed enough pressure on him to reveal his nature. The beautiful burden of leadership is a truth-character serum.

Warrior: Our failures can be the greatest teachers, if we learn to recover and grow out of them.

Guardian: This is why we study the wisdom of the warriors, sages, and saints. Their wisdom guides us to see what is truly going on around us. It gives perspective. It prepares us to meet the demands of leading. I never understood, until I started leading, the power of the sacred and wisdom canons as living guides.

Warrior: Now I understand why you emphasize that students, as a first leadership act, should listen and hear their unique calling. This is critical. It is our students' first direct experience with truth. It commands our students to initiate action on the truth they receive. This teaches students to discern the difference between truth's guidance and all other guidance.

Guardian: This is how we build the inner structure to withstand the burdens of our art. As a guide, I lean heavily on Carrol Quigley's framework for truth-seeking and apply it to developing leaders.[52]

---

[52] Carroll Quigley, *Tragedy and Hope.*

The first principle of truth-seeking–

> There is a truth to leading and developing leaders.

Warrior: This first principle leads to the practice of meditation and contemplation, to know and become this truth. We then bring the truth of leading into the domains of character development, identity development, intellectual development, and ethical development.

Guardian: Do you see the next principle? Why do you think I needed your camaraderie on the expedition?

Warrior: The second principle of truth-seeking–

> No one person or organization or university possesses the full and unabridged truth of leading.

Guardian: Yes. I know I am insignificant as a man. And I know that the call, the responsibility, is significant. I need leaders with wisdom and experience to contribute to this art, from their knowledge and experience. When we teach our students, we will be learning as much in teaching as they in studying. Together, in being and becoming, in teaching and learning, with teachers and students, we will grow deeper and deeper in our understanding.

Do you see the third principle?

Warrior: The third principle of truth-seeking–

> All teachers and students in our art, as souls of goodwill, already possess truth-potencies in their being, by virtue of their existence and their experiences. This means we all have something to contribute by virtue of the soul's will, intelligence, and spirit.

Guardian: Yes. This is how we create friendship and harmony between teachers and students. We will cultivate a flow of respect and admiration between us. We create this environment by building strong relationships with the knowledge, by building strong relationships with one another, and by maintaining an unshakeable devotion to the mission of making leaders.

We, as teachers, educators and trainers, are trusted to lead out the moral and intellectual faculties in our students by making them sharp, discerning and developed.

Warrior: This is how we honor the dignity of the souls before us. And yet, we realize that the beings before us are not all equal in expertise, experience, wisdom, and excellence.

Guardian: Alberto Coll describes here how Jacob Burkhardt warned us–

> It was one thing to argue that all men should be equal under the law, an idea Burckhardt did not find problematic, but quite another to argue that all men

are equal, and even more pernicious to suggest that all beliefs, opinions, and ways of life are of equal worth, a reduction ad absurdum that Burckhardt believed would lead to the death of culture and the return to barbarianism.

An age may have a level of material prosperity or intellectual and artistic experience lower than that of another, but it is not thereby inferior in its capacity for spiritual insight or nobility.[53]

Warrior: You are called to increase, in our leaders, the capacity for spiritual insight and nobility?

Guardian: Yes. I aim to develop leaders worthy of leading free-thinking and independent souls.

That is how our students will trust our teachers as they engage in the most strenuous spiritual and intellectual exercises.

Warrior: Is the training meant to make the act of leading seem easy, by comparison?

Guardian: Yes. The students need to learn to awaken the will to self-actualization and the will to truth. When they learn the ways of limitless being and becoming, they'll be prepared to lead.

Warrior: This is why we build deep roots of trust and friendship. So we can strike the will in our students, to ignite the drive and energy required to become proficient in this art. The challenge for the student is to learn to strike the will again and again, in seeking truth, in seeking actualization. Our art is the life-long endeavor of being and becoming.

Guardian: Yes. Once this goodwill and friendship is established, then we approach leadership development through didactic training, autodidactic training, and dialectical symposiums.

Warrior: So you integrate the core teaching methods into a unified whole, leaving nothing to chance as our leaders study with our students and show them the way?

Guardian: Yes. We seek to build leaders who are self-governing, self-correcting, and self-cultivating. Intense apprenticeship is needed for this serious and intense art. Life will challenge them after the training, but during the training, we are going to teach by example and by our presence (our being), so we can transmit knowledge in a more subtle and mystical way.

Warrior: The grace of the saint and the sage.

Guardian: Initially, our students will respond more to our being than to the knowledge and the training. The knowledge at first will seem distant, static, and obscure. The training at first will seem foreign, awkward, and meaningless. But by our presence, they will respond to our being.

---

[53] Jacob Burckhardt, *Judgments On History And Historians*. From the foreword by Alberto Coll.

By our being, we will be able to create a metaphysical container, an invisible structure, that guides them along. They will experience the light of truth before they see the light of truth. This is how we practice and teach command and leadership presence. Our energy of being initially does the heavy lifting to guide and aid them in their development.

As they mature, they will spend more time in silence and solitude, in study and practice, to learn to move from their beings, undisturbed by others. Once they learn to move from the light and truth of the soul, the knowledge will seem lively, dynamic, and energetic—as if the knowledge becomes light and truth itself, nourishing and maturing their beings. When they have mastered the fundamentals of the training, they'll see how their wills, intelligences and spirits disclose truth and actualize potential.

We need to be with them to guide them. This art lives in our character and in our intelligence as we make knowledge and expertise an extension of being. We lead out the light and truth of our students, the moral and intellectual faculties. They will see the similarity to athletics and gymnastics. Then they will learn to see how their art is more metaphysical (an art of will and intelligence) than physical.

Warrior: If I follow correctly, these are the three phases of learning that you will integrate into the training–

> The first learning style is knowledge acquisition by studying math, grammar, logic, and music as an example. This is classroom teaching with a textbook and a teacher.
>
> The second learning style is the development of intellectual skills, by exercise, practice and coaching, to learn the techniques of observing, calculating, measuring and problem solving. This style prepares our students in the art of practical judgment. This is where we begin to unite theoretical reason and practical reason.
>
> The third learning style, the style we have used most on this expedition, is dialogue and inquiry, a modified Socratic method, in which we discuss ideas and leverage our knowledge, expertise, and experience. This is when we invite our students, because they lack knowledge and experience, to begin the study of sacred and wisdom canons. We will lead symposiums based on these canons as a method to initiate our students into the pursuit of truth and the pursuit of actualization.[54]

To this, we need to add a fourth learning style–

---

[54] Mortimer Adler, *How to Speak, How to Listen.*

The style that unites the metaphysical and physical arts—meditation, contemplation, yoga, music, weight training, martial arts, and climbing.

Guardian: Do you see what is being revealed?

Warrior: Yes. It's a way of living that aims to realize our potentials through the demands of leading. Our teachers and our students will be living, training, and leading in a way of being and becoming that is limitless. What is the essence of this enterprise that we're building?

Guardian: What do you see?

Warrior: Are we, in fact, seeking, with our art, to build a true and lasting community of truth-seekers?

Guardian: Yes. I searched for this kind of leadership training and could not find it. I searched for this kind of community and could not find it. Should it be our purpose to build the training and the community?

Warrior: It is a noble goal and one I'm willing to devote my drive and energy toward manifesting.

Guardian: Do you see why our art begins and ends in a true community?

Warrior: Yes. Can you describe the true pattern we are seeking?

Guardian: Bloom sketches the ideal for us–

> The real community of man, in the midst of all the self-contradictory simulacra of community, is the community of those who seek the truth, of the potential knowers, that is, in principle, of all men to the extent they desire to know. But in fact this includes only a few, the true friends, as Plato was to Aristotle at the very moment they were disagreeing about the nature of the good. Their common concern for the good linked them; their disagreement about it proved they needed one another to understand it. They were absolutely one soul as they looked at the problem. This, according to Plato, is the only real friendship, the only real common good.[55]

Warrior: This pattern I have seen before. This pattern I have experienced. It is the pattern of the true warriors, of the warrior community. We guarded this community like a sacred vessel to keep out all pressures and demands from outside interests. It took tremendous energy to preserve the culture of this warrior community. I see how we can create this for our art. It's the same chassis, only the knowledge, training and techniques are different. Most do not have the

---

[55] Harold Bloom, *The Closing of the American Mind: How Higher Education Has Failed Democracy and Impoverished the Souls of Today's Students.*

willpower or discipline to train and live this way. Most like the "idea of it" and the "image of it," but not the "truth of it," of what it takes to realize these deep human potencies.

Guardian: Our leaders will be called. They will know.

Warrior: Yes.

Guardian: Why the seriousness? Why is devotion needed? Why is the mystical calling needed?

Warrior: Only the truth of the call can sustain our students as they crush the ego and awaken the soul. Only those who are called will undergo a training that seeks to "suffer no fiction" and "disclose truth."

Guardian: What else do you see?

Warrior: Only those who are called will become virtuous, leading with the virtues of humility and detachment, to silence the ego-body-octagon at every moment that the soul detects deception and delusion entering its mind and will. Our art reveals to the soul, in a blinding light, that truth is the master.

Guardian: There it is. Instead of the ego as master, the truth is the master of the soul. Now I understand true obedience—obedience to the commands of truth.

We are asking the soul to devote its entire being to the pursuit of truth. By this one aim, the soul devotes all its power to know truth and to act on the truth it knows. This means the soul strips the ego of its insatiable desires. The denial of the ego, creates inner turbulence, a rupture of being, as the soul transcends the grip of the ego—the self-will, the non-corresponding and non-conforming aspects of our being. It seems counter-intuitive, but, once the transcendence becomes stable, once the bridge of the transformation has been crossed, by obeying, corresponding, and conforming to objective reality (not another human being), the soul experiences its first true sense of freedom—the direct apprehension of metaphysical freedom itself—freedom as a being of light and truth.

Now we enter into the crux of our journey and what we are to learn. I see the summit, finally.

The fourth principle of truth-seeking–

> Through dialogue, the truth in each being can be realized and united with the truth of other beings. Once these truths are united, a transformation with its own energy generates deeper insights that lead to further hidden truths. These are truths with such power and wisdom that no one person could have generated them on his own. Even Plato needed Aristotle.

Warrior: Good God! Training, expertise and experience are not enough. Our leaders need communities and enterprises with human beings devoted to seeking truth. This is the real power of leading—hunting for the truth in each being, leader and followers, and letting the truth of all these beings unite to discover deeper and more necessary and essential truths.

Guardian: Yes. To lead this way, leaders and followers must learn how to make good and just contributions to good and just aims. Both leaders and followers need knowledge, expertise, and experience. Few want to lead this way because of the demands placed on the leader.

Harold Geneen[56] demonstrated the courage to lead this way, notwithstanding his attempts to use the CIA to increase his power on overseas holdings.

Warrior: What?

Guardian: Europe called him the Michelangelo of Management. As CEO, from 1961 to 1977, he transformed the International Telephone and Telegraph Corporation (ITT) into one of the first international conglomerates, growing from $765 million sales to $17 billion sales. How do you think he led?

Warrior: With a ruthless and iron fist?

Guardian: No. He led by the Socratic Method.

Warrior: What?

Guardian: For seventeen years, he led monthly General Management Meetings (GMM).

Warrior: What is a GMM?

Guardian: They were week-long operational meetings. For one week each month he met with his Europeans managers to focus on operational and strategic challenges. This meant that over 100 leaders would be in a massive boardroom, like the knights of the round table, and everyone would go over each leader's battle plan. They, as a team, would study and correct problems on the spot. Everyone would learn by studying each unit's problem-sets. To prepare for these meetings, the unit leaders would spend three weeks in preparation—doing their homework, to give fact-based opinions on how to solve operational and strategic challenges. This meant that all transactional tasks were delegated to junior managers.

Warrior: Wait, he did this each month?

Guardian: Yes. For 17 years, this is how he led.

Warrior: It seems so simple.

---

[56] Harold Geneen with Alvin Moscow, *Managing.*

Guardian: Is it? Is it simple? No, it is not. It is intellectual intensity at its apex.

Warrior: Wait, what about North American operations?

Guardian: He did the same with them; he led a week-long GMM each month.

Warrior: Are you telling me that two weeks out of every month, he led these management meetings?

Guardian: Yes. Through this practical teaching and leading style, he not only led his company to become profitable, he also developed 130 future CEOs. Here is a sketch of his character–

> A maverick and a genius, "the General Patton of industry," "the Michelangelo of management," remained a mystery, rarely appeared in public and seldom made speeches. His high energy level, natural enthusiasm and quick mind were what made him extraordinary.
>
> Because he was a good listener and loved to learn something new, this made him easy to talk too.
>
> He is very human…. He takes great care never to demean a man personally, especially a subordinate.... He can be extraordinarily kind and compassionate.
>
> Above all else he works hard. He sets a clear example for all those who work with him.
>
> Intense probing for answers in an open forum was Socratic. One question led to another. He demanded facts and opinions backed up by facts.
>
> An unstinting teacher, running a school for business managers.
>
> Extraordinary enthusiasm was highly contagious. He inspired men.[57]

Warrior: A man I would willingly follow. And you share this because it's an example of the Socratic method and the pursuit of truth by a leader in a powerful and functional domain?

Guardian: Yes. Facts are the foundations of truth. If he could develop 130 future CEOs, he inspires us to develop 130 future leaders in our art. Few have the call and the courage to lead and manage the way he did. No one trained him. He led by the full powers of his being—"instinct and intuition as much as logic and experience."[58] His calling led him into this way of leading—that of a teacher. His calling was the way of the manager, and

---

[57] Harold Geneen with Alvin Moscow, *Managing.*
[58] E. H. Edersheim, *McKinsey's Marvin Bower–Vision, Leadership, and the Creation of Management Consulting.*

he followed it to its apex, by becoming a legendary teacher—they called ITT "Geneen University," because he produced so many future CEOs. He was a student too. He leaned on Marvin Bower for expertise. Bower thought of managing as a vocation equal to the calling of the priesthood.[59]

Bower lived and led by a few principles[60]–

1. Lead a profession, not a business.
2. Put clients' interests first.
3. Be ethical at all times.
4. Only do work that provides true value.
5. Maintain independence.
6. Tell the truth.

Warrior: There it is—true value and truth-telling. It's all right there, if we have the courage to look.

Guardian: Simple to "know about." Difficult to "know." Eisenhower also leaned on Bower's expertise to build out the executive functions of the White House. Both Geneen and Bower brought the mystical call to bear in their art, the art of the manager. If I felt called to be a business leader, I would lead this way. I studied the writings of both Geneen and Bower. They were geniuses; the god-within spoke to them, and they spoke truth in their endeavors. They listened to their daemons. I bet they did not even know they were doing this.

Yet we seek to build a different kind of leader, one who cannot be beholden to organizational constraints. One who seeks perfection of being.

Warrior: Now I see your aim. Now I see why you went insane in business environments.

Guardian: Do you?

Warrior: Yes. Your aim is to develop a kind of leader that has "the capacity for spiritual insight and nobility."

I know your aim. I'll pull from two sources to highlight the kind of leader you hope to build. One source is Hart, who speaks of Lawrence of Arabia. The second source is Coll, who speaks of Burkhardt–

> Free from pettiness, freed from ambition, immeasurable in understanding, [Lawrence's] profound respect for others' freedom embodies the wisdom

---

[59] Harold Geneen with Alvin Moscow, *Managing*.
[60] E. H. Edersheim, *McKinsey's Marvin Bower: Vision, Leadership, and the Creation of Management Consulting*.

of the ages—the wisdom which reveals that life can endure, and manhood develop, only in an atmosphere of freedom…. For he was a message to mankind in freedom from possessiveness. In freedom from competitiveness. In freeing oneself from ambition, especially from the lust of power. His power sprang from knowledge and understanding, not from position. His influence is a living growth—because it is a spiritual message transmitting a spiritual force. The man was great; the message was greater. In him the Spirit of Freedom came incarnate to a world in fetters.[61]

If there was a renaissance ahead, it would come about, Burkhardt surmised, as the unexpected fruit of the human spirit and the quiet work of a few individuals—'secular monks,' he called them—who did not care about power but cherished the characteristics of the culture of 'old Europe,' foremost among these being the love of freedom and beauty.[62]

Did I hit the mark of your aim?

Guardian: Yes. I see the summit.

Warrior: You have faith in the spirits of freedom, truth, and beauty as actual facts that can be awakened in souls and directed to action—action that unites sense-perception, intellect, and primordial desire. So you focus on the nature of truth and the substance of light—these are what makes the spirit free, noble, and beautiful. And wisdom is the force-multiplier of truth.

Only the inner light can know truth–

> Coup d'oeil and coup d'esprit par excellence

Guardian: Do you see the summit as well?

Warrior: Yes, I see the summit.

Guardian: Good. You have been a strong guardian on this quest. I'm learning to see with greater insight. I just saw a deeper principle reveal itself. The concept of the GMMs disclosed the insight.

The fifth principle of truth-seeking–

> Truth must be lived. This means the truth that leads to practical action will soon become obsolete, once new information, new facts, new experiences and new situations reveal themselves in the act of leading. This initiates the

---

[61] B.H. Liddell Hart, *Lawrence of Arabia.*

[62] Jacob Burkhardt, *Judgments On History And Historians.* From the foreword by Alberto Coll.

return to dialogue to disclose new truths that lead to new actions, to adapt and respond to the challenges we face.

I lean on Pieper's sage advice to understand this principle–

> Man is positioned too much in the midst of a world that constantly deals out surprises beyond all presumed knowledge; man is living too much face to face with the absolute of it all, so that his own inner boundlessness constitutes but the counterpart to an unfathomable world.[63]

Warrior: We prepare our leaders to live in the truth of this reality—living boldly, courageously, and commandingly. To face this reality, we arm them with principles and wisdom from the timeless and eternal writings of the wise.

Guardian: That is the reason we train this way—to flourish in the act of living.

There is an inner boundlessness within us; that is why we strike the depths of the soul, to respond to an unfathomable world.

This leads us to disclose the sixth principle of truth-seeking–

> We never reach the whole truth. We progress and advance closer and closer to the truth, knowing we will never know the whole, unabridged, full, truth of it all.

This is why faith, courage, detachment and humility are essential to live this art. We must never claim to know truth in totality, but, with practical judgment, we will claim to know the art of truth-disclosing, to make manifest and actualize true aims, noble ends, and virtuous means.

These first six principles are the means to the end we seek. The end, the seventh principle of truth-seeking, is as follows–

> These principles are the foundation for all true power, strength, and wisdom.

We seek true power, strength, and wisdom as the result of living for good and true ends.

Warrior: Let us lean on Quigley to summarize the principles of truth as the source and power of western philosophy[64]–

1. "There is a truth, a reality."
2. "No person, group, or organization has the whole picture of truth."
3. "Every person of goodwill has some aspect of truth, some vision of it from the angle of their own experience. Thus each person has something to contribute."

---

[63] Josef Pieper, *Living The Truth*.
[64] Carroll Quigley, *Tragedy and Hope*.

4. "Through discussion, the aspects of truth held by many can be pooled and arranged together to form a consensus closer to truth than any of the sources that contributed to it."
5. "This consensus is a temporary approximation of the truth, which is no sooner made than new experiences and additional information make it possible for it to be reformulated in a closer approximation of the truth by continued discussion."
6. "Thus western man's picture of truth advances by successive approximations, closer and closer to the whole truth without every reaching it."
7. "This basic methodology of the west is the basic underlying foundation to the success, power, and wealth of the west. It is its source of strength."
8. "It's been attacked again and again by all kinds of conflicting methods and outlooks and all kinds of alternative attitudes based on narrowness and rigidity."

Guardian: We will live by these principles to achieve the noble ends of truth, freedom, light, and beauty for our leaders, for our enterprise and for our community of truth-seekers.

Why are these principles the core of our art?

Warrior: Because practical judgment is a truth-disclosing activity and we need to know how to disclose the truth. Full-stop, period.

Guardian: Now we turn to the Guardian Archetype. What are the means of the guardian?

Warrior: I see it now. The means of the guardian is truth. Now I can see how truth can be a form of violence—a vigorous power that destroys ignorance. It is similar to the means of the warrior, only it does not harm the soul; it frees the intellect from bondage, deception and error. The guardian lives in and through the truth's lead. Truth is the master of the Guardian. Truth is the means and end of the Guardian.

Guardian: Saint Augustine[65] mentors here–

> One must believe that the nature of the human mind is so connected with intelligible things that is gazes upon all it knows by means of a unique light.

Saint Aquinas[66] comments–

> Now, the light by whose means the soul knows all things is truth.

Warrior: We seek to know the light of truth. This is the aim and end and means of all our effort.

Guardian: Yes.

---

[65] Saint Thomas Aquinas, *Truth, Volume 1*, Translated by Robert W. Mulligan.
[66] Saint Thomas Aquinas, *Truth, Volume 1*, Translated by Robert W. Mulligan.

Writer: Dear Reader, the warrior, the guardian, and the writer are at the edge of understanding. They are limited and imperfect beings seeking principles and practices to test and verify in the art of leading and leadership development, which are one and the same. The writer is an imperfect and flawed being, who leans heavily on the wisdom literature to mentor the guardian and the warrior as they continue their journey. We need to ask ourselves, can we practice these principles? If we can practice these principles, will it result in truth revealing itself? And if truth reveals itself, do we need courage and faith to act on truth's insights? This is the crux of leadership development— through the light of truth, leaders act with wisdom and justice, and this makes them trustworthy. We know about Christ and Buddha, but, does not Colonel Lawrence (of Arabia) invite us to become the essence of the message, to become beings with the spiritual strength to act in a spirit of freedom and a spirit of courage? To learn how to live and move with this kind of spiritual strength is the purpose of this metaphysical quest. The warrior and the guardian are not only learning how to teach it; they are learning how to wield this strength themselves. Not only the warrior and the guardian, but, are not we, the reader and the writer, learning how also to wield this spiritual strength? Are we not also, in the act of living, already on a metaphysical quest? A quest that demands of us spiritual strength? Lead in the light, The Writer

Warrior: We have broken through the impasse. It seems we've been stuck here the entire time.

Guardian: We have. It took us this long to prepare our souls to move through this impasse.

Warrior: With greater understanding, from direct experience, I see why the weapons of meditation and contemplation and the canons of wisdom and sacred literature are essential for our art. This is how we prepare the soul's will and intelligence to break through reality's impasses, to allow truth to reveal itself. To transcend the restrictions of beliefs, values, and authority. To transcend the prisons of impatience, indolence, delusion, foolishness, distraction and busy-ness. To see the hidden, now unhidden.

Guardian: Yes.

Warrior: To be entrusted to teach leaders, this means that first, I need to learn and then teach meditation and contemplation as the two weapons that wield truth-seeking and truth-disclosing?

Guardian: Yes.

Warrior: Second, I need to learn and then teach the truth-seeking principles as a method to generate new insights, to teach leaders how to make good judgments—what Aquinas calls prudence, and Aristotle calls practical judgment—to command rightly?

Guardian: Yes.

Warrior: Finally, third, for operational and strategic leaders, one week a month, I need to sequester them in meetings modeled after those of Harold Geneen, and guide them to see the true obstacles and challenges they face. I will need to teach them the dialogic art and dialectical art of smashing and colliding independent thought, to disclose new insights and new understandings, to overcome the incessant assaults of uncertainties and complexities at play in the operating environment?

Guardian: Yes. The beautiful burdens endured by our leaders.

Warrior: The vision of truth—I am experiencing it now in a state of wonder. I'm experiencing deeper depths and higher heights.

Guardian: How have you achieved this state?

Warrior: On this quest, I left the known and the temporal. I allowed my intelligence to contemplate the nature of the human being and the nature of leadership. In this contemplative state, truth began to reveal itself. Because I had the courage to contemplate, because I had the courage to exercise my intelligence, truth began to disclose itself. It is our nature to see the light of truth. It seems simple now.

Guardian: And is it simple?

Warrior: No. We have traveled a rigorous and arduous pathless path, to arrive at the depths and heights of light and truth.

Guardian: Now do you see why we failed in the past?

Warrior: Yes. We led organizations and bypassed the leadership of souls. We did not educate our leaders in the spirit of freedom and the spirit of truth—The light of truth.

We reduced souls to automatons, chess pieces, and we played these pieces to hit operational and strategic targets, to win.

Guardian: Does it "pay to be a winner?"

Warrior: Good God no. No one wins in a game controlled by the ego-body-octagon and the leviathan-cube. Only war, in this game, proves to be critical, because we protect the physical nature of the soul from the wickedness of tyranny's violence and domination. Everything else that wins, loses, because it increases the delusion of the ego—wealth, stardom, image, fame, reputation, pleasure and prestige. In deception, we think we've won and achieved, but we've lost. We've lost truth. We were not playing the true game. We did not earn truth's revelations–

Truly, it pays to know truth.

Guardian: In the true game, this is why we can never gain in expediency by bypassing truth. In the true game we are the foundations, not the institutions. In the true game, we become the light, the true, the good and the noble. Institutions do not contain truth and virtue; they are inanimate containers responding to virtuous or vicious leaders. Most enterprises are containers of wealth, not truth. These enterprises can be led by virtuous or vicious leaders and achieve the same wealth-generating aims. It is the leaders, for good or for bad, and the followers, for good or for bad, that create the experience of community and culture. We seek the good. Leaders bring to life the truths that the institutions and enterprises symbolize. Institutions respond to the nature of our leaders. Our leaders, as foundations, become the unmoved movers.

Warrior: Leader as foundation? Leader as unmoved mover?

Guardian: Do you see the way? Do you see true learning? Do you see consciousness inviting us in? Do you see how we are the spirit that actualizes the forms and structures of man?

When we are immersed in the depths of the intellect itself, our physical being seems distant and far away. What is unmoved within us reveals itself. This unmoving nature moves the will, the intelligence, the sense, the emotions, and the body. Instead of experiencing life subjectively, we experience life objectively—uniting knower with the known, and becoming an unmoved mover.

Warrior: I see. I am experiencing this right now. My physical body seems light, like an iridescent cloak, something I don, like armor, to exercise the soul's powers.

Guardian: In these depths, we learn to swim in the ocean of consciousness, like orcas, with power and freedom, true metaphysical freedom. When we gaze up to the surface, we see weak and ignorant human beings clutching to the fragile rafts of the ego-body-octagon. We see, instead of truth, beliefs, fears and desires. Because they are cowards, they do not have the courage to leap from the rafts and dive into the depths of consciousness, to discover truly what they are. Only by leaping into the deep waters will they awaken their potencies. What they fear most, what the ego fears most, is the release of control. There is no control in the deep waters. One learns to become one with consciousness—an unmoved mover. This is the freedom revealed in the deep waters of truth and light.

Warrior: Truth as the killer of ignorance.

Guardian: Do we understand the principles of truth-seeking? How do these principles become intuitively embedded in our being? How do they become sealed into our consciousness, so the truth can guide us without restriction or resistance?

Warrior: Let us search for a technique that secures these principles to our being—a technique similar to the sword in martial arts. A master teaches us to wield the sword in martial combat. Do we need a master to teach us to wield the sword in metaphysical combat?

Guardian: Who is the teacher of truth's fighting skills?

Warrior: The guardian?

Guardian: Not necessarily.

Warrior: The sage?

Guardian: Yes. At the apex. At the pinnacle. For now, let us focus on the guardian.

Warrior: It will be a good day when we meet the sage.

Guardian: Indeed. Thank God we have the writings of the sages. But what is a guardian and how is a guardian different from a warrior?

Warrior: The warrior is focused on the common need, that of protecting and defending citizens from martial threats. The guardian is focused on the common good, protecting and defending citizens from non-martial threats. This is why ends focused on the common need do not live in truth-seeking. These ends are basic goods—teaching, farming, healing, building, making and creating—and these basic goods have true ends, but they are temporal ends that take care of the physical realm of being. The ends of the Guardian focus on the truth of the spiritual and intellectual realms of being.

What are the fighting skills of the guardian?

Guardian: The basic fighting skills of the guardian are meditation and contemplation, to seek wisdom and truth, and to engage in practical judgment.

Warrior: Wait. We already know the techniques?

Guardian: Yes, partially. If the fighting skills of the warrior are martial arts, weapons, tactics and strategies, we need to discover the equivalent fighting skills for the guardian.

Warrior: To keep this basic, the fighting skills of the warrior are needed to battle the adversary's will and to make the adversary powerless. To crush the adversary's will.

Guardian: Then in principle, the fighting skills of the guardian must be to harmonize independent wills and to liberate wills, instead of battling them. The aim is to build true friends, transformed by thinking, willing, and acting toward true aims, virtuous means, and noble ends.

Warrior: So the aim of the guardian is to harmonize and liberate souls, to make them powerful and free?

Guardian: Yes. Freedom, not power. Truth, not domination.

Warrior: How do we do this?

Guardian: Have we not been practicing this the entire time?

Warrior: It's too close. I don't see it.

Guardian: Distance yourself. Open up your awareness. We spoke about it when we mapped out the warrior archetype. We unite wills by two kinds of relationships. The first is by cultivating, by the guardian's lead, true friendships, a relationship that is built on what is best for the friend. Aristotle calls this the highest form of friendship. This means ego, envy, judgment and comparison are continually dissolved in the act of building a true friendship. It is a dynamic and living friendship. Aristotle said strong communities are built on friendships. And friendships take energy, endurance, tests, trials, care and concern.

Warrior: Ah. I remember. You mean that what unites the will into harmony and correspondence and consonance is Platonic love, love as an act of will, love as Peck stated–

> The will to nurture one's own or another's spiritual growth.[67]

In our art, we take this act of will with a seriousness of intent—to nurture spiritual growth is the test of true friendship. I see. Our art unites our leaders into the strongest bonds of friendship. As Plato said, a true community of true friends, who seek the truth.

Guardian: Yes. By this concept of friendship, who are your friends?

Warrior: Only my wife, my children, and the brothers I fought with.

Guardian: That is why the concept of brotherhood is critical. A fellowship of equals, united for a common purpose.

Warrior: And our common cause and purpose, the reason why we need true friendship, true fellowship, and true brotherhood, is to create enlightened leaders. Those beings who know the light of truth.

Guardian: Yes.

Warrior: The more I follow, the more I see the underlying metaphysical and mystical structures, by necessity, uniting all of this.

Guardian: Yes. As with a warrior, so with the guardian. Our friendships create a metaphysical phalanx, a union, a bond, a glue that binds one to another, without stripping one of its identity as an independent being, an unmoved mover.

To unite wills we need to create this brotherhood, this community of truth-seekers, so that our teachers and students will be united as one in the means and the ends.

---

[67] Scott Peck, *The Road Less Traveled.*

Warrior: I see it. It will be a beautiful sight if you can manifest this vision.

Guardian: With your help and with other similar natures, making this manifest will simply be a laborious and enduring effort of will, mind, and energy, no matter how long it takes.

Warrior: I will help. Let us look at the other fighting skills, aside from true friendship.

Guardian: Before we move on, we need more understanding on what we mean by friendship. Our friendships are based on the calling and the vocation, not on personal wants and needs. This means we orient our friendship not toward one another, but toward what we must do, the work and the labor. In our art we forego the conventions and covetousness of social life. This means, that we seek a freeing and healthy form of impersonal and professional friendship. It's different from personal friendship, in which there's an emotional payoff. In our art, there is no emotional payoff. The entertainment industry thrives by striking our emotions instead of our light. In our art, we take nothing from one another; we simply need one another to achieve the goals we pursue. Our friendships are born of the spirit of truth. We need this spirit to distance ourselves from the vices and indulgences of emotions—the secret and hidden emotional payoffs of comfort.

In our realm of being, the emotions, like the body, are far away, for they cloud the intelligence and obscure the experience of light and truth.

Untethered from emotions, we learn to wield the fire of spirit and the vigor of being. Is this not why detachment and humility are cardinal virtues for our work? Do not the emotions reveal one's attachments and conceitedness? Our art demands self-restraint, to reign in our emotions, to transform their energy by our spiritual powers, to give birth to compassion, intensity, concentration, and endurance. This is how we will smoke out the image-seekers and discover the truth-seekers. The truth commands our actions and we act accordingly, independent of what we feel initially. We are lovers of truth, not glory; we seek nothing. There is no reciprocity in our art.

The soul is the spirit that leads the spiritedness into the emotions. We learn to wield spirit into emotions and make the ego-body-octagon's feeling-nature vibrant, vital, and vigorous. We move from the light and truth outward, not from the emotions inward. Do you see?

Warrior: I see. You never took to the conventional wisdom of emotional intelligence?

Guardian: No. The emotions are weak, unstable and insecure. The power of spirit is strong, secure, stable, and indefatigable. The emotions need to be, not suppressed, but restrained, harnessed and directed. Does not entertainment deliver the secret emotional payoff to the craving spectator?

Warrior: Yes.

Guardian: In our art, we become free us from this payoff, so that we remain clear and on guard against the fog and storms of emotions. Instead, we focus on uniting the spirits of our leaders and directing these spirits to apply their full powers in work of true value.

Warrior: Do you have an example?

Guardian: Yes. The technique of feedback. To highlight how weak the emotions are when it comes to truth and performance, we need to become versed in a feedback style that prevents the human being from lashing out emotionally.

Warrior: What? How?

Guardian: Have you ever had to give feedback to a strong, aggressive, and competitive leader?

Warrior: Yes. All the time.

Guardian: Is it ever easy to give true feedback to these spirited warriors, the kind that stings the ego but strengthens the soul?

Warrior: No.

Guardian: Is there not often a violent emotional reaction?

Warrior: Good God, yes. I never thought about it. Everyone tends to be on edge when giving character, not performance, feedback. Feedback on character is painful. It truly stings.

Guardian: It does not need to be this way. This means that both giver and receiver have been distorted by the irrational and emotional energies. We have not taught leaders how to restrain these energies, to clear them from the intellect, so the intellect can see what is hidden and can clear out the deception and ignorance with truth and wisdom. Feedback truly is a truth-seeking and truth-telling technique. It is a weapon of the guardian.

Warrior: Feedback is a weapon of the guardian as the sword is of the warrior?

Guardian: Yes. Feedback is one of the most powerful fighting skills of the guardian. It aims to kill ignorance. It aims to increase power and freedom by removing resistance, deception and delusion. It aims for truth, wisdom, and understanding—to increase one's freedom of movements.

Warrior: Wait. For our art, feedback is to become one of our most powerful fighting skills? It is a skill that requires rigorous training and practice? It is the skill in which we truly come to know how to give and receive light and truth, from one to another? To be used as a core technique that drives the will to self-actualize and the will to seek truth?

Guardian: Yes. This is why self-knowledge is critical to our art. Feedback makes us reflect. Feedback makes us take a hard look within. Feedback is the sting of truth that awakens deeper potencies to be realized. Feedback is the way of perfection. Because most leaders have not studied themselves, they do not possess the self-knowledge required to give and receive true feedback, the kind that increases power and freedom.

Warrior: They do not know the truth? They do not know they are in bondage? They possess professional knowledge, but do not have command of human nature and how to awaken its potencies?

Guardian: Yes. Most managers, remember, live from the ego-body-octagon, and do not want free-thinking teammates. They want to dominate, manipulate and command others to achieve their targets. They want to remove any threat to their own advancement and achievement.

Warrior: It seems the current structure of organizations is in direct conflict with the way you intend to lead—truth, freedom, friendship and excellence.

Guardian: This is why I endeavor to train our leaders—to make leaders I would want to follow. It would be a blessing to find leaders that I trust enough to follow, ones who were true friends, who had the will to self-actualize and the will to truth.

Warrior: Can you describe the feedback technique with an example?

Guardian: Because I am asked to provide feedback to intense, aggressive, and competitive high performers, I have found myself in a number of situations where what I saw, I could not distill to a few key points. I could not complete the kinetic chain of what I knew tacitly and intuitively—the direct apprehension—into a linguistic statement of logic and reason that the leader could absorb intellectually. The feedback sessions proved unsuccessful. I failed. I realized standard methods of feedback were of no use to these high performers. I had to study them. I had to gain their trust. I had to make sure they knew I served them and I had only their best interests in mind.

I learned that I had to study their characters more than their performance, to complete the kinetic chain of giving and receiving, of character, expertise, and performance, into one unified thread of truth and understanding.

Warrior: Go on.

Guardian: For each true feedback session, I write up to twenty pages, a method of self-inquiry, to discover what is hidden in the individual. This is arduous, necessary and essential work, to blast through the restrictions and impasses, to discover what needs to be known. I study my writing, as if I'm mining for diamonds, until I discover three to four key insights that reveal themselves in the depth of the writing—this is truth-disclosing. I study each key insight and create a kinetic chain from character, expertise, knowledge, experience, to performance— making feedback an extension of one's being. The aim is to integrate the kinetic chain so the individual can see truth clearly because it resonates with what she is. Once I am clear, I practice a few rounds of feedback with a teammate, so I can essentially lead a feedback session as though it were a free-flowing, effortless and graceful dialogue. This is to acquire the training repetitions essential to become skilled in feedback. This makes sure I can flow in the kinetic chain, up and down the threads, gliding as needed, in the actual feedback session, like an improvisational jazz musician. What I mean is, I get these insights embedded in my being, the truth, the known and the knower—as extensions of my being. Once I've done my homework, once I'm prepared, I schedule the feedback session. I leave nothing to chance. I run feedback sessions in a massive empty room. In the room, there are only two folding chairs. The backs of the two folding chairs are up against one wall. The two chairs are separated by ten feet of empty space. When sitting in the chair, the only view an individual has is that of almost being alone, in an empty room. When the leader walks in, I shake her hand and ask her to take a seat. I take a seat. I begin by providing the guidelines of the session, the same guidelines of the dialogue technique. Except, I add one more—the individual is required to look only straight ahead, in the direction of the empty room. There is to be no turning of the head or looking at one another during the entire session. I do this to silence and disarm the ego's drive to compete and control. I begin the session by sharing the insights and asking if the insights resonate with the individual.

This is a sketch of what takes place–

> Individual: Yes, the insights resonate. I am angry right now and I want to turn and attack you. Since I'm forced to look forward into the emptiness (into the abyss), there is, however, nothing to attack. I am sitting here, listening to you, with no ability to act. All there is is openness. It's actually peaceful. How did you discover these insights?

> Guardian: I spent a few hours writing. I sought to understand what is hidden from our view, what is hidden in the kinetic chain from character to performance. I did this because it is difficult to give feedback to someone like you, with your caliber of knowledge and expertise. Because you perform at such a high level, I sought to discover insights that were hidden from you and from me. It is tough to figure out what will increase your power and freedom in your art. These insights are truth's gift to you. They are designed to guide your intelligence to remove deceptions or distortions—your blind-spots. The feedback is designed to counter any resistance that keeps you from awakening deeper potencies in your art. Know that I don't judge you. Know that I do judge the qualities or conditions that you are able to change, correct and strengthen, by your powers of will and intelligence. Because of your caliber, most do not know how to provide you true feedback. Most cannot handle this kind of true feedback. It is a testament to your character and spirit that you can handle it, learn from it, and take corrective action from it, so you can lead with increased command and power.

Individual: How did you learn to see what is hidden?

Guardian: I seek truth. I had to untether my mind from the superficial observations in your performance reviews. That is why I had an interview with you and your teammates, in preparation for this feedback session. I needed to learn to see what was hidden deeper. There is a truth to you. There is a truth to the work you do. And I had to discover the essence of that truth. I imagined, if I worked for you, what would I be afraid to tell you? Where would I discover the insights to drive the moral courage to provide you salient feedback? Feedback that you needed to hear, but was denied you, because your teammates fear an aggressive reaction from you. That is the challenge of true feedback, which is why your leaders brought in, as a trusted advisor, a person with independence and objectivity. They know your talents and they want you to reach your potential as an executive. From this perspective, I let my intellect return to the performance evaluations and the interviews, and I patiently waited for truth to reveal itself. When truth revealed itself, when I became clear, I schedule this session.

Individual: How long did it take you to prepare?

Guardian: All told over the course of three weeks, about thirty hours. Then I let the insight crystallize in my thinking.

Individual: Thirty hours of preparation for a one-hour session? I had no idea how intensive preparing for feedback is.

Guardian: I came in cold, having never met you, which required an intense ramp-up.

Individual: It is ironic that in my role, most of my mistakes are in providing feedback and in judgment calls. I know I have the knowledge, expertise and experience.

Guardian: Has anyone trained you in the art of practical judgment and the art of feedback as truth-discoing activities?

Individual: None. We never speak of truth. We speak of values, missions, targets and profit.

Guardian: Right now, how much time do you devote to preparing for feedback and judgments calls?

Individual: None. My decisions and feedback are made on-the-fly and from experience, with little deliberation or discernment.

Guardian: Is this command style effective?

Individual: Clearly not.

Guardian: What are you learning?

Individual: In my role, I need to delegate transactional work and study problem-sets with more discipline, deliberation and collaboration.

Guardian: How might you schedule working methods, to make sure you commit to the practice of building intellectual rigor to meet the demands of your role?

Individual: I'm not sure. I could use your help to map out a way forward.

Guardian: I am here to help. I hope to demystify the art of practical judgment and the art of feedback. To prepare for our next meeting, study up on the management methods of Geneen and Bower, both geniuses in the art of managing executive functions.

Individual: Homework? I like it.

Warrior: Impressive—you got her to ask for help.

Guardian: That was the aim of the session. Being outside the organization, I am no threat to her advancement. All of our work is private and not shared with her leaders.

When a person asks for help, the doors of truth open and real learning takes place. It takes trust. It takes relationships. It takes friendships.

Warrior: All of this seems so simple now.

Guardian: And is it simple?

Warrior: No.

Guardian: Only by the rigors of acquiring knowledge, expertise, and experience, does it then become simple.

Warrior: What this implies is that it's simple when the art becomes an extension of our being.

Guardian: This is why we demystify the art. So leaders know "the what" and "the how" to actualize this art in their being—known and knower—one and one.

Warrior: It does seem simple—the "knowing about."

Guardian: Most stop at "knowing about" and they never arrive at knowing. Encyclopedic knowledge instead of wisdom's excellence.

Warrior: Are we on the summit now?

Guardian: What do you see?

Warrior: The truth, the principles of the warrior and guardian that must be awakened–

> The means of the warrior is violence; the means of the guardian is truth.
>
> The warrior aims to battle wills; the guardian aims to harmonize wills.
>
> The obstacle for the warrior is friction; the obstacle for the guardian is resistance.
>
> The game for the warrior is chance; the game for the guardian is change.
>
> The object of the warrior is to make the adversary powerless; the object of the guardian is to make the individual powerful.

Guardian: There is one more principle that needs to be revealed. What is the experience of the warrior?

Warrior: It is an antagonistic experience.[68]

Guardian: How do you define antagonistic?

Warrior: This means, the warrior faces an opposing force, and adversary, that is using menace to inhibit the warrior's freedom of movement.

Guardian: What is the experience of the guardian?

Warrior: It is an agonistic experience.[69]

Guardian: How do you define this?

Warrior: This is the ideal experience in our art, of spirited debate and competition, seeking to increase truth and excellence in each leader.

Guardian: We have finally discovered the experience of this art.

Warrior: Yes. On our quest, we have been experiencing the nature of our art the entire time. What eluded us were the intelligible concepts of what we were experiencing. What we experienced in reality and knew tacitly, we now know conceptually. Our aim is to demystify what we know intuitively in order to transmit this art to others.

---

[68] O.E.D. definition of antagonistic–Mutual resistance of opposing forces; active opposition; a feeling of hostility or opposition. An opposing force or principle.

[69] O.E.D. definition of agonistic–Pertaining to athletic contests or athletic feats [good-willed competitive spirit and drive]. Striving for effect [pursuing excellence}.

Guardian: Wisdom speaks. The experience we hope to create is one of friendship, struggle, spirited debate, and spirited competition to make our students and teachers powerful.

> The experience of the warrior is antagonistic; the experience of the guardian is agonistic.

Warrior: Truly, we have discovered the core principles of the warrior archetype and the guardian archetype.

It follows–

> The means of the warrior is violence; the means of the guardian is truth.

> The warrior aims to battle wills; the guardian aims to harmonize wills.

> The obstacle for the warrior is friction; the obstacle of the guardian is resistance.

> The game for the warrior is chance; the game of the guardian is change.

> The object of the warrior is to make the adversary powerless; the object of the guardian is to make the individual powerful.

> The experience of the warrior is antagonistic; the experience of the guardian is agonistic.

Guardian: Yes. Then it is done. We have penetrated the truths of our art.

Warrior: Yes. It is done. Our leaders need to become the essence of both the warrior and the guardian. These are the patterns, the archetypes, that they aim to become.

Guardian: Yes. Though we know that this ideal is never fully realized, even if we reach the summit. We know that this truth-prototype is never fully actualized, and that our art lives in a never-ending cycle of being and becoming, and that we need the will to fortitude because we always act in a state of imperfection seeking perfection.

Warrior: Our leaders need to study, knowing they will never have the full and unabridged truth of it all.

Guardian: Our leaders know that with faith, discipline, detachment, and humility, they can move from the core of their being, from their light and truth, through meditation, contemplation, and dialogue. Only by learning to move from the nature and substance of their being, will they acquire the fortitude and endurance to act moment by moment, as they continually climb to the heights of their art, from the depths of their being. When they achieve this way of being, they will have become unmoved movers—the pinnacle of our art.

Warrior: We know there is freedom only in the activities of our art. The reward is learning the way to pursue truth, wisdom, beauty, goodness and excellence.

Guardian: There is no winning, only truth. Winning, if there is still such a thing, is a second order effect of truth. Truth always wins—it frees the soul from bondage.

Warrior: We are prepared to battle the adversary. The adversary is relentless and ruthless. We never defeat the adversary; we make it powerless. We make it powerless by the might of truth.

Guardian: It seems counter-intuitive, but the only way to render the leviathan-cube powerless is to strip it of its source of energy—the soul's will and intelligence. We see clearly that its energy comes from our energy and our energy alone.

Warrior: Now we see the adversary. It is no longer hidden. It can no longer deceive.

It is time to prepare others for battle. To render the leviathan-cube powerless by focusing on the might of the truth, the good, and the light in all our leaders.

This is why our leaders need to become stronger than a warrior and stronger than a guardian. They need to rise and become even more complete in order to strengthen their teams and combat the adversary simultaneously.

Guardian: Yes. This is why the Spartans emphasized philosophy as much as warfighting skills.

Warrior: So they would not be deceived by the cunning of their adversaries?

Guardian: Yes.

Warrior: To prepare our leaders, I now see physical development as the companion of intellectual development. Physical development strengthens the will, the mind, and the body; intellectual development strengthens the will, the mind, and the intellect. I never understood how different the mind and the intellect are.

We'll use meditation, contemplation, dialogue and wisdom literature to make the will and the intellect sharp, discerning and developed.

Guardian: Saint Matthew mentors–

> Behold, I am sending you like lambs among wolves; therefore be wise as serpents and pure as doves.[70]

Truly, this metaphysical quest has revealed the wisdom literature as one of the greatest mentors.

Warrior: Now I understand how the canons mentor us in the act of leading.

Guardian: Purification of arrogance and ignorance leads to detachment and humility; wisdom leads to discernment and practical judgment.

---

[70] Holy Bible, *Book of Matthew*, Lamsa Translation.

Truly, we are all called to become the essence of truth and wisdom, by the union of the known with the knower. Our leaders must awaken the light of wisdom in their beings and become living examples of wisdom's light of truth. We are true disciples—disciples of wisdom's being, of light and truth, of nature and substance, the whole core of our true being.

Nothing can manipulate or dominate an awakened and wise soul.

Warrior: Do you realize what this means? Our enterprises and institutions, which declare they want leadership, in reality want controlled automatons they can manipulate and control to achieve artificial aims and ends.

Truly, they do not want awakened souls—the chess players. They want chess pieces, experts, who perform their tasks with excellence and mastery, in bondage on the chess board.

Experts who give no thought to the perennial questions–

> Where did I come from?
>
> Why am I here?
>
> Where am I going when I depart from here?

Guardian: Your insights have caused me to reflect on my previous existence, when Google requested a leadership development intensive. A period of great suffering and confusion.

Warrior: You brought this to Google?

Guardian: Not exactly.

Warrior: What happened? I'm listening.

Guardian: We have travelled a long way. Before we move on, let us sit in an easeful posture, at the summit and be like–

> That man who, forsaking all desire, moves about devoid of longing, devoid of the thought of "mine," without ego-sense—he approaches peace.[71]

Warrior: Let us be in peace.

---

[71] *The Bhagavad-Gita*, Feuerstein translation.

CHAPTER TEN
ADVERSITY

Guardian: Where to start? I am cautious about flowing in this stream of inquiry because it stems from the life of the ego-body-octagon and not the soul-sphere. What I am about to share is the stream of living experiences that led to the actualization of my calling and vocation. These experiences, at the time, I took too personally. I only share them as an example to help our leaders understand how to build self-knowledge, and how to endure hardships and trials to see their truths actualized, both in potencies of soul and in excellence of skills. I'm not sure if I can do this with complete detachment and in a state of contemplation. That is the aim, when we reflect—not to make our experiences "personal" but to make them "lessons" of growth. Mind you, most of these experiences occurred in the ego-body-octagon and the leviathan-cube, not the soul-sphere and the eternal-sphere. I am at the edge of teaching this art. Should I fall into the abyss of the ego, please pull me out. If you hear any contempt in my voice, please demand that I lift my soul into contemplative wisdom and speak from those graceful and loving heights. For many years, I took my experiences too personally, living in the bondage of the ego. Now, if I am to teach this art, I must engage in a reflective style that demonstrates truth, light, and wisdom. I need to use this stream of reflection as a catharsis to clear out any remains of the ego-body-octagon's projections—memories, emotions, or experiences of self-will that keep my soul in darkness, bondage, and ignorance. I must understand these experiences of living as methods in which reality revealed my weaknesses—in which contempt and lust fueled me, instead of compassion and fortitude.

Warrior: What happened?

Guardian: Let me search my heart and speak from the depths of my being. I aim to give expression to what lives deep within, to speak from my pain, to speak from my soul, to contemplate how I recovered and responded to tests and failures. Our leaders must know how to recover from failures and falls. Honestly, I do not want to speak about this or think about it. But at this summit we've been given a deeper understanding and it's here that we begin to lay the foundations for leaders to leap from—from being into becoming. We are almost prepared to teach this art.

We are friends and I must speak truthfully. We're in the depths and I must be courageous so that I'm not a hypocrite. I'll confront, face to face, what still lurks in these depths, to continue the purification that sets the soul free.

Know that I share these experiences as one example how a leader may be formed by trials and tribulations, by suffering and pain, by failures and defeats, in order to strengthen the soul by the healing art of recovery, and the transforming art of being and becoming.

Where to begin? Let me see. Remember when I told you that I once hired a leadership coach and set these three goals–

1. Get a Master degree in leadership.
2. Move to California.
3. Get a job with a leadership firm.

Warrior: Yes, I remember.

Guardian: I hope I can see clearly and not let the emotions ensnare me. I am still learning the virtue of self-restraint, to remain detached and objective as I look within. I need to distance myself from my own experiences, almost as if they happened to another human being, so that they lose their grip on my interior being. Self-knowledge, the art of moving beyond one's self by meditation and contemplation, begins with detachment to create the distance required to open the soul's power of objectivity. I never understood the seriousness of this until I found myself ensnared in a vicious cycle of shear antagonism with reality itself.

Warrior: You mean, your self-will battled with reality's truth? A warrior at war with reality? At war with truth?

Guardian: Yes. I experienced my subjective willing at war with reality's truth. Everything seemed a struggle. I had no peace or harmony about how my life was unfolding. Had I known the seriousness of my error, I would have begun correcting it without hesitation. But I had no guide, no guardian. It seemed that even the beings I admired were of no help. Now I understand. Now I know how to correspond with reality. To swim in reality's waters. But I'm still learning. I still need to make amends with the past. I still need to exercise forgiveness of others and self, as we were all moving from an imperfect nature darkened by the ego-body-octagon and the leviathan-cube. I need to be further cleansed and purified, which is another reason for following this river of past experiences. To once and for all move on cleanly and purely from past failures and regrets. From the point of view of the soul-sphere, it's nothing, these past experiences. They are trivial and the soul teaches this, if we can learn from them. If we use them as reality's teachings, the lessons of experience will be seen as the awakeners and liberators of the soul. The experiences, the lessons, I now know, did awaken and liberate my soul. Without them I may have lived an unexamined life. And without an examined life, there is no metaphysical freedom. And so I now embark on an examined life.

I moved to California. Check.

I had a job at a consulting firm. Check.

I began a Master degree program in leadership. Check.

I began hunting for a leadership firm. Check.

Warrior: And why do you start here, instead of heading straight into your experiences with Google?

Guardian: I need to set the context to connect the threads from a number of different experiences that led to my formation and the discovery of this art.

Warrior: Then speak freely and I will listen.

Guardian: On the surface, all that I am to share is quite insignificant, except from the perspective of lessons of experience—how direct experiences awaken the truth in the soul.

Years before I found myself in front of Google executives, I worked for KPMG Consulting.

Consulting is essentially glorified blue-collar pick-and-shovel work, for the intellectual side of capitalism. Generally, consultants are middle-class kids, who don't want to be poor and want the economic route to the good life—country clubs, private schools, luxury homes and cars, and island timeshares.

Because they seek "things", they give their souls and energy to a firm, being owned by the partners, working between 70 and 90 hours a week. They don't necessarily work for the love of the profession. The work is the means and affluence is the end. I once asked 80 consultants, if they had an ATM card with unlimited funding, would they return to work the next day. Not one hand went up. Work was the means for the revenue they sought as ends. I could understand—that was why I was there too. The carrot of being a professional is financial reward.

But, behind the veil, you see, there is no difference between the physical work of a blue collared worker and the intellectual work of a white collared worker. Except one difference—one uses physical labor; the other uses intellectual labor. The intellectual labor pays. That is why people do it. The pay is good if you don't have generational wealth or own your business. It's a great profession if you don't know your calling or purpose.

That said, I never wanted to be in that kind of situation. Work as the means for ends. Because I knew my calling and vocation, my actual work was both the means and the ends—an autotelic[1] activity. I wanted important work, which is why I had served as a Marine officer. Work as Deed. Work as Act.

I got lured into consulting because—the old bait and switch—I thought we would be advising clients on management, for both their operational and their strategic challenges. I learned that the partners would "talk" and "advise" these clients, while we, the consultants, were essentially a non-physical intellectual sweat shop, producing Excel, PowerPoint, and Word documents based on our client responsibilities. I served as a risk manager, managing the cost,

---

[1] O.E.D. definition of autotelic–having or being an end in itself.

schedule and performance for a multi-year, multi-billion-dollar project. Daily, I had to track a 1,500-line item project schedule. I spent the rest of the time in client meetings and client briefings.

Warrior: Good times.

Guardian: Metaphysical Hell. I use to get emotionally disturbed when I reflected on it. Only the power of soul can keep me undisturbed and resting inwardly as I continue the examination of my experience.

Here the Angelic Doctor mentors–

> For the act of contemplation, in which the contemplative life essentially consists, is hindered both by the impetuosity of the passions and by outward disturbances. Now the moral virtues curb the impetuosity of the passions and quell the disturbance of outward occupations. Hence moral virtues belong to the contemplative life as a predisposition.[2]

I suffered unrestrained passions and allegiance to outward experiences and occupations. As you will see, this is the reason I suffered so then, and do not suffer so now. I did not know I needed moral virtues to effectively and gracefully move through these experiences.

At the time, the way I made sense of living this way, and the way I restrained the will to quit, was that I had nothing else to do, and I thought I would build my professional experience and could strengthen my mind by concentrating on things that I had no interest in, but that were intellectually demanding.

Here Mark Twain mentors–

> Do something everyday that you don't want to do; this is the golden rule for acquiring the habit of doing your duty without pain.[3]

I failed to practice this sage principle. I did work I did not want to do. But I did it with rage and contempt instead of doing it with gentleness and grace.

I increased my production by 700% and hit the revenue target of $1.2m in under one year. Why is this significant? The target to hit $1million drove me, as that target came with a promotion to manager. Why the drive to become a manager? I felt insignificant being an individual contributor instead of leading a team. Being trained and called to lead, I felt a constant discomfort not being in a leadership position. What drove me were the challenges of leading, not wealth, success or achievement, independent of leading. The best part of me was

---

[2] Aldous Huxley, *The Perennial Philosophy*. Saint Thomas Aquinas quoted.
[3] Mark Twain, *Following the Equator*.

not being engaged. That discomfort triggered the contempt and rage, as though I were in a metaphysical cage, seeking to break free.

And as you know now, this metaphysical cage is a reality—the ego-body-octagon and the leviathan-cube had captured me and held me in bondage. A bondage I did not know was a reality. I did not know of its existence and force.

While I did not know of this, I had enough wisdom to imagine that I was in prison and one day I would be released, but, I did not know when.

Let us begin to look, here, at my performance review after I hit my targets.

Warrior: Why? What happened?

Guardian: My manager not only did not promote me to manager, but he did not give me a bonus, and only gave me a slight raise, to keep up with inflation. Essentially, I received nothing for the merits of performance. I thought I worked in a meritocracy. I soon learned that I lived in the tyranny of the bureaucracy. I had no control, no power and no leverage in this situation. I wanted to reach across the desk and smack the manager with the back of my hand for his unmeasured and subjective evaluation. I thought, where is the objectivity, the cause and effect of effort and production that resulted in increased revenue and profit, by my energy, intelligence and labor?

Instead, I took the serving he dished out. I left the performance review calmly. Then I threw down the gauntlet and immediately scheduled a meeting with the partner and the manager to contest the evaluation and seek a promotion, bonus, and raise.

For the meeting, I prepared a 10-page slide-deck to cover the performance metrics that merited a promotion, a bonus, and a raise.

Warrior: You did your homework.

Guardian: Yes. I learned from Geneen[4] that when dealing with egotists (and both my partner and manager were suffering the disease of egotism) one must be armed with facts, logic, and objectivity–

> Egotism blindsides a man to the realities around him…. More and more he lives in the world of his own imagination…. He's impaired by his narcissism…unwilling to accept data and information contrary to the image he has of himself in his own mind…believes he is smarter than everyone else…that he is in control and everyone is to serve him…seeks praise and adulation…stems from deep personal insecurities.

---

[4] Harold Geneen and Alvin Moscow, *Managing*.

Warrior: This is how we learn to grow as a leader, in combat with the adversary.

Guardian: Yes. Yet maybe at the time I too suffered the disease of egotism. But I knew of the suffering and was not oblivious to it. You will see, this is where I hit rock bottom. A state of inner torment and turmoil.

Warrior: What?

Guardian: My good man, you should know that even though I crushed my performance metrics, I nightly put down a fifth of scotch to extinguish the rage. I did not remain unscathed. I became morally compromised by my own reaction to the reality of my existence.

Warrior: Painful.

Guardian: I felt shame. It was one of the few times I experienced this wicked emotion because of my weaknesses and recklessness. Having a good heart is not enough. A good heart must convert into good actions.

Warrior: A classic example of crushing performance goals and sacrificing your well-being.

Guardian: The scales of justice were at play. The madness of living incongruently—my interior nature did not correspond to my exterior nature. I lacked harmony, resonance and correspondence with life itself. I met my goals in work that I hated. I experienced life as a metaphysical hell, a prison, the leviathan-cube, a situation that I could not see and could not understand. I had allowed the structure, a fictional and fabricated exterior, to taking ownership of my will and intelligence and energy. All I had to do, if I saw truth, was turn away, walk way and leave the structure. But I did not even know truth existed. I was in ignorance. Darkness had veiled the light and truth of my soul. I wanted metaphysical freedom. Do you see?

Warrior: I see. You were on the board of a game you did not understand. You were a piece on the board, being controlled by a player who told you what to do, how to move and what targets to hit. You were, in fact, being controlled by another human being. You allowed yourself to be controlled because you sought financial compensation for your time, energy, and expertise. But you didn't resonate with the way your time, energy and expertise were being used. If you had had wealth, you would not have allowed another being to use your energy as a means for an external end.

Guardian: Yes. Making this period even more maddening, this is when I started fasting and meditating. I started to experience wild spiritual awakenings, free of the bondage and darkness. In those days my calling and purpose began to be revealed with more depth and clarity. I learned that if one is not living his purpose, but knows his purpose, then any activity separate from his purpose is experienced as pain and suffering, in his interior nature, in his soul.

Warrior: You mean, during the week you suffered rage and intoxication, and on the weekends you experienced purity and freedom?

Guardian: Yes.

Warrior: You were a fractured and non-integrated soul. It seems you were cycling in between heaven and hell, weekly.

Guardian: Yes. It's wild to reflect on. At the same time, I also pursued a Master degree in leadership.

Warrior: Wow. You were being initiated in the depths of the hero's journey.

Guardian: In reflection, is appears so. I don't know if this personal example is important. But it may help our leaders see the power of recovering from a fall from grace. We will be there to help them recover and learn from their missteps. In this period, in the depths, I ran on treadmills and hamster wheels—a cycle of futile, worthless and wasted energy. A peer coined this the cycle of futileness.[5] The master's program was worthless but I thought it would help me transition into a leadership firm. I checked out after the first semester, and did the minimum to keep high marks.

Know that I'm setting the context for when I get to Google.

Warrior: Don't be in a hurry. Describe the experience.

Guardian: This is when I crossed the threshold into the depths of the unknown. Now I'll return to the meeting I scheduled with the partner of the firm.

Warrior: And so begins the birth of truth-seeking.

Guardian: I knocked on the door and entered. Three of them, one partner and two managers, were sitting there waiting for me. They had involved another manager, unbeknownst to me. Always be prepared, I had thought; when you go through the door, have the weapon of truth ready. I steadied myself like a warrior—I will attack if provoked. The warrior in me asserted himself. For many years I had forgotten to live the warrior principles—to have contempt for death, to act boldly and courageously, to suffer no fiction, to wield power and strength by training and combat. It never occurred to me that those around me, who were not enemies, could still be nonetheless adversaries and not true friends, even though I worked side by side with them. These leaders were not my true friends. I steadied myself. I found my footing. I began to see. Conventional life had lured me into complacency. Something awakened in the depths. An energy I had not felt in a long time ignited my will and mind—I had the power, the leverage, and the control of the situation, not them, because I had nothing to lose. I could walk away at any moment. I began to experience metaphysical freedom. Insights flashed before me. I remembered the counsel of a wise leader, and now I listened in my mind–

---

[5] The Cycle–the highs and lows of unharnessed, unrestrained and dynamic energy because of indiscipline and intemperance, where one is one's own worst enemy.

"Guardian, you know you make us nervous," he said.

"Why?" I responded.

"Because we cannot control you; you are not married and do not have a mortgage," he said.

Good God, this is how managers control people who do not have generational wealth.

I remembered Proverbs–

A wise man will listen and will increase in learning; and a man of understanding shall attain to leadership.[6]

I smiled in earnest as I entered the room. I knew metaphysical bondage had already lost this battle.

Partner: Welcome guardian, take a seat. What did you want to cover with us?

Guardian: I prepared a performance evaluation that demonstrates how I've surpassed the metrics required to earn a promotion to manager, and how I merit a yearly bonus and salary increase. By this objective evaluation, I contest the evaluation of my performance manager. An evaluation that did not include a promotion, a bonus, and a true salary increase. After reviewing this performance evaluation, I hope the three of you will reconsider what I merit at this performance review.

Partner: Let's take a look at what you prepared.

Guardian: Here are the highlights. By hitting the target of $1 million, I merit a promotion to manager. By increasing revenue and profit, I merit a bonus and raise. I increased my team from 1 to 5. In actuality, on the ground, I am already managing and leading, independent of title.

Let me also remind the three of you that last year, you reluctantly promoted me to consultant because I transferred from a Midwest team. I also had to fight then for a promotion I had earned. At that time, you told me that hitting the $1 million mark would merit another promotion. The speed with which I hit this target is not relevant. As with last year, so with this year—I am fighting for what I actually earned and should not have to fight for. Further, without my effort the firm would not have increased its revenue by $1 million. As I remind you, the guy I replaced, who you promoted, did not increase revenue or profit in three years. I make this request based on the

---

[6] The Holy Bible, *Book of Proverbs*, Lamsa Translation.

virtue of justice, what one is due, what one earned, and, by earning, merits in professional rewards.

The partner looked at the two managers. Their contempt could be seen in their faces. I did not have the authority and rank to speak this way to them.

> Partner: I am responsible for our entire team. Yes, you increased revenue by $1m, but the other manager here lost $1m of revenue, and to cover him, I used your revenue to make sure everyone could sustain the P&L requirements of the partnership.

I looked at the other manager, the one who had failed. He was a coward and a snake. Time to attack.

> Guardian: We are not a firm that takes on charity cases. We are a meritocracy. This manager failed. Hold him accountable. It is not honest and it is not just how you are managing and leading. You should fire him for incompetence. If you suffer compassion (this means to suffer with), then you can demote him to a consultant, you can reduce his pay, and you can put his team under me and I will manage them, moving forward. These would be honest and just decisions.

This really fired them up. What, reduce his position and his salary, let alone, fire him?

> Partner: I am the partner and I'll do what deem best. Who do you think you are? You are nothing. You are a consultant, one of 50 on my team. I make the judgment calls, not you. I do what is best for the firm.

I witnessed the disease of egotism. Now he saw me as a threat. I had called out his lack of courage and justice. This partner suffered the bondage of the ego-body-octagon.

> Guardian: We have professional standards and metrics to hold ourselves accountable. I do not provide my energy and labor so that the manager or you or another human being may personally benefit. We have a duty to act in objectivity and not subjectivity to what is true, fair, and just. We are not a non-profit. We are a performance-based firm.

> Partner: What would you do, if you were in my position, cast this manager out on the street? He has a family he must provide for. He has personal demands and responsibilities that you do not have.

Now he tried to play to the emotions instead of reason.

> Guardian: I told you what must be done, if we are to honor the truth. I would reduce his pay and demote his role. That is fair. That is truth. Truth should guide.

Partner: You have never been in this position of responsibility, for the livelihood of others.

Guardian: Each man must carry his own burdens and responsibilities. We create an injustice when we strip the power of souls to carry their own burdens, burdens that necessitate the awakening of the soul's power to respond to reality's truth, pressure and lessons.

Now I laid it on him.

Guardian: You forget that I led Marines in my formative years, before I understood how to pursue virtues, excellence and wisdom. I led by raw potential waiting to be awakened. I led global logistics operations for 5 squadrons, 80 aircraft, and 1,000 Marines, making sure that any piece of equipment that affected mission readiness rates would be secured. This was sheer drudgery, But the mission was noble—supporting the pilots, the mechanics, and the squadrons. The mission mattered. I did this by scourging the earth to locate, and commandeer, if necessary, the equipment needed to make the mission. We had the highest mission capability rates in the entire Marine Corps and my Colonel became the future Three-Star General for all Marine Aviation. If you know anything about logistics, getting the gear is critical to supporting flight operations. In that role, I experienced more stress, intensity, purpose, and meaning in one hour than I have in 4 years of consulting. I'm wondering why I left the Marines for this kind of life and meaningless work. I thought it would be freeing; I'm finding it enslaving.

Let us be honest. Our work is insignificant. I dare say, our clients would be fine without us. This is our firm's cash cow. All four of us in this room know this to be true. That is why we do this work. We are highly paid servants to help incompetent bureaucratic managers whose organizations find it more problematic to fire them than to retain them. It is boring and futile and worthless work. I am here because I do not have generational wealth and the salary rate you pay me is better than elsewhere. I am here to improve my economic station in life. Period. This is not about charity or "your firm." I merit the promotion, the bonus, and the raise. This is the truth.

I threw a grenade into their sense of worth. I revealed how insignificant we all were.

Partner: I am in command. I'll do whatever I deem best. We are not going to change our decision. I suggest you focus on becoming a better teammate. Your self-centeredness and conceitedness is unbecoming and unprofessional.

Guardian: By looking at the truth, I am self-centered and conceited?

Partner: No. Your attitude, your tone, and your perspective is arrogant and ignorant.

Guardian: Arrogant, no. Ignorant, guilty as charged.

I saw how the partner turned the truth upside-down, to make me the villain, the egotist, the one who was arrogant and ignorant, conceited and selfish, because I did not bow and obey their authority and position, and fought for what I had in fact already earned. This was what infuriated me, the injustice. I earned it. I merited it. I did not expect what I did not deserve.

Guardian: Then is this meeting over?

Partner: Yes.

Guardian: Then, thank you for your time to meet with me and cover my concerns.

After the meeting, I felt not only rage, as righteous indignation, but I again felt the wickedness of shame. I did attack their manhood. Now, as I reflect, these managers were average and weak human beings, in will, in intelligence, and in skill. They belonged to the status quo professional environment. They were not seekers of truth and light. At the time, I could not comprehend how destiny guided me by these experiences, to turn me away from common ways of being and toward uncommon ways of being. Destiny, I learned, pointed me straight into the unknown. If I had wisdom, the kind that ignited right before the meeting, I would have simply resigned instead of fighting for a 2-bit shift of rank and pay. I felt shame because most human beings on earth live a bare-bones existence and here I am fighting for my just dessert, which is in truth nothing and insignificant.

Thoreau mentors us here–

The mass of men lead lives of quiet desperation.[7]

Instead of fighting for insignificant just desserts, I needed the wisdom to turn and walk away from the known. I did not yet have the moral courage to turn from the known to the unknown. At the time, I did not know that the hero's journey is a living reality in each soul. I know now how truth reveals itself when we continuously leap into the unknown.

Warrior: What happened next?

Guardian: Maybe divine justice. The partner, fired for incompetence, lost his partnership. Upon my departure, the client sent a note to the partner that said, "The guardian is one of the best professionals I have worked with in my 30 years of experience."

Warrior: So, you quit?

---

[7] Henry David Thoreau, *Walden*.

Guardian: Hold on. Not exactly. I'm getting ahead of the story.

As I drove home from the meeting, I thought, I have nothing to win and nothing to lose. My life had become insignificant and meaningless. This is hell for a soul who needs significant work. I realized I placed too much significance on meaningful work as the measure for happiness. I remembered a scene from movie, "Office Space," when the protagonist stopped showing up to work and no one did anything. Now I began to suffer the sin of indifference.

Warrior: Wait. You stopped showing up at work?

Guardian: Yes. I tested the principle in the film. That is how I justified staying with the firm. I still had not finished the master's degree (I am still paying off the loan, mind you), and I could essentially do my work from home, about an hour each day, the "duties" of a manager. This evolved into a great and prolonged retreat. I lived a block from the ocean, and spent the days in silence and solitude, in academic and spiritual studies, each day bookended with physical training. The discovery of freedom.

Warrior: You did this?

Guardian: Yes. The absurdity of it—paid $80k a year, for about 300 hours' worth of work. I had a team doing the work and I managed them. They were self-starters and needed little guidance.

Warrior: What about your manager?

Guardian: Initially, he called and asked why I was not in the office. I said, except for client-facing meetings, I would be working from the satellite office—my home office. He did not question it from there. I think he felt bad for the way he and his team treated me, and to throw me a bone, he let me work from home. I looked up and thanked the engineers for the advances in technology that allowed me to do this, work from my satellite office.

During this retreat, I found an opportunity at the Center for Creative Leadership. They had an opening in San Diego, seeking a strategic account manager. While I lacked specific business development experience, I could make a case that the experiences in logistics and consulting were transferable skills, and would lead to success in this role. I took a shot, applied and got an interview.

God, I hate interviews. There is no true evaluation. It's a subjective free-fall with the likes and dislikes of personality, predilections, and temperaments.

Warrior: Go on.

Guardian: I had erred in setting my goal.

Warrior: How?

Guardian: I set a goal to work with a leadership firm and that goal meant I would take any position I could get, to get in the door. Notice how the goal can affect the movements. I did not have a goal to work at a firm where I led as a leadership teacher and facilitator. From the military and consulting, I had learned just how difficult it is to get into a firm. Getting into the right firm became the goal, and not the kind of work I would be doing. This mistake was an important lesson.

Yes, I had the long-term goal to develop leaders, but this firm was not looking for teachers. Plus, I learned, at my age, if I did not have a PHD, I would not be considered by most firms to merit a teaching role. That said, I wanted out of consulting and would take any gig I could get.

The interview process was brutal, the firm had a relational culture, one I had never experienced before—likability and skill were equally valued. This meant I interviewed with dozens of employees, in both group and one-to-one interviews. There were multiple days of interviews. And what happened? I fit the likeability score; I did not fit the skill score. The potential skills, mapped out in a fit/gap analysis, on how I could contribute based upon my experience, were not enough. Christ, I thought, compared to being a Marine Officer, being a strategic account manager, in my mind, was a joke. Did they not see this? No, they did not see this.

Warrior: And?

Guardian: I did not get the job.

Warrior: Why?

Guardian: The managing director did not want to take a risk on me because I did not have specific business development experience that met her threshold. I had no experience with the type of open-ended questioning and sales consulting they were looking for, even though I essentially did consultative selling as a management consultant. It is madness. My worth getting evaluated from interviews. There was no way to tryout to prove oneself. The subjectivity of it all led me to despondency. They could not see the character or the intelligence of the person before them. I knew from experience that I could engage the work and figure out what needed to be done. The job would be simple compared to leading Marines and consulting managers.

Warrior: What did you do?

I asked the human resource manager, if any other openings came up to please keep me in mind. I then shared with him that I had already resigned from my current firm, and thought, if I did not get this job, I would travel to India for a month. I could hear his ears perk up when I said I had resigned. He asked why? And I said I had thought I would get the job. He said, I'll keep you in mind.

Warrior: Wow. You had already resigned.

Guardian: Yes, indeed. A moment of true liberation in the unknown. When I called my consulting manager to resign, I could almost feel the news hit him like a punch in the gut or a *shockabuku*. He had no idea I would resign. He thought, why would I give up this sweet gig, working from home, living by the ocean, and only working an hour a day. He knew what I was doing. He knew I could manage. He knew I would perform. And he had thought there was no way I would leave that sweet a deal.

Warrior: You truly are mad.

Guardian: He never met anyone as called to truth as I am.

Warrior: Then?

Guardian: Then, I resigned. I experienced intense uncertainty, but I felt free. A true freedom. It lasted only a month.

Warrior: Why?

Guardian: The human resources manager from the Center for Creative Leadership called, and said he had another job opening. I asked what kind of opening. He said, strategic account manager.

Warrior: What? Didn't they interview you and say you did not have enough experience?

Guardian: Yes they did, and that is what I told him. But, he said, "I think the hiring manager is looking for someone like you."

Warrior: Why?

Guardian: Because it was a new role, on the west coast, and they needed someone with courage, initiative and an adventurous spirit to map out and hunt the territory from the ground up. The manager liked my resume and liked what the other employees said about me.

I got the job. And, yes, entered into bondage again.

Warrior: What? I thought you wanted this job?

Guardian: I wanted to join the firm. For context, this is the recap of the interview, the entry point into the firm.

> Sales Manager: I need you to be able to work on your own, with little guidance or help. You need to map out the West Coast territory, and build strong client relationships that lead to clients commissioning our leadership services.

It reminded me of "The Message to Garcia."[8]

---

[8] A tale of leadership, initiation, and achieving through the unknown.

Guardian: Yes, as a former Marine, I can execute on that commander's intent.

Sales Manager: Then you have the job. I've been looking for someone like you.

Guardian: Before I accept this job, I need to be honest about my intentions. My goal is to develop leaders. This job is a means to that end. I will devote two years of my life to this role. Then, after two years, if I succeed, I will request to transition to the faculty team and begin the training to teach leaders in these services.

Sales Manager: That is fair. Thank you for your honesty, so that I know what drives you.

She was one of the best leaders I had ever met.

In two years, I operated like a big game hunter and landed Google, Microsoft, and Starbucks to name a few. These few were the bulk of the revenue I generated. I increased my revenue year over year by 120%. But I knew I was lucky. Period. The training market is a series of ups and downs, and I got lucky. I also hunted only for big game, a very risky mindset, win big or lose big, with no safety net. I did this because small organizations are tiresome; they are led by risk-averse leaders who have limited funding for training. The big firms, however, prioritize leadership training as they know don't have the skill or the time to teach leadership, being fully engaged to lead their enterprises to hit quarterly goals.

I took a $15k pay cut to get into the firm. My peers thought I was mad. That said, my performance led to bonuses that made up for the reduction in salary. To think that in a non-profit I made a $16k bonus, and in consulting I never made one!

Now for the intrinsic value of the role. I attended numerous leadership trainings, at no cost, to learn how to sell them to clients. Most leadership trainings cost between $3k and $7k for an individual. I share this because I experienced first-hand the leadership education methods developed at this firm.

Most importantly, I was taken in behind the veil of powerful companies. This experience changed my perspective on leadership development. What I saw terrified me.

Warrior: And this is where Google comes into play?

Guardian: Yes. A senior manager reached out to vet our leadership development programs. Because of their explosive growth, they needed help.

Warrior: Was it a great experience?

Guardian: Hardly.

Warrior: Why?

Guardian: I'm doing my best to explain what I experienced. I don't know if I can capture it in writing. When I speak about my experiences, I get unsettled and have to keep detaching and distancing myself from the experience to see with true insight. When I speak or seek the truth, I experience the insight as light.

Here is the experience at Google.

It started with a lead, Mary, an older woman who looked like a mystic. Light was in her eyes, and was framed by her long sliver-gray hair. She seemed like a sage amidst a bunch of young souls in the midst of their first incarnations on earth. These young souls, working at Google, treated Google like a deity and temple. It was terrifying. She managed a critical need, the training and development of Google's engineers. She invited me to visit the campus and meet with her executives.

One thing to note—it's only cool to be at Google if you are an owner or an engineer. The rest of the company is essentially a support staff, with typical management functions that you find in any organization. Highly prized sheep, the Googlers, most of them. The engineers, however, were warriors in their field, geniuses, many of them. Google attracted the most intelligent souls on earth. The place is electric.

Warrior: And?

Guardian: The experience turned out to be a defining moment in my development.

I flew to Palo Alto. Mary brought me to the campus. A team gave me a tour, highlighting all the amenities, all the nutrition and personal services—dry cleaning, transportation, exercise, mindfulness, etc.

> But, I thought, this is how they keep all these pawns on campus day and night.
> The tyranny of the leviathan-cube.

The two days I spent there, both Meg Whitman and Carly Fiorina were guest speakers during the lunch hour in their massive café auditorium. I thought, this place is powerful, in the world of business and technology. I could see the allure of power seducing all these people in its web, and how this web manipulated their wills and intelligences for corporate ends—wealth, power, control, and domination.

After the tour, I found myself in a conference room with 20 executives. The image—me, this nobody, with all these high-powered and highly paid executives responsible for leading the growth of Google. In leadership, what could I offer? What training could CCL offer?

After establishing rapport, I asked what they needed and what they were seeking in a partner.

Then I became terrified when I heard and witnessed their ignorance.

> Executive: You know, we are a flat organization, a new kind of business model, and the old leadership development models just won't do at Google. We have a different kind of employee, one who is free-thinking, incredibly intelligent, and moves in a hyper-dynamic and hyper-collaborative work environment. I'm not sure your trainings can help.

> Guardian: What are you seeing? What do you need?

> Executives: We are a young company and most of our employees are under 35. They lack professional experience and have never led or been in management positions, and they are tasked with leading their peers on innovative and world-changing projects. We have found there are communication issues between teams and between service lines. We need something that will harness and integrate all these interactions so we can accelerate the development of our products and services. But our Googlers are resistant to these soft skills of leadership and coaching and planning. They like to act and create, in a fluid, unstructured and dynamic way. They like facts and data and performance.

> Guardian: Why do they consider leadership a soft skill?

> Executive: You know, all the psychology and emotional-based stuff that it addresses.

> Guardian: I need to caution about the bias that leadership is a soft skill.

> Executive: It is a soft skill.

> Guardian: By whose standards? Your standards?

> Executive: Standards?

> Guardian: Yes. Standards. If you want performance measures, what are your measurements for leadership development and leading? At Google, you have standards for the hardware and software. What are your standards for the human beings who work at Google?

> Executive: I'm not sure what you're asking.

> Guardian: Don't let the long hair fool you, I am a former Captain in the United States Marine Corps, and warriors have stated, since the dawn of combat, that leadership is the hardest skill to develop, and it requires the most strenuous and rigorous kind of training, one that aims, first, to find each warrior's weakness in will and intellect, seeking to break the warrior then and

there. We all break. And the reason for this is that, once we break, the true task of leadership development is learning how to recover from this initial break so it never happens again. And if it does, so that we know how to recover and regain our center, and become stronger in the fight. The goal is for a leader, by the strength of his or her will and mind, to become an unmoved mover. This is essential, so a leader can rest inwardly and observe reality objectively and respond with lucidness and insight.

Executive: You have my attention now.

Guardian: Would you hire me to be an engineer if I did not have a PHD or experience in software engineering?

Executive: No. You would not have the knowledge and skill to meet our performance standards.

Guardian: Standards. And yet, now you need performance standards when it comes to leading?

Executive: Yes. Until now, I never thought about it in those terms.

Guardian: What if that's because it's the hardest skill and takes the longest to develop? And here, you expect young souls under 35 to exercise leadership? What if it's not needed in your business, but only in war? What if you only need better managers?

Executive: We need leaders.

Guardian: Why?

Executive: Google lives in creative uncertainty and complexity.

Guardian: But the search engine is your economic engine, your cash cow. The marketing revenue and the stock market fund and fuel this creativity.

Executive: Yes. We have bought over 100 companies since we started. We are a creative behemoth.

I thought, no, Google is an example of leviathan-cube bondage and they don't even know it.

Guardian: Wait. How many of you in this room have been assessed, trained, and selected for your leadership capabilities?

Not one hand went in the air.

Guardian: How many of you have attended at least one leadership training?

One hand went up in the air.

>Guardian: How many of you have read and studied and implemented the techniques of at least one leadership-specific book.

Not one hand went up.

>Guardian: Is Google special?

>Executive: Yes. We're pioneers.

>Guardian: Let me ask you, what has changed in the nature of human beings in the last 70,000 years?

Not one comment. For a chatty group of executives, they were stunned into silence.

>Guardian: The answer—nothing. Nothing has changed. We, you, me, the human beings at Google, none of us have changed in terms of what produces virtue in us. What has changed is the science and the technology, not the people wielding the science. The use of science and technology may be what distinguishes Google from its competitors, but the human beings at Google have no more special gifts than the human beings at your competitors. I've worked with them and they are no different than you. In this light, what you seek is how to grow human beings to meet the demands of working at Google. Most organizations have failed in the art of developing human nature. They have succeeded at building human expertise. The value of CCL and what we can bring to Google is to get your teammates prepared to meet the professional demands they face unceasingly, every day, here at Google.

>Executive: What do you have in mind?

>Guardian: I would like to schedule a two-day focus group and interview fifty of your engineers. From there, I will capture the findings and create of few solution sets to establish standards, as well as training methods to meet those standards.

The meeting ended. The leaders left the room intrigued. I left the room horrified. How can it be possible that no one takes this skill, leading, with the seriousness that they should? They were highly skilled workers. They were not leaders. I would not trust my soul and energy with any of them.

Warrior: What happened?

Guardian: As I left the meeting, I linked back up with my handler, Mary. She seemed distraught. A small circle formed around her and she broke down in front of her teammates. She shared that her mother had just passed away. Everyone just stood there, stunned, as she started to weep uncontrollably. No one consoled her. I could not let that stand. I stepped forward and embraced her in a gentle and consoling embrace. She put her head on my shoulder and wept. I closed my eyes and prayed. Once she let the initial grieving go and sighed relief, I looked at her and smiled. Her team looked even more stunned. The affection I gave seemed to make them uncomfortable. I thought, leading is about leading the soul, and about care and concern for the soul's well-being.

Warrior: Compassion. Then?

Guardian: Then I headed to parking lot to get my car, and I drove to the airport.

Warrior: And?

Guardian: The rest was easy. I led focus groups. I created sketches of possible leadership solutions sets. And then the firm's lead trainers took the sketches and created tangible work products in the form of trainings and simulations. Google became one of the biggest accounts for CCL.

Warrior: And they almost did not hire you, because you did not have experience. Classic.

Guardian: The reason why I share this story is that I saw the same thing at every other organization–

Highly skilled managers underdeveloped in the leadership arts.

It seemed perplexing at the time, how these powerful organizations could be successful without true leaders of the art. I began to think that business did not need good leaders, though they did need good managers.

Warrior: Why?

Guardian: Because businesses provide goods and services. The goods and services need to be competitive and excellent, but the people in the organizations do not need to be developed and good; they only need the skills to make the organization thrive. This is when I shifted gears to more intensely study the warriors, the sages, and the saints for guidance and clarity. I began to see things differently.[9]

Warrior: How?

Guardian: Instead of great products and services, I wanted to focus on serving the needs of human beings to self-actualize, to self-realize and to awaken the soul's inner faculties. I did not

---

[9] Iconoclastic Leadership–see things differently, challenge the status quo, fortitude in the face of fear, social intelligence.

think it mattered, for true business needs, if managers developed the will to actualize. But it mattered to me. I care about human beings and I love the process of self-actualization, in which the goodness and truth of the human being is what matters most. I found that professions like medicine, war, education, religion and government would benefit from this form of leadership development because their decisions impact the well-being of the people they serve—civic responsibilities. This period marked a shift in my focus, away from enterprise leadership and toward personal leadership—making human beings better. Google did not actually want this kind of leadership. They wanted chess pieces, not chess players. None of the executives attended the trainings, but their pawns did. The subordinates were required to attend the training. I learned that these powerful executives were weak in character and substance. The experience tainted me enough never to want to work for a corporation again. I found it a prison.

Warrior: That was not my experience at Google.

Guardian: Then why did you not want to work there?

Warrior: Ah. After three decades of military service, I wanted to run my own organization.

Guardian: Exactly. You wanted to lead your own enterprise. Me too.

Warrior: What happened next?

Guardian: This is when I really went off the reservation.

I spent two years at CCL as an account manager. During that two-year period, I received no training in the art of teaching leadership. I only attended commercial-off-the-self trainings built for leaders, not built for *teachers of leaders*. I was not offered the opportunity to attend these internal trainings. Remember, my goal was to transition from an account manager to a faculty member and live a calling teaching leadership

At the two-year mark, I asked my manager if I could begin to transition to a teaching position by attending their assessment-and-selection course. True to her word, she said yes.

Her support sent a rush of nerves and emotions throughout my body. I had no experience in teaching the leadership art. I suffered an extreme fear of speaking publicly. I suffered an extreme discomfort in the confinement of a formal classroom setting. Both conditions were reflections of a cerebrotonic[10] disposition. And yet, my calling placed me in the cross-hairs of this extreme fear and extreme discomfort.

What did I know? I had direct experience leading Marines and consultants. I had little experience as a teacher, transferring knowledge and understanding to others. CCL's work is

---

[10] Cerebrotonic Traits–over-sensitive introvert, no desire to dominate, passion for privacy intense, seeks solitude, primary allegiance to the internal world of consciousness, not the external world. From Huxley's *Perennial Philosophy*.

essentially in a formal classroom environment. It did seem too artificial, and I preferred the training of an athlete versus formal classroom training. But, I had to meet the reality before me, as it was, not as I wanted. I had purpose and potential; I lacked skill and experience.

Warrior: Time and again, I notice you keep entering situations where you don't have the exact experience and skill. You never stayed long enough in one domain to develop experience.

Guardian: I did not know that at the time. I kept going in the direction of the daemon's calling.

I thought, as in war, how must I prepare? I had an infinite love for the art. The calling was very significant and important to me. That is where I rested my being and moved from.

Warrior: And so it begins, learning to be an unmoved mover.

Guardian: Yes. I spent a month preparing for a one-hour audition, a lesson on human development. This included meditation, yoga, and self-reflection. I thought I could teach these techniques because they were embedded in my being from a decade of practice—they were an extension of my being. This is when I began to think of leadership development as an intellectual art, the equivalent for the mind of arts for the body. This is before I read Plato. I had already learned to move from what lived within, the source of true power. And yet, remember, this is when life thunderously thrashed me, again and again. I had moved through the thrashings of dark nights, the consulting, the master's, the account management, and I thought that finally the gateway was about to open to my calling—to develop leaders.

Warrior: Thrashed again? What happened?

Guardian: The day before the audition, after a month of preparation, the second-in-command called me. I'll recount the conversation. What I hope to show through these lessons of experience is how so much of our experience comes from our relationships with others, either helping or thwarting our efforts, regardless of potential and drive.

COO: Good morning Guardian. How are you?

Guardian: I am good. Very excited to try out tomorrow. This is something I've been working towards for the last 7 years.

COO: I know you are very excited about this opportunity. That is why I'm calling. I don't know how to say it, so I will just say it. You are doing a great job in the account manager role. You have built relationships with Google, Microsoft, and Starbucks and they have become 3 of our top 10 accounts in North America. This is a good fit for you and for us. Because of this critical need you are fulfilling, I cannot approve the transition to faculty. We need you where you are at, to best support our organization. That said, to be honest, even if you proved your potential, you don't have a PHD; you are too young, too inexperienced, too rough around the edges, for what we look for in a faculty member. You don't have the credibility in expertise and character. I am sorry to tell you this but that is why I am delivering this feedback to you. You deserve the truth, to know the breadth and depth and to understand my decision.

Guardian: I understand. Thank you for giving me the feedback and letting me know where I stand.

COO: Keep up the good work.

Warrior: Ouch. Once again, just like at KPMG Consulting, you felt the sting of not being allowed to use your energy the way you thought best.

Guardian: I became distraught. Why did I leave the Marine Corps? Maybe I'm not a good fit in business. Where do I fit in the world? Why did I have this calling? Why did I listen to it? Where was it leading? I started to let outer events affect my soul, my inner nature. This was in direct conflict with the teachings of truth[11]–

> A man whose mind is unagitated in sorrow, who is devoid of longing in his contact with pleasure, and free from passion, fear, and anger—he is called a sage steadied in vision.

> He who is unattached all-round and who neither rejoices nor dislikes when encountering this or that auspicious or inauspicious experience—his gnosis is well established.

I fell deeper into darkness with the rejections and the ensuing despondency. I started drinking daily and dating beautiful women. A desperate attempt to extinguish the rage in my soul.

Again, I felt the bondage of metaphysical prison. I had great health, great finances, a good job, and yet I experienced the hell of bondage—by the ego's attachments, passions, and desires.

I again started working from the satellite-office when not travelling to clients.

Warrior: Again? And this led to where?

Guardian: I met a leader, a world-renowned leadership trainer who needed support in a program to train diocesan priests in leadership development, commissioned by the Catholic Leadership Institute (CLI). The goal would be for CLI to hire me as a trainer, if I passed their assessment and selection. This leader saw my potential and opened the door, and I walked in. I thanked God for this opportunity. I had almost become a Catholic priest when I was younger, and I felt excited about this opportunity. My manager at CCL gave me as much leeway as I wanted, so

---

[11] *The Bhagavad Gita*, 2.56-2.57, Feuerstein Translation.

long as I met my client needs and hit my targets. She threw me the gift of freedom, thinking this organization, not hers, was giving me the chance to learn and teach the leadership art.

Warrior: That was fortuitous.

Guardian: Fortuitous that Fortuna thrashed and crushed my spirit again?

Warrior: What? How?

Guardian: I began the assessment-and-selection training program. Over the course of 6 months, I attended their train-the-trainer program and assisted in 4 trainings. Then I tried out, at a final audition, to become a lead trainer.

Warrior: You finally received the training and experience you were seeking. What happened?

Guardian: I felt I would be a great fit to serve the needs of CLI. I loved the trainings. They were held in monasteries on beautiful and sacred grounds. I prayed with the priests and attended mass daily. I loved being released from the classroom and corporate environment.

Warrior: And…

Guardian: And, I was not selected.

Warrior: Painful, another rejection.

Guardian: I seriously considered going back to the Marine Corps, the last place that had valued my work ethic, drive, and intensity.

Warrior: Yet, now you were too far off the reservation to return. You were too free of spirit to return.

Guardian: I know. I trusted that intuition. To return would be to fail completely and to settle in the known.

Warrior: What happened?

Guardian: Once again, I sought metaphysical freedom even if I abandoned all safety of economic security. I resigned. My manager knew me and saw it coming. I lost sight in the rage.

Warrior: What did you do?

Guardian: I become a professional gold caddy.

Warrior: Wow. All or nothing

Guardian *Todo y nada*.[12] All and nothing. I follow the lead of the inner voice, the daemon, to the best of my ability. The experiences that I shared with you are examples of the gatekeepers on the

---

[12] Saint John of The Cross, *The Collected Works*.

hero's journey saying "no, you can't get through, you can't go any further." Examples of not getting promoted to manager, of not being allowed to try out at CCL, of being allowed to try out but being rejected by a gatekeeper at CLI. I learned these experiences triggered the transformational experience. The rejections and the failures forced me to be bold and leap into the unknown.

At the time, I looked at my bookshelf, stacked with philosophy and metaphysical books, the sacred and wisdom canons. That is where my truth lived. I learned I'm a truth-seeker and a wisdom-seeker. I learned to sacrifice all else to realize these ends. I needed space, time and distance from outer demands. And, seeing that the daemon spoke and I listened, I finally accepted the true calling and purpose. I accepted, in truth, after the frustrations and failures. What I mean is that there is a metaphysical truth[13] to each being and I now know the truth of mine.

Warrior: Understood. What happened next?

Guardian: Being a professional golf caddy served as an experience of metaphysical freedom. My roommate and good friend was in the midst of preparing to win a coveted PGA tour card, at the yearly Qualification School, or Q-School. To prepare, he traveled up and down the west coast, entering in professional events by the process of Monday qualifications, which opened up 4 spots to professionals without a tour card. I had nothing going on and offered to be his caddy. For 6 months we drove around the west coast, in Betsy, his Buick Regal, living out of hotels, and competing for spots on tour events. This was my most freeing experience since backpacking through Europe a decade earlier. But, he did not win enough to support our expenses and I ran out of funds.

Warrior: Then what?

Guardian: For the first time, my fallback of a consulting gig failed. I could not get a job. As a middle-aged man, single with no family or roots, I left California as I had arrived, with nothing other than my jeep, some clothes, and some books. I landed penniless in Cleveland on my parents' doorstep, a failure, to regroup.

Warrior: And so you hit rock bottom.

Guardian: It appeared so. Then a mystical experience took place. On the drive cross-country, as I drove through the Rockies, I had a divine moment; I felt for the first time in my life, in the mercy and guidance of divine providence, a lovingness that came from I know not where. After a decade of failures and unmet expectations, I experienced what I searched for, true metaphysical freedom. The rest of the drive I experienced as pure contemplation, allowing the essence of metaphysical freedom to bathe my soul.

---

[13] Sister Miriam Joseph, *The Trivium–The Liberal Arts of Logic, Grammar, and Rhetoric.* Definition of metaphysical truth–The conformity of a thing to the idea of it in the minds of men. Every being has a metaphysical truth.

Warrior: You are a strange being. When you had nothing, freedom revealed itself. What happened next?

Guardian: A period of rapid development that ignited me into the calling and led me to where we are now, today, which is freedom in this art. I share my lessons of experience and development to show the nonlinear path that prepared me for the calling. Had I known the terrain, I would have moved with more ease and grace. But no one guided me with the wisdom that actualizing a calling which is to be a lifelong endeavor could take a decade of preparation, failures, and growth, as though life were assessor and selector. I move with an ease and liberation now, but back then, it seemed I was in the trenches of metaphysical hell. This is why guardians are essential to our art.

Warrior: What happened next?

Guardian: I still could not get a job, a nerve-wracking experience. Nothing. I had no idea what the future held. I could not see the next step. From caddying, I did get very good at golf. My brother said that I should train to complete. But I did not love golf. I think it's a worthless sport and a waste of energy, time, and land. Desperate, I reached out to a managing partner from my old consulting firm. She and her husband were playing golf and asked if I wanted to play. I said yes. They had no idea I had been caddying the past six months. Shot after shot, I dazzled them. They could not believe the skill I displayed, and then I smiled and said, imagine if you had six months to train only in golf, what do you think would happen? They said, maybe they would improve, but it seemed that I had a gift for golf. I did have bodily-kinesthetic gifts. They asked about my next steps. Here is the dialogue.

> Partner: How is the job searching going?

> Guardian: It is a blood bath of rejections. I just spent 7 interviews, in Detroit and Pittsburgh, interviewing with Deloitte Consulting's Human Capital Services. I brought a woman with me to ease the tensions, probably not a good idea, as I did not sleep. Why the nerves? I did not have an MBA, and partners (though not the staff) did not understand the value of an M.S. in Leadership. I created a fit/gap analysis to show how I would contribute as a utility player, and then mapped out a development plan for learning each skill expected in the role. I met with the last gatekeeper, a partner, and failed, in his eyes, as he examined me in a business case study. He gave me a case study that I did not have the background to answer, so I kept asking him questions to figure it out. Afterwards, he told the hiring manager, who wanted me on the team, "This guy does not even know elementary business case study solution frameworks." I have contempt for the guy and want to take the back of my hand to his face. People keep confusing character and competence.

I can learn anything. God, I miss leading Marines, and the seriousness of the endeavor.

Partner: You are too free-spirited to return. I remember when I hired you as you transitioned from the Marine Corps. You had fire and intensity, and you were, and still are, too rough around the edges for business life. It can be a bit unnerving meeting someone like you, with your raw energy being harnessed to land jobs you don't have the exact experience or skills for, and the confidence that you can figure it out.

Guardian: I know, I vividly remember our interview.

Partner: I, too, remember it well. You had no business or consulting experience and the hiring manager said you were not a good fit. As a partner, I had the final say, the gatekeeper as you say, and I remember when you walked in for the interview. You said, "I'm a former Marine officer and any shortfall in knowledge is no comparison to the value of leadership skills I bring to the team." My team at the time lacked an intense and aggressive personality and I thought you'd be a great utility player. And you were, until you got edgy and restless and transferred to the West Coast.

Guardian: Thank you for taking a chance on me.

Partner: We were the ones who benefited. You have a tireless work ethic and a magnetic and charismatic persona. We needed that.

Guardian: You're still one of the best managers I've ever worked for and one of the few managers I've ever trusted.

Partner: What are your next steps?

Guardian: I need a job just to stop the bleeding.

Partner: Do you want me to stop the bleeding?

Guardian: Are you serious?

Partner: Yes. If you promise to give me one year before you take off again, which I know you will.

Guardian: Deal.

And then, by the power of a gatekeeper, the bleeding stopped.

Warrior: Wow. And just like that, you had another gig in business.

Guardian: Yes. Another lesson initiated. When I left her team the first time, as I drove to the West Coast, I thought I would never work for a client like hers again. And *voila*, 5 years later, I found myself working for this same client. We shook hands on the golf course. I accepted a base pay of six figures. My good fortune I thought! I decided to live at home to stockpile my savings again. Financially, things turned around.

Warrior: This partner trusted you.

Guardian: The primacy of truth. I trusted her. But the work she hired me for was the curse of brutality's boringness. The daily cycle of purgatory—I would drive into the city, enter underground parking, and pull a ticket to pay for parking. Then I would walk to the building, wait in line, to go through security, and then enter the building. Then I would take the elevator to the 28th floor. Then, to get into the office, I would type in a security code to unlock the door. Then I would walk to my cubicle, sit down, and enter my key card to unlock my computer. Then I would log on to my computer, with a VPN pass code for extra security. Once I gained access to the computer, I would spend 8 hours doing worthless activities—documenting, scheduling, reporting, and meetings—to capture the client's operations in writing. There was no action. There was no growth. I hit another level of despondency. I hate being in a cubicle. Metaphysical prison captured me again. And a month earlier, I had experienced metaphysical freedom during the cross-country trip. Had I fallen asleep again that quickly? When would I learn the lesson?

Warrior: Good God, again? And yet, you needed a job; you were broke. Come on Guardian, you are a blessed soul.

Guardian: Maybe. But when I left her firm the first time, I said I would never find myself in that situation again.

Warrior: And there you were, reality commanded otherwise. Life seems always to be testing you. I never saw these truths until our journey. Life is growing and testing us. Living is the school.

Guardian: Indeed. I remained lost. I could not see the vision. Even if I could, would I follow it? I came back from the west coast a failure with some wild experiences. Now, to kill time, I started practicing yoga at a local studio. San Diego is a hotbed of yoga studios. There are 80 studios in a twenty-mile radius. In Cleveland, there were 4. One was 10 minutes from my parents' home. I walked through the door of this studio and life ignited, finally.

Warrior: What?

Guardian: I remember a conversation, years earlier. I met a mystical professor. One morning, while having tea, she must have read my soul and said–

    Mystic: You should become a yoga teacher.

Guardian: What? I'm called to develop leaders.

Mystic: Don't you admire the character of the Yogi from the Glass Bead Game? Have you not been practicing yoga for a few years? Don't you practice meditation and contemplation? Aren't you on the spiritual path? Aren't you reading *The Bhagavad Gita* according to Gandhi? These are your actions and interests, correct?

Guardian: Yes. But, I'd be a priest before I became a yogi.

Mystic: Are you so sure? Where is there more freedom of being?

Guardian: Yoga instructors are glorified aerobics instructors.

Mystic: You could practice the path of the yogi as a yoga teacher, not a yoga instructor, and this could be an arena that equips you to lead souls. And your aim is to teach leaders, to teach them to know their souls and to lead from their souls, and to lead the souls of others.

Guardian: Yes, but I'm not sure. I'm not good at yoga, even though I practice it.

Mystic: You don't see it yet. It's not about the physical art of yoga; it's about the intellectual and spiritual art of yoga. You are reading Huxley's *Perennial Philosophy*, correct?

Guardian: Yes.

Mystic: You don't see it yet.

Guardian: See what?

Mystic: You need to practice self-knowledge. Take a harder look within, to see and to know what you are. Then, you may become free.

Guardian: I'll increase the energy and concentration in the meditations.

Mystic: Do not give up until you see it.

Guardian: I won't give up. I won't quit the pathless path.

Mystic: Good.

I had forgotten this insightful conversation. Then, in Cleveland, when I walked into this studio, her insights blazed light into my soul. I could see. Within a few months, I headed again into the unknown, the pathless path by which we learn to see, by taking a certification course to teach yoga.

Warrior: What?

Guardian: Strange. Consultant by day, yogi by night.

The *Bhagavad Gita*[14] guides us–

> That which is night for all beings, therein is the self-controlled awake. That
> wherein beings are awake, that is night for the seeing sage.

Warrior: Good God, on the surface you seemed rudderless; in the depths, you seem anchored
to truth's commands.

Guardian: I knew none of this at the time. I did not know how to return to the depths. But, do
you not see, the nonlinear development of a soul?

Warrior: I see it because you have the wisdom of integrating the experiences. On the surface,
it seems without integration; in the depths, there is continuity—you are on the journey and the
journey does not follow a linear progression.

Guardian: Could it be that the daemon continually prompted me to lead me to freedom?

Warrior: Yes. It appears so.

Guardian: At the time, I still had failed to achieve a lifelong goal—to earn income doing
what I'm called to do. What I mean is, teaching yoga served as a means to earn a living in my
calling—developing leaders. It was one method of developing leaders, anyway—an hour of
self-inquiry in a physical, meditative and contemplative activity. I saw it as a method to make
the soul powerful by building both physical and intellectual strength. The most significant
benefit, I saw, is that yoga teaches the soul how to build self-knowledge. That is how I saw it
and that is how I taught. I used it as a leadership method.

Warrior: Understood.

Guardian: For my development and formation in the leadership arts, I saw teaching yoga
as a method to conquer my fears. To teach an activity that I did not excel at—the physical
postures. I'm not a gymnast, I lacked flexibility, and my tendons and ligaments are thrashed
from high impact activities. But, could I teach this art? Teaching yoga forced me to practice
the art of teaching, to unlock potential in others. Teaching forced me to overcome my fear of
public speaking. Teaching taught me how to communicate knowledge from one soul to another.
Teaching taught me how to connect from soul to soul, to build bonds of trust, and through trust
to create an atmosphere of openness, one that is necessary to awaken the soul's powers and to
disarm the adversary, the ego-body-octagon. Teaching yoga unlocked potencies in me that are
required to teach true leadership. I learned to unite the energy of 60 souls. I learned to unite souls
in the bonds of truth and friendship. At the same time, I learned, this union is the leaping point
for each soul to understand her own unique experience by studying her individual body, mind,

---

[14] *The Bhagavad Gita*, Feuerstein Translation.

and emotions—true self-knowledge being gained. This is where I discovered how I would teach leaders. I don't know where I'd be without the insights and foundations I gained teaching yoga. I learned a teaching method, one that is essentially an open-mic, informal dialogue, to speak truth from soul to soul—to reach true communion and understanding. Teaching and learning this way seemed natural and seemed to be the missing perspective in teaching our art. Rhythm, flow, harmony, union and power could all be used to awaken and uplift the soul.

Because I saw this, it made sense to me. My consulting peers could not see this; it seemed like madness to them.

Lastly, even though I only earned $35/hour doing something I love, I finally found a path to start earning a living engaged in my calling. Metaphysical freedom returned.

Warrior: *Voila*, and there it is, you found your footing on your pathless path for the first time and you felt free. I see it.

Guardian: The mystic saw it. Teaching yoga is a sacred endeavor when truly performed. *The Yoga Sutras*, *The Bhagavad Gita*, *The Upanishads*, are sacred canons that underlie the yoga teachings. Teaching yoga, for the first time, I felt free to speak and to lead the way I know best, from soul to soul, engaged in an activity that is autotelic. What I realized was that I love autotelic activities, activities that are ends in themselves. That is how I saw teaching and practicing yoga. That is also how I saw leading and teaching leaders. Both are where the crosshairs of means and ends become one. Yoga practitioners were having autotelic experiences, and I was there to guide and guard their individual growth, to make sure they were safe as they moved from posture to posture. I devoted myself to the art, with total abandon.

Csikszentmihalyi mentors us here–

> An autotelic person needs few material possessions and little entertainment, comfort, power, or fame because so much of what he or she does is already rewarding. Because such persons experience flow in work, in family life, when interacting with people, when eating, even when alone with nothing to do, they are less dependent on the external rewards that keep others motivated to go on with a life composed of routines. They are more autonomous and independent because they cannot be as easily manipulated with threats or rewards from the outside. At the same time, they are more involved with everything around them because they are fully immersed in the current of life.[15]

Warrior: Ah, I am learning to understand your nature better and better. This is how you live as an autotelic person—being and activity are one.

---

[15] Mihaly Csikszentmihalyi, *Creativity: Flow and the Psychology of Discovery and Invention.*

Guardian: Yes. I studied Csikszentmihalyi's writing on creativity. I created a fit/gap analysis to the way creative people live and the way I live. Then I mined and closed the gap. I worked to overhaul my entire way of being into the ways of creativity. Then I united the way of creativity with the way of the guardian. The outgrowth of all of this is our art. I've not had one moment of despondency since I launched into this way of being and this way of teaching. I struggled up until this point because my disposition is not suited to be the means to an end. I need the means and ends to be one. And I found oneness in the union of these ways—the warrior, the guardian, the saint, the sage, the philosopher—all are autotelic activities. This is where I discovered metaphysical freedom. This meant, I can learn to do any activity in peace, be it business, labor, or otherwise. All this time I thought the work set me free. I truth, metaphysical freedom sets you free. So any management or domestic activity, I can now become one with. The lessons of experience taught me that I had become disordered and not ordered on the inside, with my relation to the outside, and with my relationship between means and ends.

Our leadership art is an autotelic activity, one and one, known and knower, truth. This is how we learn to play the art, when we rise above all other functional and temporal domains—the wisdom is not in and below the clouds, but above the clouds. Look now at the heights we've reached in our journey.

Warrior: We can see. It's not hidden. It's in full view.

Guardian: You should know, this lesson of teaching yoga only occurred five years before we met.

Warrior: Ah, that is why you were still teaching yoga, but now you no longer teach.

Guardian: Yes. The truth taught me another lesson, one I resisted for two decades: I'm not the householder type. I've never had financial and professional security and certainty. I live by spirit, and when it moves I move.

Warrior: These experiences do shed light on your formation as a leader.

Guardian: That's the thing. If life is teaching us and it teaches through experiences, then we need to look at them as lessons and not take them so personally, as I did for many years. Are not experiences nothing but lessons? We need to untether ourselves from the tyranny of selective memory.

Warrior: Then what happened?

I learned I might be some sort of contemplative *ronin*.[16] I love silence, solitude, prayer, and study in between my professional work. I eat most meals alone. I train alone. I tend to teach solo. But now it's time to transition, and I need to find people to train to carry this art forward.

---

[16] O.E.D. definition of ronin–a lordless wandering samurai.

Warrior: How did you launch this leadership enterprise?

Guardian: Another guardian, a spiritual sister living in Nantucket, had an idea to open a yoga studio. She and her husband were getting certified. It's an example of synchronicity. We did not know the other was getting trained.

We formed a team to launch. I would lead the leadership services, she would lead the spiritual services, and he would lead the health services. We mapped out a twenty-year plan.

Warrior: With all your experiences as the genesis of the calling… you leaped into the unknown… the unknown as the realm where metaphysical freedom is discovered.

Guardian: Now you see. Twelve months to the day from when I shook the partner's hand, I resigned from her consulting team. She asked, "what are you doing?" I said, "heading back to the west coast to launch a human development enterprise." She smiled, "of course you are."

Warrior: And this is how I found you. When you landed in San Diego. It's good to hear and understand your story. I did not know about all the failures and wreckage. You have lived an iconoclastic life.

Guardian: Do you understand the reason why I shared these experiences?

Warrior: Yes, to demonstrate that the formation of a leader can be non-linear and must take into account the full range of experiences, not just the professional ones.

Guardian: Yes. I also sought to highlight how a leader's formation takes place, not in spite of, but *in* the failures, mistakes, wreckage and lost opportunities. We tend to focus on leaders who somehow seemed to sidestep all the failures and wreckage and who seemed to move brilliantly. And yet these brilliant leaders seem to be at a loss for how to develop new leaders, even though they led their organizations and their people to high achievement.

Warrior: Hart[17] cautions on the pressure of conformity–

> Fallacy…that, in order to command, you must learn to obey.

> A model boy rarely goes far, and even when he does, is apt to falter when severely tested.

It seems that life has severely tested you metaphysically, and now you have earned your freedom. Many would have quit, but because you experienced the bitterness of quitting in your formative years, before you experienced the limits of your potential, you armed yourself to endure—you'd rather die than quit on the truths you know and the voice that speaks within.

---

[17] B.H. Liddell Hart, *Why Don't We Learn from History?*

Guardian: Maybe. What I do know is that I found no resonance with the leaders who achieved in the status quo of the leviathan-cube. I did not resonate with most CEOs. I did not resonate with most generals. I did not resonate with most presidents. But, **I do resonate with the warriors, the saints, the philosophers and the sages—the true free spirits of the soul-sphere and the eternal-sphere.** I value and admire those who let truth lead, those who follow the truth still, even if they are put in the crosshairs of the adversary's ego-body-octagon and the tyrant's leviathan-cube.

My experiences in life and truth are where I found my center, my footing, and the true ground of my being.

Warrior: I remember when I vetted you. No academies or firms, no professors or leaders spoke like you did when it came to developing leaders. They described leading. They did not describe how to develop leaders. That is what I need—to teach leaders how to develop leaders. I need warriors to be leaders of leaders. You speak of resonance. I knew you would resonate with our warriors. It's in you. I saw it and I trusted what I saw.

Guardian: And I thank you for your trust.

Warrior: You earned it. What you did and what you created are what is missing. **You want to build free-thinking, self-cultivating and self-correcting human beings who have the courage to seek light and truth and let it guide them in the chaos of leading.** That is rare.

Guardian: I also shared this example because if we are going to ask our students to give an account of their character journey, we must give an account of ours.

Warrior: To make sure there are no blind-spots lurking in the depths.

Guardian: Yes. I had been hesitant to cover my lessons of experience, because I feared getting ensnared in the emotions of memory and the ego's personal attachment to them. This dialogue taught me to distance myself, to truly see experiences as lessons. To remove the value judgments on them as good or bad, and instead to see them as the lessons of being and becoming. The lessons of experience are what cause potential to actualize. I am clear now.

Warrior: Good.

Guardian: We have travelled a long way from the surface. We are heading into advanced weapons training in the techniques of dialogue, meditating and contemplating. I used this self-reflective practice to clear my entire being for this next training, so there is nothing obstructing my view as I teach these weapons to our students.

Huxley mentors us on the right mindset to develop, to wield these weapons–

The saint is one who knows that every moment of our human life is a moment of crisis; for at every moment we are called upon to make an all-important decision—to choose between the way that leads to death and spiritual darkness and the way that leads towards light and life; between interests exclusively temporal and the eternal order; between our personal will, or the will of some projection of our personality, and the will of God. In order to fit himself to deal with the emergencies of his way of life, the saint undertakes appropriate training of mind and body, just as the soldier does. But whereas the objectives of military training are limited and very simple, namely, to make men courageous, cool-headed and co-operatively efficient in the business of killing other men, with whom, personally, they have no quarrel, the objectives of spiritual training are much less narrowly specialized. Here the aim is primarily to bring human beings to a state in which, because there are no longer any God-eclipsing obstacles between themselves and Reality, they are able to be aware continuously of the divine Ground of their own and all other beings; secondarily, as a means to this end, to meet all, even the most trivial circumstances of daily living without malice, greed, self-assertion or voluntary ignorance, but consistently with love and understanding. Because its objectives are not limited, because, for the lover of God, every moment is a moment of crisis, spiritual training is incomparably more difficult and searching than military training. There are many good soldiers, few saints.[18]

Warrior: All in. All the time. Never ending. Go on.

---

[18] Aldous Huxley, *The Perennial Philosophy*.

CHAPTER ELEVEN
CROSS-EXAMINATIONS

Guardian: We have advanced to the edge of our understanding again and again on this quest—to the edge where leading and teaching must live. This edge is how we cut our way into deeper realms of understanding. We must learn how to cut our way in the depths, slicing our way, truth by truth. We must move in these depths and not get ensnared back into the surface. I'm cautious to explore how dialogue, meditation and contemplation guide and lead the soul to remain in the depths, as an unmoved mover.

Warrior: Why are you cautious?

Guardian: We are entering the final pitch of this quest—advanced weapons training—learning to wield the techniques of dialogue, meditation, and contemplation. As before, I need to speak from experience. I do this to make these concepts concrete and tangible, so it appears to the mind that the intelligence can grip and wield the concepts by the metaphysical swords—our techniques. I plan to leave a record for how one might progress in our art. This is our final evolution. Once it's complete, we will be prepared to train a leader. We need skill in teaching to produce knowledge and skill in another human being. Our greatest tests have yet to be faced—teaching students and combating adversaries. This is the last time we will move without those heavy responsibilities.

Warrior: I am prepared.

Guardian: Why did I rely heavily on the writings of the sages and saints?

Warrior: Our art is a truth-disclosing art. Our art demands that we become an integrated being, uniting character (the good) and intelligence (the wise). Our art demands the skill to reach into the essence of things, to reach into the essence of reality, and to lead out its truths. Our art demands intellectual and spiritual knowledge, capable of knowing the truth necessary to make practical judgments that affect the lives of human beings. Our art demands a purified soul, with the foundations of integrity and justice. I now see that our art is a sacred art, similar in rank to the call of the sage and the call of the mystic. The difference being, the call of the leader is to lead out wisdom from the chaos of conditioned-existence. Wisdom is the aim we seek.

Pieper[1] mentors us here–

> Prudence as a virtue is the art of considering, deciding, and commanding rightly.

---

[1] Josef Pieper, *Living The Truth*.

On this quest, you have set out to discover how we make our character and intelligence worthy to pursue prudence (practical judgment) and wisdom. And then you mean to discover how we, once worthy, can transmit this knowledge and excellence to students.

Guardian: Yes. The knowledge is all there if we have the courage to study it and become it. Just like in chess, few study to become masters. We now know what must be studied, to take command of knowledge and skill and make it an extension of our being. It's up to us and our students to study with rigor and intensity, to make ourselves worthy of wisdom's light and truth, to become the living light that the wisdom literature calls for us to become.

Saint Matthew mentors–

Many are called, and few are chosen.[2]

I know I am called. I do not know if I'll earn the merit to be chosen by our yet-to-be leaders, to be trusted to teach them. I live in preparation and study. Likewise, with our students, the yet-to-be leaders—we will affectionately call to them to pursue this endeavor. We will make no guarantees that they will be chosen to lead. They, too, will live in preparation and study.

The burden of the leadership journey is that it is solitary. It seems like a paradox, because leadership lives in friendship. But, as we have experienced, each leader must endure the formation and transformation, in the silence and solitude of her heart and soul.

Warrior: And why is this the case?

Guardian: Each leader is transformed by wisdom's light and truth, not by another man's light and truth. Do you see?

Warrior: Do you mean to say, even though we are teachers, we cannot give light and truth to our students—we can only show them the way to receive light and truth?

Guardian: Yes. This pathless path takes our students by a solitary route, even if we train together. It seems a paradox. Leaders are givers and receivers of light and truth, but we are not their authors or source or cause. Our students need to condition their being to see what we see, not by looking to us, but by turning to look toward the light and truth of wisdom. This is why meditation and contemplation are the swords of light and truth and wisdom. In my studies, I have seen the fear these weapons produce in students. It's fear of seeing the truth. What most moderns call meditation is simply a desperate attempt to reduce stress and anxiety and produce a sense of peace and serenity. But they stop there. That is just the first phase of preparation to clear the mind for true meditation—seeing light. I notice how most fear contemplation, because it forces one to think clearly and fully, uniting reason and intuition. It is terrifying how many souls want other human beings to do the thinking for

---

[2] The Holy Bible, *Book of Matthew,* Lamsa Translation.

them, to absolve them of the burden of thinking to realize and know what is the truth and what is to be done.

The burdens on the leader know no limit, so we must master these swords of meditation and contemplation.

The swords prepare us to battle our way through tests and trials to produce virtue and skill. You and I, and each leader, must learn, on our own, how to endure this burden with grace. We learn this endurance by slicing into the disturbances we come to know in our hearts and souls, when we are alone in silence and solitude.

The leader must come to know that, even though leading involves relationships, she does in fact carry the burden of responsibility and accountability. Her DNA, for good or for bad, cascades through the enterprise. She comes to know the full weight of this burden when reality demands that she make a judgment call. Even if it's shared leadership, which I have experienced, each leader still shoulders a burden that none other can carry. There is something about responsibility that makes this so.

Warrior: And to discover this art, you leaned on Huxley's perspective about the way of the saints not as the end point, but as a leaping point.

Guardian: Yes.

Warrior: Then leaders do not need to become saints, but the burden of their vocation is comparable to that of the saint.

Guardian: Yes.

Warrior: I revised Huxley's quote from a leadership perspective, to lead us deeper into the depths.

> The leader is one who knows that every moment of our life is a moment of crisis; for at every moment we are called upon to make an all-important decision—to choose between the way that leads to darkness and deception and the way that leads to light and truth; between interests exclusively financial or interests best for the enterprise; between our personal will, or the will of some projection of our personality, and the will of reality as light and truth, guiding our actions and aims.

Guardian: The key is that the leader, like the saint, must come into contact with wisdom's light and truth.

Warrior: Yes. That is why we emphasize the techniques of meditation and contemplation.

Guardian: As I am at the edge of understanding, I use the writings of wisdom as stepping stones, to leap into the unknown. I wonder, how did these sages discover these timeless and eternal truths? What training must they have undergone to awaken their wisdom faculties?

Warrior: Ah. They used dialogue, meditation and contemplation! And these are the techniques leaders refuse to learn. Too busy to learn, they say. Too little time to learn, they say. Not practical enough to learn, they say. They don't see their self-deception.

Guardian: What is the benefit if we learn these techniques?

Warrior: If we practice these techniques and take them seriously, is should make the burden of leading easy compared to the burden of the training. These techniques demystify truth-disclosing, which is simply the second order effect of experiencing our character and intelligence. You have reduced this art to its bare-bones nature.

Where did you first learn of these techniques?

Guardian: When did I first take sight? I remember a passage in a book that essentially weaves dialogue, contemplation, and meditation into a unified whole.

Warrior: Walk me through what you learned and how you drew out the essence from an obscure passage in a book. What book?

Guardian: *The Glass Bead Game* by Herman Hesse.

Warrior: What is the passage? How did you learn?

Guardian: I dove straight into the passage and worked out point by point.

I first read this book twenty years ago. It's strange to look back and see its influence as the leaping point of my journey into the unknown, and how it shaped my possibilities in teaching leadership.

For context, the protagonist, Joseph Knecht, is a genius (his daemon is awakening), who is being trained in the life of the mind by his Music Master. He is not just being trained in music, but in all intellectual arts, including meditation. The scene I am to cover is a dialogue between the Music Master and Joseph, in which the Music Master shares an experience when he lost his center, his ground, his ability to be an unmoved mover, and then explains how to return to one's center.

The Music Master[3] spoke–

> They probed more and more mercilessly into details, and forced me to an analysis of my whole intellectual and moral life during the past weeks and months.

---

[3] Herman Hesse, *The Glass Bead Game (Magister Ludi)*.

Warrior: Ah. Self-inquiry and dialogue. Intellectual and moral virtue. The Music Master had guardians as guides in his formative years, who forced him to practice self-knowledge to learn to see his errors for himself. This means we cannot expect our students to learn these techniques on their own. As with any art, they need guides and teachers.

Guardian: Yes. The passage continues–

> This could only have happened to someone who had submerged himself
> disproportionately in his studies and that it was high time for me to recover
> my self-control and to regain my energy with outside help.

Warrior: Ah. All of us, especially leaders, need outside help when we've lost our center, our energy, our well-being. I see how the virtue of self-knowledge leads to the virtues of self-restraint, equanimity[4] and justice (as harmony). But we do not value this tranquility nor this help. We see the need for help as weakness. We live in hyper-frenetic and hyper-intemperate organizations. We reward unbalanced and obsessive leaders who give over their souls to make mission, a way of being that essentially runs their moral, intellectual and psychological energy to empty. They only rest when they crash and burn. There is no temperance in their way of being. This is why so many leaders, who live out of control lives, seek self-indulgence and vice-laced activities away from work. Instead of gaining balance on reality's scale of justice, their egos swing between indulgence and intemperance, recklessness and obsessiveness. No one admits they are out of control until reality thrashes and smashes them. They need, we need, help that we are afraid to ask for, help that guides us to regain our center by the virtuous techniques of dialogue, meditation, and contemplation.

Guardian: Yes. If we view living from the perspective of the scales of justice, by giving and receiving, it demands for us to become balanced and harmonious in our energy and being. I never understood the primacy of maintaining personal well-being, until I learned meditation's ability to dissolve inner turbulence, weakness, disquietude, agitation and frustration.

Warrior: And, I gather, because you suffered the affliction of a wicked cycle, you experienced first-hand the toxicity of your own unbecoming and unbalanced nature.[5]

Guardian: Yes. This passage pierced into my soul. I paid attention.

The passage continues–

> I had omitted meditating for quite a while on the grounds that I had no
> time, was too distracted or out of spirits, or too busy and excited with my

---

[4] O.E.D. definition of equanimity–Tranquility of mind or temper; composure.
[5] The Cycle–the highs and lows of unharnessed, unrestrained and dynamic energy because of indiscipline and intemperance, where one is one's own worst enemy.

studies. Moreover, as time went on I had completely lost all awareness of my continuous sin of omission.

Warrior: Good God. The same excuses our executives give—too busy, not enough time, too many other priorities, not important enough. They send their acolytes to train, but they don't train. You mean to tell me that contemplation and meditation are how we nourish and strengthen our souls, the way nutrition and exercise strengthen our bodies?

Guardian: Yes, if they're done correctly. I see many move from the ego-body-octagon in these techniques and produce no true fruits. The central aim is to strike the soul, to make the moral and intellectual faculties sharp, discerning and developed. When we exercise our soul in these techniques, we learn to live and move in the flow state—a state where there is a self-forgetfulness, and a bending and release of time's pressure. It's a state where everything seems to be in slow motion and where we move with grace and ease, guided by reality's truth and wisdom.

Warrior: Is this possible?

Guardian: What has been your experience on this quest? What has been your experience in combat? In martial arts? In climbing?

Warrior: Supreme focus and attention to the activity at hand. A release from any other care and concern. Total devotion. Total concentration. Union of soul with skill. It's not the absence of rigor and struggle; it's the rigor and struggle themselves that produce this effect of flow.

Guardian: Yes. Our art is not natural; most arts are not natural. Arts must be studied and learned. We achieve flow through rigorous training. In our art we will learn to move with grace and ease, like a master swordsman, and the intelligence, the art and the skill will become one being.

Warrior: Thereby making virtue, knowledge, and excellence extensions of our being.

Guardian: Yes, the mark of transformation.

The passage from *The Glass Bead Game* continues –

> I had to return to the training routines and beginners' exercises in meditation
> in order to gradually relearn the art of composing myself and sinking into
> contemplation.

Warrior: There it is. You used this quest as the training method for our art. I see the kinetic chain that links dialogue, meditation and contemplation to make the art an extension of our being. I see how the powers of soul are on full display in these techniques We can use these techniques to build foundations and to build mastery. I think we will always be sharpening the sword. The masters never tire of the basics; they ground their art in principles and techniques. They bypass nothing in learning mastery. We've discovered the basic principles and techniques of our art. All the other domains seem simple now—character, identity, ethics, tactics, operations, management, leadership, command and strategy—because the light and truth of our soul takes command of the knowledge and wields it in the act of leading.

Guardian: You see with the light of wisdom. The passage continues–

> But the fact is, Joseph, that the more we demand of ourselves, or the more our task at any given time demands of us, the more dependent we are on meditation as a wellspring of energy, as the ever-renewing concord of mind and soul. And—I could if I wished give you quite a few more examples of this—the more intensely a task requires our energies, arousing and exalting us at one time, tiring and depressing us at another, the more easily we may come to neglect this wellspring, just as when we are carried away by some intellectual work we easily forget to attend to the body. The really great men in the history of the world have all either known how to meditate or have unconsciously found their way to the place to which meditation leads us. Even the most vigorous and gifted among the others all failed and were defeated in the end because their task or their ambitious dream seized hold of them, made them into persons so possessed that they lost the capacity for liberating themselves from present things, and attaining perspective. Well, you know all of this; it's taught during the first exercises of the course. But it is inexorably true. How inexorably true it is, one realizes only after having gone astray.

Warrior: There it is—meditation as the way to the well-spring of energy for our well-being, in mind, soul, and body. In meditation we can transcend time-space-temporal existence and enter into timeless-eternal-immortal existence. It's how we discover and return to our center, our ground, to the realm of unmoved movers. We need this well-spring of energy to lift our soul into the light and truth. Our art is a serious endeavor and meditation strengthens us for it.

Guardian: What else are you seeing?

Warrior: The reality of metaphysical quests can only be undertaken with these techniques. We left the demanding realm of physical reality and the phenomenal realm of reality. We crossed these thresholds to enter the unknown of intelligible and spiritual reality, seeking to move deeper and deeper into the sublime truths of all things. These techniques, those you coined our metaphysical swords, are like both mountaineering skills and combat skills that take us to the deepest depths and the highest heights, to teach students and to combat adversaries. Without these techniques, we'd be tethered to the surface of things—the source of disillusionment, deception, and bondage. We learned, by these techniques, to teach and fight from the abyss of the unfathomable world of consciousness. Somehow these techniques activate knowledge as knowing, and this activation creates a lucidness of mind to uncover what is hidden, to come to know wisdom's light of truth. This quest requires that we meditate on our interior natures and contemplate the exterior nature—to unite the knower to the known. I see meditation, dialogue, and contemplation as our trinity of skills to master and transmit our art. These are the swords that will take command of all other knowledge relating to the common need—be it warfighting, governing, managing, financing, educating, doctoring, innovating, farming or parenting. Good God, why is this not taught to our leaders?

Guardian: Why? Because few have the courage to be purified by the light of truth. Why? Because most find comfort being tethered to the surface. Why? Because the ego-body-octagon and the leviathan-cube reign on earth.

Are we not in the crosshairs of this conflict?

Warrior: Yes.

Guardian: Do we have the courage, as teachers, to practice with our students non-stop, day and night, until meditation and contemplation can become their way of being, at all times and in every movement of knowing, willing and acting? Will we not need to begin with the basics, teaching ourselves and our students to meditate in silence for one hour at the beginning and at the end of the day? Shouldn't this practice make up the bookends to the rigorous training that will be mapped out, hour by hour, each day?

Warrior: Are you not too idealistic and too extreme?

Guardian: No. The debt we pay for mastery is sacrifice. The Shaolin monks, with their way of preparing and training, day and night, are beings I admire.

Warrior: To suffer no fiction. To reduce one's life to minimalist essentials, to carve out the time and space to master our art. To minimize all distractions—the media's babbling-chattering-class and the marketer's advertising-class on all platforms. We will create a way of living that aims at our objectives and our object—the source of light and truth.

Guardian: Yes. The purpose is to make the body-mind-soul connection as strong as is humanly possible and our techniques aim at that end. We are not after acquiring or possessing "knowledge about"; we aim to awaken and strengthen our will and intelligence, to "know."

We have demystified the metaphysical techniques and exercises. We know what it takes to wield the metaphysical swords.

Let me ask, how do we practice detachment and humility?

Warrior: By these methods.

Guardian: How do we become virtuous?

Warrior: By these methods.

Guardian: How do we make contact with the soul's light and truth?

Warrior: By these methods.

Guardian: How do we make virtue, knowledge and skill an extension of being?

Warrior: By these methods, which are easy to discuss, but difficult to learn. Let me ask, how did you realize the significance of that passage, so long ago?

Guardian: In reflection, it's simple. It was the depths of suffering. I did not know of the elegance and simplicity of the journey we are all on. I did not have the wisdom to realize truth. By the grace of suffering, I did awaken an openness of soul and a receptivity to listen.

I read this passage as a young man stationed in Japan, missing the love of a woman, amidst an existential crisis. I suffered the pain of not-knowing, of the hiddenness of what I was and the purpose of my existence. The metaphysical pain made me receptive to truth. The pain—I wanted to know and I did not know—the suffering of ignorance. The drive to pursue truth— the wisdom to desire truth—had been ignited. Now I know why this igniting took place. Because of the suffering, I began to pursue knowing and understanding in earnest. In my desperate search, I found solace when I read Bildungsroman[6] books, of which *The Glass Bead Game* is the exemplar–

A novel "dealing with one person's formative years or spiritual education."

Yes, I learned, I am in the formative years of my spiritual education. I learned that this spiritual education is the true education. And I had no one who could mentor me.

Warrior: Why is that?

Guardian: Because leading in the military is about the "common need," not the "common good" of man.[7] The senior leaders did not possess the skill required to focus on the common good, the awakening of the soul by spiritual education. Without living mentors, the wisdom literature itself became my living teacher.

It was then that I learned of the potential to know truth and to know light. Pieper[8] mentors–

The capacity for spiritual knowledge has always been understood to mean the power of establishing relations with the whole of reality, with all things existing.

---

[6] O.E.D. definition of Bildungsroman–A novel dealing with one person's formative years or spiritual education.

[7] Josef Pieper, *The Philosophical Act.*

[8] Josef Pieper, *The Philosophical Act.*

> Spirit, it might be said, is not only defined as incorporeal, but as the power and capacity to relate itself to the totality of being.

> Spirit, in fact, is a capacity for relations of such all-embracing power that its field of relations transcends the frontiers of all and any 'environment.'

> By its very nature, it (spirit) breaks the bounds of any 'environment'; it abolishes both adaptation and imprisonment.

> Therein lies, at one and the same time, the liberating force and the danger inherent in the nature of spirit.

And, finally and most importantly–

> … the spiritual being is 'capable of grasping the whole of being.'

Your silence as you contemplate these truths is significant.

You see, we have the latent potencies to know, by the light of spirit, the ground of being. You see, we are spirit. We know this by our faculty of intelligence—the cognition to know the reality of being. And the techniques of dialogue, meditation, and contemplation are the bridges we cross to enter into this knowing—to transcend our ignorance and to behold wisdom.

Once I learned that I valued one's spiritual education over one's professional excellence. Once I learned that I followed two paths, one that led to excellence, one that led to truth. I learned to unite these paths and make them one—a relationship between virtue, excellence, and wisdom. To achieve this aim, I learned to sacrifice the primal drives—wisdom demands purification. Knowledge without purification is ignorance, deception, calculation and cunning. It took twenty years of purification to transcend these drives. They were twenty years of failures, regrets, and wreckage. I learned to recover and grow through the wreckage.

Wisdom demands sacrifice.[9] I sacrificed all else to unite these two paths and to let them lead—the way of truth and the way of excellence. This is why our art is essential. It focuses on the common good of our leaders. They are desperate to evolve.[10] They have mastered the common need and the common skills. What they intuitively want and are afraid to ask for is a spiritual education. They have mastered the ego-body-octagon and the leviathan-cube, in achievements, excellence, honors, prestige, and wealth. And yet, they are unfulfilled. This is the moment we hunt for; this is when we arrive with our art, after they have exhausted all temporal ways of meaning. What they seek is the liberation of their soul into truth and wisdom.

---

[9] Transformational Leadership–one principle is to sacrifice one's self for a great purpose.
[10] Melissa Love, a metaphysical student, helped the writer realize this truth.

It is good that you are contemplating these truths, in silence. Now you truly see the summit. Wisdom has drawn you into the beauty of her being.

Warrior: You knew, and I just realized, that I had to be awakened deeper to teach this art?

Guardian: Yes.

Warrior: How did you know?

Guardian: I possess no wisdom and excellence of my own. I only have the gift of contemplative sight—an imageless knowing that responds to the reality of being.

Warrior: The suffering you must have endured in your formative years, having this sight and not knowing what to do with it. This is why you found solace in the writings? The discovery of wisdom literature served to be a metaphysical Godsend?

Guardian: Yes. Wisdom literature is a living and perennial teacher, once the soul is admitted entrance.

When I read the passage from *The Glass Bead Game*, when I read how the Music Master's state of being was cross-examined by trusted mentors, I felt like my soul pierced through the passage and discovered truth, lying in wait. And when I set my gaze on it in kind, it returned a force with such intensity and depth and power, it seemed that my being had been branded by truth, claimed by truth, as one of its own. The branding on my soul is still there. I had been baptized into divine madness. I did not have the wisdom to comprehend the significance of this initiation.

Seeking understanding, I dove into the depths of the sacred scriptures—the gospels, *The Bhagavad Gita*, *The Upanishads*, the writings of the saints and sages. When I read, I reflected–

> If wisdom is true, if there is a metaphysical reality, why did our leaders not see
> this? Why did they create structures based on the ego-body-octagon and the
> leviathan-cube, instead of the soul-sphere and the eternal-sphere? Why did our
> leaders create weapons that assured mutual suicide[11] of the human race if ever
> used in an all-out war?

I learned one good outcome of nuclear weapons—they have deterred the human race from all-out war and now we have limited-scale and low-conflict wars. But, at the time, it terrified me that I perceived a reality different from my leaders' perceptions of reality.

Warrior: You experienced Hart's "truth is a spiral staircase."[12] Have you always suffered such despondency?

---

[11] B.H. Liddell Hart, *Strategy*, commenting on nuclear war.
[12] B.H. Liddell Hart, *Why Don't We Learn from History?*

Guardian: No, my good man. My existential nature revealed itself early and I did not even know what it meant.

I'm sharing reflections from twenty years ago that shaped my formation. Now I understand. Now I love the pursuit of wisdom and truth. I expect the tests and the trials as necessities to get through the purgative phase, to undergo the purification, to reach illumination and union, to see and know truth. But at the time, in a state of ignorance and immaturity, I did suffer despondency.

Warrior: Which is why you experienced numerous falls from grace, to numb the pain of purification. Wisdom only reveals itself to the purified soul, but you did not understand this truth, or understand that there are stages to this purification.

Guardian: Yes. I never quit the path. Seeking truth is my greatest love. Such is the mystery of sacrificing the lesser for the greater—the lesser being the primal drives, the greater being the primordial drives.

Warrior: And is it worth it, the sacrifice?

Guardian: Yes, now, with understanding I know it is. At the time, the purgative phase, metaphysically, broke me again and again, to awaken my soul's powers to transcend the vices of the primal drives. Though few, I have had enlightened moments, and those moments, the divine's consolations, affectionately call me upward along the ascent. The writings of the great sages, saints and philosophers affectionately call to all of us, all generations, in all time. How will each generation know to listen to this call? Who will teach these souls how to listen? Who will guide them on the ascent of a spiritual education?

Warrior: Each generation must begin anew, pursuing the upward path to reach wisdom— "truth is a spiral staircase."[13]

Guardian: Yes. We need not be sages to wield our art, to gracefully weather all storms of living. But we must study the art and learn its techniques.

Warrior: You speak of failures, regrets, and wreckage. It's hard to imagine you living a life of excess and indulgence, knowing the truths you learned as a young man.

Guardian: I had "knowledge about" but did not have the strength of soul to convert "knowledge about" into "knowing," to actualize the kinetic chain of known and knower, united as one being.

Warrior: So you experienced firsthand the danger of "knowledge" without "knowing." Possessing the knowledge, you were still ignorant. You lacked wisdom. But you suffered added pain by understanding truth's burden. At that time you became fractured, partitioned in an internal war between the soul-sphere and the ego-body-octagon.

[13] B.H. Liddell Hart, *Why Don't We Learn from History?*

Your "will and body," as habits, were reckless, indulging in the vices of the primal drives of thirst, hunger, and pleasure as your "will and intellect" studied to know primordial and perennial truths.

Guardian: Yes.

I needed a guardian during those volatile formative years. I had wizards as mentors professionally; I lacked sages as mentors spiritually.

Warrior: I see the difference. You were in the middle of the war between the higher and lower natures of beinghood, between the power of soul and the power of ego. You needed a guide to help you fight your way through this battle, in which the soul fought to regain her powers and take command of the primal drives—the essence of the spiritual education.

You desperately needed a guardian to guide. Now I see why you became what you needed most—a guardian—devoted to the common good of yet-to-be leaders and seekers.

Guardian: Yes. I am still purifying the stains that defiled my soul from recklessness, excess, and indulgence. The stains are the result of wasting spirit and energy in the non-essentials and non-necessities of our art.

Shakespeare[14] mentors–

> Th' expense of spirit in a waste of shame
> Is lust in action; and till action, lust
> Is perjured, murd'rous, bloody, full of blame,
> Savage, extreme, rude, cruel, not to trust,
> Enjoyed no sooner but despised straight,
> Past reason hunted, and no sooner had,
> Past reason hated as a swallowed bait
> On purpose laid to make the taker mad;
> Mad in pursuit, and in possession so,
> Had, having, and in quest to have, extreme;
> A bliss in proof, and proved, a very woe;
> Before, a joy proposed; behind, a dream.
> All this the world well knows; yet none knows well
> To shun the heaven that leads men to this hell.

Any time I numbed the pain, it made things worse. I wanted release from this hell. To free myself, I had to purify my soul.

---

[14] William Shakespeare, Sonnet 129.

The reason I share this sonnet is that it arms us when our students, who have yet to experience wreckage and moral failures, resist our methods of providing a spiritual education that leads the professional education. Character leads skill. Virtue creates a divine soul; vice creates a hellish soul.

Our art will unabashedly and unforgivingly probe our students' moral and intellectual life and force them, by cross-examinations, to clear their minds and consciences of any vicious thinking, feeling, and wanting, so they can create the interior structures to live in the light of truth.

We will ask questions that require intense reflection. This is to produce self-knowledge, a self-knowledge that leads to the liberating force of interior freedom, which is the foundation that leads to truth-disclosing and truth-knowing.

We cannot bypass the art of self-knowledge. Acquiring knowledge and skill will be the hand-maiden, not the master, of the soul. To see the truth, we must discover what we are. Self-knowledge is the knowledge that we can know most deeply, because it is knowledge of what we are. And because we are created alike in nature and essence, the more we study and know ourselves, the more we can study and understand those around us.

Warrior: The more self-knowledge we acquire, the more we can actually know another human being?

Guardian: Yes. A spiritual being creates a friendship that way, by knowing what he is and knowing what others are, to unite the knower and known. It is remarkable that we possess this power to know, which makes our art an extension of being. But this means we cannot suffer fiction, we cannot suffer lies; we need to know and speak to the truth.

Warrior: It seems strange—if we seek reality's truth when it comes to ourselves, when it comes to our friends, when it comes to knowledge, when it comes to skill, when it comes to leading, this drive to seek the truth is the cause of the effect, of truth-disclosing itself?

Guardian: That is what I see. I know no truth when it comes to medicine. I have no intuitive insights when it comes to the skills of the surgeon. I am ignorant of these truths and skills because I have never sought to know the domain of medicine or the skills of the surgeon.

But, because I sought to know the domain of leading and the way of the leader, I learned the truths, the principles, the knowledge, and the techniques both in study and in practice. And yet that is not enough. That is only knowledge and skill. What about the knowledge of the being? The self-knowledge of what it is, its true purpose and nature?

Do you see the simplicity of what I am seeing?

Warrior: Do you mean–

The root of our essence and nature is light and truth, and by self-examination, by taking a hard look within, by getting to know what we are, that knowledge leads us to the knowledge of those around us, and if we know those around us we can be better guides and leaders. It seems counterintuitive that the more we study our being the more we can understand others.

Guardian: Yes. When we learn to move from the soul, we learn to connect with the souls of those around us. And then we unite that self-knowledge to the knowledge and techniques of our art.

Warrior: How is this not psychological?

Guardian: It is psychological, but our art is not wholly psychological.

If you mean the psychological dynamics used by Socrates, Christ and Nietzsche, to awaken the soul to truth, then yes. To understand the meaning, we need to draw out the epistemological root of term psychology—the psyche[15]—which means the study of the soul.

Bloom[16] mentors us–

> Socrates said man is a 'being toward eternity.'

> Heidegger, leaping from Nietzsche, said man is a 'being toward death.'

And you, Warrior, as a lover of science, must remember one priority. Whether we turn to death or turn to eternity, or turn and unite both, we must become first-rate men. Nietzsche mentors–

> First-rate scientist, second-rate man; Second-rate artist, first-rate man.[17]

Let us become second-rate artists but end up being first-rate men. First-rate souls verify their trustworthiness to teach this art.

Warrior: Assuming these first-rate souls are competent.

Guardian: Yes. We do not follow incompetent leaders. If we do, it's the road that paves the way to hell.

I am reminded of Gandhi's insights, when it comes to becoming first-rate men.

We begin by contemplating *The Bhagavad Gita*[18]–

> The Blessed Lord said:

---

[15] O.E.D. definition of psyche–The soul, the spirit. Formerly also (rare), the animating principle of the universe.

[16] Plato, *Symposium*, Allen Bloom Translation, The Ladder of Love Essay.

[17] Fredrick Nietzsche, *Beyond Good and Evil*, Aphorism 137.

[18] *The Bhagavad Gita*, 2.55, Feuerstein Translation.

> When a man relinquishes all desires that enter the mind, and is content with
> the Self in the Self, then is he called steadied in gnosis.

The Bhagavad Gita employs the term "self" to designate the reality that is the "ground of all being" which by purification we come to know. The term "gnosis" means the wisdom-faculty, the power to know the divine ground of all being. Our wisdom-faculty is awakened by purification of the desires and the ego-body-octagon. Do you understand?

Warrior: Yes.

Guardian: Can the wisdom-faculty awaken to see wisdom, light, and truth, if it remains latent inside a soul focusing on the primal desires?

Warrior: No. But, by divine grace, a soul experiences moments of this awakening and understanding.

Guardian: Yes. To reach this state, a secure state in an awakened wisdom-faculty, Gandhi offers this insight–

> Anyone who wants to live in such a state must give up everything which is
> likely to obstruct his effort. If all that we do is merely to indulge in fancies,
> it would be better not to think at all, neither good thoughts nor bad. The road
> to hell is paved with good intentions. That is why it is said that one may cast
> into a river a ton of thoughts and cling to an ounce of practice.[19]

Your silence is good. Keep learning the contemplative art.

Warrior: Truth has wrestled me into true submission. I am a warrior. I mastered an art. I've used science to advance modern warfighting. I see, with the leadership art, science will advance the practical side, but we will lead the art by striving to become first-rate men, seeking purification and seeking the awakening of the wisdom-faculty.

> I see that to awaken the wisdom faculty, we use wisdom literature and sacred
> scripture to leap into the unfathomable abyss of truth.

> I see that we use meditation, contemplation and dialogue to awaken the soul's
> "inner boundlessness" as the light, to learn to see in truth's unfathomable
> abyss.[20]

Guardian: Wisdom speaks. And if we return again to contemplate the passages from *The Glass Bead Game*, what do you see?

---

[19] *The Bhagavad Gita* According to Gandhi.
[20] Josef Pieper, *Living the Truth*.

Warrior: I see that we need guides, not only as teachers, but as mentors, to reign us back in when we've gone astray.

Guardian: And because we don't have guardians as guides, what happens when we go astray?

Warrior: We go into lockdown. We retreat within the ego-body-octagon's prison. We shut everyone out. We close ourselves off from reality and beings. We turn from the guidance of truth and light and toward deception and darkness. We turn to recklessness, excess and indulgence to numb the pain and suffering, instead of transcending it by cross-examinations that lead to self-knowledge and the awakening of the wisdom-faculty, so the soul can exert her powers.

Guardian: Has the summit's depth let you in?

Warrior: Yes. The essence of our art is building an architecture of understanding in my intellect.[21] I see the structures of our art uniting knowledge and being. I see the need for true friends. I see the need for communities of truth-seekers. I see the underlying structures that guide the formation of a leader. I see the leadership archetype.

Guardian: What do you see in the depths?

Warrior: Here is what I see–

The call to discover the truths of teaching the leadership arts sent us on a metaphysical quest. To discover leadership truths, we first needed to discover the truths of the human being, her nature and essence. These two aims, to know nature and essence, sent us into the knowable unknown of being. To learn to see, we leaped from the speculative insights that our nature is truth and our essence is light. This led us to our guides, the writings of the sages and saints, to anchor us as we journeyed into the unfathomable abyss of being. We learned that to be true guides, we needed to discover the truths of three perennial aims–

1. How to become virtuous
2. How to know the truth
3. How to make virtue, knowledge, and excellence an extension of being

By the concepts[22] of light, truth, soul, spirit, will, intelligence, knowledge, techniques, meditation, dialogue, and contemplation, we designed a route to climb to the highest heights and the deepest depths of our nature and essence. We learned that our true aim was to awaken the wisdom-faculty, with which we could claim allegiance to the soul-sphere, transcend the

---

[21] O.E.D. definition of intellect–The faculty of knowing and reasoning; power of thought; understanding; analytic intelligence.

[22] O.E.D. definition of concept–A product of the faculty of conception; an idea of a class of objects, a general notion; a theme, a design.

ego-sphere, and conquer the deception, darkness and bondage of the ego-body-octagon. We sought to learn techniques that carried us to the source of light, truth and wisdom. To reach the depths of the wisdom-faculty, we became still, to listen to the daemon, that true power of inspiration which awakens our spiritual potencies.

I see how to teach our art. I see our art as an activity, and I can see its movement and motion and momentum. When the body becomes still, the spirit moves.

The techniques of dialogue, meditation and contemplation can awaken the wisdom-faculty. This awakening leads to the truth-disclosing art of practical judgment.

Jacques Maritain[23] mentors us here–

> Right practical knowledge, as the immediate regulator of action, is the virtue of prudence. It judges and commands what is to be done here and now. As we know, this virtue is both intellectual and moral; it is connected with the moral virtues and necessarily presupposes the rectitude of the will.

Our students can practice contemplation, even if their wisdom-faculty is not awakened. Contemplation is a skill that can be practiced, with the guidance of a guardian or a contemplative. Or by the guidance of the wisdom literature–

I see that our art is the true art—the art of truth-seeking, truth-disclosing and truth-knowing, the union of what Aristotle calls contemplative wisdom (complete sight) and practical judgment (discerning right means and ends).[24]

I see, in our art, the union of *hexis* (active condition) and *energeia* (being-at-work), as contemplation (the being-at-work-staying-itself of the intellect).[25]

I see our art as a true relationship, and I see a union of relationships. It's a union of the human being, our spiritual nature, to reality, the eternal nature. This union is what we call psychological health and metaphysical freedom. I see the union of the human being, our physical nature, to reality's natural laws. This union we call bodily health. As composite-conditioned-beings, our physical nature is being breathed by Mother Nature. Finally, by the power of our intellect, we unite and order all these relationships into a knowing being when knower and known become one. We call this oneness truth.[26]

I see how to wield the techniques as swords of light and truth. I see the beauty and elegance of the necessities and essentialities of the art, which leads to true freedom. The liberating power

---

[23] Jacques Maritain, *The Degrees of Knowledge.*
[24] Aristotle, *Nicomachean Ethics*, Sachs Translation.
[25] Aristotle, *Nicomachean Ethics*, Sachs Translation.
[26] Josef Pieper, *Living The Truth.*

of freedom demands sacrifice to gain metaphysical freedom. For we do not command light and truth; light and truth command *us* to act.

I see the answer to the question–

> Stripped of all authority and power would I be selected to lead from a group of peers?

Guardian: Who is to be selected?

Warrior: Those who see best. Those who disclose truth best. Those who light souls best. Those who lead the light of souls best. Those who display excellence and wisdom in their craft. Those who display contemplative wisdom. Those who know the best means and ends. It is these souls who I would select to lead. It is these souls I willingly follow.

Guardian: Do you see, that is why you were selected to teach this art. You see best.

Warrior: I do not see this.

Guardian: Look again, to the truth. Look again, to what drove you to study leadership, amidst warriors who were already legends in warfighting.

Warrior: Let me be silent and still.

Guardian: Close your eyes and take an easeful posture. Let the truth reveal itself.

Warrior: When I look, I see leaders who had rank and authority over these warriors, not based on merit, but based on the fiction and force of hierarchy. They commanded these warriors in the heights and depths of self-deception and self-delusion, because of their blinding darkness and denial of reality's truth. The warriors made missions in spite of these leaders, not because of them.

Guardian: Instead of seeing leaders lead warriors, you saw autocrats and tyrants commanding by authority. You saw an enemy you could not render powerless. You did not know how to defeat him. Instead, you had to wait it out until the change of command. It's genius, in this regard, the military custom of shuffling commanders every two to three years.

Warrior: It's strange to see it from this perspective, but this is what drove me to study this art, to make sure I contributed to building strong and competent leaders.

Guardian: And have you discovered what it takes to build leaders?

Warrior: I have discovered the foundations.

Guardian: And what are the distinguishing qualities of these foundations?

Warrior: The courage to lead in the light. The courage to let the light lead. The courage to know truth and to take action on the truth we know—*coup d'oeil* (inner sight) and *coup d'esprit* (determination).

Guardian: Yes. Are these qualities more than just foundations?

Warrior: Yes. They are the objects and objectives of this art.

Guardian: If they are objects and objectives, we must become one-pointed in concentration and effort to realize the nature and essence of these objects and objectives, the ends and the means, so that they become our way of being.

Warrior: How do we do this?

Guardian: Do you not see? It's all right here, in the writings of wisdom literature and sacred scripture. We must learn to see the inner sight, the insights of truth, that flash in the mind amidst times of intense training and hardship. These are the gifts we receive, when we need them most, and we must be diligent and ready to see them and respond to them.

Warrior: How?

Guardian: You know, but it's too close. Distance yourself from it. We have been practicing this way of being this entire quest. We are close to teaching this art. What we must learn is to live and move in the deep waters of consciousness.

Close your eyes again. Be still. Breathe.

We are going to breathe deeply for thirty minutes. I will lead the vision quest in meditation. We will enter into timeless time. We will enter into the fabric of being. Just contemplate what you see.

What do you see?

Warrior: We are walking on a path leading down from a mountain summit to a fjord in Norway.

Guardian: Good.

Warrior: I see the path leading us to a cabin on the banks of the fjord. It is a reclusive and desolate place. I see candles lit in the windows and smoke wafting away from the chimney. I see you about to knock on the door, as if I'm there with you, but ahead of you in time, overseeing your movements, as a guardian. It seems I can see the events unfolding. What is this realm?

Guardian: Remember when I had the existential crisis as a young leader? And I sought sages for guidance and, not knowing one, I dove into the wisdom and sacred canons?

Warrior: I remember.

Guardian: I landed here.

Warrior: In a vision?

Guardian: Yes and no. It seemed real enough. Remember, this was a period of divine madness.

This was when the nature and essence of divine madness become one with the nature and essence of my soul. Before I landed here, in my despondency I requested a meeting with my commanding officer. To anchor us, this the memory–

Guardian: Sir, permission to speak freely.

Commander: Permission granted. Please close the door and take a seat.

Guardian: Sir, as a leader of Marines, I don't understand how there can be a God, when there is so much violence and madness on Earth. I don't understand how, with the pictures from Satellites, which show the beauty and magnificence of Earth, we still wage war against each other. I don't understand modern war. There are guided missiles. There are attack fighter jets. There are nuclear weapons. How is this even war? It's human madness and assured mutual killing and suicide. In war, shouldn't the individual count for something? Shouldn't the mastery of the warfighting martial arts count for something? It seems that technology and the mechanized way of warfighting have reduced individual merit almost to insignificance. How can individual virtue, intelligence, and skill compete and fight an enemy who can uses biological, chemical, and nuclear bombs? Compounding this, how does a warrior compete against strategic bombings and air-to-ground missiles? Maybe, because of my youth and naiveté, I had a chivalrous and romantic idea about leading warriors. Now I feel weak and insignificant. My body gets weak without enough food, water, and sleep. I use coffee, cigarettes, chewing tobacco, sex and scotch as counter measures to propel my body forward. It's not working. I don't feel strong. My body is getting thrashed from the pounding and wear and tear of carrying and using the gear and weapons of warfare. My mind is strong. But my body and emotions are breaking. Instead of feeling free and strong, I feel enslaved and weak. In this age of technology, it seems the individual counts for very little. One warrior's mastery is no match for an unseen sniper a mile away. I don't see the valor in the art. I see the art as madness. How, when we know that Earth is spinning on its axis daily, and traveling and orbiting through space like a rocket, at 36,000 miles per hour, do we not take a different perspective on what we are as human beings, and what we are to learn as composite-conditioned human beings of both body and soul, sentenced to mortality?

We sat there in silence for quite a while. The Commander, a new father, contemplatively looked in my eyes as if he suffered the same preoccupations. He then looked down for a moment, took his glasses off, leaned back in his chair, and clasped his hands behind his head. He spoke.

> Commander: One good thing about the advances in technology is that it's reduced war from large-scale, high-intensity and total-conflict engagements to small-scale, low-intensity and partial-conflict engagements.

> Hart, the great strategist, can mentor us here. He said–

> If you wish for peace, understand war—particularly the guerrilla and subversive form of war.[27]

> Guardian: Good God. I never saw it that way. It seems so simple in that light. I do seek understanding. I do seek peace.

> Commander: I seek understanding too. That is why I study war, strategy, and human nature. Most of the work we do, from day to day, is a series of transactional actions to make the military machine and bureaucracy run effectively, but not necessarily efficiently—such is the price of maintaining a military. That is not where you will grow most. You must begin to study the essence of war, the essence of peace, the essence of human nature. But this study is an activity you will do throughout the course of your life. You cannot rush the understanding you seek.

> Guardian: That is what has been hidden. I have been studying the wisdom literature, but I have not been studying strategy, war, and psychology.

> Commander: I think your condition, of wanting understanding, here and now, is creating a fictional stress in your psyche and you need to spend some time to clear your mind and meet each day as it comes.

> Saint Matthew can mentor us here–

> Therefore, do not worry about tomorrow; for tomorrow will look after itself. Sufficient for each day is its own trouble.[28]

> Be in peace. Know that I am not qualified to answer your question about God. That is an individual journey each soul wills to take or wills not to take. Even

---

[27] B.H. Liddell Hart, *Strategy*.
[28] The Holy Bible, *Book of Matthew*, Lamsa Translation.

if I knew the truth, it is an intuitive and incommunicable truth, a gift of grace from spirit to soul, not soul to soul. Understand?

Guardian: Yes.

Commander: In this light, it is best to seek understanding in prayer and meditation. You must learn to wrestle with the questions, letting the questions, not the answers, guide you on this living journey. The guidance I can provide is, you have been entrusted to lead your men to the best of your ability and to complete your missions. To do this, you must learn from your mentors, you must get to know your men, the psychological nature of each, and you must study tactics so that all of this knowledge and skill gets embedded in your being, so you can focus on the immediate demands you face each day. You are not weak, you are coming to grips early on in life with your mortality and limitations as a physical being. You must learn to see and know for yourself, that you have enough strength of mind, will, and body to carry the burdens that have been entrusted to you. You have the same strength that generations before you had, and you must give this strength to leading. Let the other questions remain unanswered until you have time and space to enter their deep waters. Until then, study scriptures, study war, have faith in yourself and lead your men.

Guardian: Understood.

Warrior: Sage wisdom by your commander.

Guardian: A divine consolation. After the meeting, I spent time in silence and solitude. There's a secluded waterfall hidden deep within Okinawa's Iriomote Island. It was there that I spent time purifying my mind and body. I let the metaphysical questions remain unanswered, and I dedicated my entire being and all my energy to the task of leading. I felt an immediate release from metaphysical bondage. My energy and mind began to soar with a one-pointed focus and concentration—to learn the leadership art. The burden of leading, by necessity, led this focus of effort. For the first time I experienced potential awakening, deep within my being. For a while I was in a euphoric[29] state.

What is most important is the insight I learned at that time. The questions, I learned, not the answers, are most important. Asking the most demanding questions leads you to the depths, leads you to the unknown, leads you to truth and light. Meditation and contemplation are the two swords that can cut through these demanding questions. They're questions for courageous spirits.

Warrior: Wait, what's going on? The cabin in the fjord…I see the door opening.

---

[29] O.E.D. definition of euphoria–strong feeling of well-being, cheerfulness, and optimism.

Guardian: This realm is deeper than memories, as though it's the realm of the undercurrents of being. What do you see?

Warrior: I see the most beautiful being, in body and soul, appearing before you.

Guardian: But, you don't see you any longer, correct?

Warrior: Yes. I see only you before the being, a being of surpassing beauty, radiating a profound spiritual love. What am I seeing?

Guardian: As a guardian, you are seeing the depths of being. These are the visualizations in the depths of my being.

Warrior: How is this possible?

Guardian: There are unseen realms to reality's truth. We need faith until we learn to see in these realms.

Daemon[30]: Greetings Guardian.

Guardian: It is good to see you again.

> Warrior: Of course your daemon appears as a divine Goddess.
>
> Guardian: What I needed and what I did not know, and what the daemon taught me, is that I needed divine comfort because my destiny would deprive me of a woman's love. I had been blessed in my formative years with two great loves, and not having a great love in my life would be the greatest test that I had to overcome. And that lack, that deprivation, raged like a war in my being. I did not know that I needed faith, not only courage, to seek divine comfort, to learn to become an unmoved mover.

Daemon: In that period of purification you lacked faith and that doubt halted your ascent. You felt weak and that weakness made you feel ashamed. Only in time did you learn that in your imperfections, in your weaknesses, your soul opened to the doors of truth. You needed to learn that yes, the conditioned-temporal-being is weak and mortal, but your spirit, as light and truth, in will and intelligence, has the strength to achieve metaphysical freedom.

On divine comfort, Meister Eckhart mentors you–

> Thus, I say that in God there is no sorrow or suffering or distress. If you would be free from all adversity and pain, turn and cleave entirely to God. Assuredly, all your ills are because you do not turn to God and God alone.

---

[30] O.E.D. definition of Daemon–1: Greek Mythology. A divinity or supernatural being of a nature between gods and humans. 2: An inner or attendant spirit or inspiring force.

Therefore, a man should strive earnestly to de-form himself of himself and of all creatures, and know no father but God alone.

But when nothing can comfort you but God, then God *will* comfort you, and with Him and in Him all that is bliss.[31]

Guardian: Now I know this to be truth. When I met you, I had courage but I lacked faith. I lacked faith capable of "giving substance to things not yet seen."[32] That lack of faith halted my ascent, and I experienced pain and suffering. I did not believe in these possibilities. I needed to exhaust all other potential realms of meaning and purpose.

The silence and stillness and beauty of this place helped me come to know these principles and truths. Now my challenge is to make manifest this beauty.

Warrior: This place is beautiful. I see leather-bound books lined from floor to ceiling. I see crystals of beautiful light shining everywhere. I see light emanating. I see truth emanating. I see beinghood.

Daemon: Why have you returned? Did you ever learn why your experts and you, the most highly skilled professionals, made so few operational mistakes and made so many character mistakes?

Warrior: I, too, wondered why the most highly skilled warriors made so few mistakes in battle and made so many mistakes on liberty.

Guardian: I have learned why.

Daemon: And what have you learned?

Guardian: We succeeded in meeting the demands of the common need. But we failed to meet the demands of the common good.

Daemon: What does this mean?

Guardian: We failed in their spiritual formation. I failed in my own spiritual formation. The days were pure; the nights were vile. I should have stayed with you and trained. I did not understand the truths you shared. No. I did not believe the truths you shared. I resisted the purification of being and becoming, of learning to see and then learning to know. Instead, I wanted to know before I learned to see. I thought I could find the answers to all my questions in the sacred canons. Only in pain and suffering, did I learn to leap from these canons, instead of staying in their security and comfort. I learned I needed to embrace the insecurities, uncertainties and discomforts of purification.

---

[31] Meister Eckhart, *The Complete Mystical Works, Treaty–The Book of Divine Comfort.*
[32] Barbara Y. Martin's definition of faith.

Daemon: Now Emerson mentors you–

> The world is young: the former great men call to us affectionately. We too must write Bibles, to unite again the heavens and the earthly world. The secret of genius is to suffer no fiction to exist for us, to realize all that we know.[33]

You failed in conduct and character because you focused intense training only on specialized knowledge and skills. You did not make mature and whole and complete human beings, in and of themselves. You are having your reckoning. Achievement is only a temporal and fleeting measure; you are seeking true measures. Soon you will experience your day of redemption, by teaching this art to yet-to-be-leaders.

This is why your quest led to the discovery of the intellectual and spiritual gymnastics. It was in these that you learned to transcend the fictional realm of the ego.

It was in this training that you experienced for yourself the spiritual war raging in each and every soul, not just your own. Most are unconscious of this war. Most mistake the effects for causes—the anxiety, the doubt, the uncertainty, the fear. These are the effects, not the causes, of the interior war. Most do not know that in this war, peace only comes by victory. Victory is the effect of the cause of true education and spiritual formation.

On this quest, you learned of the soul's nature as truth and the soul's essence as light. You learned to awaken the soul's powers, and how the soul grows by training in the techniques of dialogue, contemplation, and meditation. You learned to release yourself from the ego's prison, and what it takes to experience metaphysical freedom—it is here where you discovered redemption. This is what you were really asking your commander twenty years ago, only you did not know the question; you only knew the bondage. You knew you were not free. All these years, you have been seeking true freedom. Has it been worth the effort, energy, and sacrifice?

Guardian: Yes.

Daemon: And now you are here, as the final stage before you train students and combat adversaries?

Guardian: Yes.

Daemon: And on this quest, you sought not knowledge, but knowing as seeing, as contemplation?

Guardian: Yes.

---

[33] Ralph Waldo Emerson, "Representative Men."

Daemon: And you learned that you need to turn inward, to the source of light and truth and, at the same time, turn away from the self, from the ego, from the fiction of what you thought you were.

Guardian: Yes.

Daemon: You sought what cannot be seen with the physical eyes? You sought what cannot be grasped and possessed and acquired? You sought to be a conduit, a receiving and giver of light and truth?

Guardian: Yes.

Daemon: And what do you see now, with the inner sight, the *coup d'oeil*?

Guardian: I am no *doctor of light* like Aquinas. It seems as though I'm a contemplative, pursuing the *doctor of night*, like Saint John of the Cross.[34] I live in an imagelessness that can see.[35] It's been this way for as long as I can remember. I pray and I am given, but I see nothing. I study and train and write, and yet in my being, I see an abyss of nothingness. I still do not know nor understand the truth of all things. And yet I hear the calls and see them—they appear in the nothingness of the soul. It is these calls I respond to. That is all I know—the calling and the demands of the calling.

Daemon: You understand enough.

Guardian: Are the calls transmitted intuitively? As an intuitive knowingness?

Daemon: Yes. That is the gift to your soul. You have the gift intuitively to know the callings.

> Warrior: Is this how you received the call from the eternal-sphere, by the intermediaries and emissaries of wisdom's light of truth?
>
> Guardian: I don't know. I'm on a vision quest to help me see clearly the primacy of our techniques. Keep documenting what you see and hear.

Guardian: It is the one gift I have trusted most—to be able to listen to the deep and quiet voice that reveals itself in periods of prolonged silence, solitude, prayer, and contemplation. The voice speaks when I detach from the ego's desires and conditioned existence. It also reveals itself as flashes of understanding in periods of intense hardship.

Daemon: You learned to hear this inner voice in the early period of divine madness, by the drive to become free?

Guardian: Yes.

---

[34] Jacques Maritain, *The Degrees of Knowledge*.
[35] Aldous Huxley, *The Perennial Philosophy*.

Daemon: You knew anxiety and fear and doubt assaulted your psychological state, and that these emotions could paralyze the powers of your mind and intelligence.

Guardian: Yes.

Daemon: You knew that in this war the assaults of the enemy rendered you almost powerless and restricted your freedom of movement. You knew your bondage.

Guardian: Yes.

Daemon: How did you learn to break free from this prison?

Guardian: I did think I was going insane or having a nervous breakdown. By necessity, I started the practice of meditation. I could barely sit still for one minute. I would progress each week, minute by minute. I had broken my back and experienced too much pain in a seated meditation. I learned to lay on the floor. I would begin by saying, "I am not these thoughts. I don't know where these thoughts come from. I did not create the ability to think. I do not have command over the assault of thoughts penetrating my mind and well-being." I thought, "I am not these feelings. I am not these emotions. I am something before and beyond the feelings and emotions." I learned to see the emotions. I learned to see the thoughts. When I saw them, they lost their power over me. I did learn that my emotions and thoughts were an effect, not the cause, of my state of being. I learned to use them as a signal as to the state of my well-being. I practiced until I could be in silence and stillness for an hour. It is then that I learned the metaphysical power of visualization. I saw myself lying in stillness. I saw a metaphysical samurai sword present itself. I gripped the sword with both hands. It is then that I learned the power of soul. I learned to be on guard. Any time a thought, negative or positive, appeared, I would use the sword to slice it in half, and watch it dissolve and disappear. I learned to slice any positive or negative feeling and watch it dissolve and disappear. I did this because I wanted to be beyond good and bad, positive and negative. I wanted to move from cause, from being, not from effects. I did this for months, until I entered into a state of imagelessness and peace. From this state, I learned to wield light and truth into my thinking and into my feeling. It is here, in silence and solitude, that I learned to do this. Then I learned to do this in an active state, when engaged with the activities of living. This is how I first discovered metaphysical freedom.

Daemon: What do you see?

Guardian: I see and know in nothingness.

Daemon: Explain.

Guardian: I don't see the soul. I don't grasp the soul. I did not create the soul. But I know the soul. I connect with the soul. I connect with spirit. I know this connection by the techniques.

I know the techniques of dialogue, contemplation and meditation awaken the inner light and truth, to come into knowing, to see with the inner eye. I know them by direct experience.

But I don't have proof.

Daemon: Why is that?

Guardian: Each soul must reach up into spirit, by spiritual exercises, to come to know for herself?

Daemon: You mean, to learn to see, they need to cross the threshold into the knowable unknown? And they cross this threshold by using these techniques in spiritual exercises?

Guardian: Yes. I'm calling yet-to-be leaders to undergo rigorous training to see, to realize and to act on the truth and light they come to know.

> Warrior: Ego-shedding is more than mindfulness and feedback?

> Guardian: Yes. To see light and truth, we must crush egos and awaken our souls.

> Warrior: How is this not religious?

> Guardian: We are only interested in results. Our aim is light and truth. We don't need to become saints or priests or rabbis or sheikhs for our endeavor. We don't need to prove God or Religion or adhere to one. But we must make our leaders wise and just and compassionate, so that they won't seek to control the minds and wills of human beings. Religious and government institutions have failed because they cannot give the human being the virtue necessary for metaphysical freedom. Each soul must learn to undergo the trials of her own spiritual formation.

Daemon: Each being is on a journey. Each being must become good, wise, just, and beautiful. Look at the source of what you are afraid to call God, as the being of light and truth. Earth orbits in the heavens, a vision of beauty, eternity, and magnificence. Diotima is one of beauty's handmaidens. You seek the essence of beauty, not the physical effects of beauty.

Guardian: Yes. What remains to be uncovered, before we turn to teaching leaders? Before we teach the contemplative and intellectual arts?

Daemon: There are some experiences whose significance you have not yet learned. Where did you hear the call to seek light and truth? Where did you hear the call to become their vessel? How did life break you, so that you became receptive? Where have you failed? Do not wait until perfection to teach. Become the student known as a teacher. You will learn more from teaching this art than by simply practicing its skills. The art demands that you serve and give to others, to walk with them as a guide during the trials and hardships of their transformation and formation. You must undergo the same kind of training as the saints, though you do not need to become one. You must undergo additional periods of deeper purifications.

Guardian: Why? Why must we undergo these trials to teach this art?

Daemon: You must become purified to see the illumination in the souls you teach.

Guardian: And have I been hesitant because I'm waiting for purification's perfection?

Daemon: Yes. Simply walk the way of perfection.

Guardian: This is why humility, detachment, and faith are anchors in this teaching art?

Daemon: Yes. The courage to act and teach as an imperfect being, being perfected. As with the wreckage you experienced in the traps of the ego, you will still experience wreckage as you make mistakes teaching this art. You will fail your students. Students will fail you. You will be betrayed. You must endure and will the courage to live your calling. What remains to be uncovered? To accept the burden to "become the light unto yourself" and live in the chaos, darkness, deception, and delusion all around you and in the beings you encounter, and yet still to remain one with the truth you come to know. This is the Buddha's final message–

> Therefore, O Ananda, be ye lamps unto yourselves. Rely on yourselves, and do not rely on external help. Hold fast to the truth as a lamp. Seek salvation alone in the truth. Look not for assistance to any one besides yourselves.[36]

As a guide, it is not in your power to give this truth. It is in your power to teach souls the techniques with which one learns to be self-reliant and free, by seeking the light of truth. If your students fail, it is not your fault. If you fail in your call to become a vessel of truth, it is your fault. It is your failure. Your call is simply to remind souls of the truth and light that it is their destiny to come to know.

Guardian: Then the essence of this art is the way of self-reliance. Both Emerson and Musashi speak of this.

Daemon: Yes. Once a student's basic needs are met, it must be made clear where to focus the effort—the effort of growing the spirit in light and truth.

Saint Matthew mentors–

> You are indeed the light of the world; a city that is built upon a mountain cannot be hidden. Nor do they light a lamp and put it under a basket, but on a lamp stand, so that it gives light to all who are in the house.[37]

Beings of light and power need minimal external goods. Look at the examples of Christ, Buddha, Socrates, Plato, Aristotle, Aquinas, Augustine, Saint John of the Cross, Saint Teresa

---

[36] Paul Carus, *The Gospel of Buddha*.
[37] The Holy Bible, *Book of Matthew*, Lamsa Translation.

of Avila, Averroes, Avicenna, Plotinus, Lao Tzu, Confucius, Dalai Lama, Martin Luther King, Malcom X, Gandhi, and Mother Teresa. These are the great-souled beings relying on no economic or military power. These great souls led souls by wisdom's light, not the mind's light. They are the receivers and givers of wisdom. That is why you must rest inwardly, and live from the depths, and remain in the depths. You must live deeply. You must journey deeply.

Your leaders must become the true lights.

> Warrior: I must become a true light?

> Guardian: You are a true light.

> Warrior: No. I am too imperfect.

> Guardian: I, too, am too imperfect. All these beings of wisdom are imperfect beings. They had the courage to endure the purification of wisdom's light and truth.

> Warrior: Which is why we must learn to wield detachment, humility and fortitude?

> Guardian: Yes. The mystery of redemption and atonement.

Daemon: Warrior, look in the mirror. What do you see?

> Warrior: The guardian archetype.

Daemon: Warrior, look into the deep waters.

> Warrior: I see the guardian and you, about fifty feet below me.

Daemon: Warrior, when you journey into the depths, no one comes with you, but you will find you are not alone. The guardian has learned to move in these depths. You have been his anchor on this quest, witnessing his exploring as he shares what he is seeing. This is why few undergo the training—they won't detach from the bondage of the fictions believed to be true.

When you begin to teach this art, you will be in the depths, to model for your students how to reach the essence and nature of being. You will teach them to see and know the light of truth for themselves. When the guardian and you teach the first student, the three of you will experience a multi-layered-consciousness experience—the guardian in depths deeper than you, and you in depths deeper than the leader. The mystery is how all this is connected and transmitted, to meet souls as they are, not as you wish them to be—the maxim "as above, so below," because the essence and nature of the soul is one and the same light and truth, emanated uniquely and individually in the composite-conditioned existence of each human being.

Guardian: Warrior, the depths speak, with the voice of the stillness of being. The mind is clear and free in the depths. There is no disturbance there. There is no conflict. There is no chaos. There is no complexity. There is no suffering. There is friction. There is no fiction. There is no winning. There is no achieving. There is no sin in the essence and nature of light and truth. There is awakening. There is morality—to manage the means and ends of living. There is perfecting. There is being and there is becoming.

Daemon: And what do you come to know in the depths?

Pieper mentors you–

> Spirit, which corresponds to the totality of being, is also the highest form of inwardness, what Goethe called '*wohnen in sich selbst*'—dwelling in oneself. The more embracing the power with which to relate oneself to objective being, the more deeply that power needs to be anchored in the inner self of the subject so as to counterbalance the step it takes outside. And where this step attains a world that is in principle complete (with totality as its aim) the reflective self, characteristic of spirit, is also reached. The two together constitute one spirit: not only the capacity to relate oneself to the whole of reality, to the whole world, but an unlimited capacity of living in oneself, the gift of self-reliance and independence...[38]

Guardian: This is one of the objectives of our teaching art—to become self-reliant and independent, free from the wills and judgments of other human beings. We achieve this state of being by the techniques of dialogue, meditation, and contemplation, as we study our domain, as we study our students, as we study objective reality, and as we study ourselves. In this way, we come to know not only reality, but truly we come to know ourselves. And this coming to know ourselves, by the gift of self-knowledge, results in self-reliance and independence. This is how we become unmoved movers, and can rest inwardly, in the depths of our beings, and reach the heights of this inwardness, by the techniques, knowledge, and object that is our art—truth's light as wisdom.

Daemon: You do see, Warrior, that your art is a "practically practical science of human action"?[39] It's a science of human willing, knowing, and acting. You are a man of science, and this art is based on the science of human actions.

Maritain provides an insight into the nature of this science–

> The very method of science is reversed. The whole mode of science is practical. What does that mean? It means that there is no question here of explaining and resolving a truth, even a practical truth, into its reasons and principles. The

---

[38] Josef Pieper, *Leisure–The Basic of Culture*.
[39] Jacques Maritain, *The Degrees of Knowledge*.

question is to prepare for action and to assign its proximate rules. And, since action is a concrete thing which must be thought in its concretion before being posited in being, knowledge here, instead of analyzing, composes; I refer to the fashion in which the relation of truth is established between this knowledge and its object. It gathers together everything that is already known, all the explanations, principles and *raisons d'etre*[40] (but in order to organize them all from new points of view which provide what is needed to posit the concrete act, as they are furnished directly by experience, whose role here is primary).[41]

Few have the discipline to study your art. They turn away from it, to avoid the trials and hardships of learning the knowledge, learning the techniques, and then practicing the techniques to become proficient. Instead, they lead by authority, rank and coercive power. Their excuse for not learning the art? They say the art is too abstract, too philosophical, too theoretical and too academic. In these statements they reveal their indolence (inclination to avoid exertion or trouble) and cowardice (lack of courage). This is why the guardian sought out warriors to train in this art. The virtues of self-discipline and fortitude are already an active condition (*hexis*) of their character.

If you are serious ["a truly serious person takes few things seriously"[42]] about teaching this art, remember–

> Throughout the study of this subject...[a leader] must constantly seek to combine theory with practice, in order that practice may make theory more intelligible, and in order that theory may make practice more profitable.[43]

If you are serious about teaching this art, remember–

> That the art of [leading] includes many difficult and technical theories that he [the student] must master; and that in order to acquire proficiency in their use, he must enter upon a long period of training, involving the most rigid self-discipline, with its keynote expressed in the words of Demosthenes: 'Practice! Practice! Practice!'.[44]

Guardian: Warrior, this is how the writings of the sages and saints guide us. When we study the wisdom literature, the question at the forefront of our thinking is, how do these truths and wisdom guide us to achieve our three teaching aims–

---

[40] O.E.D. definition for raisons d'etre–reason for being. A purpose or reason accounting for or justifying the existence of a thing.
[41] Jacques Maritain, *The Degrees of Knowledge.*
[42] Aristotle, *Nicomachean Ethics*, Sachs Translation, definition of serious (spoudaios).
[43] Warren Choate Shaw, *The Art of Debate.* I've replaced "debater" with "leader."
[44] Warren Choate Shaw, *The Art of Debate.* I've replaced "debate" with "leading", and added "the student."

1. How to become virtuous?
2. How to know truth?
3. How to make virtue, knowledge, and excellence an extension of being?

Do you see it now? The union of the common need and the common good? Do you see, we focus on the common good to lead the common need?

> Warrior: I see and I know. I have always known. I have always seen. While Plato coined the term "philosopher kings," we are taking that intent further; we seek what is best in both the leader and the followers, creating "sagacious leadership" as the union of souls to respond to the demands and challenges of living. I see a few levels of correspondence. First, each human being must learn to be self-governing and self-correcting. This is when the inner nature of the soul comes into harmony with the outer nature of objective reality. We learn to do this, first by seated meditation, in silence and solitude, and then as an active meditation in the activities of our calling and vocation (say, uniting the vocation of parenting and the vocation of leading). Then, I see how you unite the energy of the souls through the practice of yoga. This is the same as meditation, only it's a moving meditation with a group of souls. This is a method to unite the inner nature of all these souls with the outer nature, the objective experience of practicing yoga. This is how you first teach souls, together, to enter the depths of being, and when it's done correctly it's the experience of making an activity an extension of being. Then I see, in the study of the domain of leadership, how the practice of contemplation unites the inner nature of the soul with the outer nature of objective knowledge. By contemplation, the soul learns to make knowledge an extension of being. And finally, weaving this all together, I see how leadership is the union of souls, and how dialogue unites souls in knowing, willing and acting, to respond in harmony to the demands of objective reality. How do I know this? How do I see this? I know that the experience of warriors training for combat and engaging in combat reaches such a heightened state. The example of an orchestra might hold as well, except in our art, we are always playing new music, in an improvised fashion, because the demands of living take us straight into the unknown. It is strange to reflect on this truth—each new day is a day living in the unknown, and by the end of the day it becomes known. The knowable unknown.

Daemon: You see with the light of wisdom. This is what makes you trustworthy to guide students as they learn this art.

Guardian: Are we at the summit?

Daemon: For the summit of this art, yes. But there are always new quests and new summits to reach.

Guardian: Have we discovered the core truths of this art?

Daemon: Yes—If you teach the means and the way, the ends will follow your lead.

> Warrior: This is how we become unmoved movers. This is the principle of detachment from results. The ends follow our lead. This is metaphysical freedom.

Guardian: Yes. Now I see why I resonated more with the teachings of Saint John of the Cross than the teachings of Saint Thomas Aquinas. Now I see the connection.

> Warrior: What?

Guardian: When it came to practicing our art, I kept returning to the example of Jimi Hendrix. He lived his music. Being left-handed–

> Jimi Hendrix had a hard time finding left-handed guitars, so he flipped over and restrung standard right-handed Fender Stratocasters. That changed the string tension and microphone location and produced Hendrix's signature mix of bright highs and delicate lows.[45]

He adapted the instruments to fit his style. He lived his music. His musical genius, born from the marriage of daemon and muse, awakened and actualized his potencies.

I'm reminded of Santana's insight into Hendrix's musical genius–

> Jimi Hendrix was like a Da Vinci. Leonardo Da Vinci of electric music… he knew how to paint with a different canvas…. Only Buddy Guy and Jimi Hendrix, they—they literally sound like they…they wait for a lightning… and they grab it and they go, 'Stay there. You will sustain until I tell you, so stay there…'. And Buddy Guy and Jimi Hendrix are the only musicians with electric guitar that I know…to will the guitar to do what they want 'em to do as long as they want them to do it.[46]

I finally understand. Our leaders, by the virtue of patience, wait for the lightning of truth's wisdom. And when they see the lightning of truth, they need to reach up to the heavens and bring it down, and wield it as inspiration, as divine madness, to make manifest their art.

---

[45] Kevin Dupzyk, www.popularmechanics.com/culture/music/a17922/jimi-hendrix-backwards-stratocaster/.
[46] Dan Rather, *The Big Interview*, with Carlos Santana.

This is why Saint John of the Cross[47] models our teaching art–

> Saint John of the Cross is "not so much interested in telling us what perfection is, as in leading us to it. This is the science of the master of spirituality, the practitioner of the soul, the artisan of sanctity…he wants at all costs to lead [us] to… supreme joy."
>
> Saint Thomas Aquinas "explains and makes us see."
>
> Saint John of the Cross "guides and leads us."
>
> Saint Thomas Aquinas "casts every intelligible light upon being."
>
> Saint John of the Cross "leads liberty through all the nights of renunciation."
>
> Saint Thomas Aquinas "by his teaching mission…is a demonstrator."
>
> Saint John of the Cross "by his teaching mission…is…a practitioner of wisdom."

Warrior: There it is, the understanding, the courage to become a practitioner of wisdom. The truths you sought to discover on this metaphysical quest have been revealed. Your journey is not about knowledge and knowing; your journey is to discover how to be a teacher and practitioner. This is how you reached into the teachings of the sages and saints, and led out the techniques and practices of our art.

The Daemon has departed. You have returned from the deeper depths.

Guardian: I do not have the power and strength to remain there. Only in short and intense bursts can I gain access to those creative depths. I am at the edge of understanding. To gain clarity and insight, I use an imaginative meditation technique to help me see and understand. I needed to see what still remained unhidden before we move to teach our students, the ones called to lead.

Warrior: The meditation served as an example of a teacher cross-examining a student?

Guardian: Partially—what I needed to remember, even though we guide and teach students, is that our art is an auto-didactic (self-taught) method in practice. I am reminded of the distinguishing characteristic in the way expert violinists train. They spend more time in solitary practice, known as deliberate practice.[48] In deliberate practice they create training goals that lead to greater mastery and greater abilities. Our art also demands solitary practice, once the basic knowledge and techniques are learned. Our art is self-taught (by practice), self-

---

[47] Jacques Maritain, *The Degrees of Knowledge.*
[48] K. Anders Ericsson, *The Cambridge Handbook of Expertise and Expert Performance.*

correcting (by insight) and self-cultivating (by clear aims). And it demands a self-knowledge that leads each student in the formation of her goals, to use the method of deliberate practice to increase her abilities and awaken her potencies.

Warrior: Our art is founded in a self-knowledge that leads to self-correcting studies and training. I see the primacy of yoga and meditation as the means to self-knowledge.

Guardian: That is how I've studied and trained. Each book I study and each technique I practice is for a training goal. The calling leads and I follow its lead. The calling lets me know my deficiencies; the deficiencies lead the training—the cycle of being and becoming.

Warrior: You understood the purpose of one-pointed concentration to achieve your aim. This is how you discovered the primacy of self-reflection and self-knowledge. This is how you knew the value of the ways of the warriors, sages, and saints.

And yet, what I keep seeing in your story is that knowledge is not enough. The kinetic chain of knowing-to-being, in being and becoming, is the challenge and burden of this art.

You "knew" the truths of this art; you continually failed to *become* the truths of this art. Your lessons of experience reveal the truth of the passage you read so long ago–

How inexorably true it is, one realizes only after having gone astray.[49]

Guardian: And I have gone astray, again and again, until I started teaching this art. By the grace of God, it seems by divine intervention, living guardians appeared to awaken my soul from the sleep that lead to its going astray. It seems I had the good fortune to be cross-examined by mentors during those periods of straying from the truth.

Warrior: How?

Guardian: Our challenge is to be a living example, to share with our students our falls from grace, the wreckage the falls created, and then how to recover from the wreckage and grow stronger because of the failures.

Warrior: Go on.

Guardian: After military service, I found myself in the prison of conventional life. You remember when I shared my experiences in consulting?

Warrior: Yes.

Guardian: Years earlier, in my first year as a consultant, I entered into a living purgatory. I felt like a metaphysical container had imprisoned me. At the time, I had a great job and

---

[49] Herman Hesse, *The Glass Bead Game (Magister Ludi)*.

great finances, but found the work meaningless. In despondency, I sought the comfort of beautiful women. This led to increased bondage. In despondency, I sought the comfort of whiskey. This led to increased bondage. In despondency, I stopped training. This led to increased bondage. I needed help to see. I needed grace. I needed light. I needed truth. But I did not know. I again suffered the bondage of ignorance. I had fallen asleep. I needed to be awakened again.

In this period I felt enslaved. I felt that my "will" or my "being" was not "free." I describe this period as my first experience with the truth of our inward nature—that it can be a heaven or a hell. I felt a polarity I had never experienced before. I had never felt the bondage and enslavement of a "want" not being met; I wanted, but I didn't know what I wanted. The condition of "wanting" imprisoned me. I could not shake it. I'm struggling to find the words to express this, but I will speak spontaneously—spontaneity is the will's act of love. The reason why it revealed itself so powerfully then was that I had transitioned from the military, and the experience of one-pointed concentration to meet the demands of leading had released itself. I needed external pressure and stress to demand excellence and energy and effort of myself, to feel significance and purpose. A conventional job seemed to be the exact opposite of this, with long hours of work, but no true pressure or stress dedicated to a worthy aim, for a worthy mission. I felt insignificant. I lived in support of bureaucratic functions. I had no one to lead, and I felt insignificant without the demands and burdens of leading. Life was teaching me that my interior nature had become disordered, and that I had become too dependent on work for meaning. I did not know that I had invested my well-being in the common need instead of the common good. I was not secure in my being; I had lost my sense of inwardness. I had become attached to the mirage—a mirage that, every time I reached for it, disappeared. I had lost my center and my way. I needed to be cross-examined. I needed to return to the practices.

How could I be in such despondency with a good family, good friends, a good job and good enough health?

Warrior: You, by your will, had become spiritually darkened.

Guardian: I let the ego-body-octagon assault the powers of my soul. Only a boring person experiences true boredom. I felt bored. That terrified me. Life seemed boring; life seemed without challenge. I was not being tested. I was not being grown. That meant that I was, in fact, boring as a being. It's a terrifying place to be.

Warrior: And yet, you were being tested. You had entered the unknown and did not know.

Guardian: Yes. And then, by divine grace, a mentor, a former pilot, a warrior, appeared as a performance manager to provide my yearly performance review. He reviewed my performance and I received high marks in all areas. This is the memory–

Mentor: You strike me as a professional who will always achieve your performance goals. You move with an audacious intensity and tenacity, as though you're fighting for your life, to prove something, to achieve something, for yourself. A self-driven measure not accountable to any outside measure. But I am concerned. Like you, I am a former military officer. When I entered our profession, I needed to learn not to be in such a hurry in this kind of work. I needed to temper the aggression and tenacity that the warrior class values. It took me a while to adjust after leading men in war. You need to be patient and gentle during this adjustment. You need to slow down. You need to find a rhythm and harmony that is aligned to the nature of this work.

I lost my bearing and responded spontaneously, as though I were speaking to a confessor.

Guardian: I do suffer the sin of intemperance and the sin of fury. I hate this job. A year ago, I backpacked through Europe. At the San Fermin Festival, in Pamplona, I ran with the bulls, fell, and was almost trampled to death, if not for a Spaniard who leaped over the fence and pulled me to safety, moments before the bulls ran by. In Cinque Terre, by day, I ran miles, from village to village, with an Olympian on holiday. By night, we drank bottles of wine and engaged in conversations that led to passionate nights with beautiful women. In Amsterdam, by day, I made love with a Norwegian goddess; by night I lost my mind. In Prague, I read Kafka and wrote fiction as I drank absinthe. Every day was an adventure. Every day, something unexpected occurred. Before this, years earlier, I was leading Marines, deployed in Japan, being tested daily in my leadership abilities—every day mattered and took on significance. Now, let me look at the present. What do I see in my new found freedom? I feel enslaved. My days are meaningless. Each day I sit here, all day, in this cubicle on the 28th floor, in a sterile and lifeless building, simply engaged in meetings, risk management, project management and reporting management. This is a waste of my energy and my talents. On weeknights, I numb the pain with whiskey. On weekend nights, I numb the pain again and read Nietzsche until dawn. I am a fractured being. I wonder why I stopped traveling. I guess I felt the pull to get serous again. But this work is not serious. I wonder why I got out of the Corps. I guess I sought freedom. But I experienced more freedom in the Corps than here. It was the freedom of purpose.

Warrior: You do have the ability to speak your mind, especially when backed into a corner, fighting for freedom.

Guardian: Just like the Commander, the Mentor remained in a silent reflection before he spoke, as though he had thought the same thoughts, earlier in his life, except he had bypassed the fall into darkness. He contemplatively looked at me, as though he could read my soul. Then he spoke–

Mentor: You do know you intimidate most of us?

Guardian: What? I'm the lowest on the totem pole. I lead no one. I have no authority.

Mentor: That's not what I mean. What do you think drives us to work here, in this environment?

Guardian: Clearly, I have no idea.

Mentor: You intimidate us because we cannot control you. We have no incentives to control you. You don't need the income. See, we control people and I'm controlled too, because we don't have generational wealth and we need a strong source of revenue and income. To achieve this, I invest, and I work as a consultant. Everyone on this team, except you, has spouses, children, mortgages, loans, insurance, healthcare, and living expenses, to support and care for the needs of our families—we are householders. What drives us is the vocation of marriage and the vocation of parenting. We were concerned to hire you because you don't own a home, you don't have a spouse, and you don't have children. You don't need the income of this job. You wanted to become a consultant. You were seeking important and meaningful work as the means and ends. You have discovered that, in this profession, most of us use it as the means to provide the ends of security and stability for our families. That is what drives us. That is not what drives you. Freedom drives you. Your free-spirited nature intimidates us. What you are reminds us to awaken and remember the adventure of living. Look at me. I wear a suit. I've got short hair, I'm clean cut. I shave each morning. You? You're iconoclastic. You don't play by artificial and conventional rules. You are not trying to fit in. You are not trying to impress people. You are driven by your work or by challenges or by adventure. Your drive is different. You are a free spirit. Your spirit intimidates us—you can't be controlled. Look at you. For shoes, you wear black Vans instead of winged-tip leather shoes. You don't wear a suit. You wear simple charcoal grey pants, with a 3-inch slit on the inseam to make a boot cut. You wear a black long-sleeve t-shirt instead of a shirt and tie. You are unshaven, with long hair. You arrive when you want. You take breaks when you want. You leave when you want. There's no controlling you. And why do we leave you alone? Because you perform your duties with seriousness and intensity, as though something inside you refuses to fail, even at work you find meaningless. You don't play the game. You seek to live boldly and purposefully. You intimidate people because you remind them that they are not living boldly and purposefully. They are seeking comfort and security…two things that, I gather, you find contemptible."

My God, I thought, I did not have this awareness. By his mentoring he was helping me see the disconnect between my inner nature and my outer nature, and the relationship between the state of my soul and the state of reality I found myself in. I just sat there in silence. How could I not see this? After a minute of silence, he spoke.

Mentor: How is your journey with Christ?

Warrior: Good God, he had moral courage, to ask such a question amidst a performance review.

Guardian: The question sent me into a deeper contemplative silence. I had not meditated, contemplated, or prayed for a long time. It seemed the question had awakened me from a dream. I saw the meaninglessness of my escapades in Europe. I saw how as a Marine I compartmentalized the spiritual side of being, as I focused singularly on the demands of leading. In this cross-examination, I learned how truly I had gone astray, and how long I had been astray. Straying from truth's path resulted in this condition of soul. Only by returning to the true path would I find the freedom I sought.

Warrior: Go on.

Guardian: I've not had a walk with Christ for quite some time.

Mentor: Have you been to church?

Guardian: No.

Mentor: You carry a rosary, but do not use it? I noticed it almost falling out of your pocket.

Guardian: I use it. I pray the "Hail Mary" and "Our Father" when I'm about to explode in frustration during our meetings.

Mentor: Do you read sacred scripture?

Guardian: Not currently.

Mentor: Do you pray?

Guardian: No.

Mentor: Do you contemplate the principles of truth?

Guardian: No.

Mentor: Do you not see the true source of your despondency?

Warrior: He knew, lo and behold, you had gone astray! My God, the beauty of truth.

Mentor: You are in bondage because you keep seeking freedom outside of yourself. You seek metaphysical freedom. It is best for you to return to the simple practices that lead to liberation's freedom.

Guardian: What do you recommend?

Mentor: Look out your window, to the right. What do you see?

Guardian: A beautiful cathedral.

Mentor: It is beautiful. Let us, each day, attend Holy Mass, and spend time in meditation, prayer, and contemplation. Just test the practices and see if they help reorder your soul.

Guardian: And he was right. I had become attached and enslaved to external measures. I needed to clear out my interior nature. The first time I set foot in the cathedral and kneeled to pray, the rush of discomfort led to a torrent of tears in purification. I returned to the light and the truth. I started to feel light again.

Warrior: This is the period right before you moved to the West Coast?

Guardian: Yes.

Warrior: Wild. You knew, but you could not convert knowing into being. You continued to experience a wide range of highs and lows before you finally learned to rest inwardly.

Guardian: Yes. What is the significance of sharing these lessons with our students?

Warrior: To guide them to transcend the internal pressures of the ego-body-octagon to be perfect. To teach them the way of perfection as the cycle of being and becoming, a cycle of limitlessness. To teach them how to learn from mistakes as lessons of experience. To prepare them for life's greatest teachable moments—the trials, the hardships, the mistakes, the failures and the wreckage.

Guardian: Yes. This means that it is our nature, as imperfect beings, to learn from the cycles of being and becoming. Our aim is to guide students to learn, first, from our mistakes, with the hope that they will sidestep character mistakes because we've trained them in the practices of virtues. Second, when they do make mistakes, in character and skill, they will have the practices to recover and grow stronger through them, not in spite of them. Third, the hope is that the training will make the challenges of living seem simple, because they have learned to unite virtue and excellence to guide their actions.

Warrior: And why do we stress mediation and contemplation?

Guardian: We cannot give to our students what they and we seek most, wisdom's light and truth.

Warrior: Which is why we teach students to take a hard look within—the way to self-knowledge.

Guardian: Yes. We are guides, but they must do the work to strike the powers of their souls with the swords of meditation and contemplation.

Warrior: Can you explain?

Guardian: The Mentor used dialogue to awaken me from my sleep, after I had gone astray. But to reorder the soul, to get to the innermost nature of being, only meditation and contemplation could provide the bridge for light and truth to pour in.

For a few months, I attended Holy Mass every single day. I needed the structure. I needed to remember the basic practices of prayer and meditation. After Mass, I would spend another 30 minutes contemplating a passage from Psalms or Proverbs. And then it happened.

Warrior: What happened?

Guardian: The anguish from deep within, from my ignorance, from my lack of understanding, erupted. I truly experienced the depths of separation from truth. I cried out to God for wisdom's guidance. I began to weep. My nose began to run. I had finally broken open.

In that moment, I entered into a state of complete peace—a state free from conditioned existence. It seemed that God lifted my soul out of my body, to let me experience eternal existence. I don't know how long it lasted, but when I came out of that state, still kneeling, I thought, this is the state we go to at death. Without body, and with a freedom of being.

Caussade mentors us here–

> No matter what troubles, unhappiness, worries, upsets, doubts, and needs harass souls who have lost confidence in their own powers, they can all be overcome by the marvelous hidden and unknown powers of the divine action.[50]

At that moment of divine action, I heard the call to seek truth and the call to develop leaders. I've been listening to these two calls for 20 years. A week later, I set in motion the activities to head west.

---

[50] Jean-Pierre De Caussade, *Abandonment to Divine Providence.*

Warrior: And yet, even though you heard the call, it took another decade to make it manifest, to convert the calling into a vocation, to turn the concept into concrete actions.

Guardian: Yes. This is the critical point for our students. They need the patience and endurance to continue until the calling is made manifest. It may take 10–20 years, but if it is a calling, they will arrive. Do you understand?

Warrior: Yes. And some may arrive at the calling sooner than others.

Guardian: Yes. That is why each student needs to learn to be self-correcting as he carves out his own river of being.

Warrior: And how do you prove this?

Guardian: You don't. It must be discovered in each soul, by the techniques and disciplines of our art.

Warrior: I know of the techniques. What are the disciplines?

Guardian: For truth-seekers on the ascent to truth, Merton recommends a few disciplines. These disciplines are the practices–

> The Disciplines of Contemplation[51]
>
> 1. Recollection
> 2. Meditation
> 3. Prayer
> 4. Study
> 5. Mortification of the Desires
> 6. Measure of Solitude
> 7. Measure of Retirement

Warrior: And these disciplines strike our soul, to train the soul's powers of will and intelligence to become virtuous?

Guardian: Look closely at these disciplines. Have we not been practicing them the entire time?

Warrior: Yes. All but prayer.

Guardian: You still don't see. We have been praying. Our way of being, on this metaphysical quest, has been our life as a prayer, a prayer to know wisdom's light of truth.

---

[51] Thomas Merton, *The Ascent to Truth*.

Merton mentors–

> When faith opens out into a deep spiritual understanding and advances beyond the range of concepts into a darkness which can only be enlightened by the fire of love, man truly begins to know God in the only way that can satisfy his soul.[52]

Warrior: Maybe for you, but not for me. I am agnostic at best.

Guardian: But now do you see with more wisdom?

Warrior: Yes.

Guardian: Do you see with more light?

Warrior: Yes.

Guardian: Do you see with more truth?

Warrior: Yes.

Guardian: Then do not get hung up and distracted by the theological concepts and proofs of God. We are after light, truth, and wisdom as gifts—gifts that we receive by the courage to seek truth.

Tell me, this activity, to seek truth, to seek wisdom, what term do you use for this activity?

Warrior: Contemplation.

Guardian: And contemplation is an activity to penetrate past the surface of things, to reach the depths and essence of a thing?

Warrior: Yes.

Guardian: And contemplation demands that we strike the powers of our will and intelligence, to awaken the wisdom-faculty, the discerning powers to make the depths unhidden, to make the unknown knowable?

Warrior: Yes.

Guardian: And what is another term for this ability to see the intelligible truths that remain hidden from sense-perception?

Warrior: Good God! Another name for contemplation is prayer?

Guardian: Yes.

---

[52] Thomas Merton, *The Ascent to Truth*.

410

Warrior: But not the prayer of petition. We are not seeking to bend light and truth for some physical advantage.

Guardian: True.

Warrior: Now I remember. It's been a long time since I've studied the contemplative sciences and the metaphysical sciences. But I did, long ago, before the burdens of war required total devotion to make missions.

Huxley mentors–

> The word "prayer" is applied to at least four distinct procedures–petition, intercession, adoration, contemplation…. Contemplation is that condition of alert passivity, in which the soul lays itself open to the divine Ground within and without, the immanent and the transcendent Godhead.[53]

Guardian: Do you see it now?

Warrior: I see it now.

Guardian: I see life as a living prayer for truth-seekers, in the activity of dialogue, meditation and contemplation. That is what I meant by becoming receivers and givers of light and truth. On this quest, we needed to become receptive. Have we become receptive?

Warrior: Yes.

Guardian: And how did we become receptive?

Warrior: By contemplation—one kind of prayer.

Guardian: Now do you see the value of our techniques?

Warrior: Yes.

Guardian: Do you see why terms matter? Why contemplation is distinguished from other forms of prayer?

Warrior: Yes.

Guardian: Do you see that not all of our contemplative acts are prayerful acts?

Warrior: Yes. It's how we direct the soul's will and intelligence.

Guardian: Do you see how there's a progression to using our swords of truth?

Warrior: Yes. My concern has been resolved.

_____

[53] Aldous Huxley, *The Perennial Philosophy*.

Guardian: How?

Warrior: On this quest, I have been concerned by your approach because it seems religious and theistic.

Guardian: I hunt for truth, wherever it leads. And now?

Warrior: I see you are a practitioner of wisdom. I see our art as the practice of wisdom as prudence, the art of truth-disclosing that practical judgment demands.

I see we can use these techniques in the study of knowledge and science, in the study of character and leadership. You live the way of the contemplative. I live the way of the scientist. We are united in the same calling, to develop leaders. We are united in the same techniques, to wield light and truth. As Plato and Aristotle needed one another to discover the truth of the good, we need one another to discover the truth of leading.

Guardian: Yes. And as truth-seekers, are we now prepared to guide and teach yet-to-be leaders?

Warrior: Yes.

Guardian: And in our art, we are hunters—we hunt for leadership genius in the soul?

Warrior: Yes.

Guardian: And to liberate the soul, we must teach students the metaphysical swords of dialogue, meditation, and contemplation?

Warrior: Yes.

Guardian: Is our art a war?

Warrior: Yes.

Guardian: Is our art violent?

Warrior: Yes.

Guardian: How is our art violent?

Warrior: The liberation of metaphysical freedom is a violent and rugged path, to become the known truth, to make virtue, knowledge, and excellence an extension of being.

Heidegger mentors–

> The transition to what is now unhidden happens with force. Liberation, in the sense of turning around towards the light of the sun, is violent. Attaining what is now unhidden involves violence, thus resistance, such that the one to

be freed is forced up a rugged path. The ascent demands work and exertion, causing strain and suffering.

The genuine liberation does not only depend on an act of violence, but requires persistence and courage to endure the individual adaptation to the light, the strident courage that can also wait, that is not deterred by reversals, that knows that, in all genuine becoming and growing, no stage can be leapt over, that empty busy-ness is just as useless and disastrous as blind enthusiasm.[54]

Guardian: And this is why most souls fail to become liberated?

Warrior: Yes. The don't trust the guides, nor do they follow the guides on the ascent that leads to freedom.

Guardian: And we lead our students, as guides, up this liberating ascent? Teaching them how to overcome their imperfection by the cycle of being and becoming?

Warrior: Yes. I am now concerned. Where do we find souls with the courage to train this way? To trust us and follow our lead?

Guardian: They will find us. We do not need to find them.

Warrior: How?

Guardian: We have left the metaphysical footprint on this quest. A courageous and seeking soul will follow the imprints we left.

Warrior: How is this possible?

Guardian: Truth claims its own.

Warrior: I see the summit.

Guardian: What do you see?

Warrior: All and Nothing.

Guardian: And in that void what do you see?

Warrior: Now I see that, as a being, I am in the unfathomable abyss, where–

The Genuine liberation of man [turns] to the primordial light.[55]

Guardian: You see the depths and heights of the summit as the summit of one's being.

---

[54] Martin Heidegger, *The Essence of Truth*.
[55] Martin Heidegger, *The Essence of Truth*.

Warrior: I see and I know.

Guardian: Good. Let us sit in an easeful posture and contemplate the primordial light—the light that awakens the primordial powers of the soul's will and intelligence as the wisdom-faculty.

Warrior: All this exertion, to learn to become the wisdom of the wisdom literature, as a fact of beinghood.

Guardian: Yes. Let us be still. Let us be silent.

Warrior: So be it.

CHAPTER TWELVE
NEW BEGINNINGS

Guardian: Now it is clear. Let us move. We are being invited upward to complete this quest. Do you see the final summit?

Warrior: No. What do you see?

Guardian: Warrior, look again with your wisdom-faculty. What do you see?

Warrior: Now it's clear. We're at the peak. I see an inscription carved in the stones.

Guardian: Read the ethos.

Warrior: It is written–

> A [leader] does not abide within his tent while his men bleed and die upon the field. A [leader] does not dine while his men go hungry, nor sleep when they stand at watch upon the wall. A [leader] does not command his men's loyalty through fear nor purchase it with gold; he earns their love by the sweat of his own back and the pains he endures for their sake. That which comprises the harshest burden, a [leader] lifts first and sets down last. A [leader] does not require service of those he leads but provides it to them. He serves them, not they him. A leader [does] not expend his substance to enslave men, but by his conduct and example makes them free.[1]

You've seen this ethos before?

Guardian: Yes.

Warrior: How do we define the term "ethos"?

Guardian: Aristotle mentors–

> Character (ethos): A stable condition of the soul that makes someone apt to choose in a consistent way…active conditions determined by deliberate choices to form oneself in particular ways…character involves taking hold of things toward which one has been passive, and forming the rational and irrational parts of the soul into a single whole.[2]

---

[1] Steven Pressfield, *Gates of Fire*, I've replaced "king" with "leader."
[2] Aristotle, *Nicomachean Ethics*, Sachs translation, Glossary definition–character (ethos).

Warrior: And this is why you sought to know the nature of truth and the essence of light. Light and truth are what set men free. In our art, the first freedom is our metaphysical freedom, and the first obstacle to overcome is metaphysical bondage.

Guardian: Yes. This is what makes our leaders trustworthy. Do you see where the summit's gateway leads us?

Warrior: Yes. At the peak, I see the architecture to develop leaders in our art. I see the depths and heights of our three aims–

1. Become virtuous.
2. Seek truth.
3. Make virtue, excellence, and wisdom an extension of being.

Guardian: And why do you see it?

Warrior: On this quest, I've united knowing and being to experience.

Guardian: Then, it is done. At this peak, let us sit in an easeful posture and contemplate wisdom's light of truth

Warrior: It is done?

Guardian: It is done, but it is not finished. Soon we must begin again.

Warrior: What must begin again?

Guardian: Another quest.

Warrior: Another quest?

Guardian: Yes. Now we turn to teach a worthy student.

Warrior: Now? Is there no rest?

Guardian: Did we not travel at a leisurely pace? Were you ever fatigued on this journey?

Warrior: We did, and I never fatigue, and yet the quest felt demanding on my mind and will.

Guardian: Truth is demanding—the beautiful burden.

> Take my yoke upon you, and learn from me, for I am gentle and meek in heart, and you will find rest for your souls. For my yoke is pleasant and my burden is light.[3]

---

[3] The Holy Bible, *Book of Matthew 11.29-30*, Lamsa Translation.

We are always at rest now, resting inwardly as we move with light and truth, so the wisdom-faculty can discern and lead us, from truth to truth, in a never-ending cycle of being and becoming.

Warrior: Are we ready? To rest inwardly and act truthfully?

Guardian: Yes. Do you trust your worthiness to teach a worthy student?

Warrior: Yes.

Guardian: Then we are ready.

Warrior: How do you know we're ready?

Guardian: Before this quest, I needed two elements integrated before we initiated this teaching art—I needed a warrior to transform to a guardian, and I needed a worthy student to find us.

Warrior: Why did you need another teacher? Why did you not begin this quest with a worthy student?

Guardian: I needed a trustworthy soul to make me give an account. I'm more of an artist, a mystical writer and thinker, and I needed a scientific mind to document where I explored and what I discovered, and what I intended to teach. You provided this measure of accountability.

I also trust the trinity concept of teaching.

Warrior: The trinity concept of teaching?

Guardian: Yes. On this quest, we had the Warrior, the Guardian, and the mentors (the wisdom and sacred canons). The trinity concept is what propelled us forward, by creating a dynamic cycle of being and becoming, as we sought the highest heights and the deepest depths. Did you not notice, our abilities, not our aims, are what opened up further growth? This is the experience of learning at a natural pace, based upon our own abilities. We did not force the learning; we learned first, then we understood, then we moved forward, moment by moment on this quest. This style of learning is how one strips the ego of desire to learn and desire to know.

Saint John of the Cross mentors here–

> To come to the knowledge of all, desire the knowledge of nothing.[4]

Warrior: Which is why, even in learning, we practice detachment, to overcome the bondage of desire. This is the true reason for our techniques—to make us trustworthy, and to know

---

[4] Saint John of the Cross, *The Collected Works*.

and love truth, a quality of unconditional love. I see how meditation, contemplation, and dialogue are the techniques to overcome the ego-body-octagon. They make us detached and unconditional beings, to be receivers and givers of wisdom's light of truth.

Guardian: Yes. The trinity concept is the beautiful art of teaching and leading souls. This model aims to teach teachers and students how to learn by the soul's powers in a rhythmic, dynamic, and unique relationship between each soul-student and her receptivity to light and truth. The teacher is there to create the architecture that is best suited to each student. Remember, in our art the underlying fabric is a relation, a bond, that unites teachers and students to truth and light.

Warrior: And because our art is about the spiritual formation of the student, we have two teachers for every one student, to create the trinity concept in actuality?

Guardian: Yes. That is what our art demands. That is what I wanted in my formative years. And I did have that for the briefest of time.

Warrior: How?

Guardian: My first guardians were peers.

The first, a warrior and strategist. From him I learned the power of physical strength and the power of mental strength. His teachings leaned heavily on Musashi (way of the sword), Lycurgus (way of the warrior), and Sun Tzu (way of the strategist). The virtues I learned were fortitude, loyalty and temperance. I learned the light and truth of inner sight (*coup d'oeil*) and determination (*coup d'esprit*). I learned I needed to strengthen my power of will and my power of mind.

The second, a sage and adventurer. From him I learned the power of logic, the power of reason, and the power of intelligence to combat the ways of the leviathan-cube. His teachings leaned heavily on Plato (way of truth-seeking), Aristotle (way of practical judgment), and Nietzsche (way of overcoming). The virtues I learned were justice, discernment, and practical judgment. I learned the light and truth of reason and intuition. I learned I needed to strengthen my power of intelligence (uniting reason and intuition).

The third, a saint and mathematician. From him I learned the power of calculation, the power of contemplation, the power of the spiritual ascent, and the power of seeking God revealed as light and truth. His teaching leaned heavily on Saint Thomas Aquinas (demonstrator of truth) and Saint John of the Cross (practitioner of wisdom). The virtues I learned were humility, detachment, charity, hope, faith and wisdom. I learned the light and truth of soul and spirit. I learned I needed to become receptive to the gift of wisdom's light of truth by purification.

Warrior: At one period in your life, you had three teachers focused on your development?

Guardian: Yes. But we did not train and study together. I sought the teachings of each one, independent of the others. I experienced tremendous growth by their mentoring and by their ruthless and unapologetic feedback, the feedback that stings, the feedback that few have the courage to provide to students. And few students have the courage to receive this feedback; it requires both teacher and student to practice the virtue of fortitude as moral courage.

Most importantly, I learned that these teachers were each incomplete. To become complete, I sought to integrate the teachings of all three.

> By integrating these teachings, I discovered the heart of leadership—wisdom's light of truth.

Warrior: How do we actualize the trinity concept in our teaching methods?

Guardian: First, I need you and the student to join me to make the trinity. Second, the trinity provides three perspectives, three points of view, and three levels of dynamic feedback. Third, by colliding our perspectives, we will learn to practice truth-seeking principles. Fourth, because of the primacy of feedback, you will be on point to give both the student and me ruthless feedback. When the student observes how I respond to your feedback, he will learn to embrace feedback instead of fearing it. The feedback will help the student and me unite light and truth by the dynamics of friendship, knowledge, excellence, and wisdom.

Warrior: And the reason for the intensity and intimacy of a trinity teaching model?

Guardian: First, to eradicate the ego's illusion of vulnerability.[5] With trusted friends who manage their boundaries, the emotion of vulnerability does not even come to light. But most of us do not have true friends, so the emotion of vulnerability builds a metaphysical armor around our emotional nature, our intellectual nature and our physical nature. Then, instead of speaking freely and cultivating the spirit of truth by dialogue, we suppress our true thinking and use language to protect and separate ourselves from truth, instead of uniting with it. We need one another to seek the truth and make it unhidden by truth-disclosing practices. To transcend all these obstacles and challenges, we build a trinity structure that is indefatigable, as we aim to make our art an extension of being. Remember that as teachers we will be challenged more than the student.

Warrior: I can't help but be reminded of the writings of Saint Paul in Ephesians, as the antidote to the emotion of vulnerability and the bondage of the ego. Saint Paul says–

> From henceforth, my brethren, be strong in our Lord and in the power of his might. Put on the whole armor of God, that you may be able to stand against the wiles of the devil. For your conflict is not only with flesh and blood, but also with the angels, and with powers, with the rulers of this world of

---

[5] O.E.D. definition of vulnerability–Able to be wounded; (of a person) able to be physically or emotionally hurt; liable to damage or harm, esp. from aggression or attack, assailable.

darkness, and with the evil spirits under the heavens. Therefore, put on the whole armor of God, that you may be able to meet the evil one and being prepared you shall prevail. Arise, therefore, gird your loins with truth and put on the breastplate of righteousness; And have your feet shod with the preparation of the gospel of peace; Together with these, take for yourselves the shield of faith, for with it you shall be able to quench all the flaming darts of the wicked. Put on the helmet of salvation and take the sword of Spirit, which is the word of God; And pray always, will all prayer and supplication for all the saints. And for me also, that words may be given to me as soon as I open my mouth, so that I may boldly preach the mystery of the gospel, for which I am a messenger in chains, that I may speak openly about it, as I ought to speak.[6]

As a warrior, I see the swords and the armor have a dual purpose. One purpose is to unite friends in truth; the other is to combat the adversary. The challenge is to know how to use these swords and armor for their dual aims—one aim leads to metaphysical freedom; one aim leads to metaphysical bondage.

Guardian: To clarify, you mean that with our adversaries, we use these weapons to render them powerless (bondage) and with our leaders, we use them to make them powerful (freedom).

Warrior: Yes. The whole armor of a leader is the development and union of virtue (character), excellence (skill) and wisdom (knowledge). The techniques (dialogue, meditation, and contemplation) are the swords of truth. The virtues (humility, detachment, fortitude, justice, temperance, wisdom, faith, hope, love) are the swords of light. The wisdom and sacred canons (knowledge) are the swords of spirit. Finally I can see the aims of this art. I see how to train students and combat adversaries.

Guardian: Has the veil been lifted?

Warrior: Yes. I see the two underlying dynamics governing the human being—one that leads to freedom, one that leads to bondage.

Guardian: Then it is done.

Warrior. It is done.

Guardian: And now?

Warrior: Now we devote ourselves, as teachers and as servants, to worthy students.

Guardian: Let us begin–

---

[6] The Holy Bible, Lamsa Translation.

What is more demanding? To be a teacher leading a student on a metaphysical quest, or to be a student being led by a teacher on a metaphysical quest?

Warrior: To be a teacher.

Guardian: Why?

Warrior: The teacher creates the structure for the student to know and love the light and truth. We lead their spiritual formation. We guide them to make their character, excellence, and wisdom powerful. We train them to make their faculties (powers of being) sharp, discerning, and developed. In our art, we lead the soul to metaphysical freedom.

Guardian: Yes. The beautiful burden of true teachers, the true leaders.

Do you understand, the burdens you are about to shoulder?

Warrior: The burden to create the structure, the container, for light and truth to guide the student?

Guardian: Yes. The demands on you, as the third point, are to discern what you are seeing and to provide feedback that leads to greater depths and heights.

Warrior: I'll be responsible to discern and to disclose truths that are hidden from students and you?

Guardian: Yes. There is much subtlety in this art of the objective observer, monitoring the dynamics between teacher, student, knowledge, skill, light, and truth. By your contemplative abilities, you need to discern hidden truths that both the student and I need to see. Do you understand?

Warrior: I understand. You are on point and you need a "third point" to monitor the progression of the student in relation to you, as a being and as a teacher, and in relation to knowledge and skill.

Guardian: Yes, as on this quest, I need you to document what you witness to keep a record—a record that we can study and build from as we progress in our teaching art. The reason why I need you as the observer is that the student and the teacher will be living and moving in the unknown. Our subjective experience will be taking a thrashing as we form our souls in friendship with one another and in friendship with the work. You need to catch us if we fall into a crevasse or veer off course. By my estimation, you have the key responsibility as a guardian, to watch over the dynamics of teaching and learning between the student and teacher.

Warrior: I understand. What now?

Guardian: Remember when I said, we will not leave the depths of our being nor the heights of our knowledge, but will remain here and wait?

Warrior: Yes. Do you mean, we are to wait here for the student, the yet-to-be leader, to find us?

Guardian: Yes.

Warrior: Did you plan this from the start?

Guardian: Yes.

Warrior: How did you know? How did you trust?

Guardian: As we headed out on a metaphysical expedition, we left a trail for a certain kind of human being to follow after us.

Warrior: What?

Guardian: We left a trail of markers at every point, similar to creating a mountain path, for others to follow. A discerning person will see the path, for it is a reflection of the knowledge and patterns we discovered on our expedition.

Warrior: How is this possible?

Guardian: Some truths are beyond direct perception. Some truths are beyond empirical verification. Some truths are beyond the reasoning mind—faith-infused reasoning will reveal itself to a discerning mind. In this light, some truths must be realized.

Warrior: What must we do?

Guardian: Patiently wait.

Warrior: For how long?

Guardian: There is no time in the eternal waters, in the abyss of consciousness. Let us take an easeful posture and meditate on the journey we have taken, viewing it from the end to the beginning instead of the beginning to the end.

Warrior: Studying the quest, in reverse order?

Guardian: Yes. Let us meditate and contemplate, in reverse order, how we got here. Now there is very little we need to do. We've exercised our potencies and have been led to a level of understanding that now makes us wait for a student with the right nature and character to find us.

Warrior: I'm too action-oriented to sit here and wait.

Guardian: Close your eyes, and return to the depths. The soul exerts her powers in stillness. Focus on this activity to reign in the drive to act, to do something. Instead, focus on your beinghood.

Warrior: I returned to the depths. Again, and again, I need to remember how the wisdom-faculty awakens in stillness when my being rests inwardly. I see nothing. What are you seeing?

Guardian: Let your wisdom-faculty learn to see the intelligible images that come before your mind. Let them reveal themselves. Inner sight is a different kind of sight, more like knowing than seeing.

Warrior: I am seeing a continuity and integration of human nature, as a cycle of being and becoming, always moving from being, as the moral and the intellectual faculties are continually made sharp, discerning and developed. I see this as the proper aim of our art. The ways of being, the ways of callings, the ways of vocations, are all secondary in nature. I see the growth, the true growth, of the human being as the most important and critical aspect in our art. We seek a student who is inherently not interested in winning and achievement, but who is inherently interested in truth.

Guardian: You see correctly. You will know when a true student appears. Saint John of the Cross Mentors–

> To lose always and let everyone else win is a trait of valiant souls, generous
> spirits, and unselfish hearts; it is their manner to give rather than receive even
> to the extent of giving themselves.[7]

Warrior: Good God! If not for this expedition, I would have thought you insane for seeking such a nature, but know that I now see that this nature is fitted to learn and teach our art.

Guardian: Why?

Warrior: Because we, our teachers and our students, seek a harmony of wills, directing our desires toward truth and light, to share in the truth and light, and to live according to what we learn from the truth and light. I see how, in our art, we need to flush out the egotists and the narcissists. I've never seen with the clarity that I do now—why you demand a certain character, even if that character lacks talents.

Guardian: Why?

Warrior: There is no winning in our art. There is only truth and ignorance.

Goethe mentors–

---

[7] Saint John of the Cross, *The Sayings of Light and Love*.

There is nothing more frightful than ignorance in action.[8]

Our goal is to eradicate ignorance and disclose truth. In our training, I learned that our intelligence can come into an aspect of the truth, and that our will needs the courage to act on that truth. Our art aims not to win, but to serve the spiritual and intellectual needs of humanity. Metaphysical freedom is our aim, for all human beings. Leaders must condition themselves by exercising their faculties to awaken the potencies that lead to this freedom.

Guardian: You see correctly. That is why we must wait. Only a certain kind of character would follow the patterns and markers we left, as we deepened our being and heightened our understanding. Only a yet-to-be leader who has the mind and will to follow in pursuit will be open and receptive to learn this art. And the path we left will serve as the foundation for a student's spiritual formation. Our journey prepared the foundation.

Warrior: Your intuition is leading you to this conclusion? You can have no proof because you've never done this before.

Guardian: Yes. We live in the realm of probable truths, of inferences, that cannot be claimed by empirical facts. That is why I wield the virtue of faith, so my intelligence will give substance to what is not yet seen. I have faith that a leader will find us, just as I had faith in you, to journey on this quest, just as I had the faith to listen to the calling and make it manifest in reality. We need faith because there is no certainty of victory in leading.

Writer: Dear Reader, it is true, a yet-to-be leader has been pursuing the Warrior and Guardian for this entire quest. At last, the yet-to-be leader is about to reach them. When this takes place, a new metaphysical quest will begin. Both the student and the teachers will undergo rigorous training and trials. Both student and teachers shoulder a burden, but they are different burdens. The student's burden is to endure the training not knowing if he will be chosen to lead; the teacher's burden is to endure the training, not knowing if he can teach this art to the student. Both need one another, to actualize a probable truth—teaching leaders. The student and teacher either succeed together or fail together. Such is the nature of this art, when two beings of goodwill seek to know truth and light and wield it. The teacher wields the swords in the act of teaching; the student wields the swords it in the act of learning. If they succeed, the student, as his final test, will face an adversary. Success leads to metaphysical freedom; failure leads to metaphysical bondage. Failure will prove this is no art at all, but only a ghost, a fiction, an image with no merit or truth in objective reality. But success will prove the truth, merit, and importance of this art.

Guardian: Rest inwardly, brother. I hear the leader coming. Follow my lead.

Leader: Guardian is that you? Or it this another pattern or marker that you left?

---

[8] Arthur Kruger, *Modern Debate–Its Logic and Strategy*, Goethe quoted in book.

Guardian: It is us. You have reached the summit.

Warrior: You knew he would be in pursuit?

Guardian: Yes. I felt his soul's presence the entire time.

Leader: It's strange. I've been following you alone for so long, but I've been studying your markings and patterns and the trail you left, and I feel like I've never been alone or without your guidance the entire time.

Guardian: Why is that?

Leader: We are never alone. Truth and light and wisdom never leave us. I wasn't prepared to understand the wisdom literature that you used for mentoring and guidance. But your dialogue and commentary on the depths and heights, and your personal examples, I think, served to mentor and guide me the entire time. And most importantly, they inspired me to follow in pursuit, any time I felt despondency.

Guardian: Wisdom speaks in you Leader. Our quest aimed to prepare the way for you.

Leader: How did you know I was en route following you?

Guardian: I must be honest. To both you and the Warrior.

Warrior: What? Have you not been honest? You spoke of light and truth the entire time.

Guardian: Do you know that being truthful sometimes means to withhold truths until others are ready to receive them?

Warrior: What? What about ruthless and unapologetic feedback?

Guardian: When the receiver is ready, yes. When the receiver is not ready, no.

Warrior: What must you share now that you did not share before?

Guardian: The Leader's daemon, his genius, his God-within, speaks, and I hear it speak. Light and truth know no time and distance. If he were not on our trail, I would have still heard. The silence and the stillness speak, if we listen.

Warrior: Then, did you hear my daemon speak? And is that why you invited me on this quest?

Guardian: Yes.

Warrior: And when consciousness expands and is in harmony, when souls are in correspondence, there is a convergence, a harmony, a union of wills and spirit?

Guardian: Yes.

Warrior: And it follows that truth and light disclose themselves?

Guardian: Yes.

Leader: I don't follow.

Guardian: Yes, you do. You know intuitively and tacitly what you do yet not understand logically and empirically. The proof is that you followed in pursuit. The daemon, the god-within, spoke and you listened.

Let me ask, why did you follow?

Leader: I'm seeking something deeper and more meaningful. I'm seeking a purpose and a mission and a challenge that takes all of my being. I heard from an instructor that you had left the academy in search of the truth about teaching leadership, and I want someone to teach me.

I am lost. I don't trust my teachers or admire them. I don't trust my friends. It seems everyone is trying to sell something, be it physical or spiritual. It seems everyone is cloaking their true being in a marketing character, in an image. I see right through the façade, the faking-Facebook image, the sin of a brand image, the sin of flattery. I want to live truthfully. I want to speak truthfully. I want to serve truthfully. I don't want to gain or control by preying on the weakness and desperation of other souls. I hate what I see. Everyone seems to be putting on an image, an image that I have always seen as untrue, as fake.

Warrior: It's impressive, your self-awareness.

Leader: It seems, when I look at people, that they are somehow asleep while they are awake. And if I notice they are actually asleep but seem to be awake, how do I know if I don't suffer the same sleeping wakefulness? I want to be awakened. Somehow, I know I'm not awakened. I know I am asleep. Or maybe I'm awake but still veiled in darkness. I don't understand what is going on. I don't fit in. I don't resonate with the way most people live. I think it's meaningless. I don't want a job; I want adventure. No, on this quest I learned I wanted a calling and a vocation. But I'm not sure how to discover it. I've travelled to dozens of countries and have gone on dozens of physical adventures. I keep getting the sense that these travels and adventures have turned into a kind of perennial distraction. Something is still missing. I feel incomplete. I don't feel whole. Not knowing and desiring to know sent me on the pursuit of you.

Guardian: What is the quality that drove you to pursue us?

Leader: The desire for truth.

Guardian: Holy desire?

Leaders: Maybe, I don't know.

On the hunt, when I reached each marker, each pitch, on the ascent, I experienced moments of intense exhilaration. That is what I wanted, the experience of knowing, the vigorousness of an experience, the inner expansion of the heights and depths of being. That is what I truly sought, the visceral and direct experience of the potential actualizing itself. I could experience and witness it taking place in my being. It is difficult to speak with language of the experience, but that is what I sought and that is what beckoned me onward. The experience of light and truth awakened in my being, and that is what I wanted.

Guardian: And what do we call that kind of experience?

Leader: Peak experiences of metaphysical freedom?

Guardian: Yes.

Leader: As I continued to ascend, the frustration turned into a longing. As I had deeper experiences, the longing turned into loving, and I learned I love the pursuit of truth.

As I progressed, I become more serene and focused as my senses and spirit heightened in awareness and understanding. I experience a state of freedom by devoting all my energy and concentration to the pursuit of truth, as I followed the markings you left.

The more I journeyed, I learned the freedom of resting inwardly, to awaken the powers of soul. I experienced a lightness of being. I learned how the emotions and the mind, if they are not purified, can create a heaviness of being. I'm after a lightness of being; I'm after a truthfulness of being. I needed both. And this ascent gave me the experiences I sought.

Even though I had no idea what was going on, I had the visceral experience. And that is what mattered most—the experience of something deeper and truer occurring in my being. It was the direct experience that fueled me, to follow the pathless path that you left. The experience gave me hope that I'd be led to meet you. I did not know where it would lead; I just kept going, because you kept going.

Guardian: You had direct experiences because the pathless path demanded virtuous acting, knowing and willing. What virtues did you display on the ascent?

Leader: Fortitude and faith. Wait—is it by the power of soul that the experience of virtue is the result of my search for freedom?

Guardian: Yes.

Leader: Are you saying that what I love is the experience of becoming virtuous?

Guardian: Yes, that is what I'm saying. Continue your reflection. What else did you experience?

Leader: I loved the experience of my intelligence and will being united and strengthened with one aim on this endeavor—not to quit until I reached you. I learned the freedom of focus and concentration as one-pointedness of mind in one endeavor.

Guardian: What is this direct experience?

Leader: The virtues of self-discipline and concentration. I love the experience of these virtues. I had to wield self-discipline. No one outside my being commanded my will and intelligence to make me pursue you. I had to command my will and intelligence at every moment on this path.

Guardian: And when you say, "pursue you," do you know what you are really saying?

Leader: I don't follow.

Guardian: It is not true that you were following the Warrior and the Guardian.

Leader: Yes, it is true. My goal was to reach you, and I followed in pursuit on the trail you left.

Guardian: Can I give you feedback?

Leader: Yes, lay it on me.

Guardian: You did not follow us.

Leader: If I did not follow you, what did I follow?

Guardian: What you sought.

Leader: Ah. Metaphysical freedom. Are you saying that I knew my bondage and I sought freedom?

Guardian: Yes. You never sought us. You sought light and truth. Light and truth left the markers and created the path. The Warrior and I are insignificant to your quest; we are simply the means to the ends you seek. What are the ends you seek?

Leader: I seek truth.

Guardian: And in seeking truth, what do you need?

Leader: Trustworthy teachers.

Guardian: Then what is the correct answer to the question, "what did you follow?"

Leader: I followed the truth's lead, as you followed the truth's lead.

Guardian: Yes. You see correctly.

Leader: Then is it correct to say, that I need teachers to guide me to seek and know truth?

Guardian: Yes. And where are the first and last teachers to guide you?

Leader: The wisdom and sacred canons.

Guardian: Yes. Where does this lead you?

Leader: To leap from the teachings and teachers, to know, experientially, viscerally, wisdom's light and truth.

Guardian: Yes. And what reveals itself when this happens?

Leader: Truth as knowing. I will know, because by realization and actualization of the soul's powers I will make contact with light and truth.

Guardian: Yes. And what are the means to actualization and realization?

Leader: Completing the kinetic chain to make truth and light an extension of being, by activating the soul's powers of will, intelligence, and spiritedness. Being as the union of knowing, willing, and acting as one—as complete wholeness.

Guardian: Then do you still need us as teachers?

Leader: Yes.

Guardian: What do you need from us?

Leader: I need mentoring and guidance to learn this art and make it an extension of being.

Guardian: What do you seek?

Leader: I want you to teach me. I no longer seek adventure or achievement. When you shared the concept of metaphysical freedom, that hit my core and awakened a deeper part of my being. I want my being to be awakened. I don't want to be just a guardian and I don't want to be just a warrior; I want to create a new archetype by integrating both of your callings and vocations. By training and studying both of your archetypes, I hope to create an archetype that is already taking shape in my being. I can see it.

Guardian: What do you see?

Leader: I am experiencing fear as I want to speak my mind. But you taught me to speak with courage, so I will try. I love human beings and it kills me that so many suffer and so many have not become their potential, including me. We don't teach human beings to train to perfection. I want to train to perfection, knowing that the way of perfection is a path that never reaches its end or attains its goal. I don't mean the sin of perfectionism. I mean I want to train and test, and fail and recover, and live continually at the edge of my limits, to drive the cycle of being and becoming. I want to learn to master and wield this cycle, which is the means to growth. What this metaphysical quest proved to me is that I love the experience of growing; I love the experience of developing virtues by striking the powers of soul to create them!

The reason I need your guidance is that I first need to learn how to be free. I need to become free of the ego-body-octagon and the bondage of insatiable desires, cravings, wants and feelings. This is why we rest inwardly—to re-order our powers, from desiring what is outside of our being, to desiring the potencies within our being. Then, if I am worthy, I want to lead, as you do, souls on metaphysical quests. I don't see anything more important. I am not interested in anything other than living the contemplative life in the active life of leading.

Guardian: In this light, you seek to unite the active and contemplative ways of being?

Leader: Yes.

Guardian: Who do you plan to teach, if you become a teacher of leaders?

Leader: Everyone.

Warrior: Leader, look around. Who is here?

Leader: The three of us.

Warrior: Who followed you?

Leader: No one. I never thought about that, the implications of no one following with me. I did think it strange, once I got some distance from the surface, that no one else followed in pursuit.

Guardian: What if it's just the three of us. The Warrior. The Guardian. The Leader. Is that enough?

Leader: I don't understand?

Guardian: What if you awaken your wisdom-faculty and the light of truth reveals itself to you? What then?

Leader: I learned from you that if I act like a torch bearer instead of a light bearer, I'll be martyred. The torch bearer tells souls they are ignorant; the light bearer teaches souls to see their own ignorance.

Guardian: Yes. What else?

Leader: Independent of my calling to serve the welfare of humanity, I must train this way.

Guardian: What does this imply?

Leader: That I can still serve others, solely and justly, by being what I am. I need no other activities that involve other human beings. I could be what I am and live any number of vocations.

Guardian: And why is this important?

Leader: I want to remain independent of the wills and judgments of others. Truth does not get rewarded. Image, wealth, and winning get rewarded.

Guardian: And why is this critical?

Leader: In our art, we follow the lead of Saint John of the Cross–

> To lose always and let everyone else win is a trait of valiant souls, generous spirits, and unselfish hearts; it is their manner to give rather than receive even to the extent of giving themselves.[9]

Guardian: In our art, we do not seek winning. We seek truth, and seek to become the truth. This seeking and becoming truth by light is non-stop and non-ending. There is no finish; there is no completion. We are always a work in progress.

Saint Thomas Aquinas mentors us here–

> Every being is perfect insofar as it is realized, and imperfection lies in this, that its potentiality is not realized.[10]

Leader: So be it. I want you to teach me this art. I want to learn this art.

Guardian: So be it. Are you determined to learn? As determined as the Warrior and I are to teach this art?

Leader: I think so.

Warrior: You think so, but you don't know.

Leader: I don't know with certainty. But I am here.

Warrior: Then, learn this—*coup d'oeil* and *coup d'esprit* anchor our every movement of willing, knowing and acting.

Leader: **The courage and determination to follow our inner light no matter where it leads.**

Guardian: Yes. This is the first principle.

---

[9] Saint John of the Cross, *The Sayings of Light and Love*.
[10] Josef Pieper, *Living the Truth*, Saint Thomas quoted.

Leader: I studied every mark you left on the trail.

Guardian: Then shall we begin?

Leader: Yes.

Guardian: As the Warrior and I did, you and I will begin a metaphysical journey.

Leader: I don't want separation. I want to revise the trinity concept.

Guardian: How?

Leader: The three of us, not the two of us, must train and study together. That is what you needed in your formative years, and what I need now. The three of us can begin another metaphysical quest.

Guardian: Warrior, your thoughts?

Warrior: I never wanted to be solely an observer, though, that is how the Guardian commissioned my service. I'm best on the hunt, on the quest.

Guardian: So be it.

We are students, teachers, and advisors to one another. The goal of the leader is to learn this art. The goal of the warrior is to teach this art. The goal of the guardian is to transcend this art. We will serve as anchors to catch one another if we fall in a crevasse or slip on a cliff. We will provide feedback every step of the way, from our unique insights and perspectives. Our challenge is to connect spirit to soul, as we build a relationship with the knowledge and the techniques of this art.

We begin with three central aims–

1. We must learn to make ourselves virtuous.
2. We must learn to seek the truth, disclose the truth, and act on the truth we know.
3. We must learn to make virtue, knowledge, and expertise an extension of our being.

Metaphysical freedom comes from virtue, excellence, and wisdom by way of disciplined skill in the performance of actions. All deeds, all thinking, all loving, being directed as one by the power of the soul.

These are the ends we seek. On the quest, we will learn and master the ways and means to these ends.

I am on point. I will serve as the guide and study how we actualize each of these aims in our being. My purpose is to study and understand with greater depth and breadth how we become one with the knowledge and techniques, and to discover where, when and how our potencies are being awakened and actualized by the training. Warrior, you are on point to document everything you see, hear, know, and experience. Leader, you are here to awaken and actualize your faculties of will, intelligence and spirit.

We will treat each other as brothers. We will never force our will on one another. We seek truth as metaphysical freedom. We are united in this common aim and we will always keep our mind focused on it.

We serve truth.

Leader, you're the reason that we take this quest. Your spiritual formation is the aim of the quest. We are here as guides. Do you understand?

Leader: Yes.

Guardian: What does this mean?

Leader: It means, my search for truth leads this quest; we only progress if I learn and understand. It means that when I'm not clear, we do not move forward. I must build foundations of understanding every step of the way.

Guardian: Yes. To this end, I've created the learning structure that will guide you on your metaphysical quest. The stress on the warrior and the guardian is to continually adapt our teaching methods to the way you most naturally learn. You have the drive and the knowledge; now you seek "knowing" as being. This means that the Warrior and I will see what's coming at you before you see it. You need to trust us that we are leading you in the best methods for you, as a unique individual, to learn this art. We will see what you cannot see, but we will not tell you what we see. The purpose is for you to learn to see and to know. Once you see and know it, we will verify that you have seen correctly. This can be frustrating for a student. Be on guard against the tendency to want us to tell you what we see before you've seen it. We cannot do this. You'll want feedback but you won't be ready for it. We will use silence and stillness and be with you as you explore. To tell you before you've seen is to kill the soul's potential to see.

Let me ask, what kills learning between the teacher and student?

Leader: I'm not sure. The wrong student? The wrong teacher?

Guardian: Suppose we have an ideal teacher and ideal student. What kills the teaching dynamic?

Leader: Lack of trust?

Guardian: Yes.

In your initial reflection, you spoke of trust as something you have struggled with your entire life–

> I don't trust my teachers…. I don't trust my friends.

Leader: Yes.

Guardian: How do we practice trust on this metaphysical journey?

Leader: I can trust you. I can trust the Warrior. And I can trust in my abilities.

Guardian: What does this mean?

Leader: It means I can wield faith and loyalty as virtues. The effect of these virtues is trust. I did not understand this before the quest.

I know that the light and truth in my soul can transform faith into trust by slowly building relationships with the techniques, with the knowledge, with the Warrior and with you.

Guardian: Yes. Why do we start with faith?

Leader: We are on a journey. There is no guarantee. We are moving into the unfathomable abyss of consciousness, into the knowable unknown, and I need faith "to give substance to things (and beings) not yet seen."[11]

Guardian: Where did you learn that definition?

Leader: A metaphysical teacher.

Guardian: You are a blessed soul. Why else do you need faith?

Leader: Our art demands we must establish true friendships. We must establish friendships that are based on the dignity of each being as an entity unto itself. We must build true friendships with peers both junior and senior, to make sure we receive true feedback that helps us grow into a flourishing and freeing state of being. We need faith to build friendships that lead to and create bonds of trust to thrive in the chaos and uncertainty of leading. Most importantly, we need faith because it leads to trust and certainty in the relationships between people, knowledge, expertise, aims, and goals, even when we lead in uncertainty. What I mean is, faith leads to a bond, a relationship that creates a strength in union, in a fellowship, without submission or subordination to one another as beings, even though within our endeavor there is a hierarchy, when it comes to expertise, knowledge, character and experience. We don't look to another human being as our savior. We must become free by a light and truth that leads to metaphysical freedom, and transcends metaphysical bondage. This means that each leader

---

[11] Barbara Martin's definition of faith.

in our endeavor aims to become an unmoved mover as we enter chaos and lead order out of it. Chaos[12] is the perfect environment for our art. Without chaos there's no need for leaders, no need for teaching leaders, no need for us. The beautiful burden is the courage to endure the chaos that is the cycle of being and becoming.

Warrior: Then, to be clear, what do you seek?

Leader: I seek to become an unmoved mover in the dynamic cycle of being and becoming.

Warrior: You are wise for your age. You see the ways and means and ends as a united activity.

Leader: Don't let me fool you. Make me give an account. Train me so that I know by being, not by knowledge. The reason I can answer your questions is that I've studied both of you in the trail you left as you blazed forward. You did the hard work and I am benefiting from it. But my interior nature is still disturbed, unsettled and not at rest. I know I am not mature. I know I am not purified. I know I am not realized. I seek the true way. I know I do not see the light and truth. I don't even know what I am or how I got to Earth. I'm seeking your guidance. I need to be taught true courage and true discipline. I need to be taught the principles to seek truth!

Warrior: Now we're getting to the truth, the true voice speaking from the depths of the soul. You needed to trust us to take off the armor and experience the freedom of the soul's nakedness.

Guardian: One last time, are you sure you desire the training to become a leader?

Leader: Yes. I have nowhere else to turn. I have nowhere else to go. I need a guide.

Guardian: So be it. To set guidelines on your quest, from your understanding, what are the cardinal leadership acts?

Leaders: There are seven cardinal leadership acts–

1. Awakening and actualizing an individual's potential
2. Awakening and actualizing an enterprise's potential
3. Realizing basic human needs, and, if possible, wants
4. Recognizing and solving identity crises
5. Recognizing and solving enterprise crises
6. Managing individual expectations
7. Managing enterprise expectations

Warrior: Impressive. You united individual and enterprise demands.

Guardian: Where do we begin?

---

[12] O.E.D. definition of chaos–1: A gaping void, yawning gulf, chasm, abyss. 2: Formless primordial matter.

Leader: We begin and end with number one–

    Awakening and actualizing an individual's potential.

Guardian: What does this imply?

Leader: Every leadership quest is anchored to cardinal act one.

Guardian: Why?

Leader: To master the art of being an unmoved mover in the dynamic cycle of being and becoming.

Guardian: What are you seeing?

Leader: If I learn to master this, every other cardinal act will seem an extension of this first one. I see this as the keystone. And I see most leaders avoiding this and thereby becoming lost in the acts and activities of leading.

Guardian: Why do you think this is?

Leader: The first cardinal act is the foundation of learning the art of practical judgment. Without this foundation, I am speculating, leaders lack the skill to disclose the truth.

Guardian: You see correctly. What does this imply?

Leader: The first cardinal act becomes the foundation and structure that supports the remaining cardinal acts of leading.

Guardian: You see correctly. Then, for this first quest, should we focus on the cardinal leadership act of awakening and actualizing your potential?

Leader: Yes.

Guardian: This means that in the future you will also endure metaphysical quests to see and know the truths of the remaining cardinal leadership acts?

Leader: Yes. I see these quests being initiated when I'm selected to lead individuals or an enterprise.

Guardian: You mean, to lead any individual or any level in an enterprise?

Leader: Yes. For individual, I mean to serve a friend or a teammate. For an enterprise, I mean at any level, in the beginning, as an individual contributor or a utility player.

Guardian: What are the cardinal leadership categories?

Leader: There are six cardinal leadership activities–

1. Tactical
2. Operational
3. Strategic
4. Management
5. Leadership
6. Command

Guardian: On this quest, where do we begin?

Leader: I've axed activities one through four.

Guardian: Why?

Leader: The are domain-specific to leading an enterprise. I am not headed into an enterprise any time soon. I intend to train with you for a decade. I see command as the art of commanding the soul's faculties to be sharp, discerning, and developed.

Guardian: What about leadership?

Leader: In the context of my quest, I'm studying the etymological roots of the concept "leadership."

Guardian: What are you seeing?

Leader: I am in need of a true education, which would serve to develop my moral and intellectual powers. This is the essence of my quest. I need the Warrior and you to teach me to make my intellectual and moral faculties sharp. In my studies of the concept of "leadership" thus far, I've discovered several interesting related roots. The concept "educate" comes from the Latin *educare*, which springs from the Latin *educere*, which means "educe". "Educe" means to develop from latency or potential. Our art is to awaken potential, which means it's the art of transforming "potential being" into "actualized being." And this is what caught my attention—*educere*, the root of "educe," springs from the Latin *ducere*.[13]

And the Latin *ducere* means "to lead."

Guardian: There it is, the wellspring of understanding. By education, you seek to lead out your moral and intellectual faculties to be sharp, discerning and developed. By leading, you seek to understand first how to make your faculties powerful, and second, how to make the faculties of others powerful.

---

[13] O.E.D. definitions and etymology of "educate" and "educe."

Then you seek to unite the first leadership act (awakening) and first leadership activities (leading) as an extension of being in the soul. Once this is understood, you will unite the first act and first activities with the remaining acts and activities, thereby living as an unmoved mover? Is this what you are seeing?

Leader: That is what I am seeing. I make the mistake of learning knowledge and skills without having command of them by uniting them to my being. I seek to live and lead from the core of my being.

Guardian: Then training will focus on making your will, intelligence, spirit, and body powerful, strong, and developed.

Leader: That is what I am seeking. The rest will follow from the strength of my being. This will make me centered. I want to make sure, when I engaged the chaos of leading, that I do not lose my center. This training will teach me to rest inwardly, from the center of my being.

Guardian: What are you seeking?

Leader: More than training, I seek tests and trials to prove to myself that my faculties have been awakened and developed.

Guardian: What do you need to prepare for the tests and trials?

Leader: I need knowledge and skill. I seek the essence of leadership–

> Disciplined skill in the performance of actions.

Guardian: How do you realize this knowledge and this essence?

Leader: By moving from the soul's light and truth into the soul's powers of will and intelligence, and into knowledge, techniques, training, tests, and experiences.

Guardian: What is the equation, the matter and form of what you see?

Leader: The equation–

> Spirit [light and truth] x Soul [will x intelligence x spiritedness] x Skill [knowledge x techniques] x Experiences [training x tests x trials] = Soul [awakened and actualized]

Simplified, the equation–

> [Spirit] x [Soul] x [Skill] x [Experiences] = [Actualization]

Warrior: Impressive.

Guardian: Then what are the swords of truth and light that wield the potential to actualize?

Leader: The swords of light and truth and spirit are the techniques of meditation, contemplation, and dialogue. The swords are techniques of spirit to awaken the wisdom-faculty—an awakening that leads to the highest happiness as contemplative wisdom.

Guardian: "Omne Ens Est Verum."[14]

Leader: "Everything that is, is true."

Guardian: Based on the cardinal acts of leading, where do you seek guidance?

Leader: I need guidance on the path to **realize potencies** and **solve my identity (existential) crisis** by discovering my calling.

Guardian: Then, for this metaphysical expedition, we will focus on character development, intellectual development, identity development, and spiritual development. This is the essence of the metaphysical quest.

Leader: Why is that?

Guardian: We need to grow your being, and you need to become secure in your being, and rest in your being as an unmoved mover. Once you achieve this foundation, everything else you do in the world will seem simple and yet arduous, in that you will become a student of truth. And truth is a relentless teacher.

Leader: Why is that?

Guardian: No matter what we achieve externally, our potencies are unlimited. Awakening and realizing your potential is a non-stop process of being and becoming. Looking back years from now on this training, it will seem that you were doing very little in the hustle and bustle of the world of human activity. But your inner nature, the nature of the soul, will be led into deeper and deeper experiences of metaphysical freedom. Enjoy this period of training, when you are the seeker and student instead of the teacher.

Leader: Why is that?

Guardian: In the beginning, you are the central aim; it's all about your awakening and realizing your potential. Later, it's all about serving others to guide their awakenings. Essentially you will transition from self-focused to others-focused. The would-be teachers fail because they never mature out of this self-focused perspective. Now is the time to focus on you. The Warrior and I are here to guide and see you through this transformation. Are you ready to begin?

Leader: I thought we already started?

Warrior: You're not as wise as I thought.

---

[14] Josef Pieper, *Living the Truth*.

Leader: What?

Guardian: How do you know when we've started?

Leader: Good God. My ego. We are not even in the depths yet.

Guardian: What do you admire?

Leader: Human beings who seek truth, wisdom, and justice. Human beings who take personal risks for a worthy endeavor. Human beings who sacrifice themselves, engaged in important work.

Guardian: Do you possess these qualities—truth, wisdom, justice, sacrifice, fortitude, endurance?

Leader: I don't know what I possess. I've never been examined and I've never taken a hard look within. I don't know my strengths and my weaknesses.

Warrior: How old are you?

Leader: Twenty-six.

Guardian: This is a good age to begin.

Leader: Why is that?

Warrior: Our character, for good or for bad, gets formed and hardened between the ages of 18 and 26. This is when most follies of life occur, and if we don't mature out of them, the follies turn into vices and addictions, which are pernicious states of being to work one's way out of.

Guardian: The truth will hunt for our weaknesses and make us pay in purification to get to the essentials of being.

I suffered from a lot of wreckage, which is why I am so determined to teach this art.

Warrior: At the age when we were most vulnerable to character lapses and falls from grace, ages 18–26, we were most left alone. We should have had mentors and guides, safeguarding us against every temptation, because we had not yet grown the character to unite knowing, willing and acting. We are here to correct this. It's absurd to ask an 18-year-old what his aim is in life. What we should ask is, what is striking your interest? What appears, then, are natural talents and aptitudes, and we slowly work from there. We aim to correct this by walking the path with you.

Leader: I've not suffered those experiences. My father and mother divorced and I had to take care of my brother and sister until they could take care of themselves. I had little guidance from my parents.

Guardian: This is actually a good sign. Howard Gardner studied leaders, and many leaders grew up in similar situations, although they usually lost a parent early in life.

Leader: Wait, so this helped me grow into a leader sooner? The experiences of my formative years?

Guardian: Yes, it taught you self-reliance. This self-reliance is what you displayed when you came in pursuit of us. We look for free and independent thinkers in their formative years, because they show the promise to be able to withstand, later in life, the wills and judgments of others in the acts of leading.

What don't you admire?

Leader: I hate social clubs. I hate the inequalities between wealth and poverty. I hate people who think they are superior to other people. I hate image seekers. I hate pop stars. I hate movie stars. I hate TV news outlets. I hate celebrities. I hate non-essential and non-necessary things and products.

Guardian: Who do you admire?

I admire important endeavors (civic leadership). I admire the adventurers (Reinhold Messner). I admire musicians (Beethoven to Jimi Hendrix). I admire literature (Shakespeare). I admire sacred and wisdom literature (Plato and Saint John of the Cross). I admire thespians (Peter O'Toole and Orson Welles). I admire the warriors (Spartans and Samurais) and I admire the Saints and Sages (Christ, Lao Tzu, St. John, St. Theresa). Most of all, I admire leaders, any leader worthy of the designator.

Guardian: Why the leaders?

Leader: No matter their talents, they engage in the chaos of living. They engage other human beings. They accept the burden. They engage the friction, the resistance, the ugliness, and wield grace, and ease, and beauty.

Guardian: So, am I seeing correctly—you admire leaders in any field, be it artistic, civic, economic, or industrial?

Leader: Yes.

Guardian: And, are you open to leading in any field that calls to your true purpose?

Leader: Yes.

Guardian: And you want to know how to make your inner nature worthy of the designator of leader?

Leader: Yes.

Guardian: If you exercise patience and devote yourself to twenty years of training, you will one day become what you admire in these leaders—their attributes of being—cardinally stated as beauty, truth, and goodness. Can you practice this kind of patience and devotion?

Leader: Yes.

Guardian: Then, to best serve and guide you, my mission is to give an account of what we are doing and why we are doing it, and its significance. At any time, make me give an account. I can handle the hard questions, and I grow as a teacher by addressing the hard questions. We want to see something together, and if we can see it, we may be able to make contact with it. If we can make contact with it, we may become it.

Leader: The known and the knower become one.

Guardian: Yes. Such is the beauty of truth's light on our intelligence. Let me ask–

What makes a leader dangerous?

Leader: When he thinks he knows but has no idea.

Guardian: Good. What is a possible solution to this greatest of leadership sins?

Leader: The solution would be to remove ignorance by seeking truth and conforming to the truth that he seeks.

Guardian: Good. Let me ask–

What leads the leader?

Leader: The truth leads the leader. This is granted to souls who know to disclose the truth.

Guardian: Good. How might a leader learn to disclose the truth?

Leader: By training in the swords of truth (meditation, contemplation, and dialogue) and by seeking feedback to eradicate ignorance.

Warrior: Outstanding. What does this lead to?

Leader: Detachment and humility. To shift from the subjective to the objective. To become the observing observer. To conform the will to truth. To free truth from unhiddenness. To bond the will to truth.

Guardian: It is good to see that you've studied on your own and that you're prepared for this training.

Leader: I studied while my peers hid from the burden of freedom. I went running in the direction of freedom. I seek metaphysical freedom, a flourishing state of potential awakening.

Guardian: Why do you think your peers hid from the burden?

Leader: Good God. An insight—they are not called to the way of the leader?

Guardian: I suspect this is the case. They act out "the image" of one who is called, but when we study them they act very differently. The do not act in the way of the leader. They act in the way of the ego-body-octagon. In their hearts, they actually seek power and dominance and wealth and pleasure. In seeking those ends, they do not pursue the studies, they do not pursue truth, they do not pursue freedom.

Warrior: That is why the Guardian sees our art as a practical, mystical art, in the realm of leading democratic citizens—the art of leading souls.

Leader: Is this similar to Plato's concept of the Philosopher Kings?

Guardian: Let us look at this passage from the *Republic*[15] to guide us–

> "Unless," I said, "the philosophers rule as kings or those now called kings and chiefs genuinely and adequately philosophize, and political power and philosophy coincide in the same place, while the many natures now making their way to either apart from the other are by necessity excluded, there is no rest from ills for the cities, my dear Glaucon, nor I think for human kind, nor will the regime we have now described in speech ever come forth from nature, insofar as possible, and see the light of the sun."

Have you read the *Republic*?

Leader: I started to read by only lasted a few days. The book seemed to be a walled-off fortress of opaque granite. I could not enter. I read the words but could not understand and make sense of what I read. It was as if my intelligence could not comprehend the concepts.

Warrior: This makes sense, if we are honest. You were not ready; your consciousness was not ready, to let you in. The same thing happened to the Guardian at your age, but not to me.

Guardian: The Warrior is a polymath, born with innate intellectual gifts. I had to work tirelessly, for years, before the wisdom literature let me in.

Leader: Wait, so your abilities are not innate? I mean, not natural?

Guardian: I'm more a contemplative than a philosopher. With the writings of the saints, I had a natural ability to grasp the essence. The philosophers were a bit more difficult because my mind is more intuitive than logical.

Leader: Which is why you are teammates with the Warrior?

---

[15] Plato, *The Republic*, Allan Bloom, translated.

Guardian: Indeed. I surround myself with beings who have talents that I do not have.

Leader: So I don't need to have natural abilities?

Guardian: In our art, no. You need basic abilities, but you need a strong will and spirit to endure. You've proven you have the will and the spirit. Now we simply need to strengthen it.

Let me ask–

What must you pay to lead truthfully and effectively?

Leader: I learned this from the writings of the transcendentalist Emerson–

The price I must pay is to suffer no fiction.

Guardian: What is the exact passage from Emerson?

Leader: It reads–

The world is young: the former great men call to us affectionately. We too must write Bibles, to unite again the heavens and the earthly world. The secret of genius is to suffer no fiction to exist for us, to realize all that we know.[16]

Warrior: We have been seeking souls like you. Your preparation, for your age, is inspiring.

Leader: Rage spurred me on. I want freedom. I want truth and peace and love as a state of being.

Guardian: Why don't you seek the contemplative life?

Leader: Why can't I live both the active and the contemplative life?

Guardian: What is it again you are seeking?

Leader: Truth. The courage to follow the truth I know.

Guardian: Do you remember the moment you had your first awakening?

Leader: I do.

Guardian: Can you share the experience?

Leader: I was travelling through Rome and stumbled upon a rare copy of *Meditations* by Marcus Aurelius. I had never read wisdom or sacred literature. I did not even know such books existed. When I set my eyes on the book, it called to me. I opened up to the page where he

---

[16] Ralph Waldo Emerson, "Representative Men."

remembers what he learned and what he admired in his "father", Emperor Antonius Pius. This is what I read, and I have never been the same–

> There was in him nothing harsh, or implacable, or violent, or, as one may say, anything carried to the sweating point; but he examined things one by one, as if he had plenty of time, and without confusion, in an orderly way, vigorously and consistently. And that might be applied to him which is recorded of Socrates, that he was able either to leave or to take those things which many are too weak to abstain from, and cannot enjoy in moderation. But to be strong enough either to do the first or to be sober in the second is the mark of a man who has a perfect and invincible soul...[17]

Guardian: Why did that strike you?

Leader: This was four years ago. I too served as an officer in the military and did not see officers leading this way. Everyone rushed. Everyone hurried. No one deliberated in an unhurried, masterful and invincible way. The writing struck my soul. It was the first time I had the thought—is it possible that what I am is a soul? That question continues to strike my consciousness—am I a soul? Life on earth makes sense if I AM A SOUL. Death is nothing.

When I landed at the military academy and heard what you two were exploring, I followed suit. I may be twenty years younger than you, but I know I'm called. I want command of my soul. I want to know the light as substance and the truth as nature of my soul.

Warrior: So you're seeking the summit of 'Mount Carmel'?

Leader: What?

Warrior: Saint John of the Cross described this mount, this summit of being–

> Here there is no longer any way because for the just man there is no law, he is a law unto himself.[18]

Leader: You mean at the summit of perfection?

Warrior: Yes. The soul is released from being and becoming and lives in perfect divine union.

No need to force, control, or dominate. Instead, simply the immortal essence that is.

Leader: Is this possible?

Guardian: The saints claim this is a possibility.

---

[17] Marcus Aurelius, *Meditations*.
[18] Saint John of the Cross, *The Complete Works of Saint John of the Cross*.

Leader: If it is possible to train for it, I want to receive that kind of training.

Warrior: I'd caution you on the further pursuit of this calling.

Leader: Why?

Warrior: The price you pay is to suffer no fiction. What does this mean?

Leader: The death of the ego. The death of the personality. The baptism of spirit in light and truth.

Guardian: Yes.

Leader: Have either of you reached this summit?

Guardian: No. But I'm pursuing this possibility.

Leader: Then I'm in good company. I need ultimate meaning and purpose. I am young enough that if I am instructed wisely, if I go methodically and deliberately, if I grow day after day, year after year, maybe I'll reach the summit of being before I pass from this mortal existence.

Guardian: I thought you wanted to be a leader.

Leader: This is what I'll do, to contribute to the well-being of our citizens as I progress and mature in character, intelligence, and spirit. I imagine, training to lead is no big deal, compared to the rigors of perfecting the soul, **to become an invincible soul.** That is the perennial aim that will serve me as a motivation to endure day after day.

Warrior: We are fortunate you found us. We're learning about the type of character and nature who will thrive in our training methods.

Guardian: Let me ask–

Where do we hunt for leadership genius?

Leader: Where do you look for leadership geniuses?

Guardian: No. In our art, we are hunters. Where do we hunt to discover the genius of leadership?

Leader: In the truth?

Guardian: No. But, in our art, it is as simple and it is as difficult as being truthful in all that we do.

Leader: I don't follow?

Guardian: What do want to make perfect and invincible? What drives you?

Leader: Ah. The soul. I wanted to know if I am a soul. And to realize the answer to this question, I need to realize the truth that I am a soul. This training helps me to realize the answer to a truth I seek–

Is it true that what I am is a soul?

And you hunt for leadership genius in the soul and in the spirit of the man!

Guardian: Yes. To realize this is the path of self-knowledge. To see the best and worst in us. We aim to strengthen what is best and to eradicate what is worst. This is how we realize the soul and its powers—its ability to eradicate ignorance and darkness, and awaken truth and light. This is how you realize and listen to the inner voice, the God-within, the daemon. A piece of the cosmic light and truth is found in every human heart.

We seek what is ancient and oldest in us—the wisdom that is eternal. We seek to ignite what is oldest and truest in the nature of soul—will and intelligence. Both are indefatigable and undefeatable. They can withstand any assault once they are sharpened and developed. They cannot be defeated because they do not engage in winning and losing; they engage in truth-seeking and truth-knowing. Be on guard until you strike the genius within.

Bloom cautions us–

> If genius is the God within, I need to seek it there, in the abyss of the aboriginal self, an entity unknown to nearly all of our current explainers, in the intellectually forlorn universities and in the media's dark Satanic mills.[19]

Leader: This is a lot to follow. I will do my best to keep up.

Guardian: This is all I did, with the Warrior, on the path you followed. A path to seek the genius within, the God-within, you. What I did was, I led you into the depths of your being, simply by leading the way. The depths of soul, both yours and mine, are the same in essence and nature. We are only distinguished by individual existence. By being an individual being. One and one. One nature and essence. Yet still, each is one individual being, a soul. I honor the dignity of the soul in each human being.

Do not try to keep up. Go at your own pace. Learn your own rhythm. I will adjust to your rhythm and make sure you experience the harmony, elegance, and grace of your potencies being awakened. My purpose is to demystify what is taking place in the transformation of knowledge into your being as it awakens your will, spirit, and intelligence. You need to learn to see what is going on in your interior nature; this seeing is intuitive. This intuition will allow you to see it taking place in the souls of others.

---

[19] Harold Bloom, *Genius*.

Warrior: Nothing remains hidden. You'll be able to see. You may not know specifics, but you will see the inner natures of the beings around you.

Guardian: Remember, we are leading you on a metaphysical expedition. Anything that takes place is to reveal what is taking place in you, in the inner reality. We do this by striking the powers of soul. There are no temporal concerns here. It is best to imagine you are a spirit and your body is a translucent cloak to distinguish you from other beings, including us. You need to learn what can only be seen with the discerning eye. The Warrior and I are hunting to strike your genius and lead it. When we do, you will experience a true education.

Leader: Then I'll have reached the ability to lead; the aim of a true leadership (*ducere*) is liberating the soul.

Guardian: Yes. This is how we teach leadership from the inside out, starting from your inner nature, from your powers of will and intelligence that form and shape your character and your intellect. This is how you learn to rest inwardly and deeply, and how to build a perfect and invincible soul.

Warrior: We are brothers by truth, not by blood. It's a bond stronger than blood. The truth binds us. The truth liberates us. All we ask is for you to be truthful, to speak your mind, to share what is living in your mind, heart, and will. It's the only way for us to come into harmony.

Leader: Some things I am not ready to share and don't feel comfortable sharing.

Guardian: Remember, go at your own pace. You do not need to share your innermost secrets. What we mean to discover is how you are coming into contact with truth and how you are building a friendship with us. Twenty years ago, I experienced the ugliness of shame, and luckily, I had priests and mentors, as confessors, to share my heart and clear it, without being too close to any one person.

Warrior: The Guardian shares this in case you need an outlet other than us. Confessors are a key to making sure you eradicate any self-defeating emotions and energies that live in the deep waters of the soul. We need to clear the soul of these torments because they affect the deep motives that convert intentions, feelings, and thinking into action. As for me, I journaled. Others trust their spouse. Others lean on a psychologist or a coach. Just make sure you practice the art of cleansing weekly. You'll need it. Our art lives in the ugliness and the beauty of the human existence.

Guardian: In time, you may learn to trust us. We will earn that trust slowly. Know that we will not judge your soul or your dignity; we will only judge the qualities you exhibit. Qualities are malleable. This is how we pursue perfection, in the cycle of being and becoming, by perfecting the qualities of our interior nature.

> Know that, for the first time in your life, you have guardians who serve as your guardsmen and watchmen, standing at the ready, to act when needed.

We will not let you fall too far, only enough for teachable points. These falls and failures prepare you to listen. And when you learn to listen, you will grow in the light of wisdom's truth.

Deal?

Leader: Deal. I have nowhere else to go.

Guardian: To begin, you should know that I'm not only seeking light and truth, I'm seeking holiness. I share this because I'm in the midst of my own transformation, from following the way of the guardian to following the way of the saint.

It's been twenty years in the making, and now that the Warrior and you are here, I may transmit the way of leadership development to you.

I too, am undergoing the rigors of the training required for another calling.

I share this because you are seeking perfection, and the way of perfection is never-ending; the callings may change, but the way stays the same–

> The pathless path of the unmoved movers in the knowable unknown.

Know that by your presence, the Warrior and you are helping me to become a better human being.

In this light, there is a shared undertaking in our arts. There is a unitive thread connecting the leader-warrior-guardian-philosopher-saint-sage-mystic in one and the same nature and essence.

These archetypes all spring from the soul's nature and essence, truth and light.

Warrior: I too, am undergoing the rigors of a transformation, from a warrior to a guardian. I lived for thirty years as a warrior. I've just begun the way of the guardian. We are better for training together. We create a trinity—Leader, Warrior, and Guardian.

Guardian: *Vos Estis Tam Sancti Sicut Vultis.*

Leader: You are only as holy as you will to be.

Guardian: Now, we begin the quest.

Warrior: Our art as the experience of the eternal return?

Guardian: Yes.

Warrior: So be it. Onward and upwards my brothers.

Leader: I will seek truth. I will follow your lead until I can follow truth's lead.

Guardian: It is good this is so. So be it. Wisdom mentors–

Now commences the exposition of purification, illumination, and union.

Writer: Dear Reader, these guardians travel the pathless path of truth and light, wherever it may lead. This is the pathless path of the unmoved movers in the knowable unknown. This is the path of the soul. This is the path of all souls. The Guardian. The Warrior. The Leader. The Writer. The Reader.

As our guardians embarked on their metaphysical quest, when they crossed the threshold and entered the unknown, they saw an invocation inscribed in the stones—an invocation meant for all of us. All souls.

The Guardian Invocation

The guardian accepts the call and walks the rigorous and arduous path of becoming truth, justice, and wisdom.

The guardian questions all authority and all conventional wisdom that is spoken in the course of his life.

The guardian seeks to understand and explore all worldviews, all religions, all cultures, all histories and all legacies of truth to understand fully what he is, his nature and his essence.

The guardian knows what he must contribute, then leaves generations to come with strong, universal, and life-affirming foundations.

The guardian explores the interior and the exterior worlds, integrating and harmonizing both.

The guardian takes an eternal perspective.

The guardian loves as fully as possible; this love comes from his soul; this love is light and truth united.

The guardian creates lasting communities of truth-seekers; the aim is freedom.

The guardian knows suffering; his virtue is compassion.

The guardian knows love as both intimacy and rapture.

The guardian enters darkness with the soul's light.

The guardian embraces chaos; chaos initiates the transformation.

The guardian is a scholar of living; his being becomes an instrument of spirit.

The guardian walks alone, though he is never alone.

The guardian heals and expands the gentleness of his heart.

The guardian lives in the mystery; the guardian goes into the abyss of truth; the guardian lives in faith; the guardian is a testament of spirit.

The guardian knows he is a creature; the Creator made his spirit and being.

The guardian seeks union of the soul with spirit; the guardian knows only by crossing the purgative, illuminative, and unitive gates can he achieve this union; the guardian devotes his life to this aim.

The guardian looks you in the eyes, sees your soul, and reminds you, all souls are called to become the living light of truth itself, expressed here and now as love, goodness, truth, and beauty.

The guardian leads with the maxims—Be Bold, Be Courageous, Be Noble, Be Silent.

THE END

IS THE BEGINNING

CPSIA information can be obtained
at www.ICGtesting.com
Printed in the USA
FSHW02n0648111018
52928FS

9 781457 565267